Tropicus Cancri

is minute and insignificant primitive
which is actually only about 2 mm
elongs to a family w'ich has done untold
e by spoiling old valuable books but
ately it numbers seem to be declining. This
view of a wingless booklouse Lepinotus
lis.

"For you and me,
and all brave
men, my brother,"
said Wayne, in his
strange chant,
"there is good
wine poured in
the inn at the end
of the world."

G. K. Chesterton
**THE NAPOLEON OF
NOTTING HILL 1904**

"Although my
tale is a dry and
unexciting one,
chiefly dealing
with local politics
and city history, I
am sure it will
assist in passing a
few idle
moments..."

The Cluracan of Faerie
in conversation, recently.

QUOTES

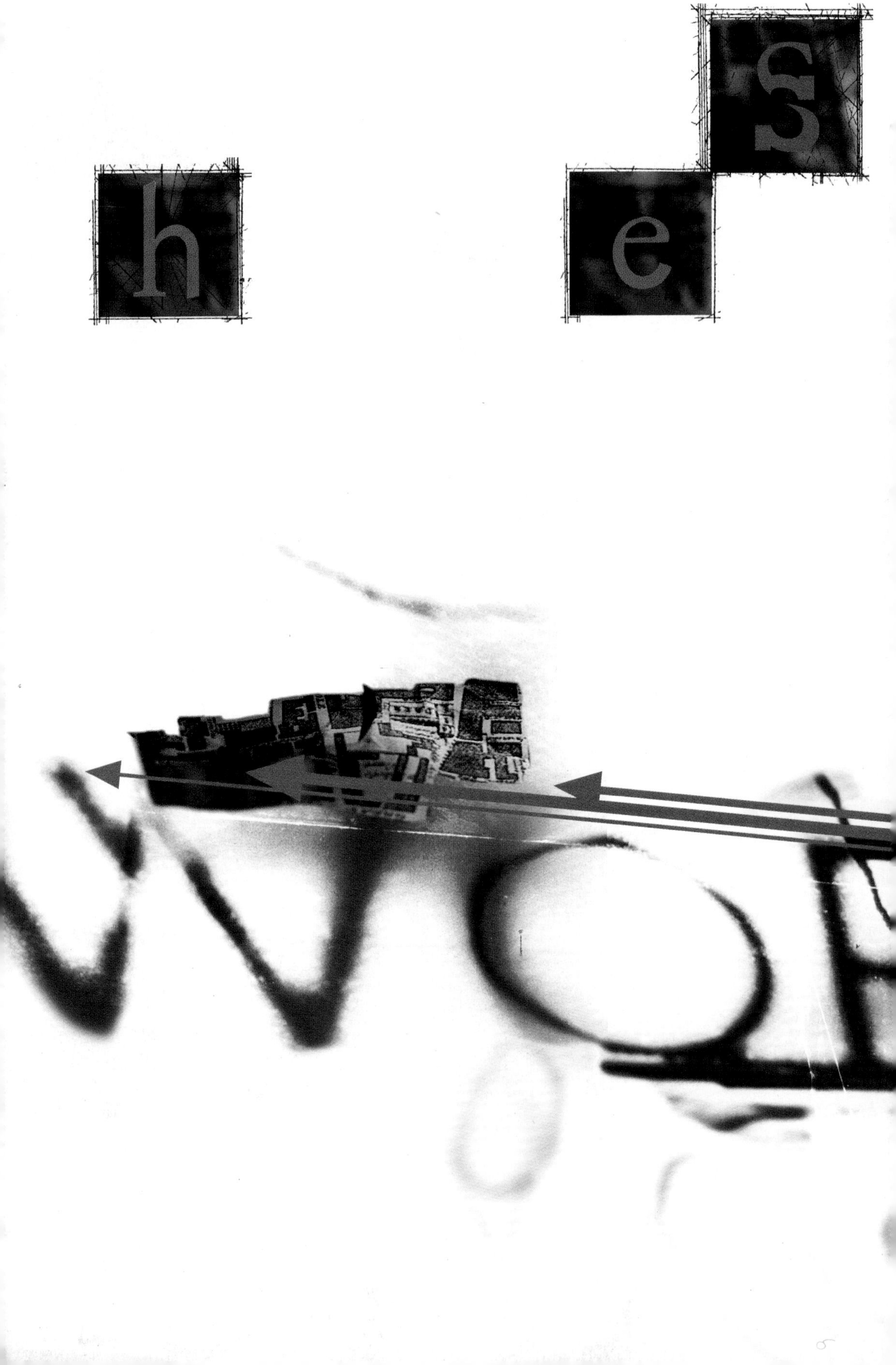

THE SANDMAN: WORLDS' END

Published by DC Comics.
Cover and compilation Copyright
© 2012 DC Comics. All Rights Reserved.
Introduction Copyright © 1994 Stephen King.

Originally published in single magazine form as
THE SANDMAN 51-56. Copyright © 1993 DC Comics.
All Rights Reserved. VERTIGO and all characters, their
distinctive likenesses and related elements featured in
this publication are trademarks of DC Comics.
The stories, characters, and incidents
featured in this publication are entirely fictional.
DC Comics does not read or accept unsolicited
submissions of ideas, stories, or artwork.

Prez created by Joe Simon and Jerry Grandenetti.

DC Comics, 1700 Broadway, New York, NY 10019
A Warner Bros. Entertainment Company.
Printed in the USA. Third Printing.
ISBN: 978-1-4012-3402-7

Cover art, interior illustrations and
publication design by Dave McKean.

Cover design by Richard Bruning.

Library of Congress Cataloging-in-Publication Data

Gaiman, Neil.
 The sandman. Vol. 8, Worlds' end / Neil Gaiman, Michael Allred ...
[et al.].
   p. cm.
"Originally published in single magazine form as The Sandman 51-56."
 ISBN 978-1-4012-3402-7 (alk. paper)
 1. Graphic novels. I. Allred, Mike (Mike Dalton) II. Title. III. Title:
World's end.
 PN6728.S26G458 2012
 741.5'973--dc23
                    2012027196

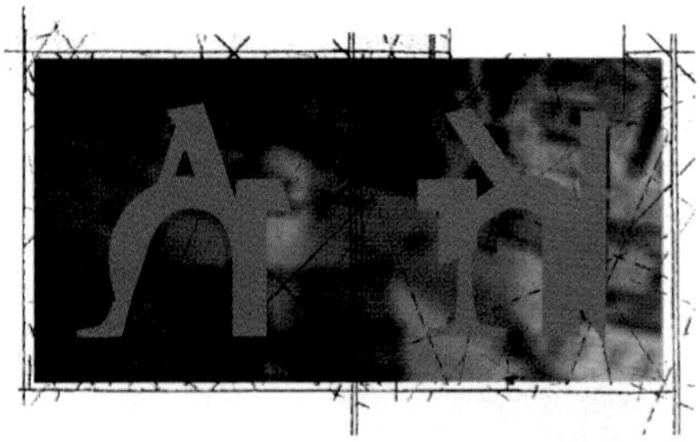

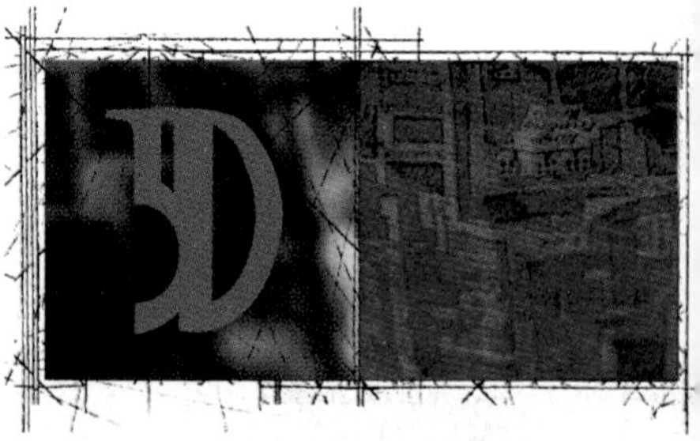

credits

Written by Neil Gaiman
Pencilled by Bryan Talbot
John Watkiss
Michael Allred
Michael Zulli
Shea Anton Pensa
Alec Stevens
Gary Amaro
Inked by Dick Giordano
Mark Buckingham
John Watkiss
Michael Allred
Vince Locke
Alec Stevens
Tony Harris
Steve Leialoha
Colored by Danny Vozzo
Color Separation by Android Images
Digital Chameleon
Lettered by Todd Klein

Covers and Design by Dave McKean
Introduction by Stephen King
Featuring characters created by
Gaiman, Kieth and Dringenberg

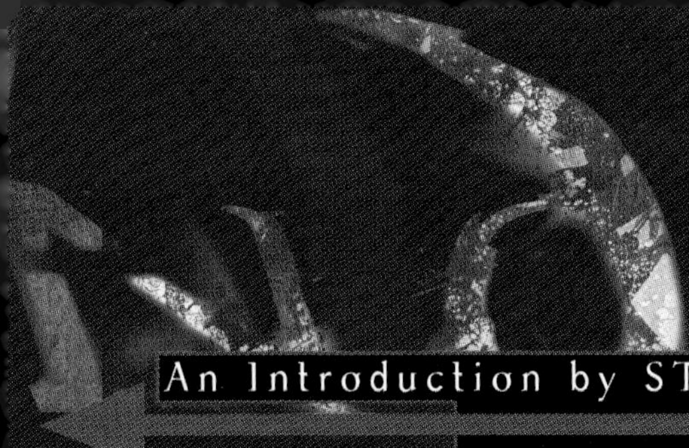

An Introduction by STEPHEN KING

Can I say anything new about the Sandman, Death's dark brother, at this point, or add to the cartography of his legend? Doubt it, Constant Reader. Doubt it very much. I got to this introducin' party rather late, you see, and some of the people who got here first are pretty awesome heads.

Neil Gaiman is a pretty awesome head himself, but those of you who have been following the series through its many odd - *very* odd, *extremely* odd, *ultimately* odd - twists and turns hardly need me to tell you that. Which is part of the problem. I should give you a bunch of reheated leftovers when *this* guy (not to mention Bryan Talbot, Mark Buckingham, Shea Anton Pensa, and all the other pencil people and inkfolk here represented) is going to follow me? I mean, jeez, Louise. Gimme a froggin' break.

What I *do* know about is story. I'm a fan of story. In fact, it might not be going too far to say that story is my life; certainly those lovely figures that dance in the smoke have saved my life from time to time. Neil Gaiman also knows story. He is, simply put, a treasure house of story, and we are lucky to have him in any medium. His fecundity, coupled with the overall quality of his work, is both wonderful and a little intimidating.

So is his workmanship.

contents

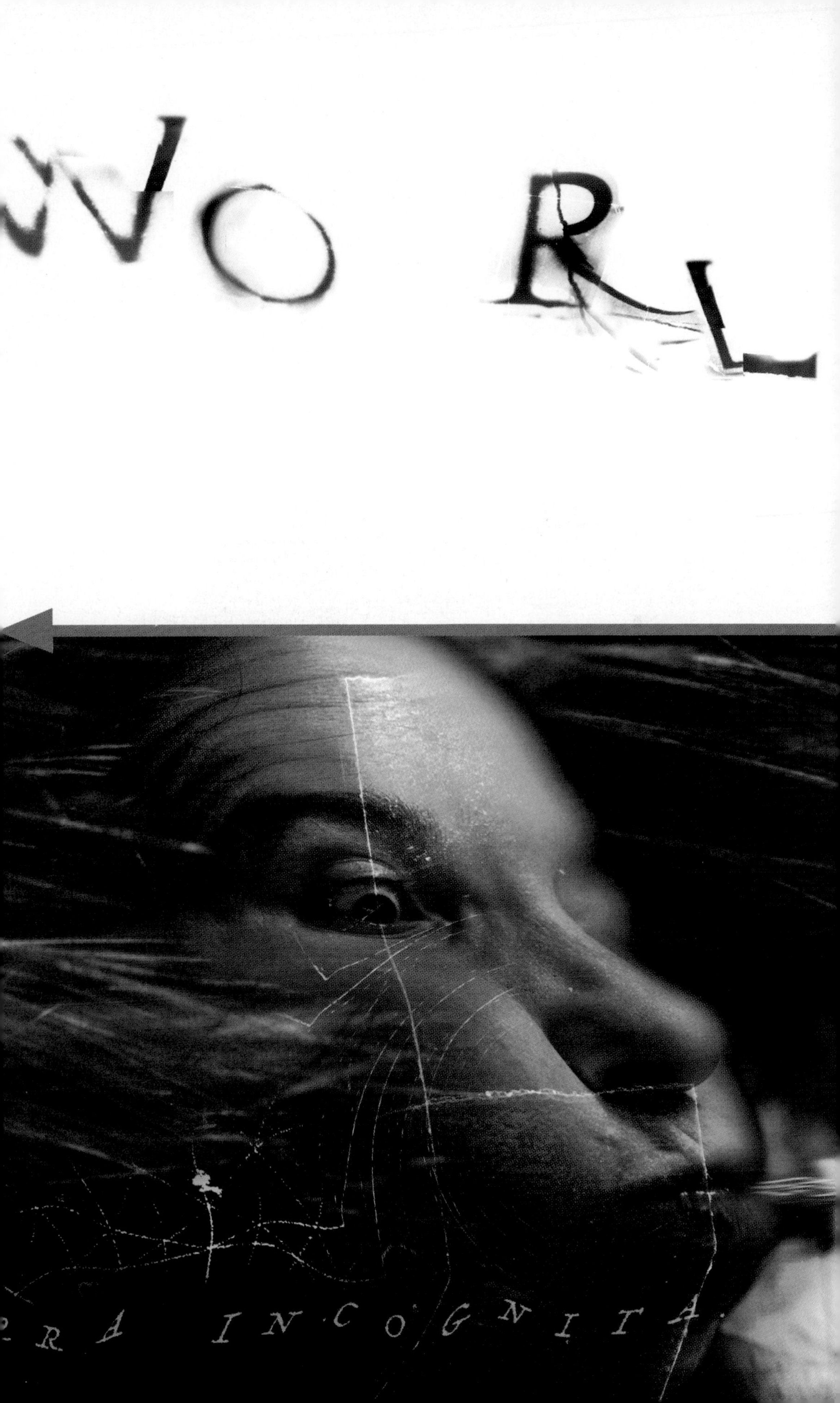
WO RL
INCOGNITA

Karen Berger
Editor - Original Series

Shelly Roeberg
Assistant Editor - Original Series

Bob Kahan   Scott Nybakken
Editors

Robbin Brosterman
Design Director - Books

Shelly Bond
Executive Editor - Vertigo

Hank Kanalz
Senior VP - Vertigo & Integrated Publishing

Diane Nelson
President

Dan DiDio & Jim Lee
Co-Publishers

Geoff Johns
Chief Creative Officer

John Rood
Executive VP - Sales, Marketing & Business Development

Amy Genkins
Senior VP - Business & Legal Affairs

Nairi Gardiner
Senior VP - Finance

Jeff Boison
VP - Publishing Planning

Mark Chiarello
VP - Art Direction & Design

John Cunningham
VP - Marketing

Terri Cunningham
VP - Editorial Administration

Alison Gill
Senior VP - Manufacturing & Operations

Jay Kogan
VP - Business & Legal Affairs, Publishing

Jack Mahan
VP - Business Affairs, Talent

Nick Napolitano
VP - Manufacturing Administration

Sue Pohja
VP - Book Sales

Courtney Simmons
Senior VP - Publicity

Bob Wayne
Senior VP - Sales

mast
head

VENATICI

Equator

VIRGO

COMA

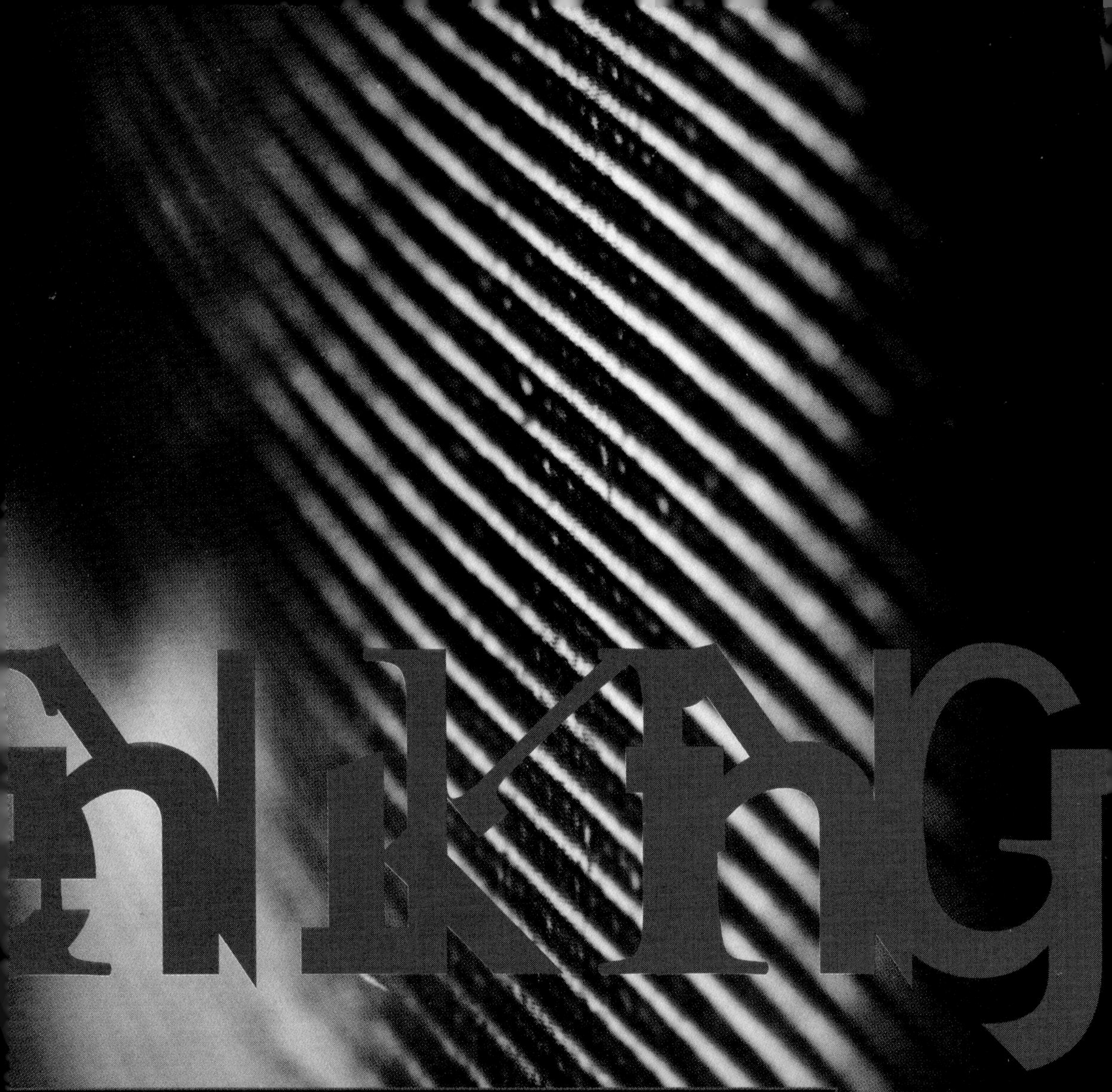

Look: **Worlds' End** was originally published in six issues of what me and my be-bop buddies used to call comic books. Yet these six books are actually installments in a longer, unified tale, which is here being published as it was meant to be read, in six chapters that make a whole. That makes them like six eggs in a single basket, right? Yet there are eggs *inside* eggs here, because **Worlds' End** is a Chaucerian tale in which travellers - this time stranded at an inn rather than clopping down the road to Canterbury - take turns passing a stormy night by telling tales. It is a classic format, but in several of them there are stories *within* the stories, like eggs within eggs, or, more properly, nested Chinese boxes.

The best example of this is in what Chaucer might have called The Sexton's Tale. In it, a man - well, *sort* of a man; his skin is an uneasy greenish-white that recalls the ghouls I glimpsed as a child in the pages of my E.C. comics - named Petrefax tells his tale. He is the apprentice of a master necropolitan (yes, that's what these people call themselves, and it's a word that certainly fits) in the City of the Dead, where honorable burial is the chief - perhaps the only - occupation.

Petrefax is sent to assist with an air burial (there are five forms of final placement practiced in the necropolis: earth burial, water burial, cremation, and mummification are the other four), following which each member of the party tells a story. They're all good, but the best is probably the story of Mistress Veltis and her withered hand...a story that *she* tells, which is within the story told by a member of the air burial party, which is within the story told by Petrefax in the Worlds' End Inn, which is, of course, within the story Neil Gaiman is telling us.

This is challenging stuff. I'm not saying it's so challenging that my old be-bop buddies wouldn't have dug it, reading our comics up in the sweltering storage space above Chrissie Essigian's garage on a rainy summer afternoon, but it's challenging - sophisticated storytelling on a level practiced by Raymond Carver, Joyce Carol Oates, or (and perhaps this is closer to the mark) John Fowles.

On the cover of each SANDMAN issue the phrase "Suggested for Mature Readers" appears, and I'd argue that that doesn't mean it's full of gore, sex, and naughty words (although there are some of *all* those things, thank heavens); it means that if you're not old enough to chew this stuff for yourself, maybe you'd better go back to Spider-Man and the X-Men and the Fantastic Four a little longer. Otherwise you're going to be puzzled. "Country don't mean dumb," Stu Redman tells the agents of the government before he's dragged off to temporary cold storage in *The Stand*; that could be amended here to "Pictures and word-balloons don't mean dumb." And amen to that, brother.

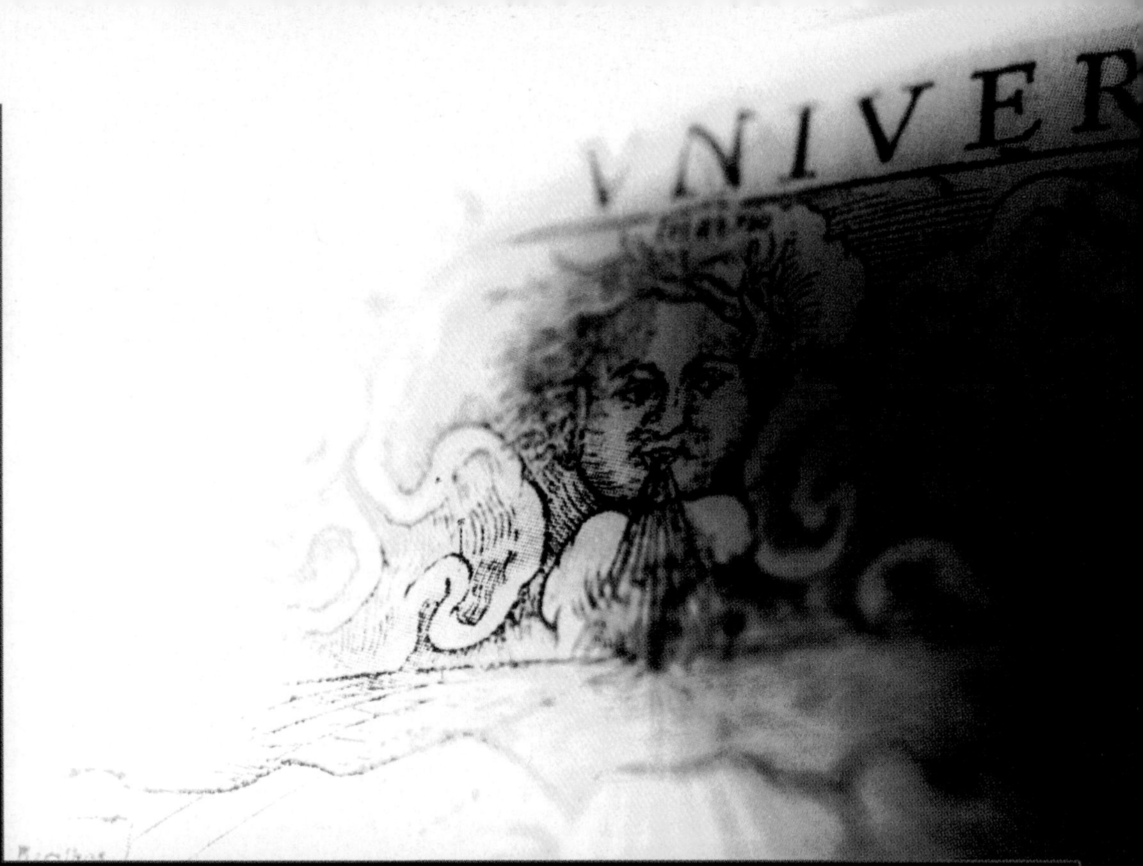
VNIVER

So these are smart stories, and cunningly crafted stories. Fortunately for us, they are also *good* stories, little wonders of economy and surprise. They never get lost in the technicalities, they are never what English villagers would deprecatingly label as "too clever by 'alf."

Probably the most satisfying thing about Gaiman's work - the thing that keeps me coming back - is that he has found his way around the standard "snapper ending" without sacrificing the sense of wonder and amazement that make fantasy so satisfying and essential. He gets those things into the hearts of the stories rather than into their conclusions, that's all; there's no feeling here of reading elaborate horror-jokes with splatters of gore for the punchlines. There's a helluva monster in one of these tales - it has to do with a deeply weird sea voyage - but it shows up nearer the middle than the end (and in a later story, one of the Worlds' End company actually refers to it as "a giant dick," which perfectly displays Gaiman's confidence in his own abilities). In fact, these stories work as well as any I have read, in any medium, over the last half a dozen years of my life. Better than most.

hink I know why, too. In most word-only short fiction, both instream and genre, there is sometimes a sense of self-awareness d a feeling that the work is meaningful...but there is hardly ever any nse of humor. In words-and-pictures fiction - comic books, in other rds - there's usually a *lot* of humor...but no sense of self-awareness, feeling that the work needs to be taken seriously on its own ms...that it has merit as art. The stories presented in **Worlds' End** n on both power sources at the same time, and the result is works th the clarity of fairy tales and the subversive undertone of)-drawer modern fiction. This is necessary stuff, and Gaiman knows pretty well what he's up to. Check the names of the places and characters if you don't believe me; there's so much referral - self and otherwise - and cross-referencing going on here that it's damned near Joycean.

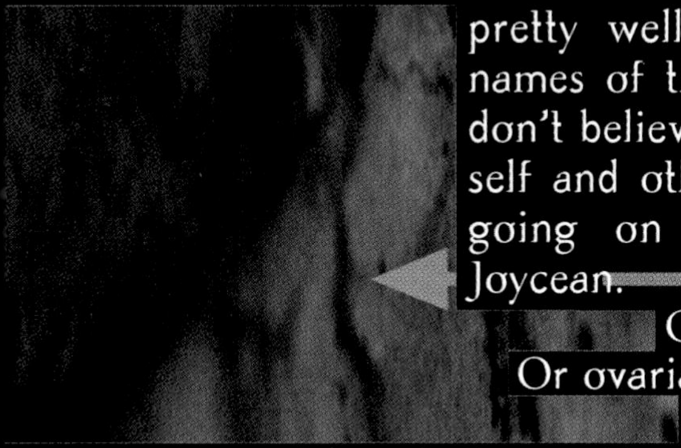

Or Proustian.

Or ovarian.

Or one of those damned things they're always nattering on about in English 202. All I know for sure is that when

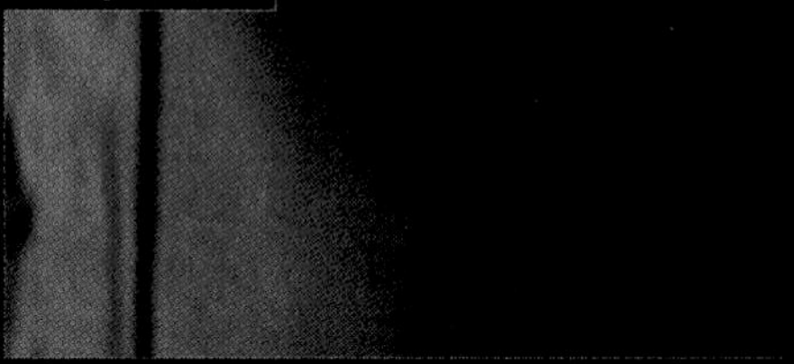

the narrator of the sea story runs away, this young gypsy first takes ship on *The Spirit of Whitby*. The reference is to Bram Stoker's **Dracula**, of course, and there are hundreds of similar references scattered through **Worlds' End**, semiprecious literary gems deliberately half-hidden, like prizes in a scavenger hunt. Gaiman doesn't do it pretentiously, thank God; that would be boring (and a little mean). It's for fun, like the scribbles of marginalia in *Mad* magazine.

One other thing, an important thing: there is an enormous sense of kindness in these stories, a sense that people are, by and large, good and worthy of some sort of salvation. Worthy, if you like, of the shelter from the storm they find in the inn at Worlds' End.

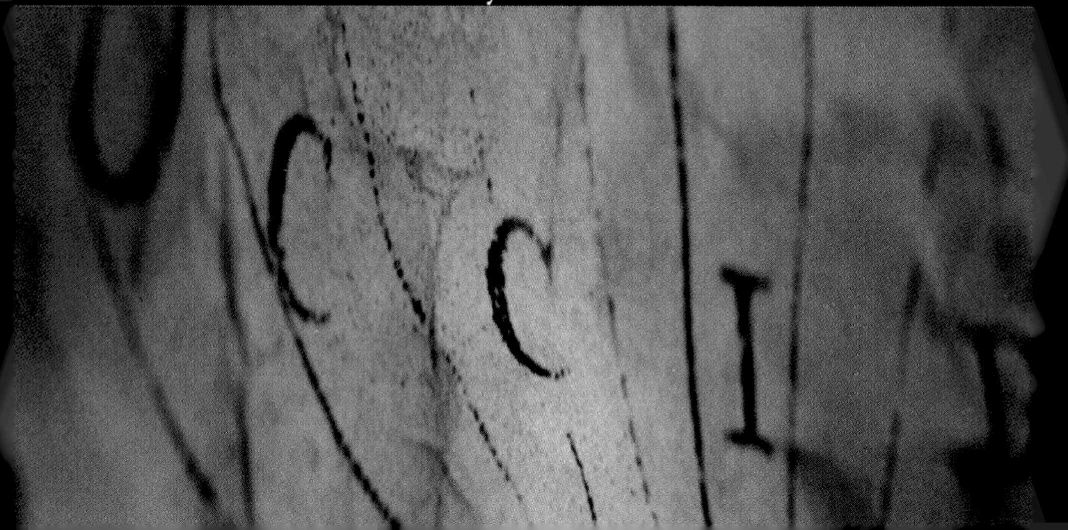

Gaiman's characters are always more than bugs running around in a tin can, to be skewered or let loose at the writer's whim. He takes each one on his or her own terms, so we feel their pride, their terror, their cunning, and their sadness; check out the cautionary tale of Prez Rickard, if you don't believe me, or Charlene Mooney's scathing soliloquy in the last tale). You come to the end feeling that you've had a *meal*, not just a meaningless assortment of high-cholesterol appetizers.

I didn't mean to go on so long, or get so wound up, but it's like I said back at the start: I'm a fan of story. It's what gets me on, gets me up, gets me through the night.

These are great stories, and we're all lucky to have them.

To read Now, and maybe again Then, later on, when we need what only a good story has the power to do: to take us away to worlds that never existed, in the company of people we *wish* we were...or thank God we aren't.

That's enough from this end, I think. All of you turn the page, like good little girls and boys...

...and pleasant dreams.

Bangor, Maine - June 9, 1994

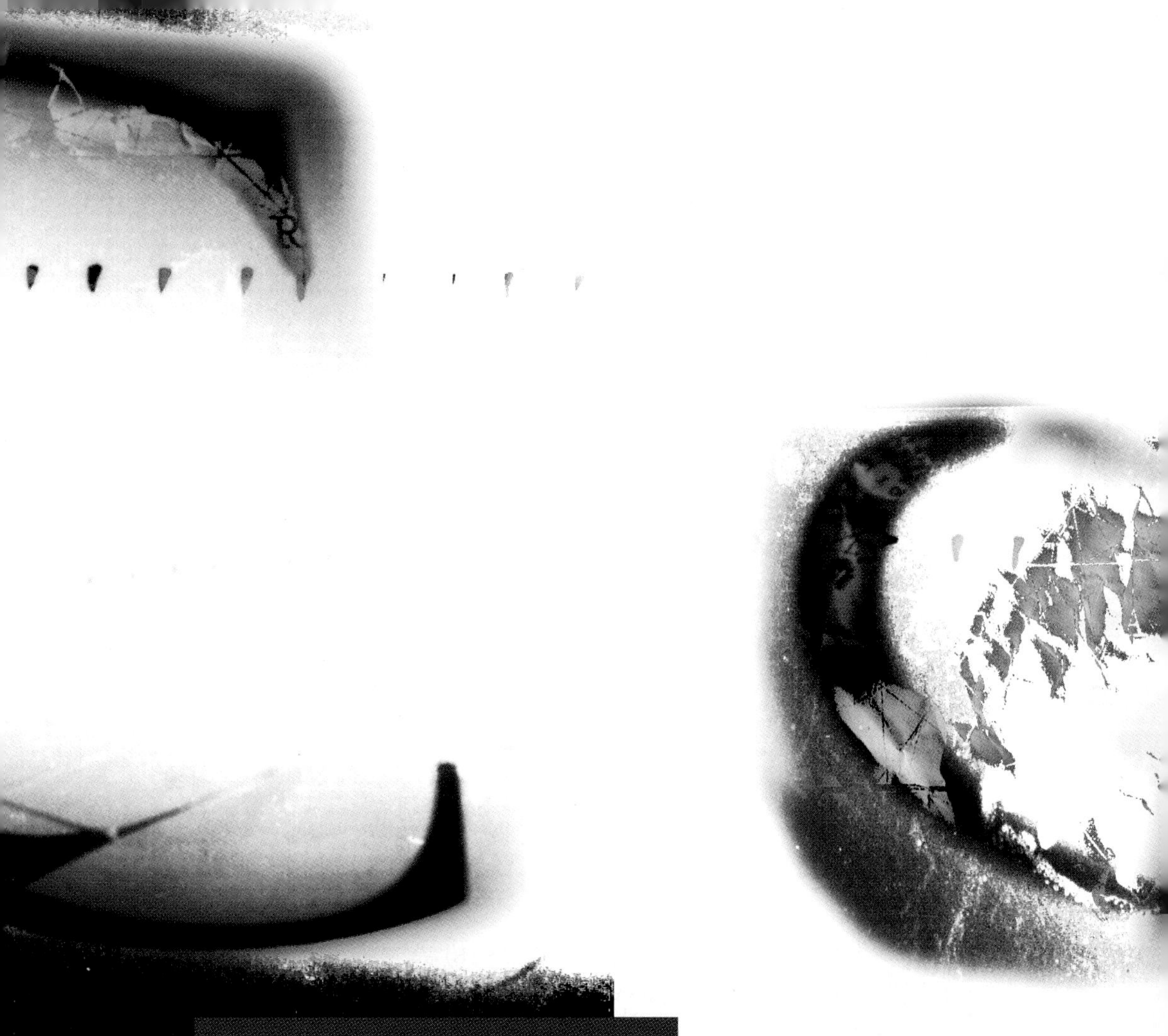

DEDICATION

This book's for

MADDY,

pink and tiny, born one hour and ten minutes ago, who has spent most of the intervening time sucking vigorously on my fingers in the mistaken belief that they provide a viable source of nutrition. I give you all your tomorrows, and these small stories. With my love,

NEIL GAIMAN

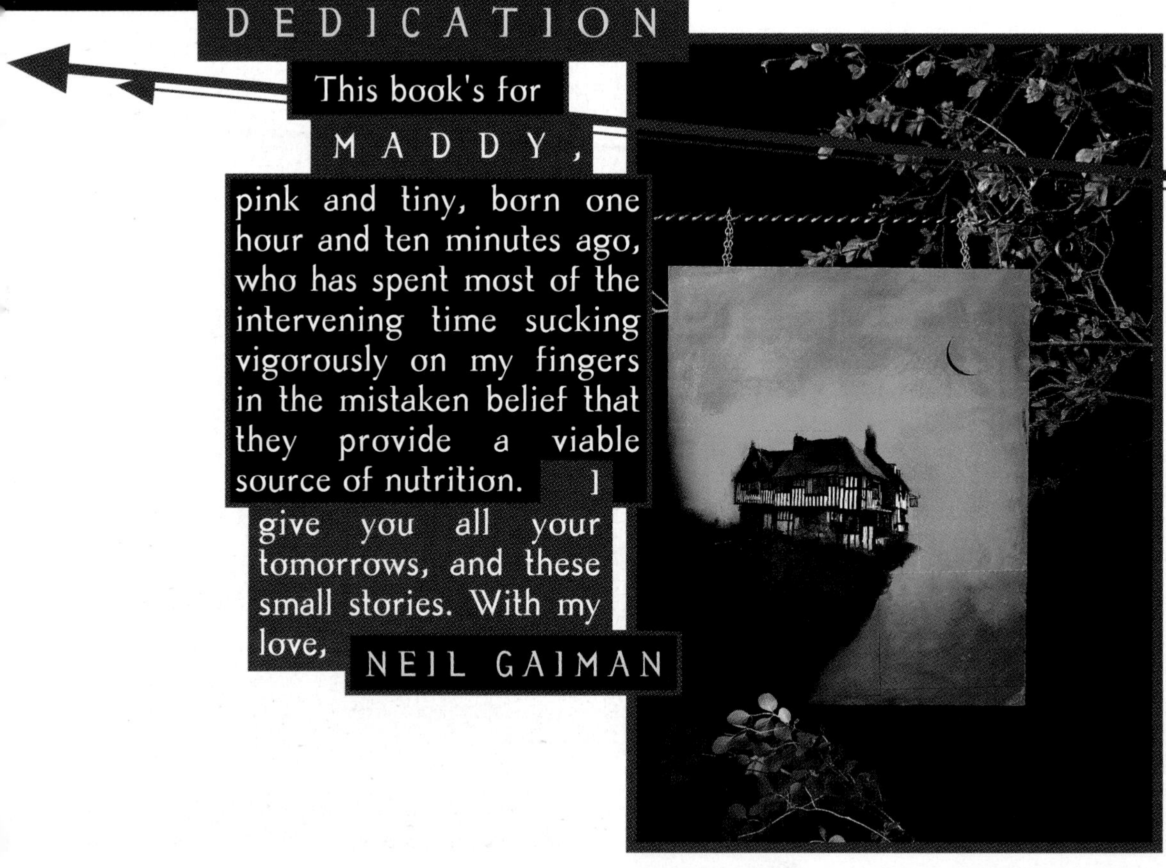

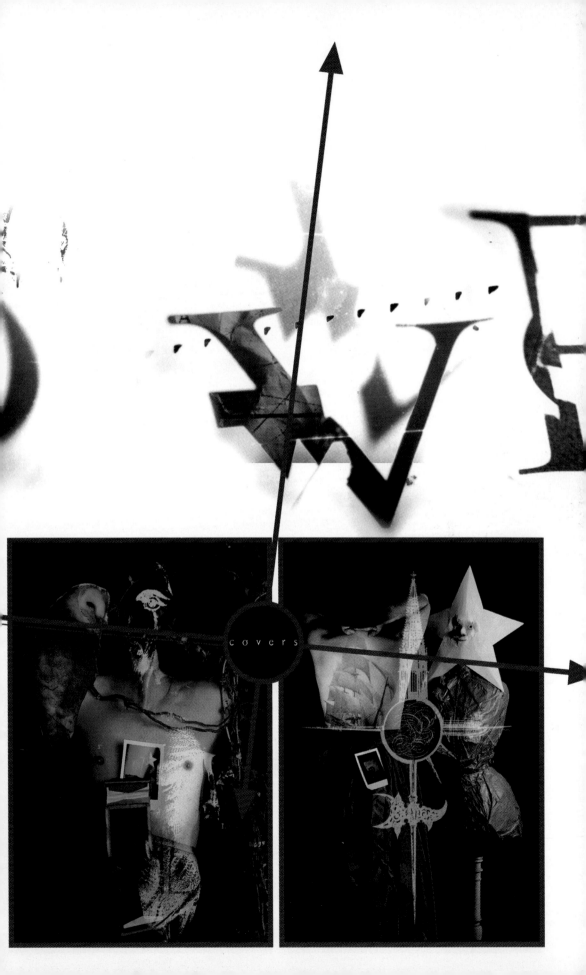

covers

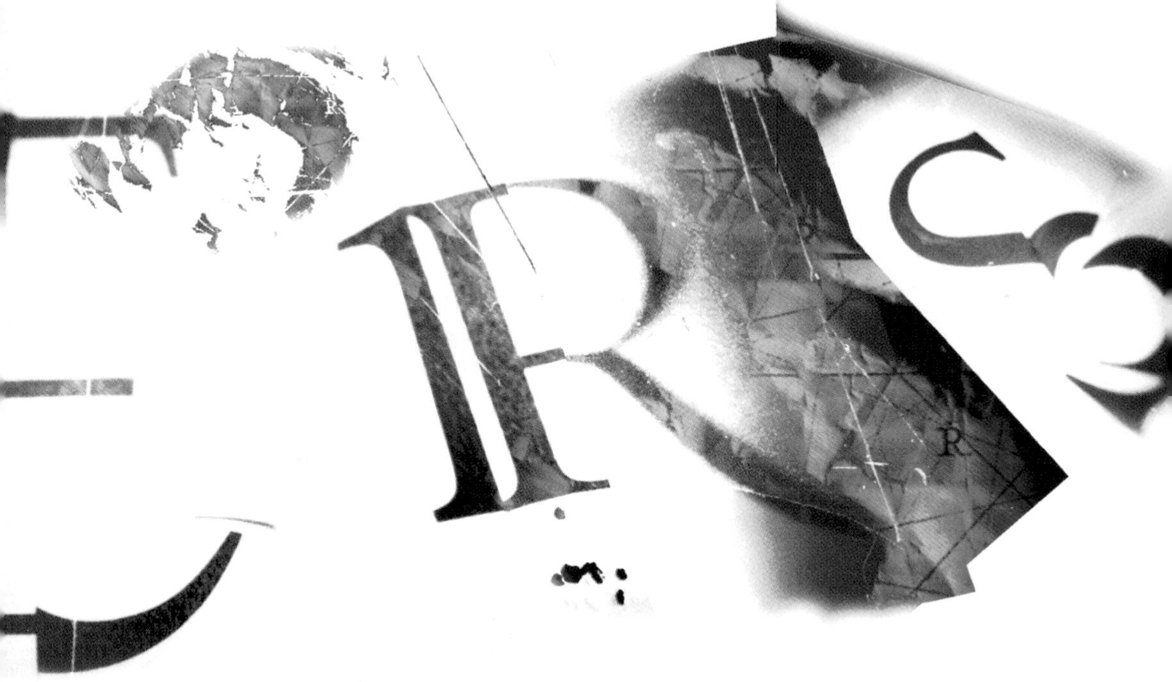

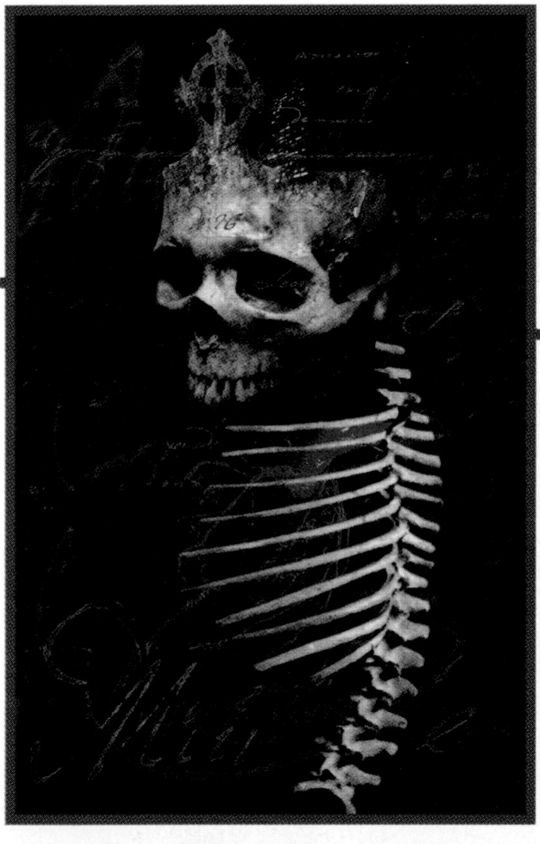

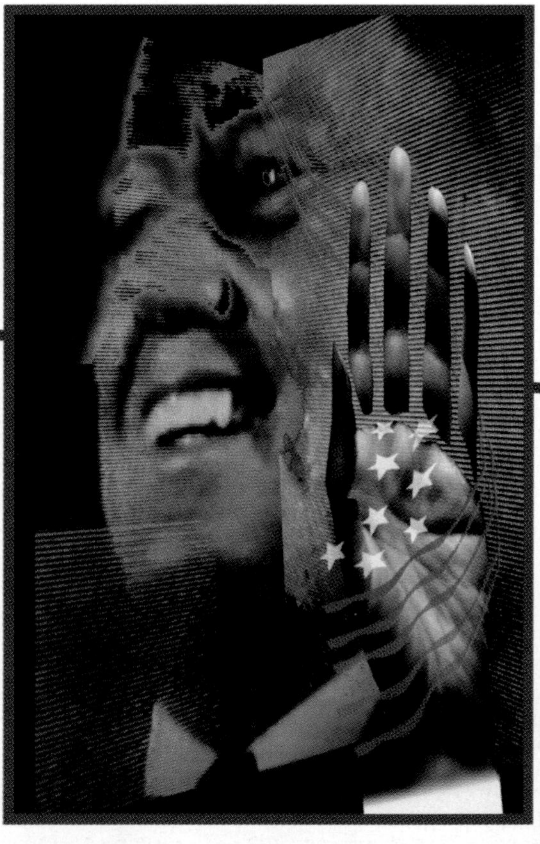

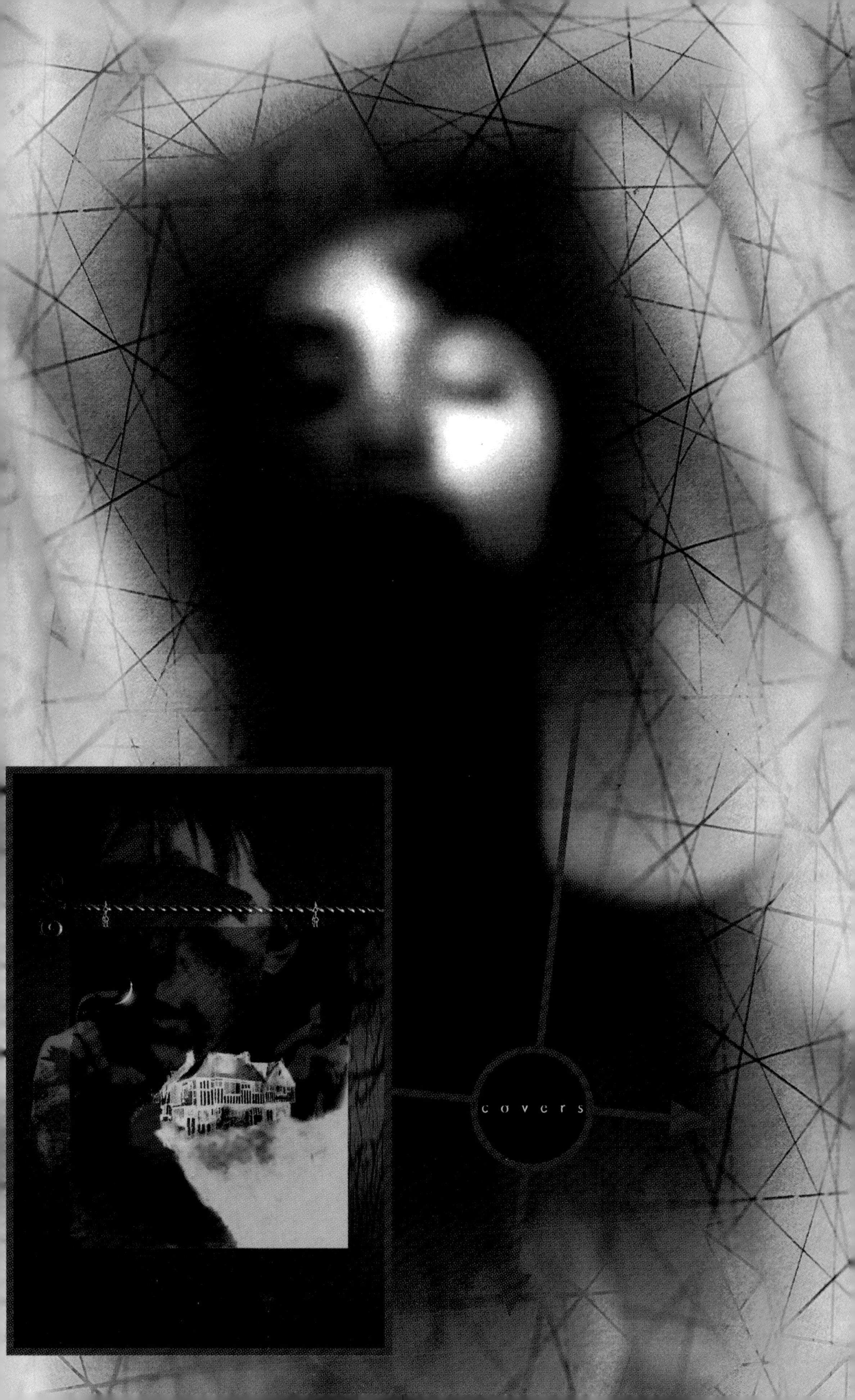
covers

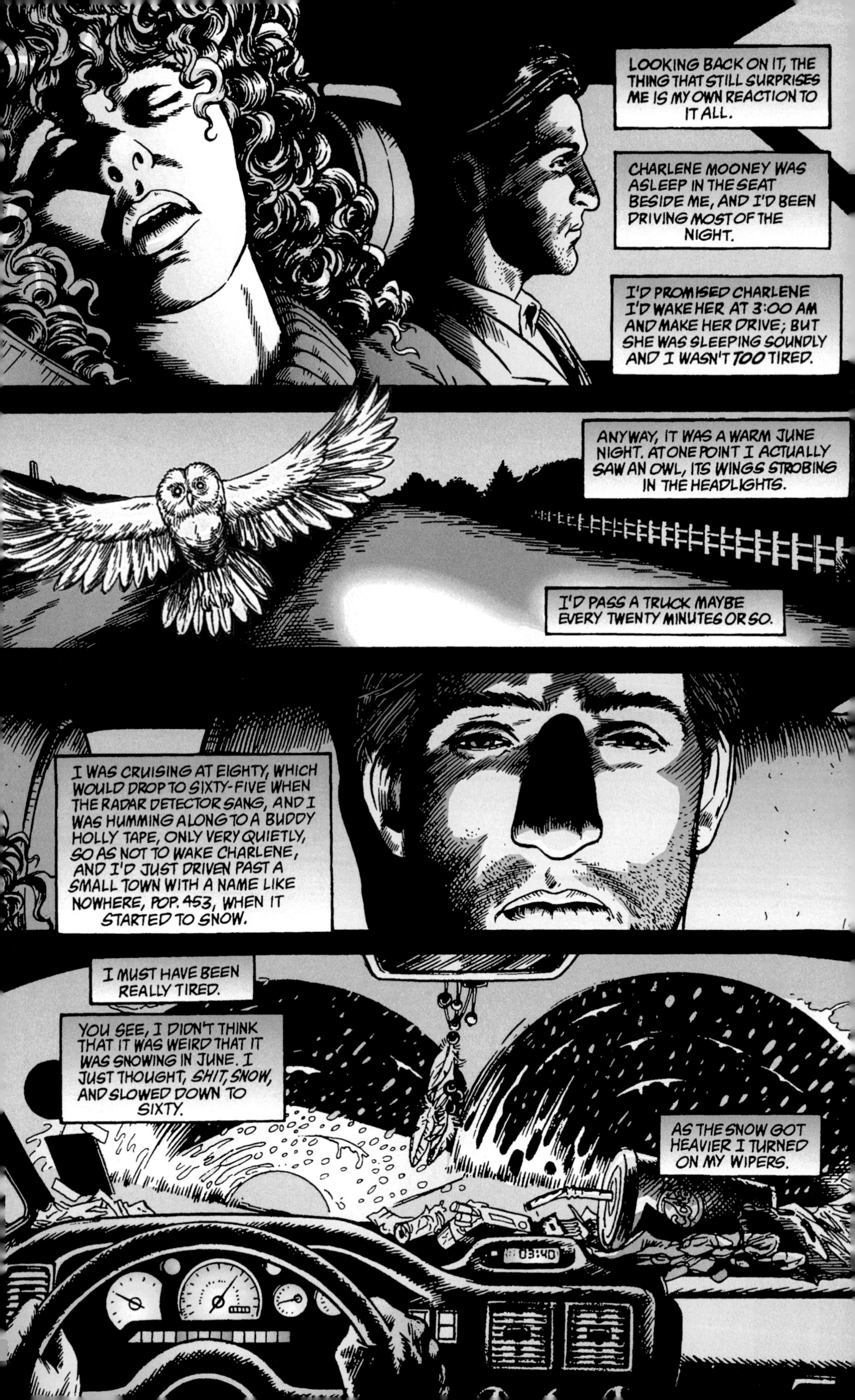
LOOKING BACK ON IT, THE THING THAT STILL SURPRISES ME IS MY OWN REACTION TO IT ALL.
CHARLENE MOONEY WAS ASLEEP IN THE SEAT BESIDE ME, AND I'D BEEN DRIVING MOST OF THE NIGHT.
I'D PROMISED CHARLENE I'D WAKE HER AT 3:00 AM AND MAKE HER DRIVE; BUT SHE WAS SLEEPING SOUNDLY AND I WASN'T TOO TIRED.
ANYWAY, IT WAS A WARM JUNE NIGHT. AT ONE POINT I ACTUALLY SAW AN OWL, ITS WINGS STROBING IN THE HEADLIGHTS.
I'D PASS A TRUCK MAYBE EVERY TWENTY MINUTES OR SO.
I WAS CRUISING AT EIGHTY, WHICH WOULD DROP TO SIXTY-FIVE WHEN THE RADAR DETECTOR SANG, AND I WAS HUMMING ALONG TO A BUDDY HOLLY TAPE, ONLY VERY QUIETLY, SO AS NOT TO WAKE CHARLENE, AND I'D JUST DRIVEN PAST A SMALL TOWN WITH A NAME LIKE NOWHERE, POP. 453, WHEN IT STARTED TO SNOW.
I MUST HAVE BEEN REALLY TIRED.
YOU SEE, I DIDN'T THINK THAT IT WAS WEIRD THAT IT WAS SNOWING IN JUNE. I JUST THOUGHT, SHIT, SNOW, AND SLOWED DOWN TO SIXTY.
AS THE SNOW GOT HEAVIER I TURNED ON MY WIPERS.
03:40

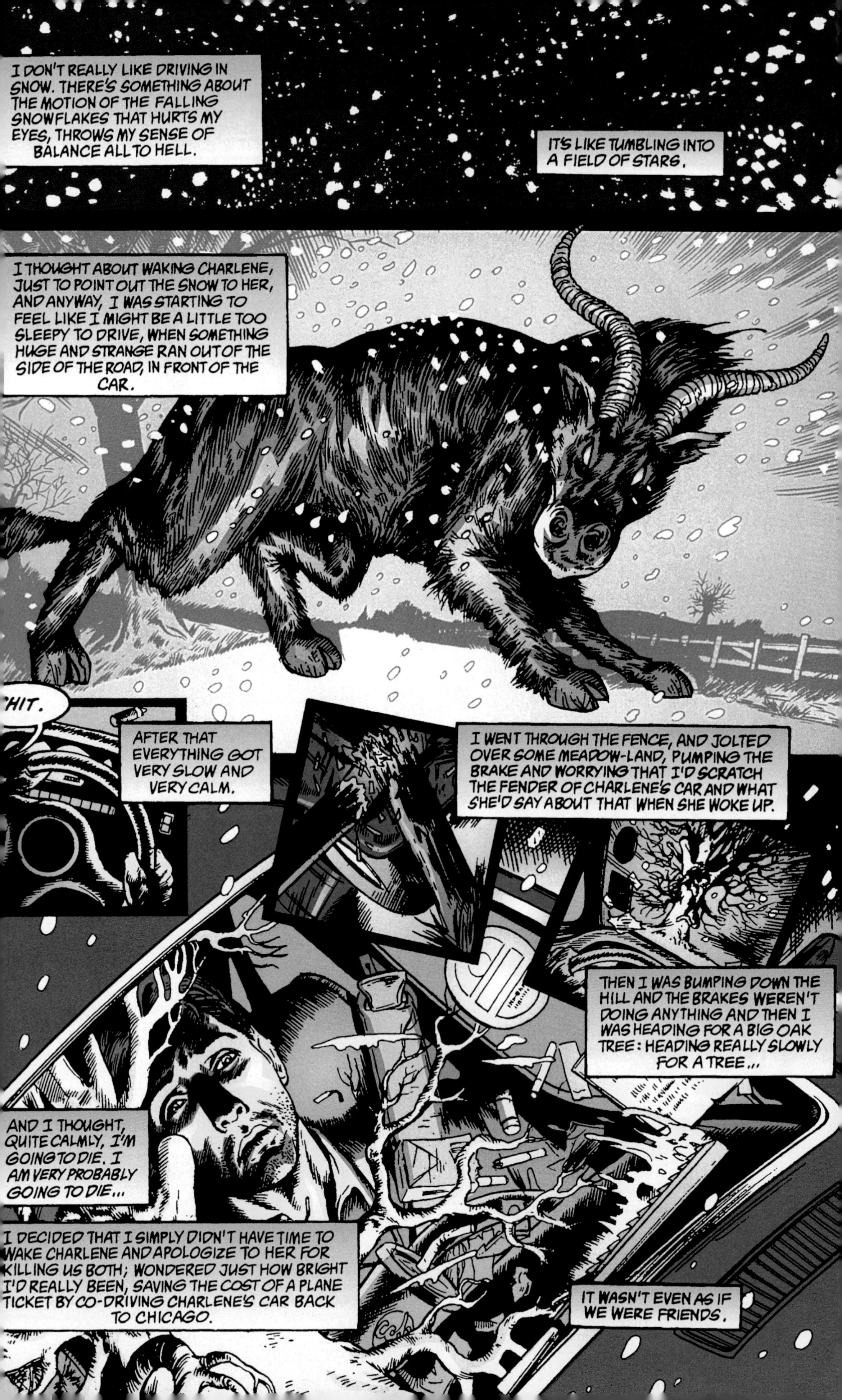
I DON'T REALLY LIKE DRIVING IN SNOW. THERE'S SOMETHING ABOUT THE MOTION OF THE FALLING SNOWFLAKES THAT HURTS MY EYES, THROWS MY SENSE OF BALANCE ALL TO HELL.
IT'S LIKE TUMBLING INTO A FIELD OF STARS.
I THOUGHT ABOUT WAKING CHARLENE, JUST TO POINT OUT THE SNOW TO HER, AND ANYWAY, I WAS STARTING TO FEEL LIKE I MIGHT BE A LITTLE TOO SLEEPY TO DRIVE, WHEN SOMETHING HUGE AND STRANGE RAN OUT OF THE SIDE OF THE ROAD, IN FRONT OF THE CAR.
HIT.
AFTER THAT EVERYTHING GOT VERY SLOW AND VERY CALM.
I WENT THROUGH THE FENCE, AND JOLTED OVER SOME MEADOW-LAND, PUMPING THE BRAKE AND WORRYING THAT I'D SCRATCH THE FENDER OF CHARLENE'S CAR AND WHAT SHE'D SAY ABOUT THAT WHEN SHE WOKE UP.
THEN I WAS BUMPING DOWN THE HILL AND THE BRAKES WEREN'T DOING ANYTHING AND THEN I WAS HEADING FOR A BIG OAK TREE: HEADING REALLY SLOWLY FOR A TREE...
AND I THOUGHT, QUITE CALMLY, I'M GOING TO DIE. I AM VERY PROBABLY GOING TO DIE...
I DECIDED THAT I SIMPLY DIDN'T HAVE TIME TO WAKE CHARLENE AND APOLOGIZE TO HER FOR KILLING US BOTH; WONDERED JUST HOW BRIGHT I'D REALLY BEEN, SAVING THE COST OF A PLANE TICKET BY CO-DRIVING CHARLENE'S CAR BACK TO CHICAGO.
IT WASN'T EVEN AS IF WE WERE FRIENDS.

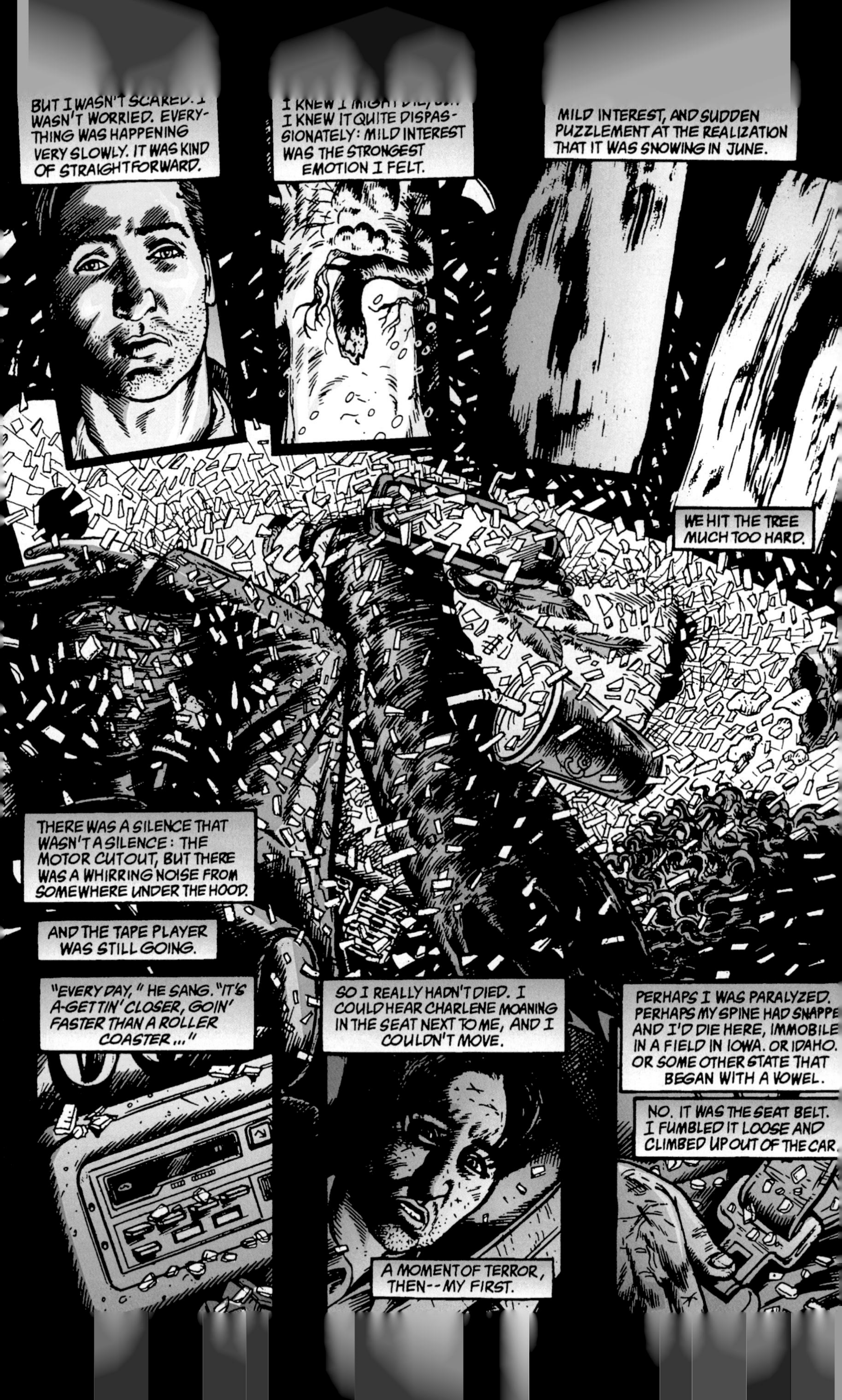
BUT I WASN'T SCARED. I WASN'T WORRIED. EVERYTHING WAS HAPPENING VERY SLOWLY. IT WAS KIND OF STRAIGHTFORWARD.
I KNEW I MIGHT DIE, I KNEW IT QUITE DISPASSIONATELY: MILD INTEREST WAS THE STRONGEST EMOTION I FELT.
MILD INTEREST, AND SUDDEN PUZZLEMENT AT THE REALIZATION THAT IT WAS SNOWING IN JUNE.
WE HIT THE TREE MUCH TOO HARD.
THERE WAS A SILENCE THAT WASN'T A SILENCE: THE MOTOR CUT OUT, BUT THERE WAS A WHIRRING NOISE FROM SOMEWHERE UNDER THE HOOD.
AND THE TAPE PLAYER WAS STILL GOING.
"EVERY DAY," HE SANG. "IT'S A-GETTIN' CLOSER, GOIN' FASTER THAN A ROLLER COASTER..."
SO I REALLY HADN'T DIED. I COULD HEAR CHARLENE MOANING IN THE SEAT NEXT TO ME, AND I COULDN'T MOVE.
A MOMENT OF TERROR, THEN--MY FIRST.
PERHAPS I WAS PARALYZED. PERHAPS MY SPINE HAD SNAPPE AND I'D DIE HERE, IMMOBILE IN A FIELD IN IOWA. OR IDAHO. OR SOME OTHER STATE THAT BEGAN WITH A VOWEL.
NO. IT WAS THE SEAT BELT. I FUMBLED IT LOOSE AND CLIMBED UP OUT OF THE CAR.

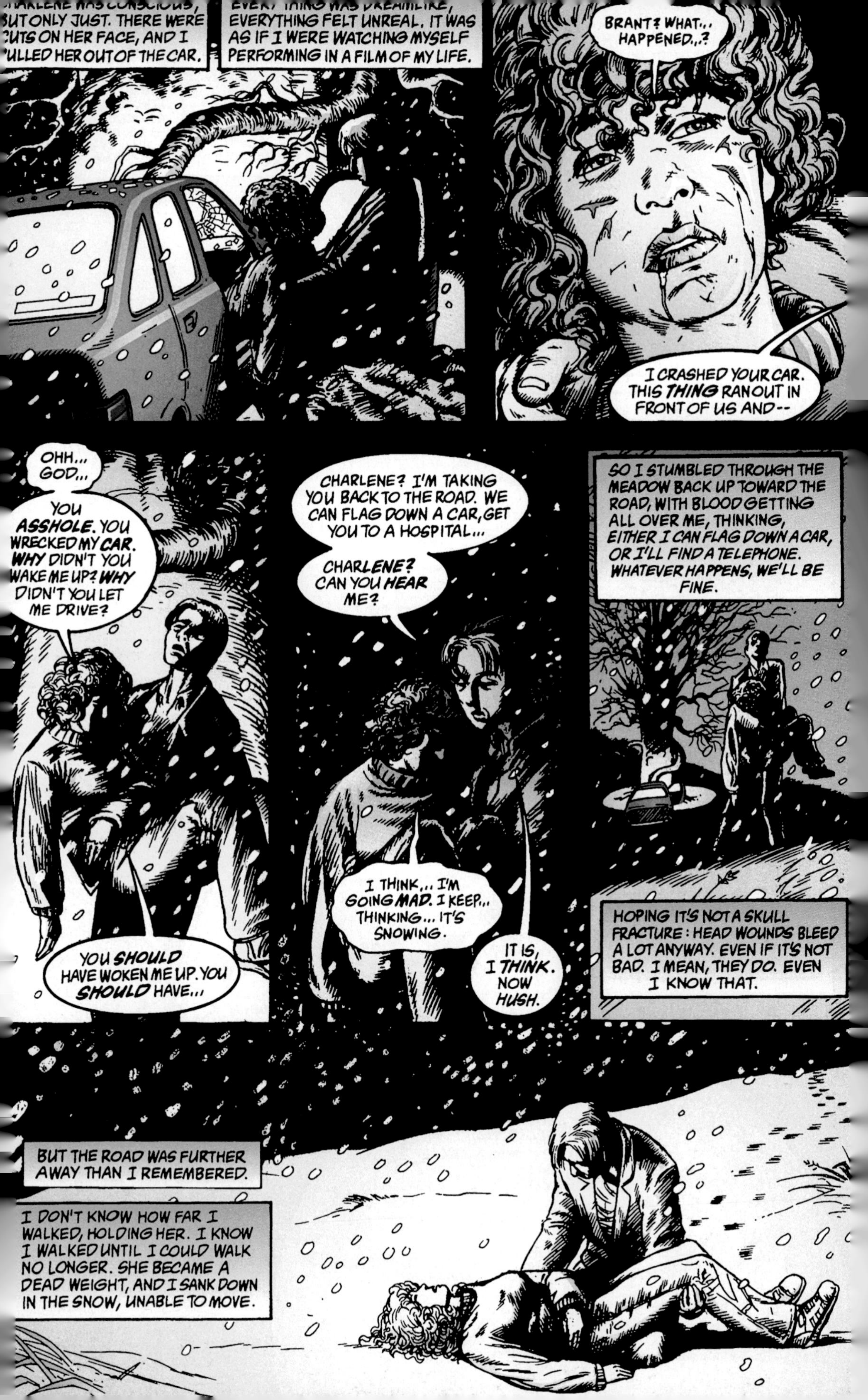
CHARLENE WAS CONSCIOUS, BUT ONLY JUST. THERE WERE CUTS ON HER FACE, AND I PULLED HER OUT OF THE CAR.
EVERYTHING WAS DREAMLIKE, EVERYTHING FELT UNREAL. IT WAS AS IF I WERE WATCHING MYSELF PERFORMING IN A FILM OF MY LIFE.
BRANT? WHAT... HAPPENED...?
I CRASHED YOUR CAR. THIS THING RAN OUT IN FRONT OF US AND--
OHH... GOD...
YOU ASSHOLE. YOU WRECKED MY CAR. WHY DIDN'T YOU WAKE ME UP? WHY DIDN'T YOU LET ME DRIVE?
YOU SHOULD HAVE WOKEN ME UP. YOU SHOULD HAVE...
CHARLENE? I'M TAKING YOU BACK TO THE ROAD. WE CAN FLAG DOWN A CAR, GET YOU TO A HOSPITAL...
CHARLENE? CAN YOU HEAR ME?
I THINK... I'M GOING MAD. I KEEP... THINKING... IT'S SNOWING.
IT IS, I THINK. NOW HUSH.
SO I STUMBLED THROUGH THE MEADOW BACK UP TOWARD THE ROAD, WITH BLOOD GETTING ALL OVER ME, THINKING, EITHER I CAN FLAG DOWN A CAR, OR I'LL FIND A TELEPHONE. WHATEVER HAPPENS, WE'LL BE FINE.
HOPING IT'S NOT A SKULL FRACTURE: HEAD WOUNDS BLEED A LOT ANYWAY. EVEN IF IT'S NOT BAD. I MEAN, THEY DO. EVEN I KNOW THAT.
BUT THE ROAD WAS FURTHER AWAY THAN I REMEMBERED.
I DON'T KNOW HOW FAR I WALKED, HOLDING HER. I KNOW I WALKED UNTIL I COULD WALK NO LONGER. SHE BECAME A DEAD WEIGHT, AND I SANK DOWN IN THE SNOW, UNABLE TO MOVE.

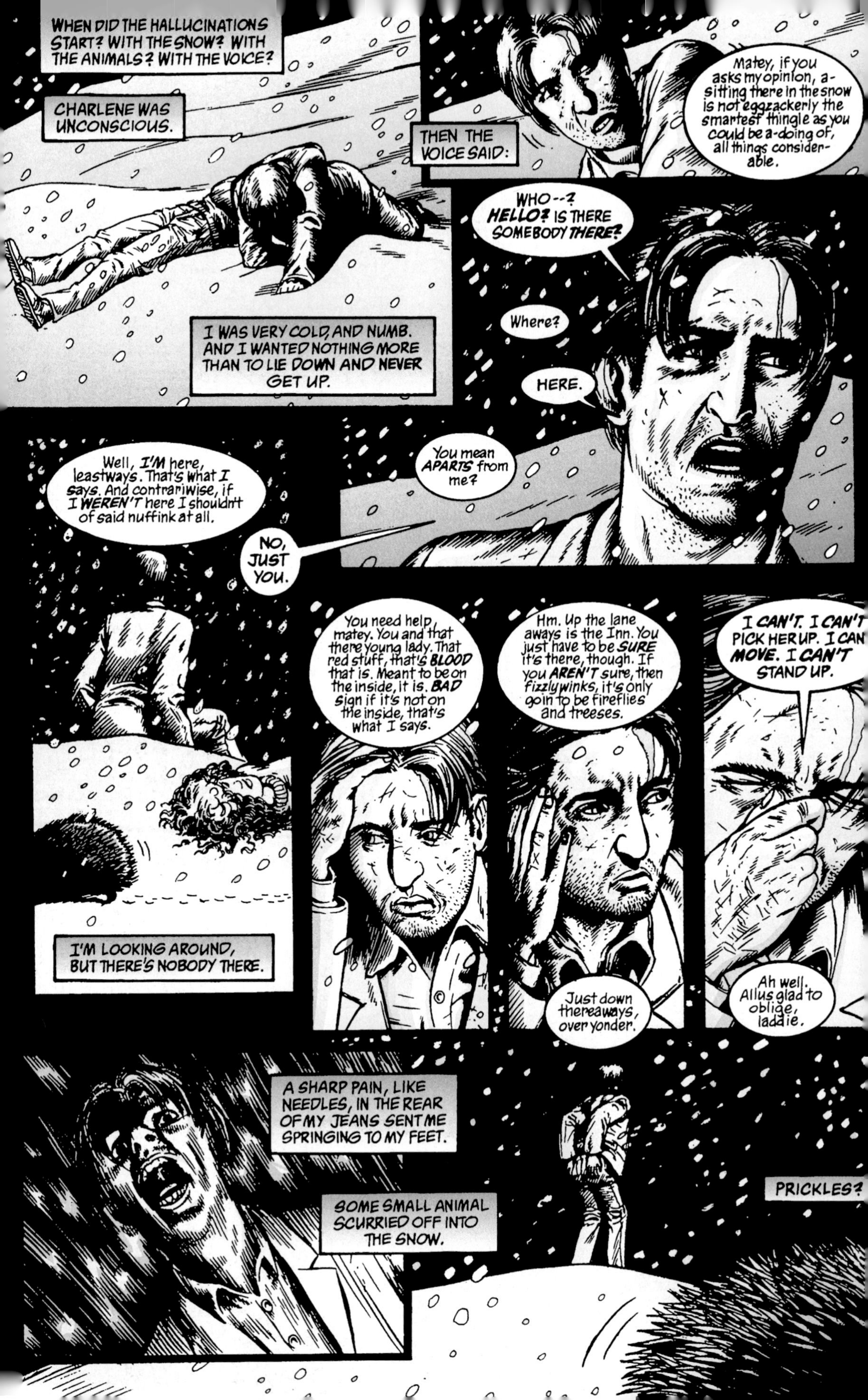
WHEN DID THE HALLUCINATIONS START? WITH THE SNOW? WITH THE ANIMALS? WITH THE VOICE?
CHARLENE WAS UNCONSCIOUS.
I WAS VERY COLD, AND NUMB. AND I WANTED NOTHING MORE THAN TO LIE DOWN AND NEVER GET UP.
THEN THE VOICE SAID:
Matey, if you asks my opinion, a-sitting there in the snow is not eggzackerly the smartest thingle as you could be a-doing of, all things consider-able.
WHO--? HELLO? IS THERE SOMEBODY THERE?
Where?
HERE.
You mean APARTS from me?
Well, I'M here, leastways. That's what I says. And contrariwise, if I WEREN'T here I shouldn't of said nuffink at all.
NO, JUST YOU.
I'M LOOKING AROUND, BUT THERE'S NOBODY THERE.
You need help, matey. You and that there young lady. That red stuff, that's BLOOD that is. Meant to be on the inside, it is. BAD sign if it's not on the inside, that's what I says.
Hm. Up the lane aways is the Inn. You just have to be SURE it's there, though. If you AREN'T sure, then fizzlywinks, it's only goin to be fireflies and treeses.
Just down thereaways, over yonder.
I CAN'T. I CAN'T PICK HER UP. I CAN'T MOVE. I CAN'T STAND UP.
Ah well. Allus glad to oblige, laddie.
A SHARP PAIN, LIKE NEEDLES, IN THE REAR OF MY JEANS SENT ME SPRINGING TO MY FEET.
SOME SMALL ANIMAL SCURRIED OFF INTO THE SNOW.
PRICKLES?

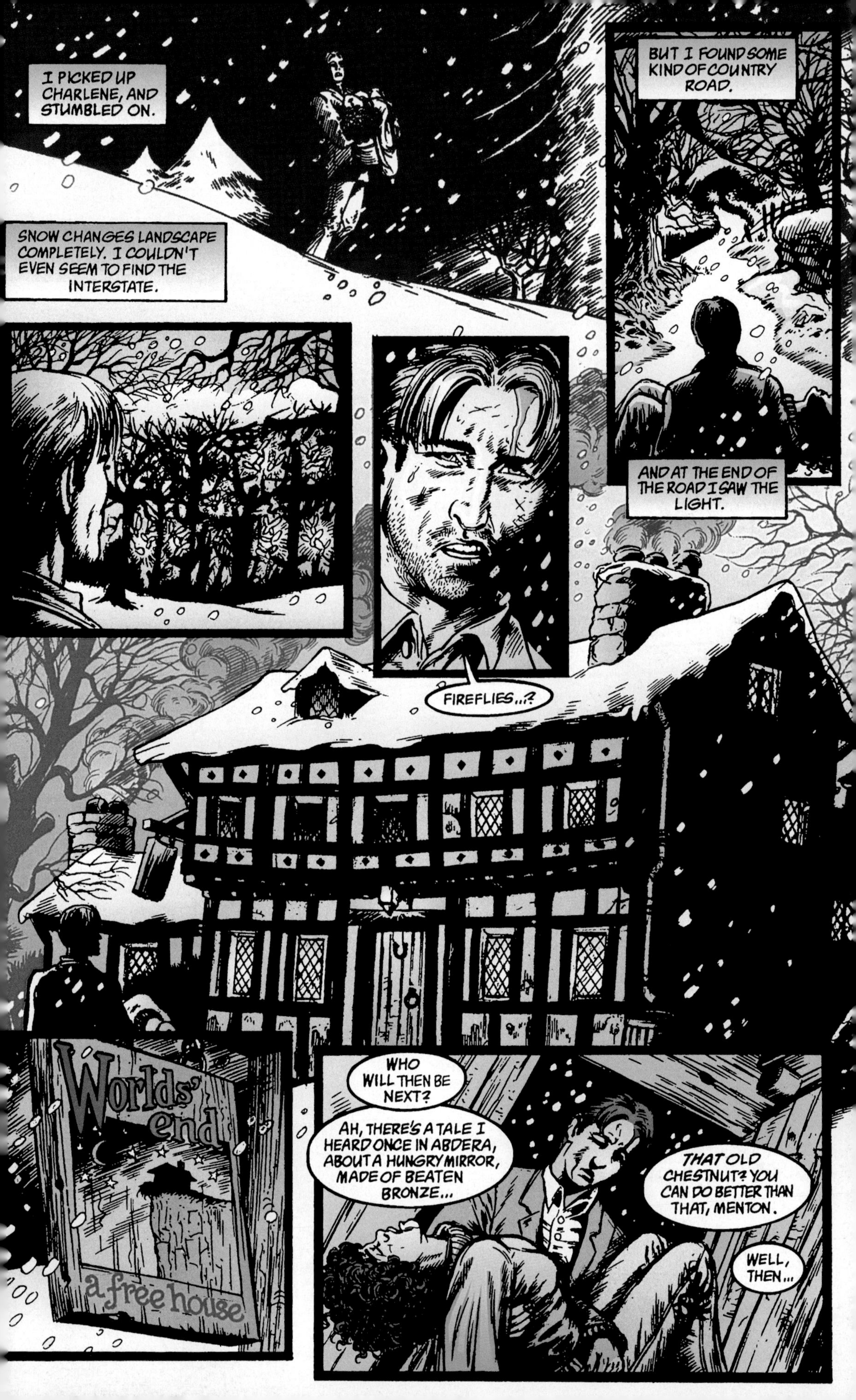
I PICKED UP CHARLENE, AND STUMBLED ON.
SNOW CHANGES LANDSCAPE COMPLETELY. I COULDN'T EVEN SEEM TO FIND THE INTERSTATE.
BUT I FOUND SOME KIND OF COUNTRY ROAD.
AND AT THE END OF THE ROAD I SAW THE LIGHT.
FIREFLIES...?
Worlds' end
a free house
WHO WILL THEN BE NEXT?
AH, THERE'S A TALE I HEARD ONCE IN ABDERA, ABOUT A HUNGRY MIRROR, MADE OF BEATEN BRONZE...
THAT OLD CHESTNUT? YOU CAN DO BETTER THAN THAT, MENTON.
WELL, THEN...

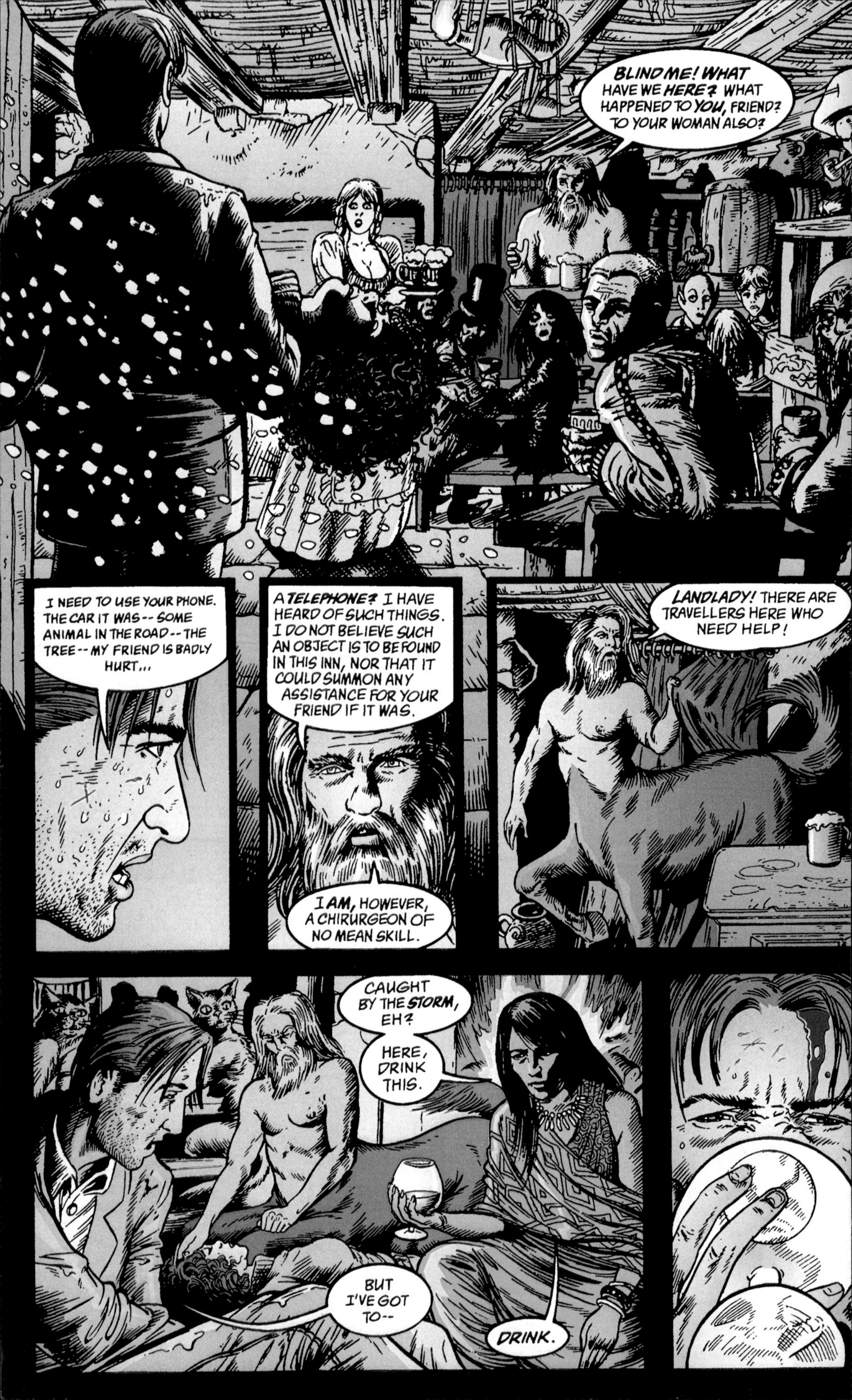
BLIND ME! WHAT HAVE WE HERE? WHAT HAPPENED TO YOU, FRIEND? TO YOUR WOMAN ALSO?
I NEED TO USE YOUR PHONE. THE CAR IT WAS-- SOME ANIMAL IN THE ROAD-- THE TREE-- MY FRIEND IS BADLY HURT...
A TELEPHONE? I HAVE HEARD OF SUCH THINGS. I DO NOT BELIEVE SUCH AN OBJECT IS TO BE FOUND IN THIS INN, NOR THAT IT COULD SUMMON ANY ASSISTANCE FOR YOUR FRIEND IF IT WAS.
I AM, HOWEVER, A CHIRURGEON OF NO MEAN SKILL.
LANDLADY! THERE ARE TRAVELLERS HERE WHO NEED HELP!
CAUGHT BY THE STORM, EH?
HERE, DRINK THIS.
BUT I'VE GOT TO--
DRINK.

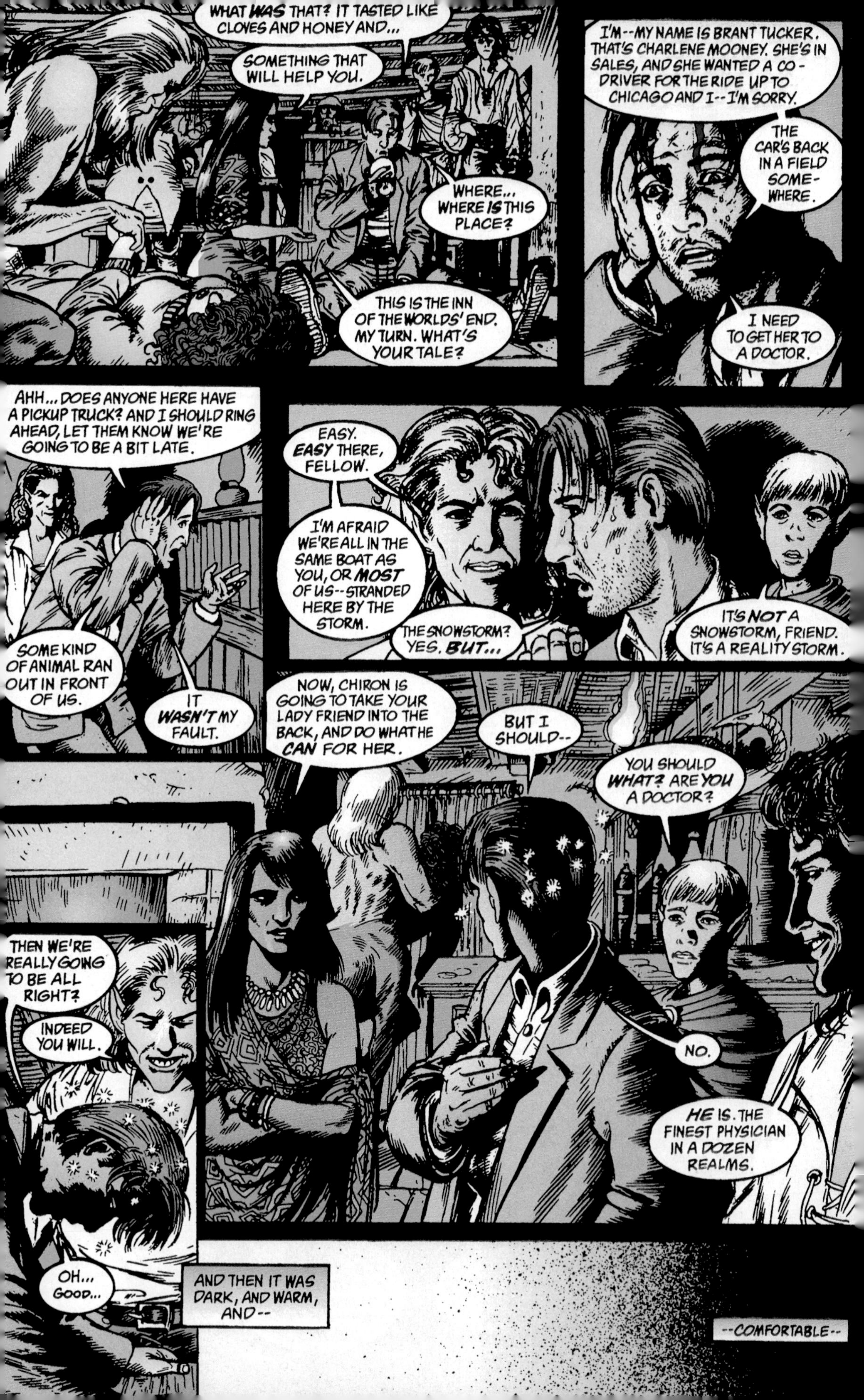
WHAT WAS THAT? IT TASTED LIKE CLOVES AND HONEY AND...
SOMETHING THAT WILL HELP YOU.
WHERE... WHERE IS THIS PLACE?
THIS IS THE INN OF THE WORLDS' END. MY TURN. WHAT'S YOUR TALE?
I'M--MY NAME IS BRANT TUCKER. THAT'S CHARLENE MOONEY. SHE'S IN SALES, AND SHE WANTED A CO-DRIVER FOR THE RIDE UP TO CHICAGO AND I--I'M SORRY.
THE CAR'S BACK IN A FIELD SOME-WHERE.
I NEED TO GET HER TO A DOCTOR.
AHH... DOES ANYONE HERE HAVE A PICKUP TRUCK? AND I SHOULD RING AHEAD, LET THEM KNOW WE'RE GOING TO BE A BIT LATE.
SOME KIND OF ANIMAL RAN OUT IN FRONT OF US.
IT WASN'T MY FAULT.
EASY. EASY THERE, FELLOW.
I'M AFRAID WE'RE ALL IN THE SAME BOAT AS YOU, OR MOST OF US--STRANDED HERE BY THE STORM.
THE SNOWSTORM? YES. BUT...
IT'S NOT A SNOWSTORM, FRIEND. IT'S A REALITY STORM.
NOW, CHIRON IS GOING TO TAKE YOUR LADY FRIEND INTO THE BACK, AND DO WHAT HE CAN FOR HER.
BUT I SHOULD--
YOU SHOULD WHAT? ARE YOU A DOCTOR?
NO.
HE IS. THE FINEST PHYSICIAN IN A DOZEN REALMS.
THEN WE'RE REALLY GOING TO BE ALL RIGHT?
INDEED YOU WILL.
OH... GOOD...
AND THEN IT WAS DARK, AND WARM, AND--
--COMFORTABLE--

WAKEY WAKEY.

STEW?

WHERE AM I?

HEY. MISTER TUCKER. I GOT YOU SOME STEW.

YOU'RE IN THE INN, SIR. YOU'VE BEEN ASLEEP FOR ABOUT 15 HOURS, GIVE OR TAKE.

YOU'RE LIKE THE REST OF 'EM: WAITING FOR THE STORM TO END, BEFORE THEY CAN GO ON THEIR WAY.

CHARLENE?

THE *LADY* YOU WERE WITH? SHE'S NONE THE WORSE FOR WEAR. THE HORSE-MAN FIXED HER UP.

SHE'S IN THE *CORNER* OVER THERE. SEE?

CHARLENE?

WHAT ARE THEY DOING?

KILLING TIME. *HUH?*

BRANT. YOU'RE AWAKE. *GOOD.* EAT YOUR STEW.

WHAT'S GOING ON?

WE'RE TELLING *STORIES.* YOU JUST MISSED A REALLY GOOD ONE ABOUT A MAN WHO WON NOVEMBER 1937 IN A POKER GAME.

LOOK, YOUR CAR. EVERYTHING THAT HAPPENED...

IT CAN *WAIT,* BRANT. WE AREN'T GOING ANYWHERE, NOT FOR A WHILE AT LEAST.

ANYWAY, MISTER GAHERIS WAS ABOUT TO BEGIN.

I CALL THIS TALE, IN DEFERENCE TO ANOTHER, RATHER LONGER STORY, A TALE OF TWO

ALTHOUGH HOW MANY CI THERE ARE IN TRULY, I MUST CONFESS I D NOT KNOW

THERE WAS ONCE A MAN WHO LIVED IN A CITY, AND HE HAD LIVED IN THAT CITY ALL HIS LIFE.

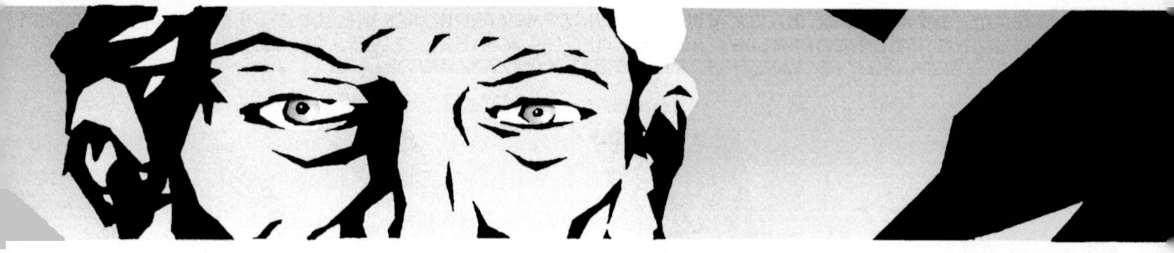

IT WAS NOT THAT HE HAD NEVER LEFT THAT CITY; HE HAD HOLIDAYED BY THE SEA, AND, ON THE OCCASION OF HIS PARENTS' DEATH, HE TOOK HIS SMALL INHERITANCE AND SPENT TWO WEEKS ON A TROPICAL ISLAND, ON WHICH HE CONTRACTED A NASTY CASE OF SUNBURN.

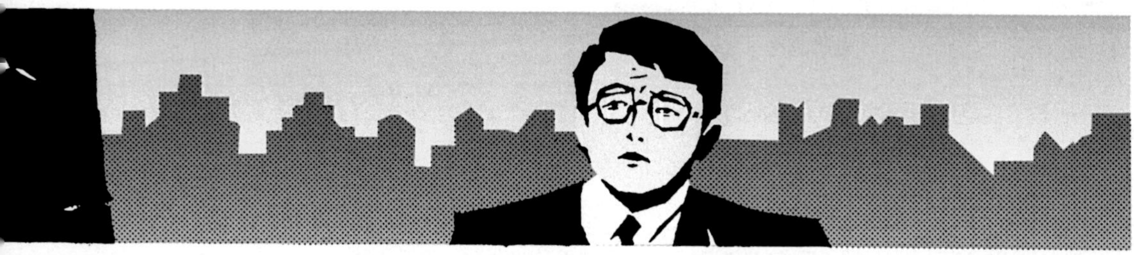

HE HAD A JOB IN THE CITY CENTER, AND HE COMMUTED TO WORK EACH MORNING FROM THE CITY SUBURBS, RETURNED HOME AGAIN IN THE EVENING.

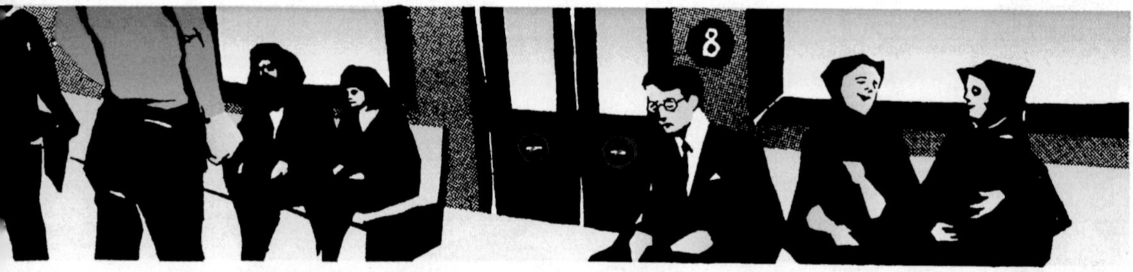
8

IN THE SUBWAY TRAIN, IN THE MORNING, HE WOULD READ A NEWSPAPER, AND WONDER WHAT WOULD HAPPEN WERE THE SUBWAY CARRIAGE SUDDENLY TO BE TRANSPORTED TO A DISTANT PLANET: HOW LONG IT WOULD TAKE BEFORE THE PASSENGERS BEGAN TO SPEAK, ONE TO ANOTHER; WHO WOULD MAKE LOVE TO WHOM; WHO WOULD BE EATEN SHOULD THEY RUN OUT OF FOOD.

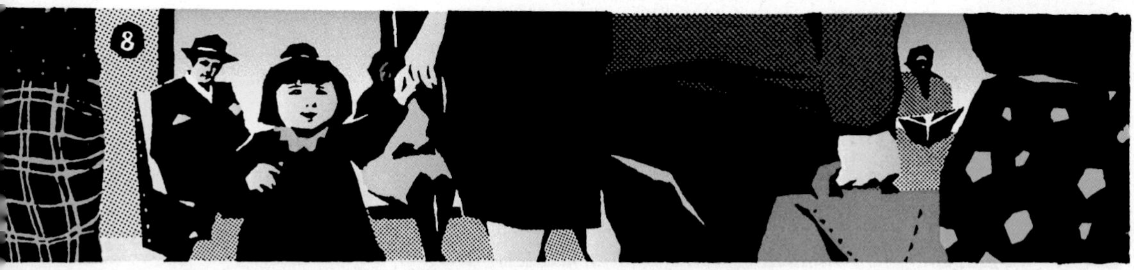
8

HE FELT VAGUELY ASHAMED OF THESE DAYDREAMS.

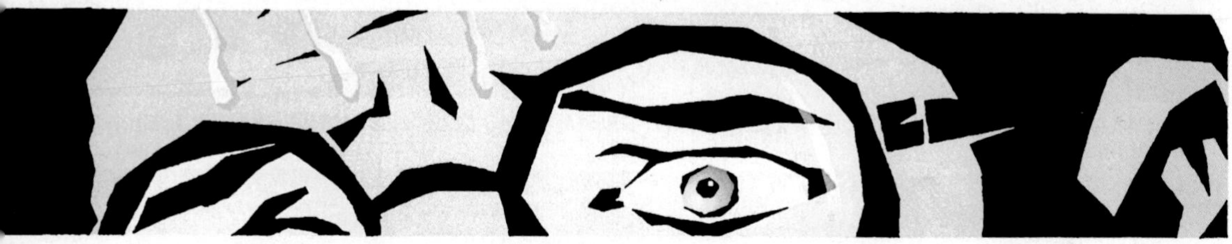

HE WORKED ALL DAY AT A DESK, IN A ROOM WITH DOZENS OF MEN AND WOMEN WHO SAT AT DESKS LIKE HIS AND DID JOBS MUCH LIKE HIS. HE NEITHER LIKED NOR DISLIKED HIS JOB: HE HAD TAKEN THE JOB BECAUSE IT WAS A JOB FOR LIFE, BECAUSE IT PROVIDED HIM WITH STABILITY AND SECURITY.

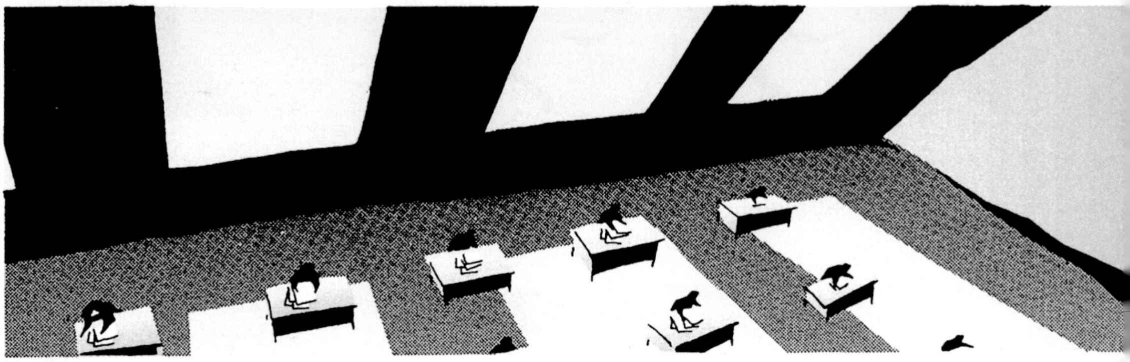

BUT ON HIS LUNCH BREAK, WHILE HIS FELLOW WORKERS WENT OFF TO A CAFETERIA ON ANOTHER FLOOR, TO EAT SUBSIDIZED LUNCHES AND EXCHANGE GOSSIP, THE MAN, WHOSE NAME WAS ROBERT, WOULD TAKE A SANDWICH FROM HIS BRIEFCASE, AND, FOR AN HOUR, EXPLORE THE BYWAYS OF THE CITY.

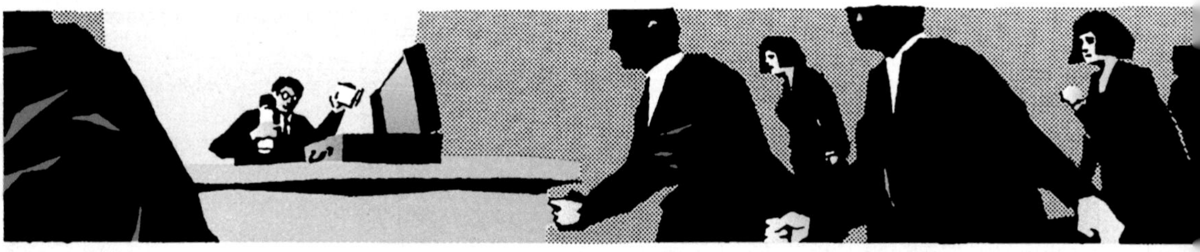

HE WOULD WALK, OR RIDE A BUS, AND HE WOULD STARE AT HIS CITY, AND THIS MADE HIM HAPPY.

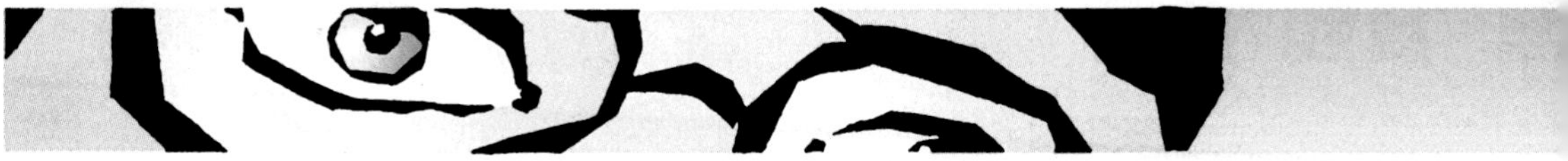

A CARVING ON A WALL ABOVE A DOOR ON A CONDEMNED HOUSE; A BRIGHT FLASH OF SUNLIGHT REFLECTING OFF THE RAILINGS OF A PARK, MAKING THEM SERRIED SPEARS TO GUARD THE GREEN GRASS AND RUNNING CHILDREN; A GRAVESTONE IN A CHURCHYARD, ERODED BY WIND AND RAIN AND TIME UNTIL THE WORDS ON THE STONE HAD BEEN LOST BUT THE MOSSES AND LICHENS STILL SPELLED OUT LETTERS FROM FORGOTTEN ALPHABETS...

ALL THESE SIGHTS, AND MANY OTHERS, HE TREASURED AND COLLECTED.

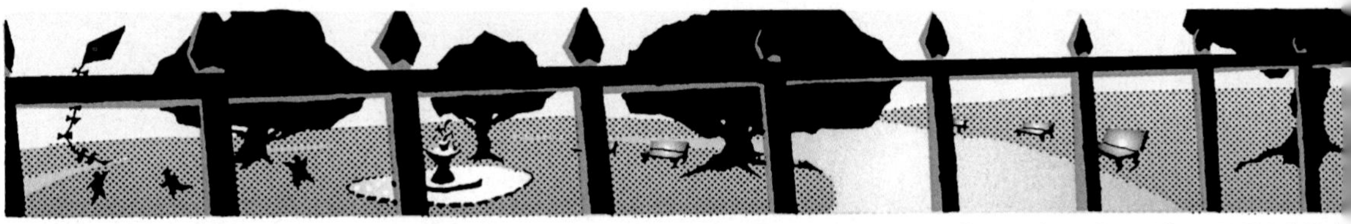

ROBERT SAW THE CITY AS A HUGE JEWEL, AND THE TINY MOMENTS OF REALITY HE FOUND IN HIS LUNCH-HOURS AS FACETS, CUT AND GLITTERING, OF THE WHOLE.

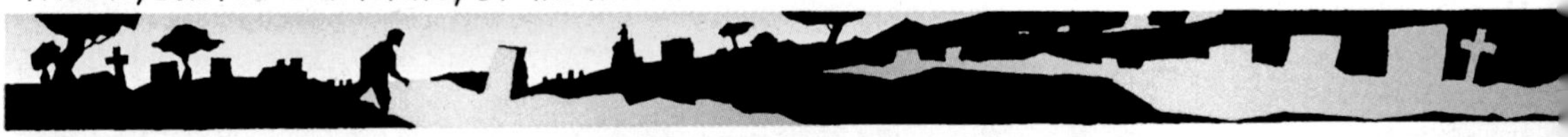

IS THERE ANY PERSON IN THE WORLD WHO DOES NOT DREAM? WHO DOES NOT CONTAIN WITHIN THEM WORLDS UNIMAGINED?

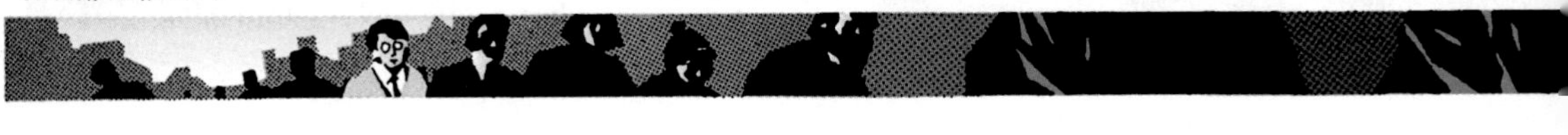

IT DID NOT OCCUR TO ROBERT THAT EACH OF HIS WORKMATES HAD SOMETHING THAT MADE THEM, ALSO, UNIQUE; NOR DID IT OCCUR TO HIM THAT HIS PASSION FOR THE CITY WAS IN ITSELF OUT OF THE ORDINARY.

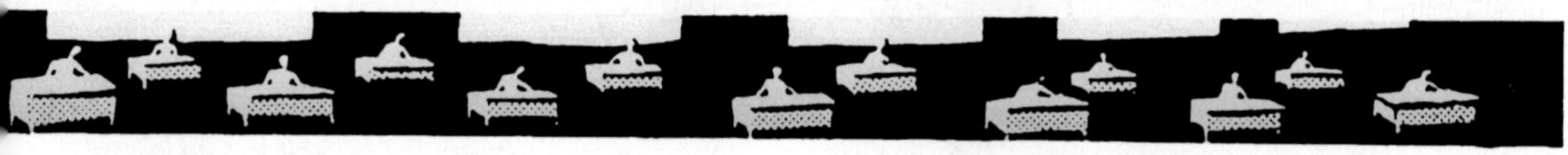

SOMETIMES ROBERT WOULD WALK ALONE IN THE CITY AT NIGHT, WHEN HE COULD NOT SLEEP, TO SEE THE FACE THE CITY PRESENTED AFTER DARK, WHICH WAS NOT ITS DAYTIME FACE. ONCE HE SHIVERED TO HEAR, THROUGH A WINDOW, SOMEONE SCREAMING--LOST IN A NIGHTMARE, PERHAPS, OR WAKING FROM HORRORS THEY WERE UNABLE TO FACE.

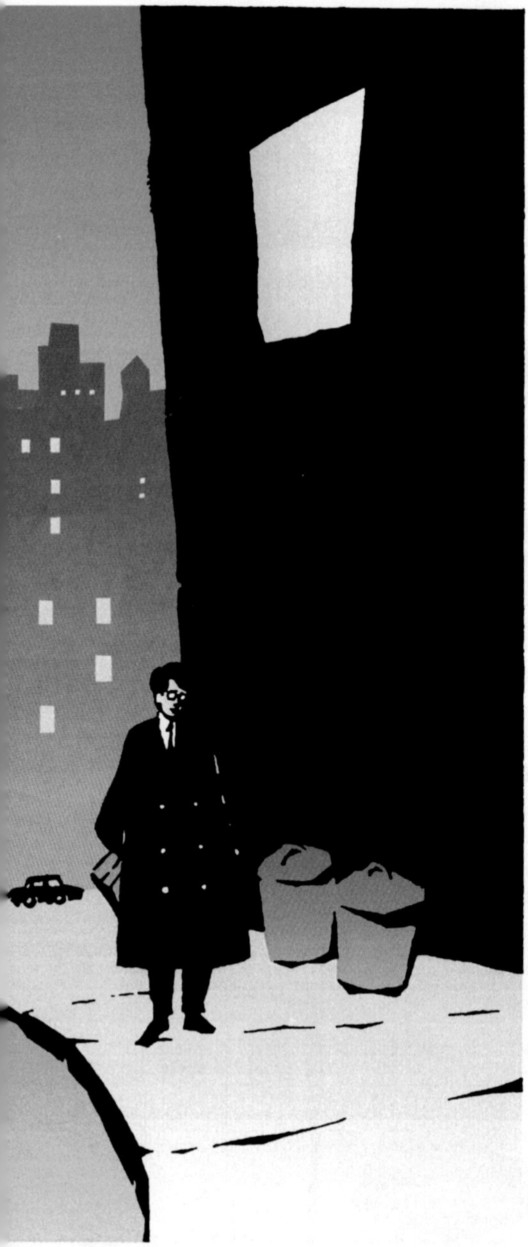

THERE WAS A RIVER THAT RAN THROUGH THE CITY, AND DURING HIS NIGHT WALKS ROBERT WOULD STARE INTO THE RIVER, AND WATCH THE LIGHTS OF THE CITY REFLECTED IN THE WATER.

THE NEXT DAY AT WORK HE WOULD BE TIRED.

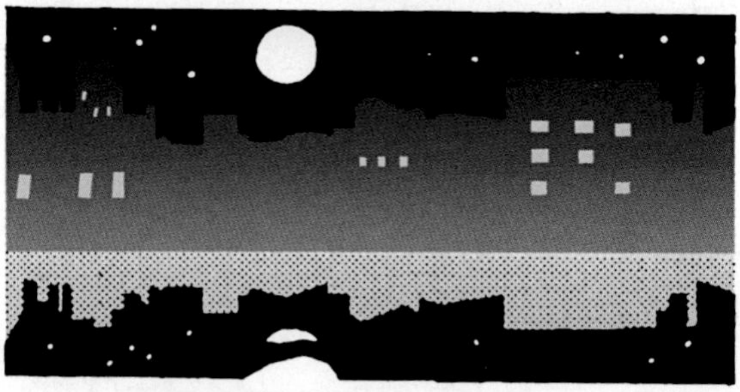

ONE MORNING HE TOOK THE SUBWAY TO WORK AS HE USUALLY DID, SPENT HIS DAY TOILING IN THE ROOM OF DESKS. ON HIS LUNCH HOUR HE WALKED THROUGH THE SHOPPING DISTRICT.

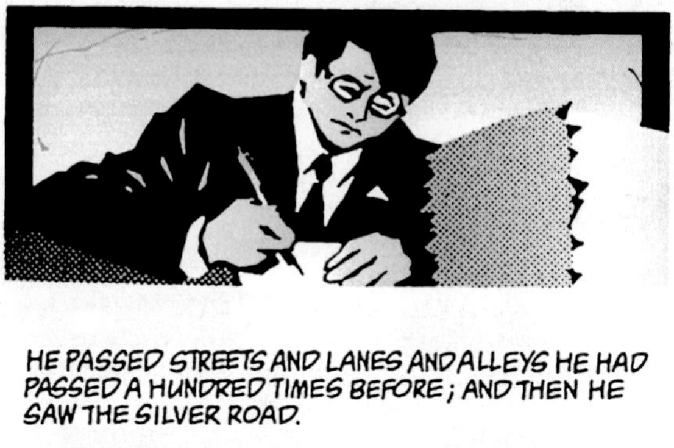

HE PASSED STREETS AND LANES AND ALLEYS HE HAD PASSED A HUNDRED TIMES BEFORE; AND THEN HE SAW THE SILVER ROAD.

IT GLITTERED AND GLIMMERED AWAY BEYOND A STREET MARKET.

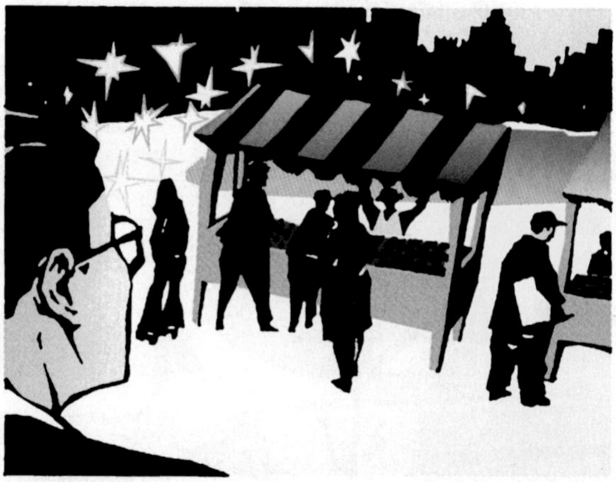

ROBERT RAN THROUGH THE MARKET, BUT WHEN HE REACHED THE END OF THE STREET HE FOUND ONLY AN ALLEYWAY, AND THE SILVER ROAD WAS NOWHERE TO BE SEEN.

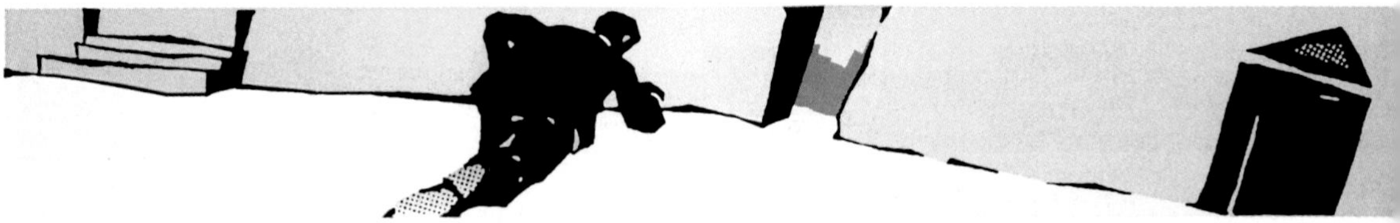

HE RETURNED TO WORK, BUT FOUND HIMSELF UNABLE TO CONCENTRATE. TWO HOURS' WORK STRETCHED INTO THREE AND FOUR, AND BY THE TIME HE HAD FINISHED HE WAS ALONE IN AN EMPTY OFFICE.

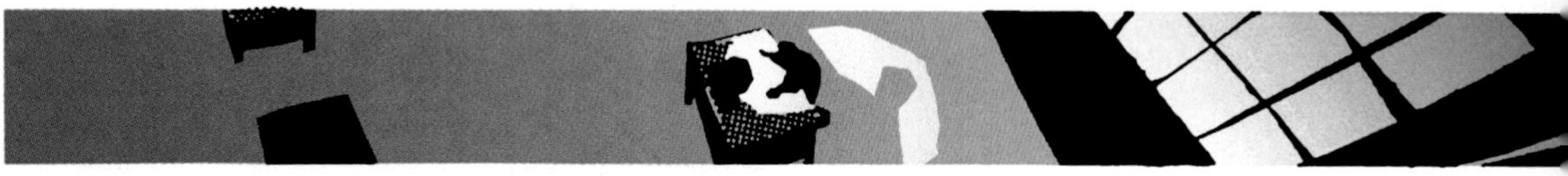

THE SUN HAD SET, AND HE HAD MISSED HIS USUAL TRAIN HOME.

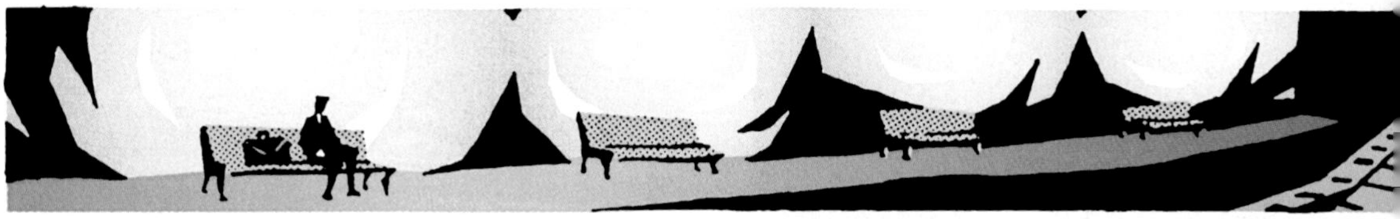

ROBERT WAITED ON AN EMPTY PLATFORM; AND DAYDREAMED ABOUT THE SILVER ROAD THROUGH THE CITY.

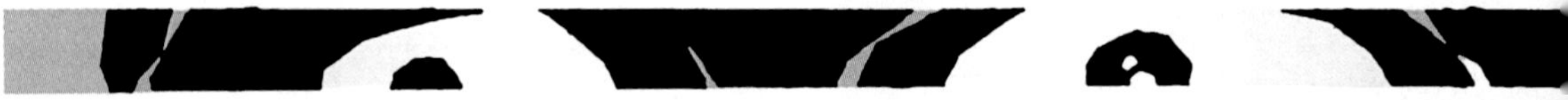

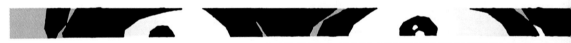

PERHAPS HE DOZED, PERHAPS NOT; ANYWAY, HE WAS JERKED OUT OF HIS REVERIE BY THE ARRIVAL OF THE TRAIN

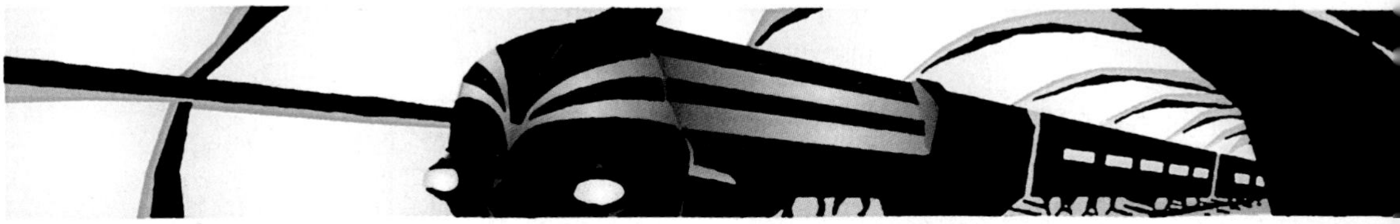

IT WAS UNLIKE ANY UNDERGROUND TRAIN HE HAD SEEN BEFORE; THE LINES OF IT WERE SLEEK AND STRANGE.

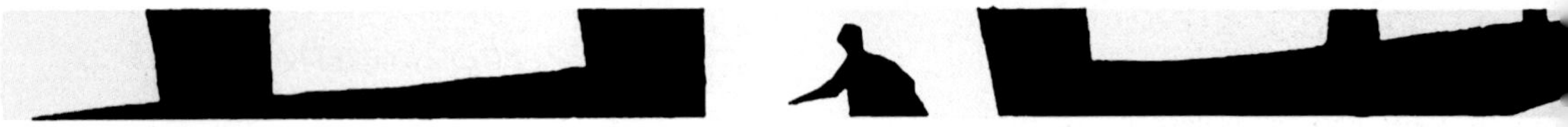

IT ARRIVED SILENTLY,
AND ROBERT GOT ON.

THERE WAS ONLY ONE OTHER PASSENGER ON THE TRAIN.

HE WAS STANDING, SOLITARY, IN THE COMPARTMENT ROBERT HAD ENTERED: A PALE MAN, WITH WILD, BLACK HAIR, DRESSED IN A LON BLACK COAT.

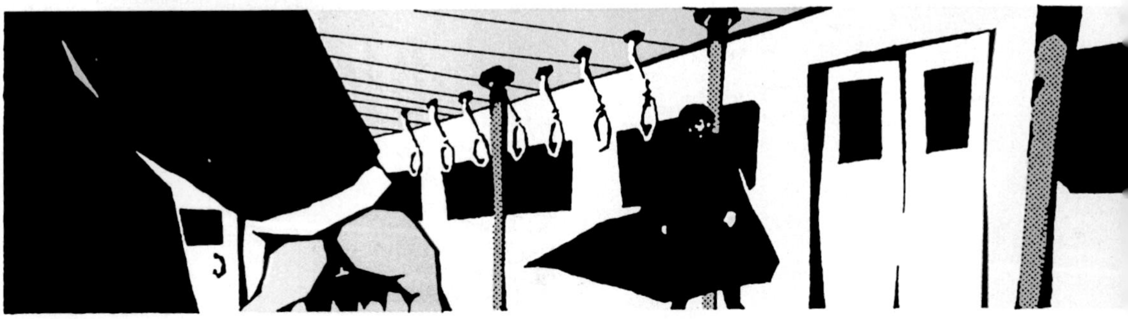

IT TOOK ONLY A FEW MINUTES FOR ROBERT TO REALIZE SOMETHING WAS WRONG: THE TRAIN WAS NOT STOPPING AT ANY STATIONS. IT WAS INSTEAD SPEEDING ONWARD SILENTLY BENEATH THE CITY.

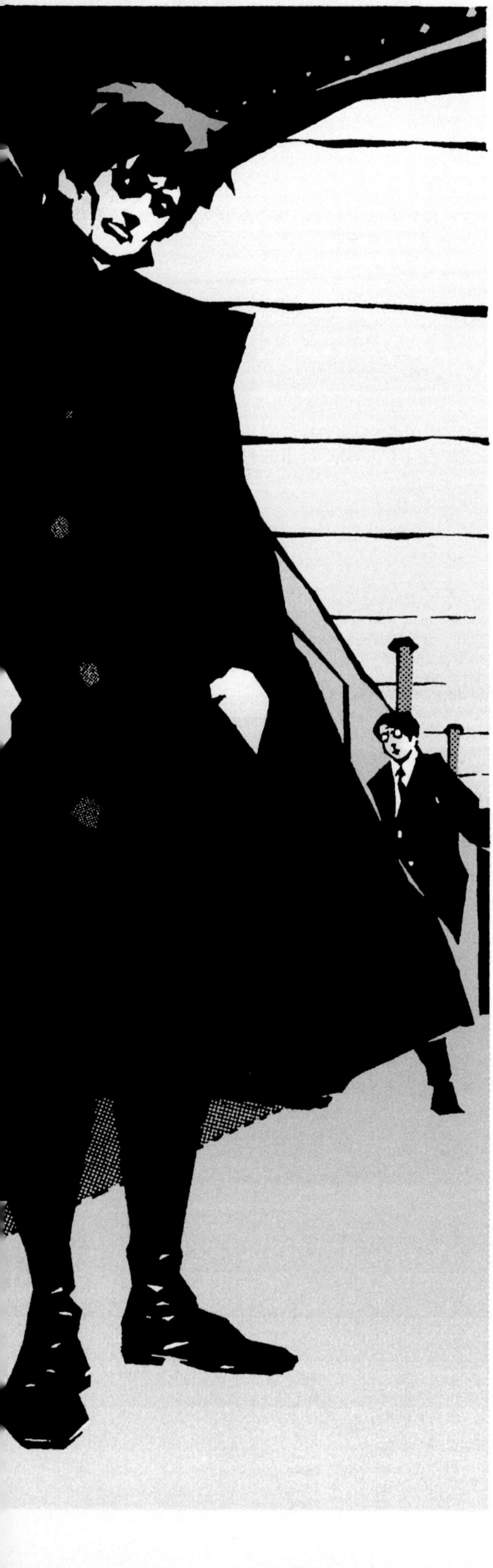

"EXCUSE ME? IS *THIS* TRAIN GOING TO *STOP?* IS THIS THE CITY LINE? I'M AFRAID I GOT ON THE WRONG *TRAIN*. I'M AFRAID..."

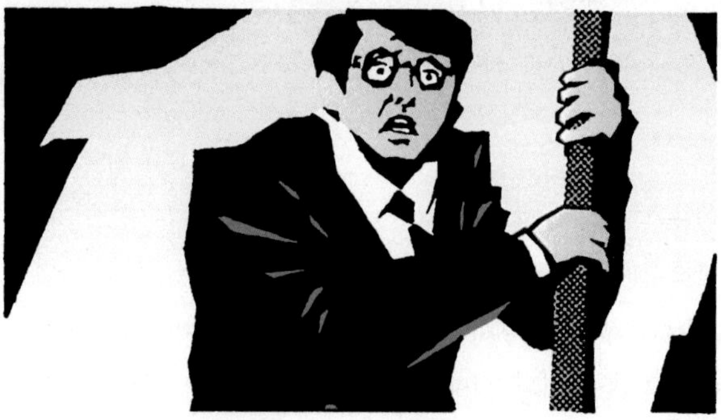

THE STRANGER SIMPLY STARED AT HIM. DARK EYES, LIKE POOLS OF NIGHT.

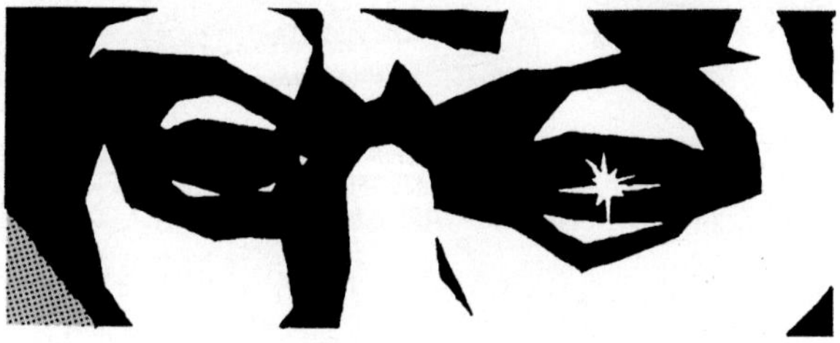

ROBERT TOOK A STEP BACKWARD THEN, NERVOUSLY, AND, AS HE DID, HE FELT THE TRAIN BEGIN TO SLOW.

THE LIGHTS OF A STATION GLIMMERED THROUGH THE WINDOWS OF THE TRAIN.

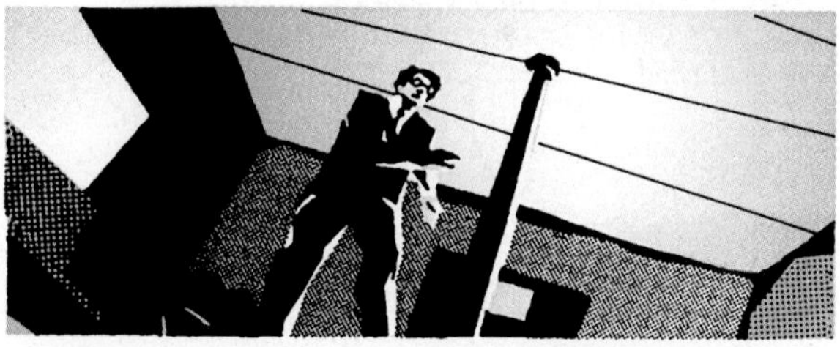

THE DOORS HISSED OPEN, AND ROBERT STUMBLED OUT.

HE DID NOT RECOGNIZE THE STATION. THERE WAS NO SIGN INDICATING ITS NAME, AND IT WAS POORLY LIT.

HE HURRIED UP THE STAIRS. ROBERT WAS CERTAIN ENOUGH OF HIS FAMILIARITY WITH THE CITY TO KNOW THAT ONCE ON THE STREETS IT WOULD BE A SIMPLE THING FOR HIM TO ORIENT HIMSELF.

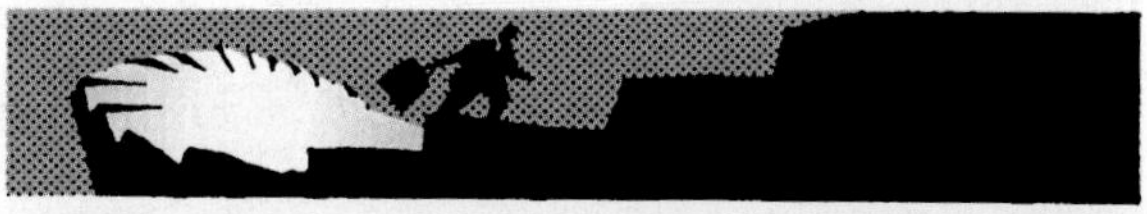

HE WOULD GET A TAXI HOME. CERTAINLY IT WOULD BE EXPENSIVE, BUT IT WAS AN EXPENSE HE WOULD WILLINGLY BEAR. HE STEPPED THROUGH AN ARCHWAY ONTO THE STREET.

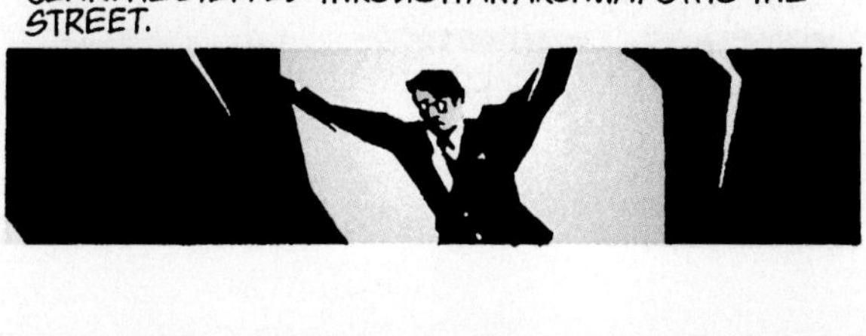

THERE WAS SOMETHING MORE THAN FAMILIAR ABOUT THE STREET HE STOOD IN. SOMETHING HE FOUND IMPOSSIBLE TO PLACE; AND HE FOUND HIMSELF UNABLE TO NAME THE STREET.

HE TURNED, BUT THE ARCHWAY WAS GONE.

BUILDINGS LOOMED ABOVE HIM, HIGH AND LIGHTLESS.

ROBERT HURRIED THROUGH THE CITY-- IF HE WAS STILL IN THE CITY, FOR HE WAS IN TWO MINDS ABOUT THIS.

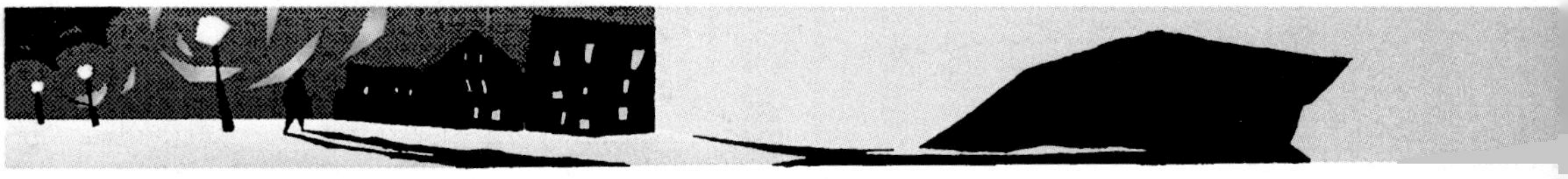

A COLD WIND BLEW DOWN THE THOROUGHFARES AND AVENUES, BRINGING WITH IT FAMILIAR SCENTS: THE MEAT MARKET AT DAWN; HOT TELEVISION SETS FROM THE ELECTRICAL DISTRICT; THE SMELL OF EARTH FRESH-DUG, AND OF BURNING TAR, OF SEWERS AND SUBWAYS.

ROBERT BEGAN TO RUN, CERTAIN THAT, EVENTUALLY, HE WOULD SEE A STREET OR BUILDING HE RECOGNIZED.

HE DIDN'T. EVENTUALLY HE COLLAPSED, BREATHLESS AGAINST A CONCRETE WALL.

FROM TIME TO TIME, ROBERT COULD FEEL EYES ON HIM FROM THE WINDOWS AND DOORWAYS. BUT THE FACES HE SAW, WHEN HE SAW FACES, WERE LOST AND SCARED AND DISTANT, AND NO ONE EVER CAME CLOSE ENOUGH TO HIM TO TALK.

THERE WERE ALSO CERTAIN OTHER PEOPLE IN THE CITY, BUT THEY WERE BRIEF, FLEETING PEOPLE WHO SHIMMERED AND VANISHED.

FROM TIME TO TIME THE SKY WOULD LIGHTEN; AT OTHER TIMES IT WENT DARK. BUT THERE WERE NO STARS OR MOON IN THE SKY IN THE DARKNESS, NO SUN BY DAY.

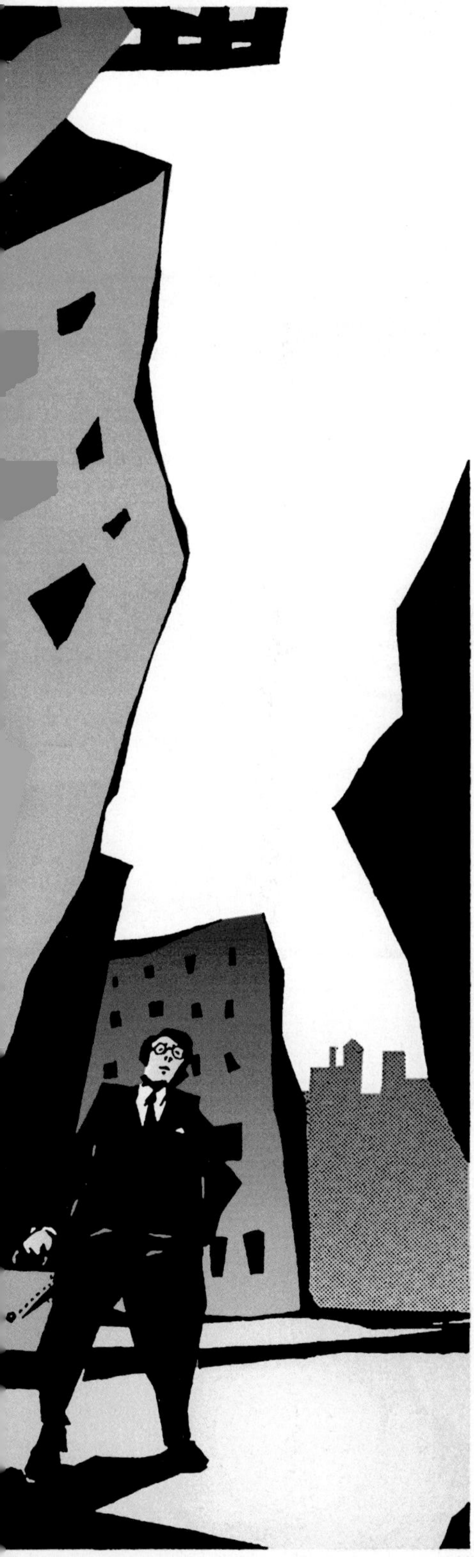

THE ROADS MIXED HIM UP, TURNED HIM AROUND. HERE, HE WOULD PASS A CATHEDRAL OR MUSEUM, THERE, A SKYSCRAPER OR A FOUNTAIN --ALWAYS HAUNTINGLY FAMILIAR. BUT HE NEVER PASSED THE SAME LANDMARK TWICE, COULD NEVER FIND THE ROAD TO RETURN HIM TO THE LANDMARK AGAIN.

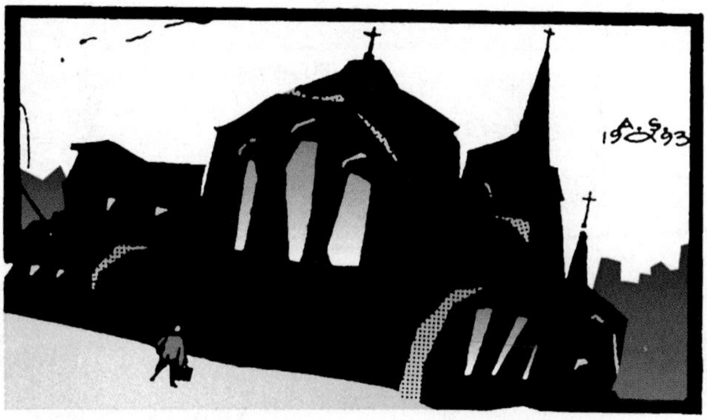

NOR WAS HE EVER ABLE TO FIND THE SUBWAY STATION FROM WHICH HE HAD ENTERED THIS DISTORTED ECHO OF HIS CITY.

HE HAD BEEN IN THE CITY FOR DAYS, OR FOR WEEKS, OR PERHAPS EVEN MONTHS. HE HAD NO WAY OF KNOWING.

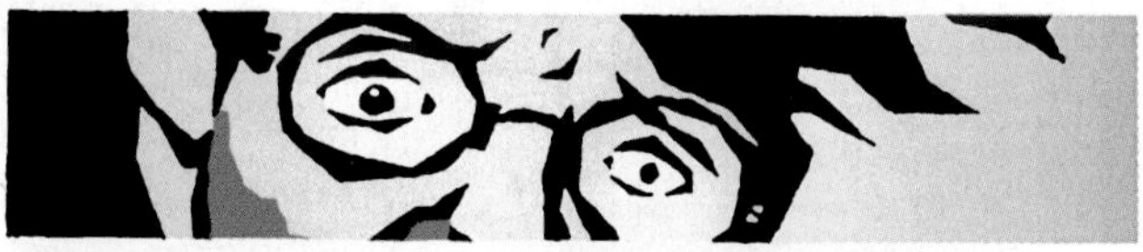

IT WAS SUNRISE, ALTHOUGH NO SUN ROSE, WHEN ROBERT FOUND THE RIVER. IT SHIMMERED AND SHIVERED LIKE A SILVER RIBBON. THERE WAS A BRIDGE ABOVE THE RIVER, AN ELEGANT CURVING ARCH MADE OF STONE AND METAL.

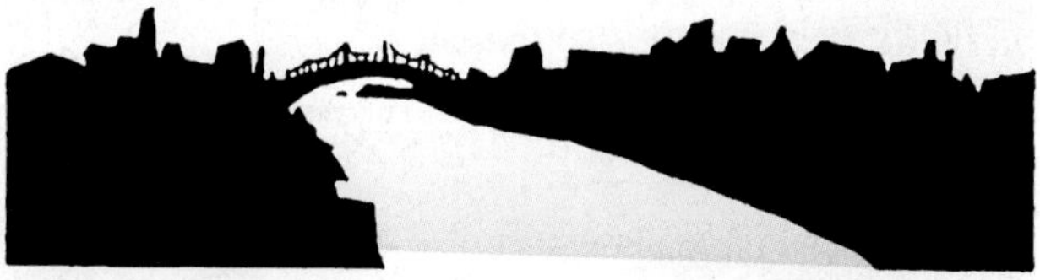

HE WALKED UP TO THE TOP OF THE BRIDGE, AND STARED AT THE CITY.

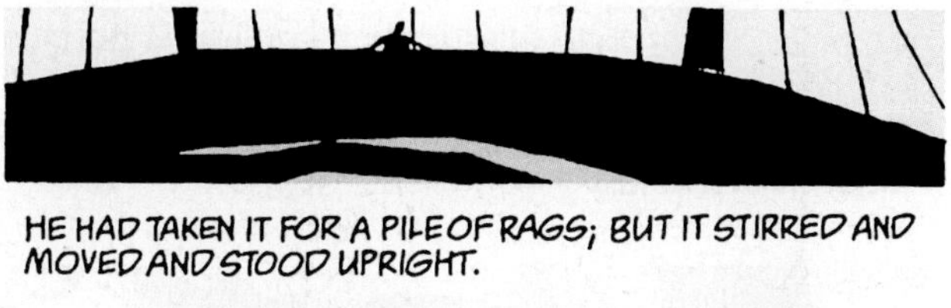

HE HAD TAKEN IT FOR A PILE OF RAGS; BUT IT STIRRED AND MOVED AND STOOD UPRIGHT.

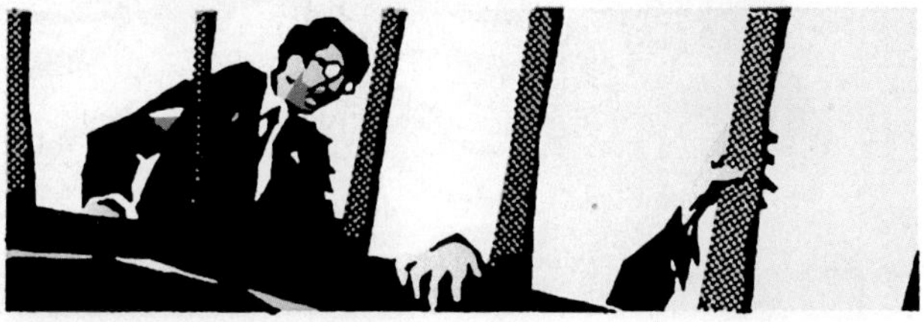

THE OLD MAN WALKED OVER TO ROBERT. "IT'S **BEAUTIFUL**, ISN'T IT?"

"YES," SAID ROBERT. "IT IS."

THEY STOOD THERE, ON THE BRIDGE TOGETHER, LOOKING OUT.

"WHERE **ARE** WE?" ASKED ROBERT.

"IN THE CITY," SAID THE OLD MAN.

ROBERT SHOOK HIS HEAD. "I HAVE WALKED THE CITY ALL OF MY LIFE. THIS IS **NOT** THE CITY, ALTHOUGH THERE ARE MOMENTS WHEN I SEEM TO RECOGNIZE FRAGMENTS OF THE CITY, IN THE MANNER OF ONE RECOGNIZING A LINE FROM A FAMILIAR POEM IN A STRANGE BOOK."

THE OLD MAN TOOK ROBERT BY THE SHOULDER.

"THIS **IS** THE CITY," HE REPEATED.

"THEN ... WHERE IN THE CITY ARE WE?"

"I THINK ..." THE OLD MAN PAUSED. THERE WAS A COLD WIND, UP THERE ON THE BRIDGE.

"I HAVE BEEN HERE FOR MANY, MANY YEARS. HOW MANY, I DO NOT KNOW. AND IN THAT TIME I HAVE HAD MUCH TIME FOR THINKING."

"PERHAPS A CITY IS A LIVING THING. EACH CITY HAS ITS OWN PERSONALITY, AFTER ALL.

"LOS ANGELES IS NOT VIENNA. LONDON IS NOT MOSCOW. CHICAGO IS NOT PARIS. EACH CITY IS A COLLECTION OF LIVES AND BUILDINGS AND IT HAS ITS OWN PERSONALITY."

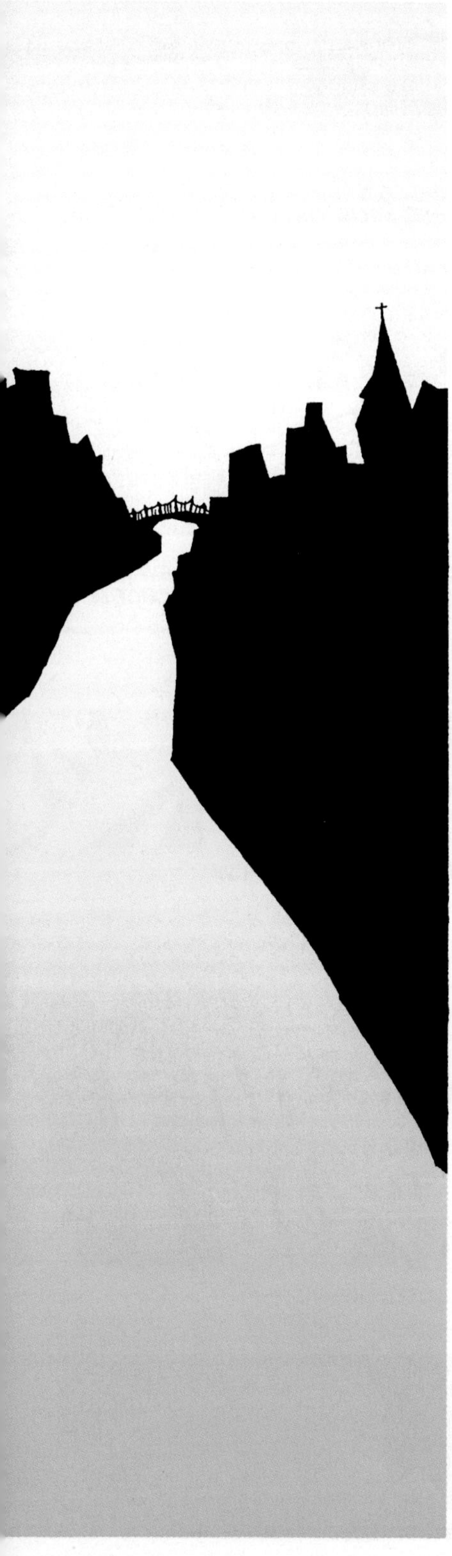

"SO?"

"SO, IF A CITY HAS A PERSONALITY, MAYBE IT ALSO HAS A SOUL. MAYBE IT DREAMS.

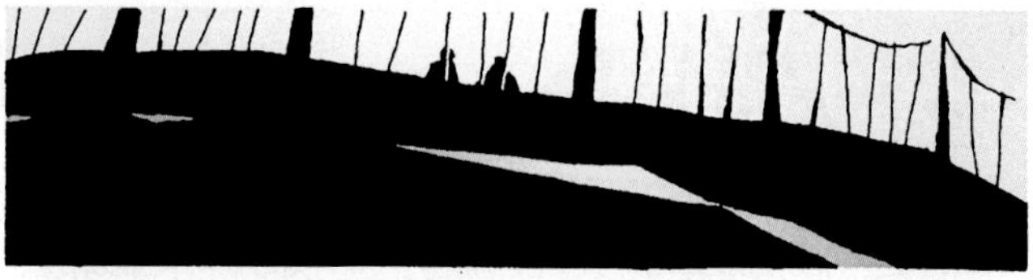

"***THAT*** IS WHERE I BELIEVE WE HAVE COME. WE ARE IN THE DREAMS OF THE CITY. THAT'S WHY CERTAIN PLACES HOVER ON THE BRINK OF RECOGNITION; WHY WE ALMOST KNOW WHERE WE ARE."

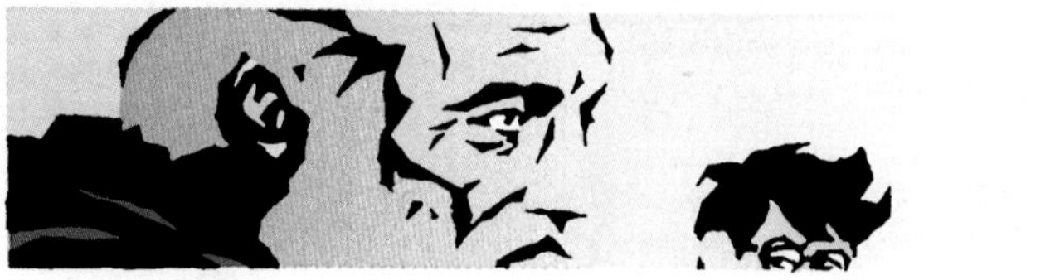

"YOU MEAN THAT WE'RE ASLEEP?"

"NO. WE ARE AWAKE, OR SO I BELIEVE. I MEAN THAT THE CITY IS ASLEEP. AND THAT WE ARE ALL STUMBLING THROUGH THE CITY'S DREAM."

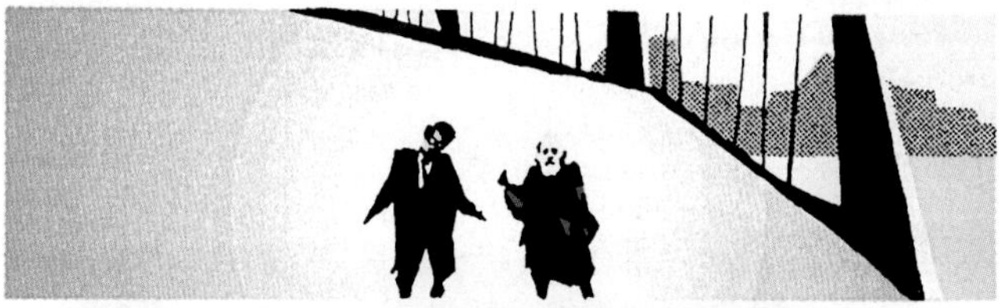

TOGETHER THE TWO MEN CROSSED THE BRIDGE, AND REENTERED THE CITY.

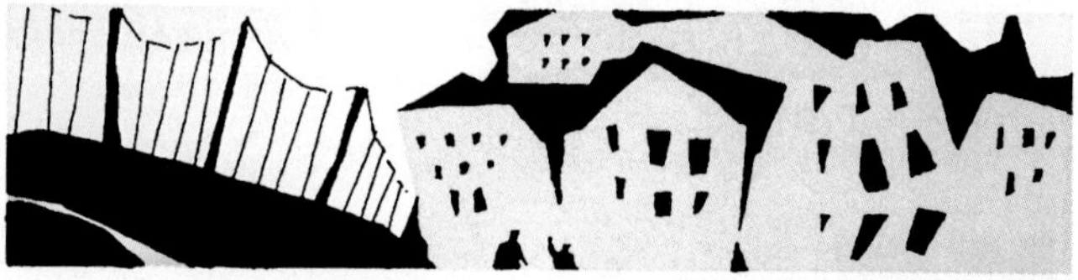

"THE ***FLICKER*** PEOPLE--WHO ARE THEY?"

"WHO KNOWS? PERHAPS THEY ARE WAKING PEOPLE, FLICKERING THROUGH OUR WORLD. FOR ONE FRACTIONAL MOMENT THEY ENTER THE CITY'S DREAM, AND SEE THE CITY THE WAY WE SEE IT. OR PERHAPS THEY ARE PEOPLE THE CITY IS DREAMING OF--"

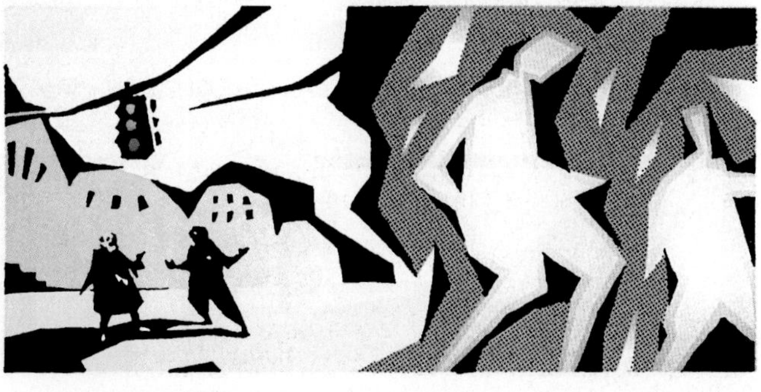

ABOVE THEM VAST, CYCLOPEAN WALLS LOOMED AND TOWERED. LIGHTS FLICKERED ON AND OFF IN DISTANT BUILDINGS, AS IF THEY WERE SPELLING OUT MESSAGES IN SOME UNCERTAIN CODE FOR A FAR-OFF OBSERVER.

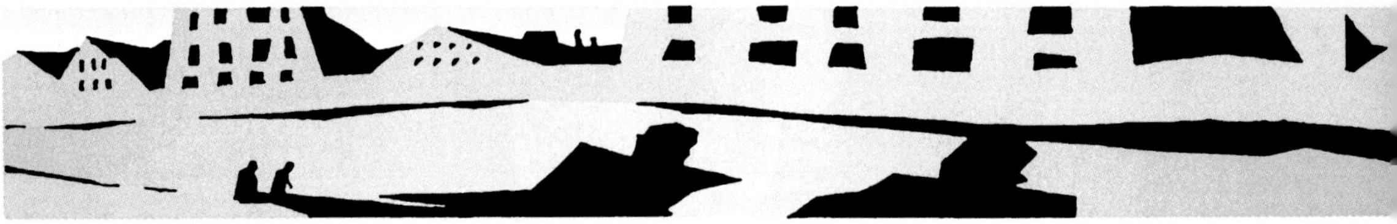

"WHAT WILL HAPPEN TO ME?" ASKED ROBERT.

THE OLD MAN SHRUGGED. "I HAVE MET MANY PEOPLE IN MY TIME IN THE CITY," HE SAID. "BUT IT IS A BIG CITY, AND THERE ARE FEW OF US. I DO NOT KNOW WHAT WILL BECOME OF YOU. FOR MYSELF, I AM CONTENT TO WANDER THE STREETS.

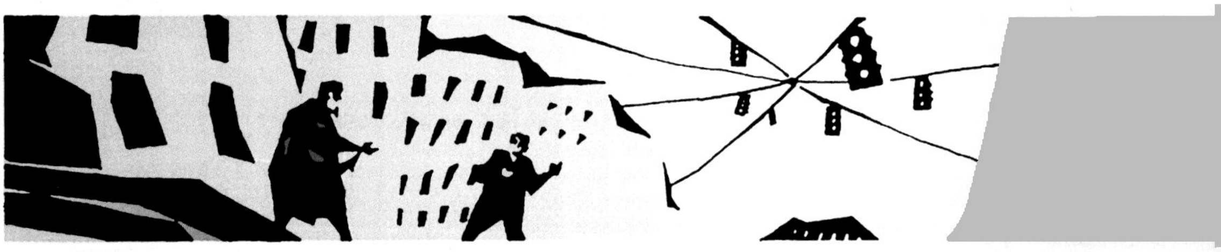

"PERHAPS ONE DAY I SHALL RETURN TO THE WAKING WORLD. I AM SEARCHING FOR A ROAD I KNEW IN THE REAL CITY--AND WHEN I FIND IT, I SHALL WALK DOWN IT AND FIND MYSELF IN THE REAL WORLD ONCE MORE.

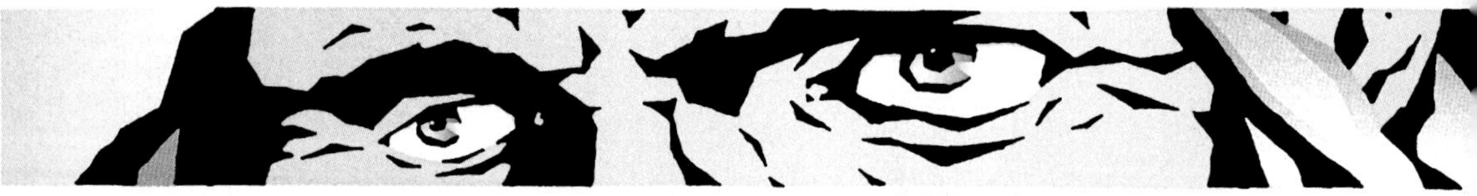

"THIS IS WHAT I HOPE AND PRAY FOR; IT IS, AFTER ALL, PREFERABLE TO THE ALTERNATIVE.

"AND THAT *IS*?"

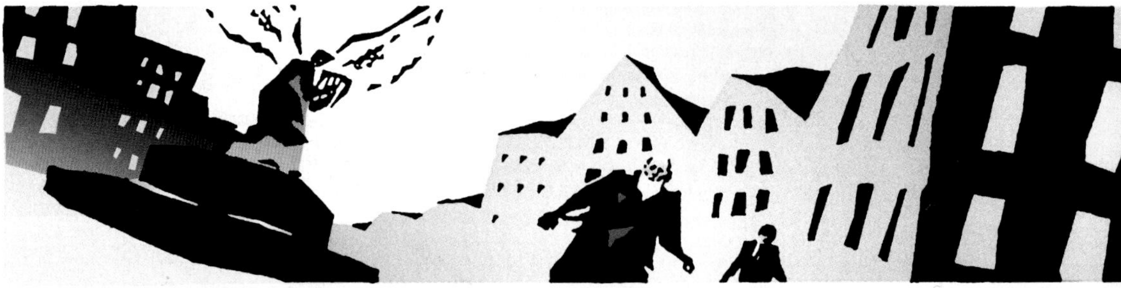

"THAT THE CITY SHOULD WAKE," SAID THE OLD MAN. "THAT IT SHOULD WAKE AND--"

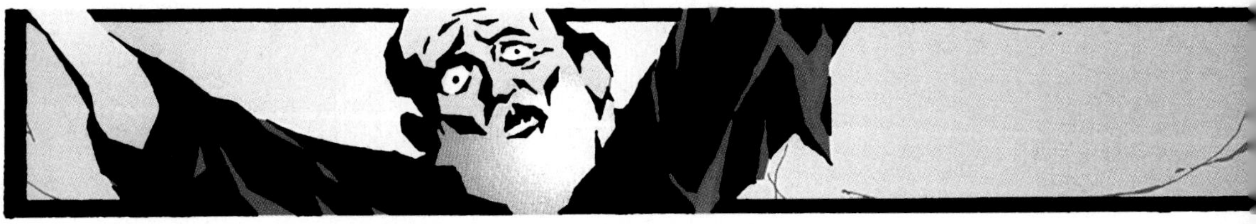

BUT HE BROKE OFF THERE, AND POINTED WILDLY. "***LOOK!***" HE EXCLAIMED. "DO YOU NOT ***SEE*** IT? THAT CORNER, THERE, BETWEEN THE WALL AND THE OLD HOUSE? IS IT NOT ***FAMILIAR?***"

ROBERT STARED, PUZZLED.

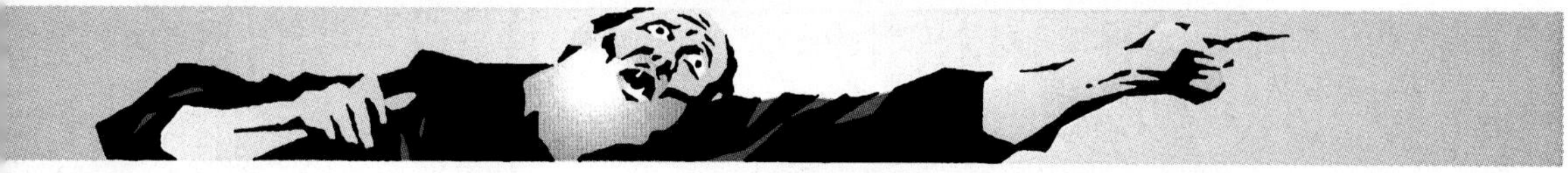

BUT ALREADY THE OLD MAN WAS RUNNING ACROSS THE STREET.

"***WAIT! WAIT*** FOR ***ME!***" THE OLD MAN WAS SHOUTING.

THE OLD MAN DARTED ACROSS THE STREET AND INTO AN ALLEYWAY AND WAS GONE.

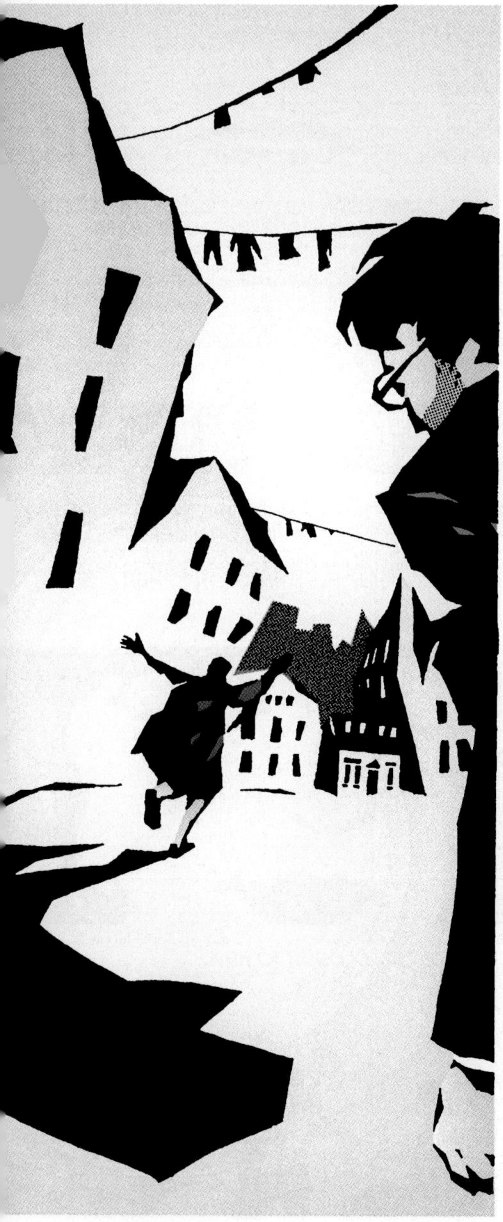

WHEN ROBERT REACHED THE ENTRANCE TO THE ALLEYWAY HE FOUND IT TO BE A DEAD END, AND QUITE EMPTY. HE NEVER SAW THE OLD MAN AGAIN.

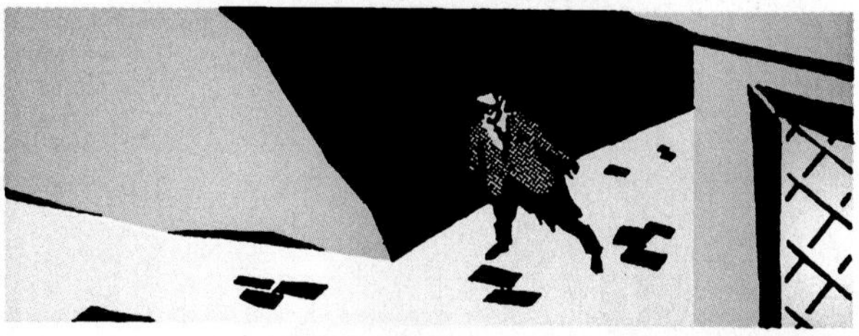

BUT NOW ROBERT HAD A PURPOSE. HE LOOKED FOR SOMETHING HE KNEW: A PATH, OR STREET OR ALLEY; HE WALKED THE CITY OF DREAMS HUNTING FOR SOMETHING HE RECOGNIZED: SEARCHING FOR THE REAL.

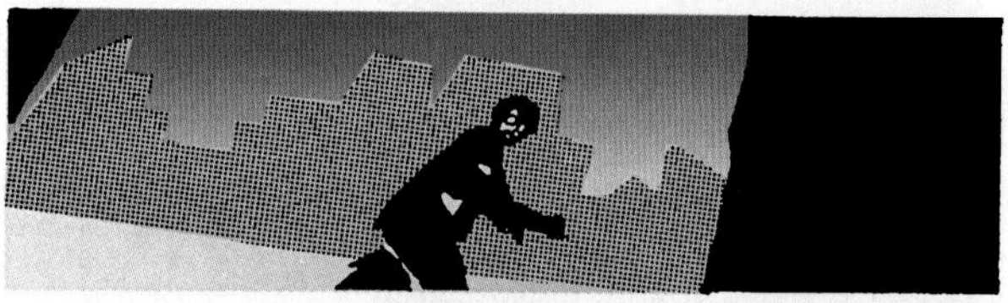

HE WOULD CLIMB THE STAIRS OF SKYSCRAPERS HUNTING FOR A DOORWAY HE HAD SEEN BEFORE.

HE WOULD DESCEND BELOW THE CITY, FOLLOWING IMAGINARY TRAILS DOWN WET DANK STEPS THAT LED HIM NOWHERE.

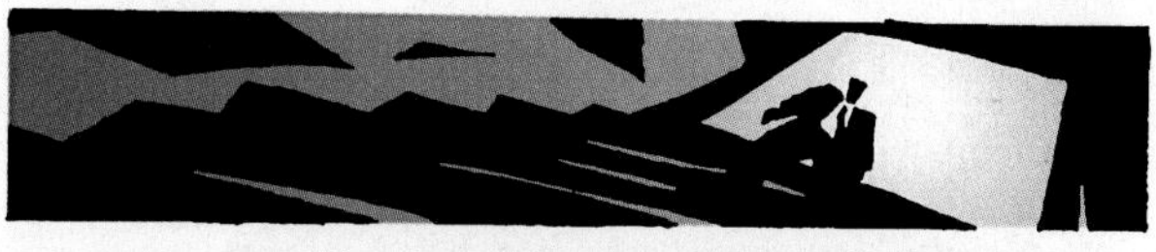

HE WALKED TINY BACKSTREETS, PASSING RESTAURANTS FOREVER CLOSED, OR SMALL STORES THAT, FROM ALL HE COULD SEE THROUGH THEIR WINDOWS, SOLD MARVELS, BUT WHICH WERE NEVER OPEN FOR BUSINESS.

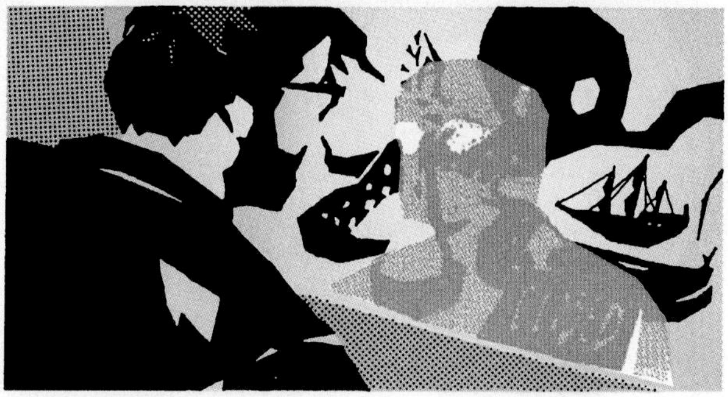

HE WALKED PERHAPS FOR MONTHS, SPEAKING TO NO ONE, UNTIL THE DAY HE ENCOUNTERED A WOMAN IN THE ROOF GARDEN OF A BUILDING THAT JUTTED UP FROM THE CITY LIKE A BLACK TOOTH.

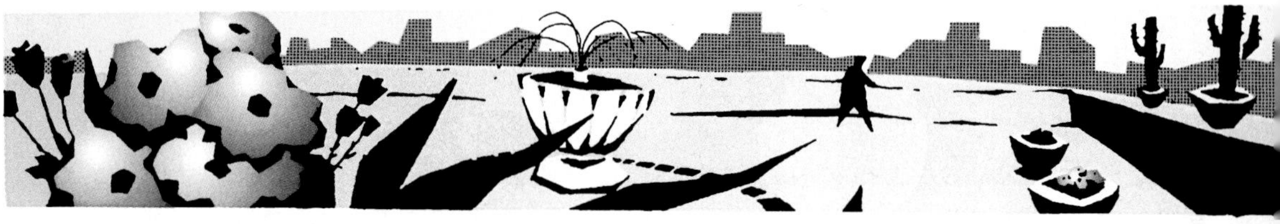

SHE WAS SITTING BY A SMALL FOUNTAIN, AND LOOKED UP AT HIM AS HE APPROACHED.

"***SIR***-- IF YOU ARE REAL, AND NOT A THING OF FIGMENT AND FANTASY-- WHERE ***ARE*** WE?" SHE ASKED HIM.

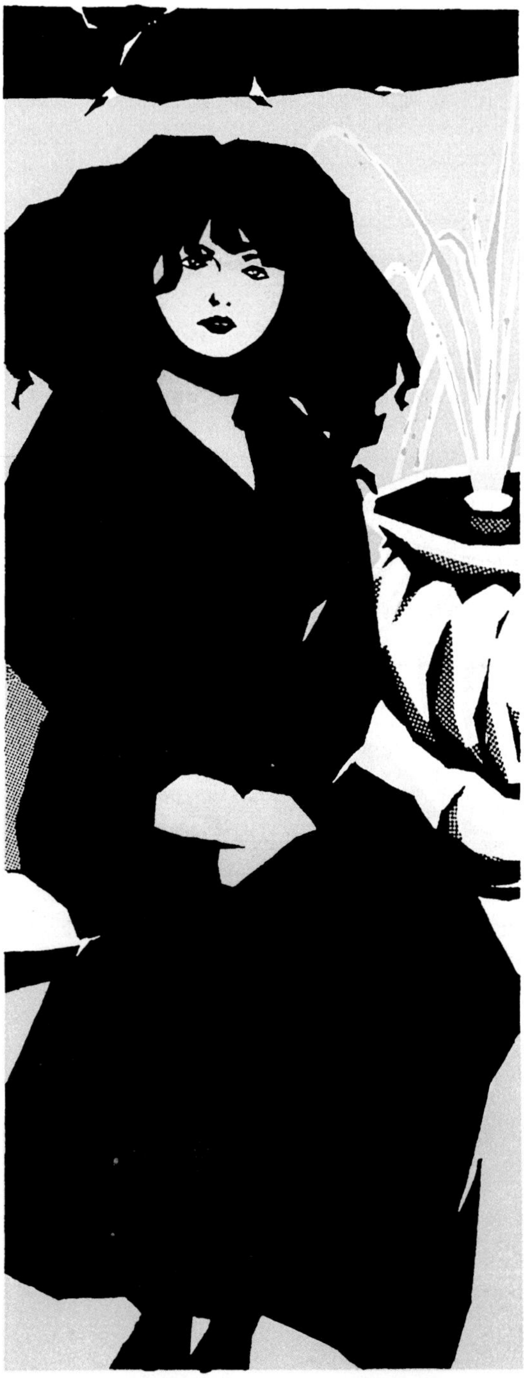

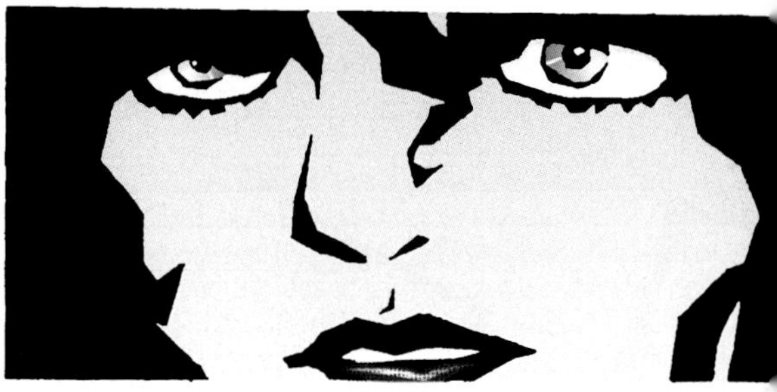

"HOW REAL I AM I CAN NO LONGER SAY," HE TOLD HER. "BUT WE ***ARE*** IN THE CITY, OR SO I HAVE BEEN ASSURED."

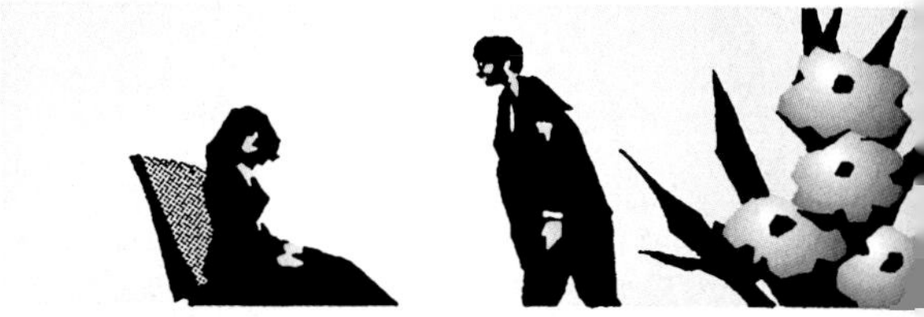

THERE WAS SOMETHING ABOUT THE WOMAN; THE WAY SHE HELD HER HEAD, PERHAPS, OR A CERTAIN COLOR TO HER EYES, OR THE LINE A CURL TRACED AS IT TUMBLED FROM HER FOREHEAD ONTO HER CHEEK.

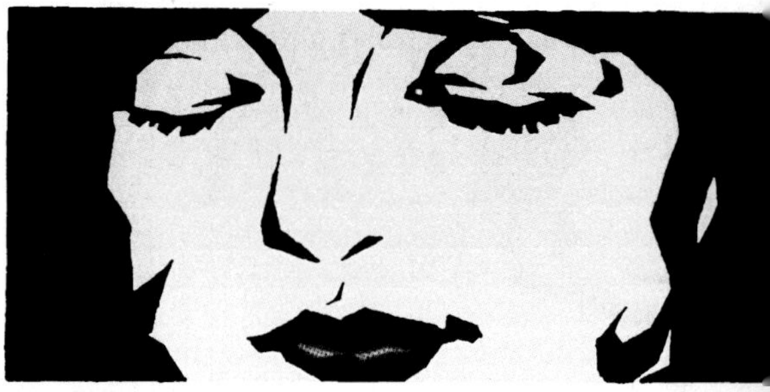

ROBERT STEPPED CLOSER TO HER.

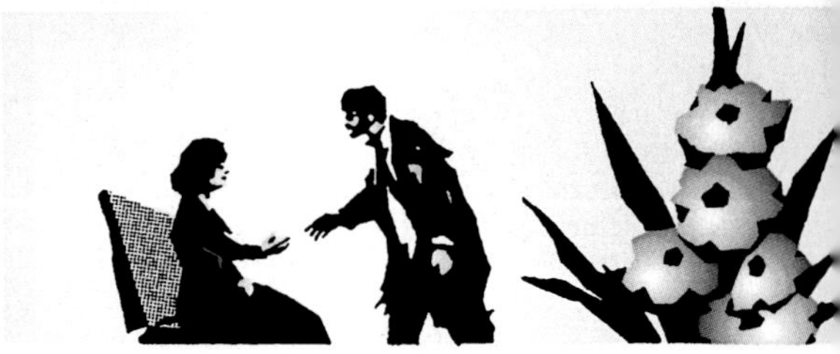

IT WAS THEN, BEHIND THE FLOWERS AND POTTED PLANTS (SOME PROSAIC, SOME POSSESSING A STRANGE AND EXOTIC QUALITY THAT WAS ALMOST ALIEN), HE NOTICED A DOORWAY.

IT WAS A DOOR OF ALMOST UNBEARABLE FAMILIARITY; HE HAD PASSED IT EACH DAY, ON HIS WAY TO WORK, IN A LIFE THAT NOW SEEMED DISTANT AND IMAGINARY AS THE MOON.

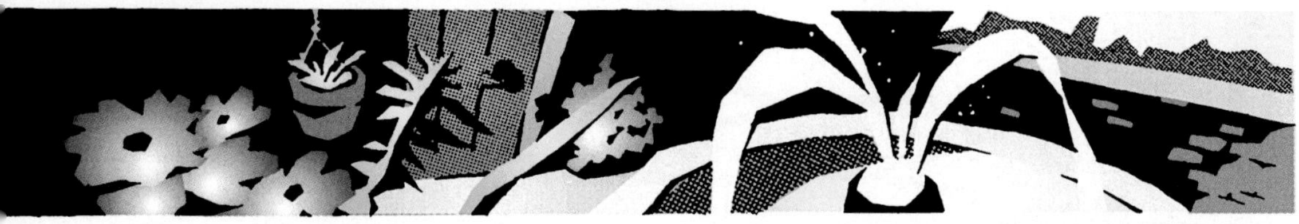

"WHAT IS YOUR NAME?" SHE ASKED HIM.

THE WOMAN REACHED OUT A HAND. ROBERT THOUGHT THAT SHE WAS GOING TO TOUCH HIM; AND HAD SHE TOUCHED HIM HE WOULD HAVE BEEN LOST FOREVER.

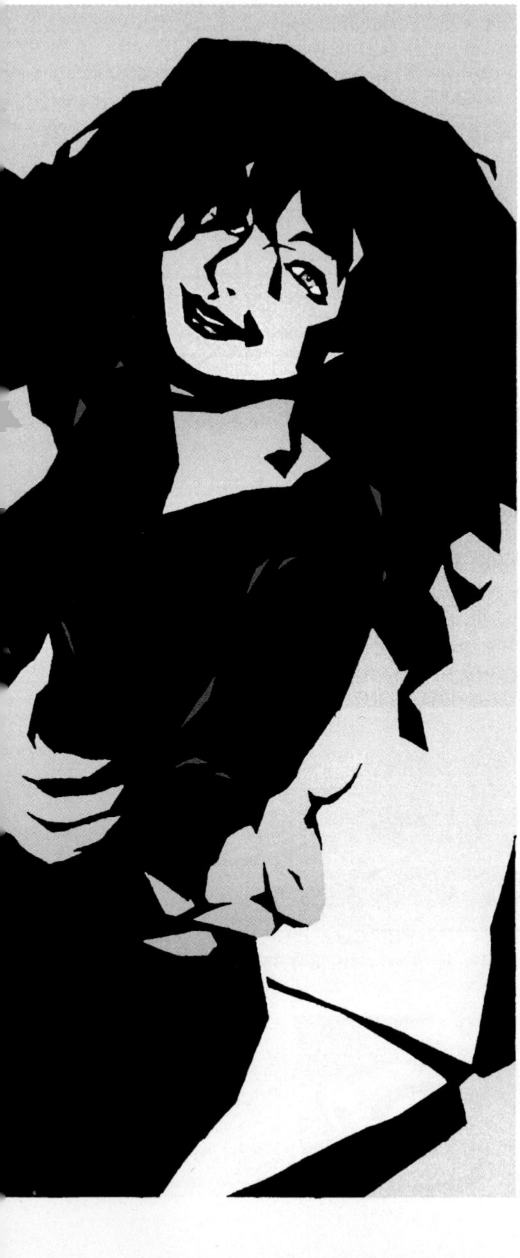

HE RAN HEADLONG ACROSS THE ROOF-GARDEN, KNOCKING PLANTS OVER AS HE WENT, RUNNING HEADLONG, PELL-MELL, HELTER-SKELTER, WITHOUT LOOKING BACK.

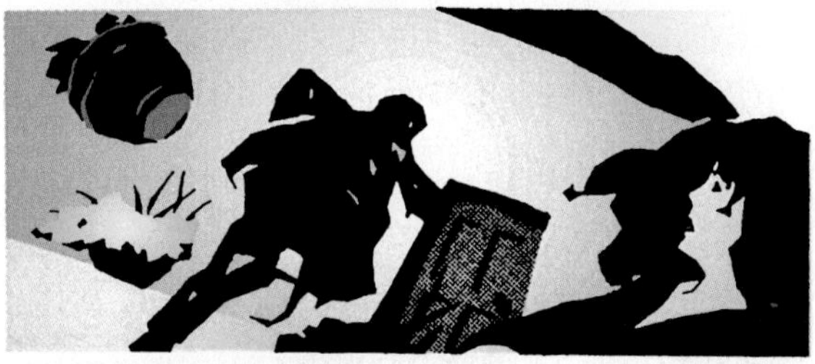

THROUGH THE DOORWAY, THEN.

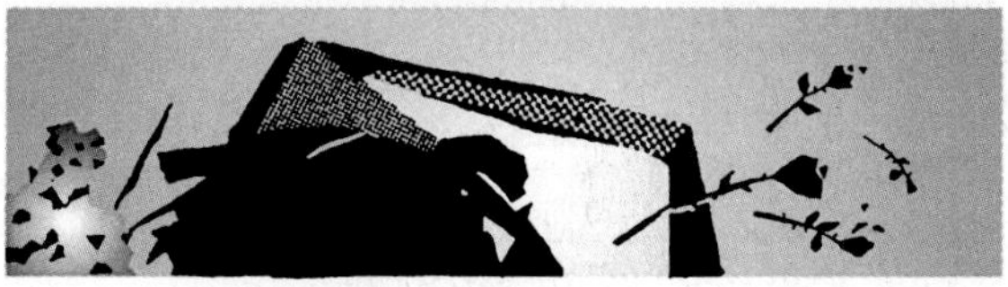

AND HE WAS BLINDED.

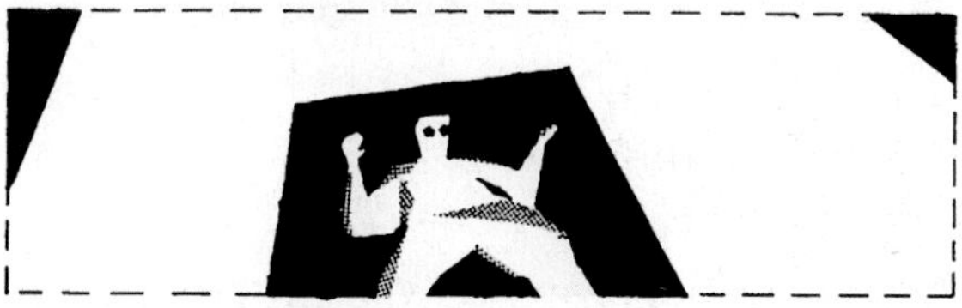

"ARE YOU ALL RIGHT?"

ROBERT LOOKED AROUND HIM, BLINKING IN THE SUNLIGHT.

"THANK YOU," HE SAID. "I AM FINE."

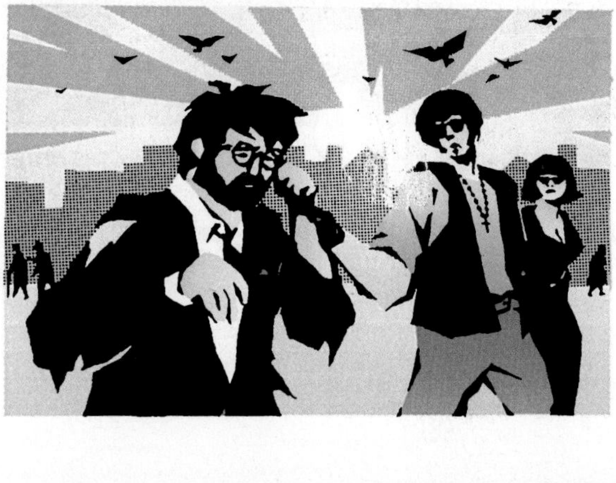

I MET ROBERT IN A SMALL VILLAGE OFF THE COAST OF SCOTLAND, SOME YEARS AFTER THE EVENTS I HAVE MENTIONED HERE.

IT WAS A VERY SMALL VILLAGE HE LIVED IN, CONSISTING OF A FEW SCATTERED HOUSES AND FARMS, AND A SHOP THAT SERVED AS POST OFFICE, VILLAGE STORE, AND INN. OTHER THAN THAT THERE WERE ONLY STUNTED SHEEP AND BLASTED TREES, AND THE CONSTANT LOW SUSURRUS OF THE SEA.

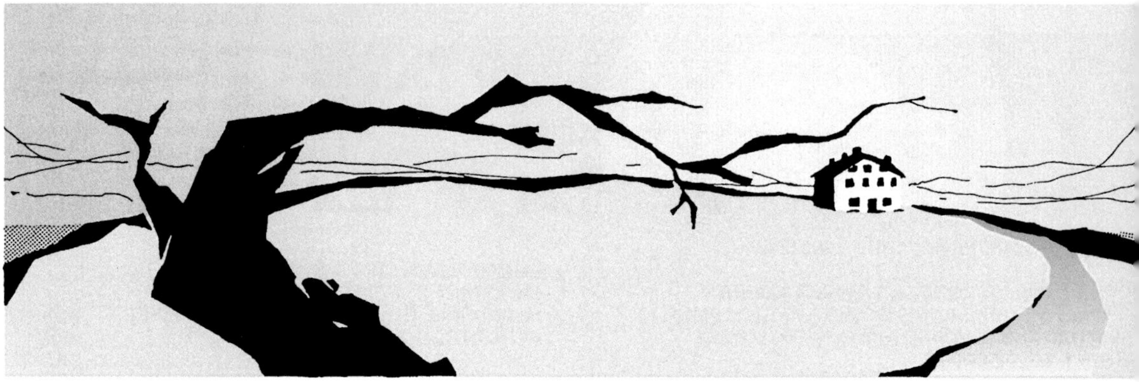

IT WAS IN THAT INN THAT HE TOLD ME THE TALE I HAVE TOLD YOU.

HE WAS A MOST FRIGHTENED MAN.

"DO YOU FEAR THAT ONE DAY YOU WILL RETURN TO THE DREAMS OF THE CITY?" I ASKED HIM. "IS ***THAT*** WHY YOU LIVE OUT HERE?"

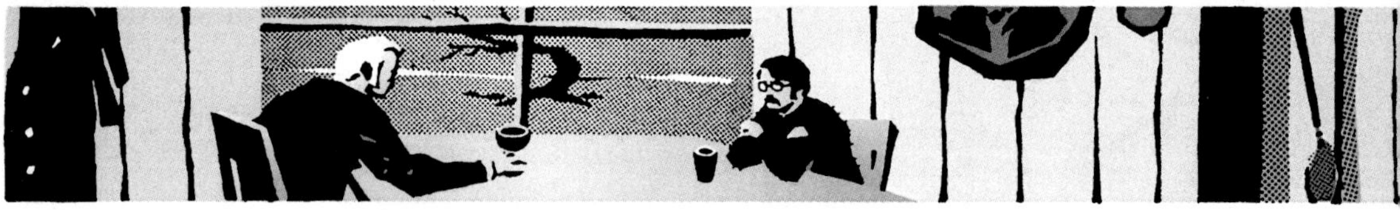

HE SHOOK HIS HEAD, AND WE WALKED OUTSIDE. THE MIST HUNG LOW AND WHITE AND THICK AND WE MIGHT AS WELL HAVE BEEN NOWHERE AT ALL.

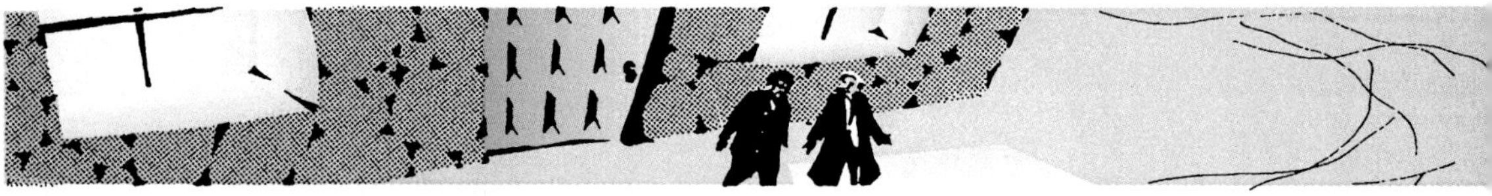

"IF THE CITY WAS DREAMING," HE TOLD ME, "THEN THE CITY IS ASLEEP. AND I DO NOT FEAR CITIES SLEEPING, STRETCHED OUT UNCONSCIOUS AROUND THEIR RIVERS AND ESTUARIES, LIKE CATS IN THE MOONLIGHT. SLEEPING CITIES ARE TAME AND HARMLESS THINGS."

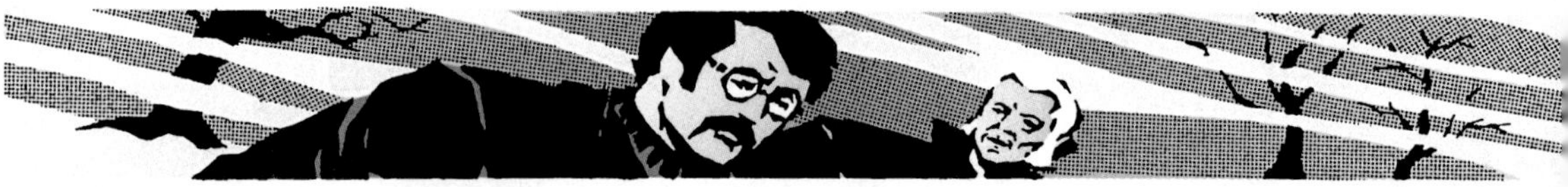

"WHAT I FEAR," HE SAID, "IS THAT ONE DAY THE CITIES WILL WAKEN. THAT ONE DAY THE CITIES WILL RISE."

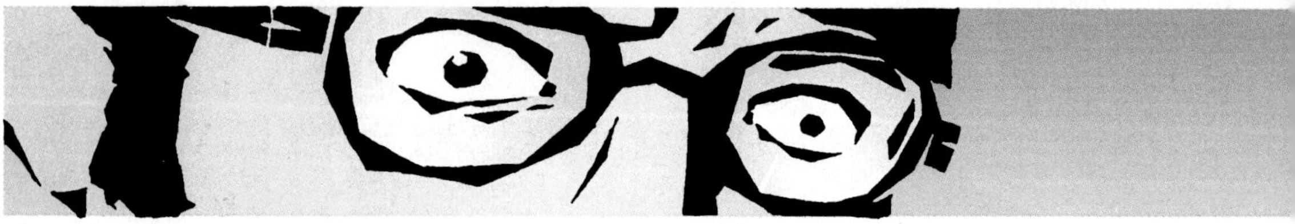

I LIKE TO BELIEVE IT WAS ONLY THE COLD THAT MADE ME SHIVER, ONLY A STRAND OF FOG IN MY THROAT THAT CAUSED ME TO CATCH MY BREATH.

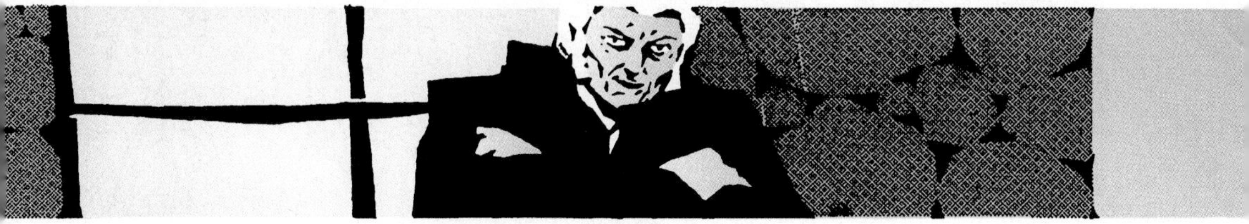

ROBERT WALKED AWAY ACROSS THE MOOR AND I NEVER SAW HIM AGAIN.

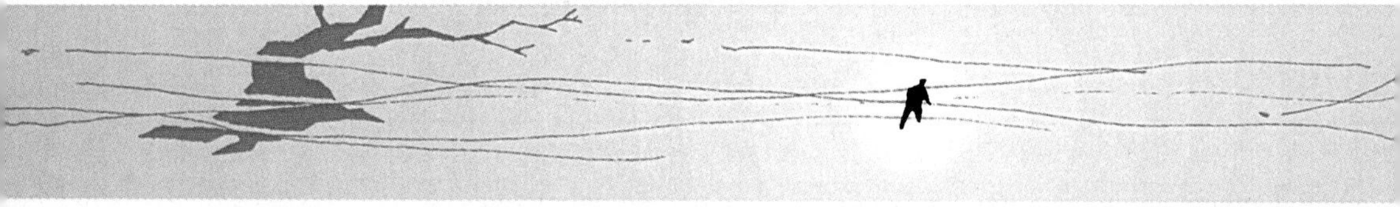

SINCE THAT TIME I HAVE WALKED WITH LESS COMFORT IN CITIES,

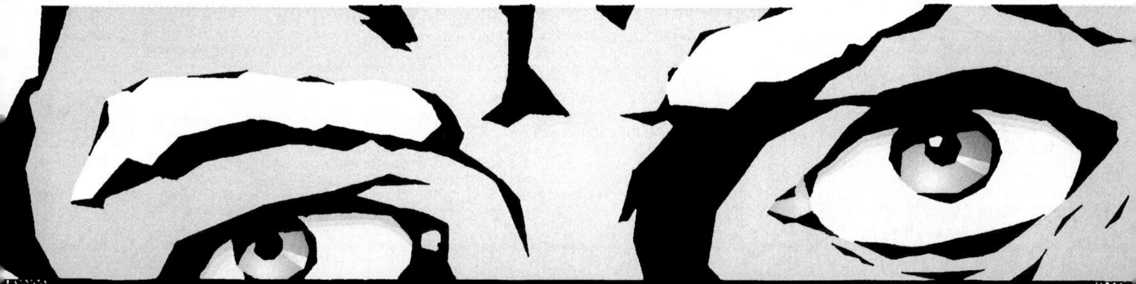

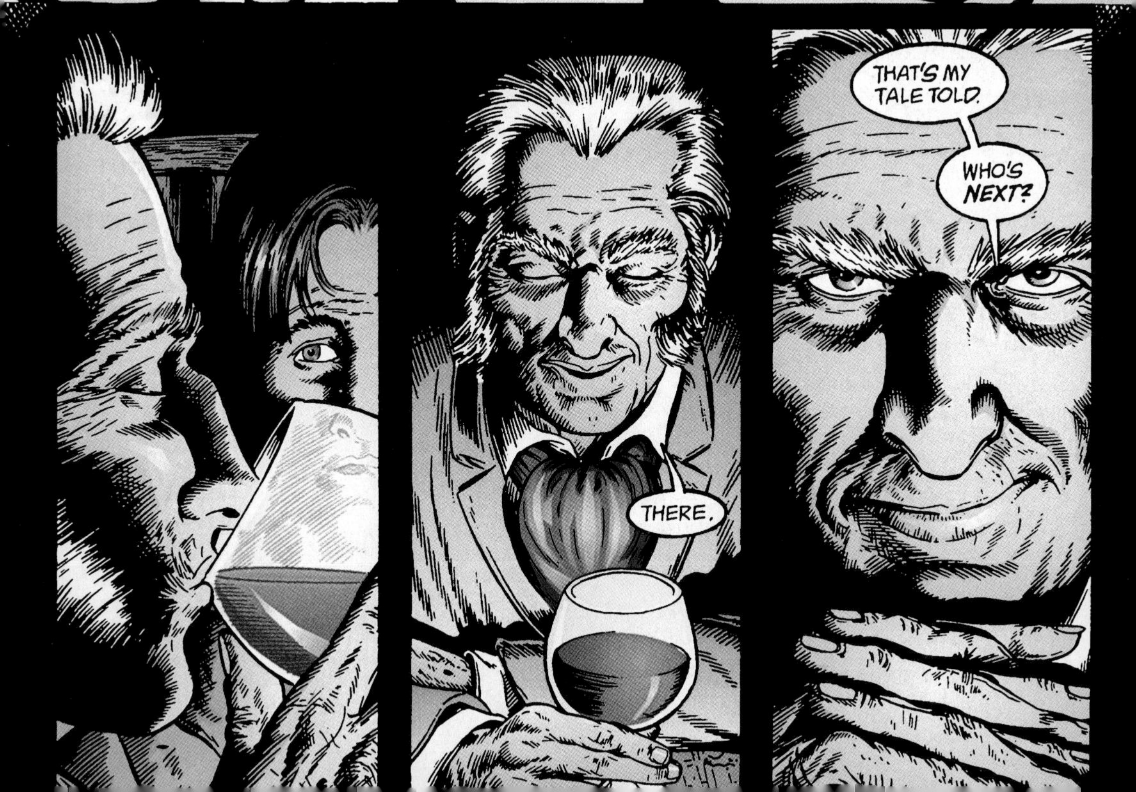
THERE.
THAT'S MY TALE TOLD.
WHO'S NEXT?

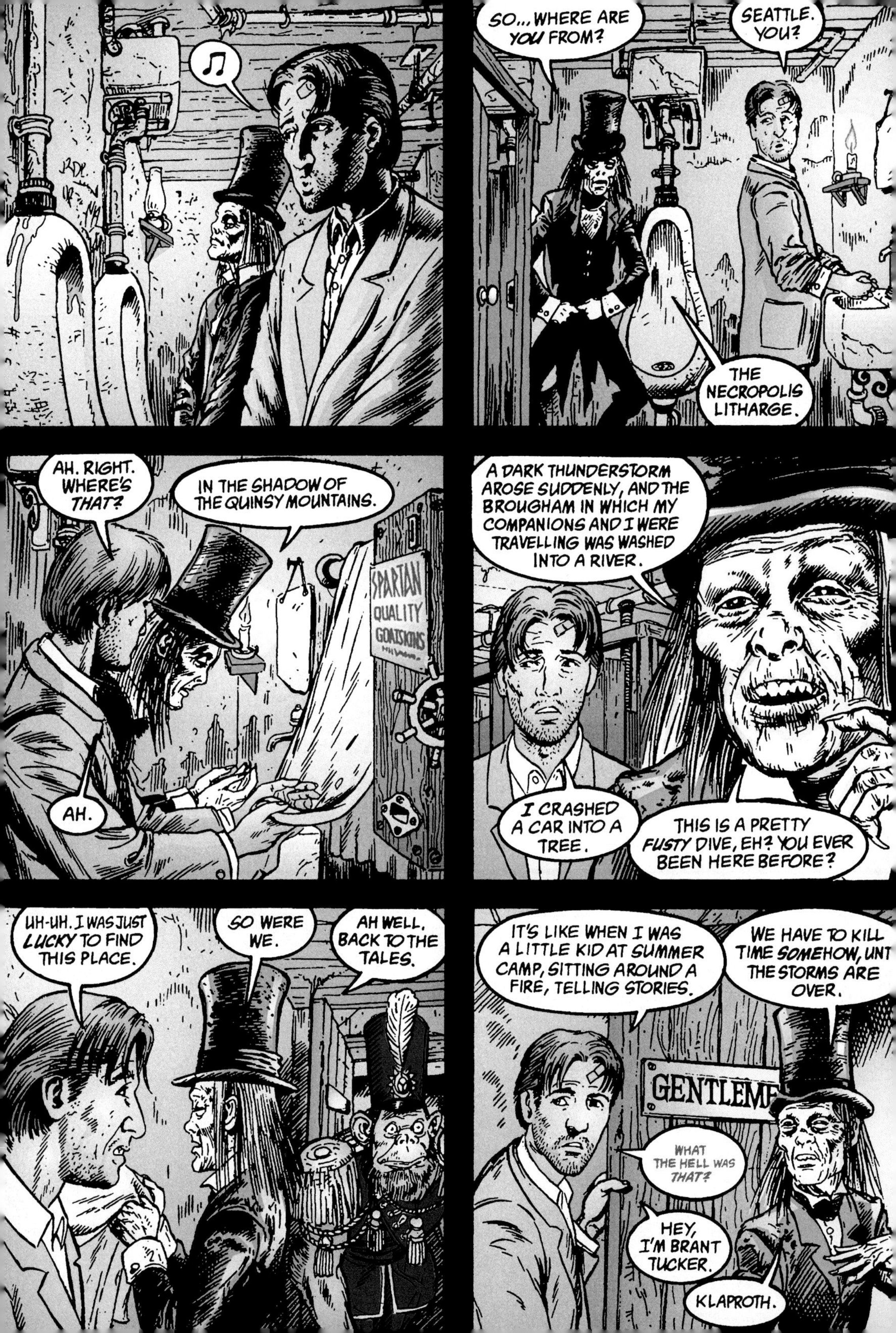
♫
SO... WHERE ARE YOU FROM?
SEATTLE. YOU?
THE NECROPOLIS LITHARGE.
AH. RIGHT. WHERE'S THAT?
IN THE SHADOW OF THE QUINSY MOUNTAINS.
SPARTAN QUALITY GONISKINS
AH.
A DARK THUNDERSTORM AROSE SUDDENLY, AND THE BROUGHAM IN WHICH MY COMPANIONS AND I WERE TRAVELLING WAS WASHED INTO A RIVER.
I CRASHED A CAR INTO A TREE.
THIS IS A PRETTY FUSTY DIVE, EH? YOU EVER BEEN HERE BEFORE?
UH-UH. I WAS JUST LUCKY TO FIND THIS PLACE.
SO WERE WE.
AH WELL. BACK TO THE TALES.
IT'S LIKE WHEN I WAS A LITTLE KID AT SUMMER CAMP, SITTING AROUND A FIRE, TELLING STORIES.
WE HAVE TO KILL TIME SOMEHOW, UNT THE STORMS ARE OVER.
GENTLEME
WHAT THE HELL WAS THAT?
HEY, I'M BRANT TUCKER.
KLAPROTH.

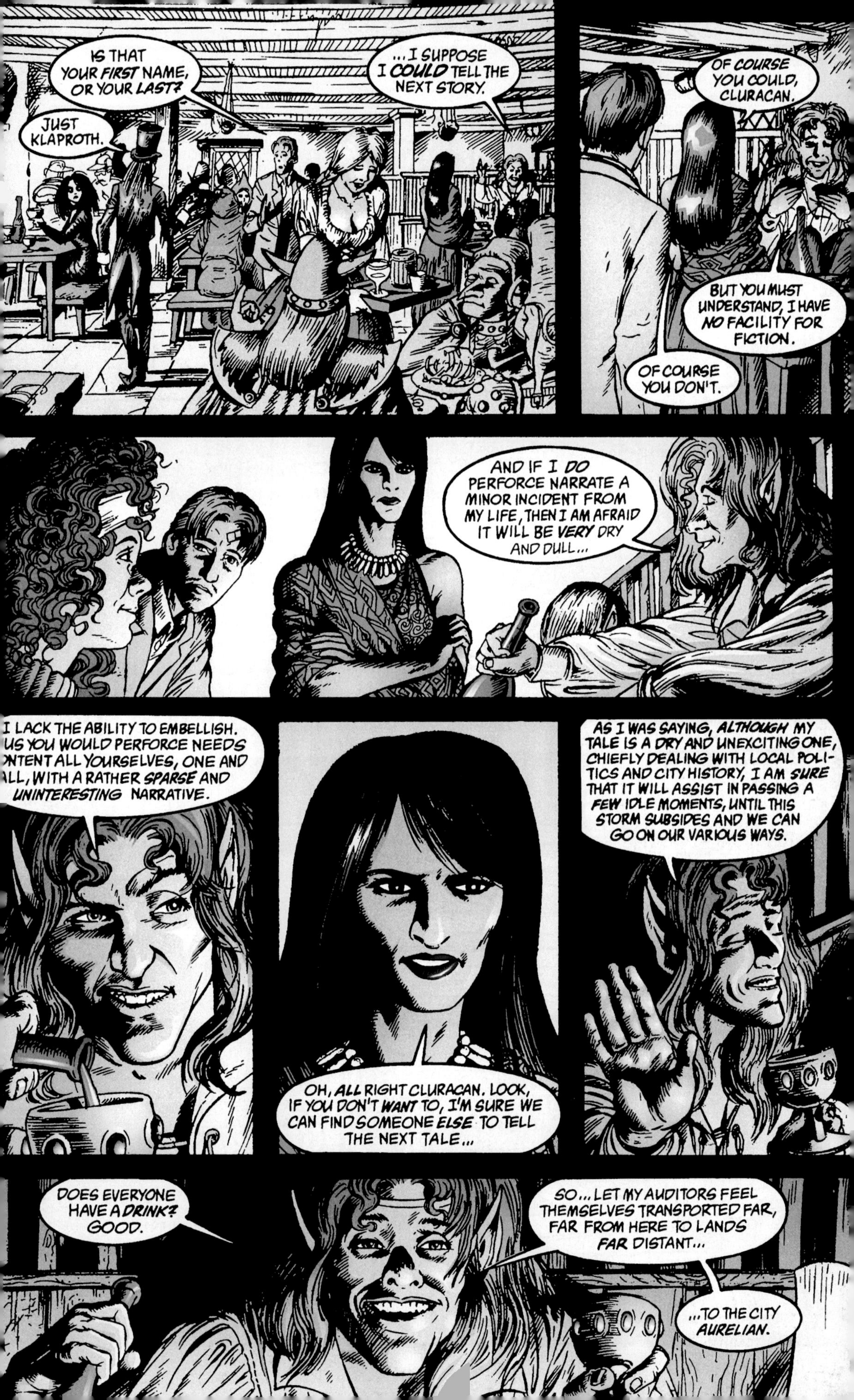
IS THAT YOUR FIRST NAME, OR YOUR LAST?
JUST KLAPROTH.
...I SUPPOSE I COULD TELL THE NEXT STORY.
OF COURSE YOU COULD, CLURACAN.
BUT YOU MUST UNDERSTAND, I HAVE NO FACILITY FOR FICTION.
OF COURSE YOU DON'T.
AND IF I DO PERFORCE NARRATE A MINOR INCIDENT FROM MY LIFE, THEN I AM AFRAID IT WILL BE VERY DRY AND DULL...
I LACK THE ABILITY TO EMBELLISH. US YOU WOULD PERFORCE NEEDS NTENT ALL YOURSELVES, ONE AND LL, WITH A RATHER SPARSE AND UNINTERESTING NARRATIVE.
OH, ALL RIGHT CLURACAN. LOOK, IF YOU DON'T WANT TO, I'M SURE WE CAN FIND SOMEONE ELSE TO TELL THE NEXT TALE...
AS I WAS SAYING, ALTHOUGH MY TALE IS A DRY AND UNEXCITING ONE, CHIEFLY DEALING WITH LOCAL POLITICS AND CITY HISTORY, I AM SURE THAT IT WILL ASSIST IN PASSING A FEW IDLE MOMENTS, UNTIL THIS STORM SUBSIDES AND WE CAN GO ON OUR VARIOUS WAYS.
DOES EVERYONE HAVE A DRINK? GOOD.
SO... LET MY AUDITORS FEEL THEMSELVES TRANSPORTED FAR, FAR FROM HERE TO LANDS FAR DISTANT...
...TO THE CITY AURELIAN.

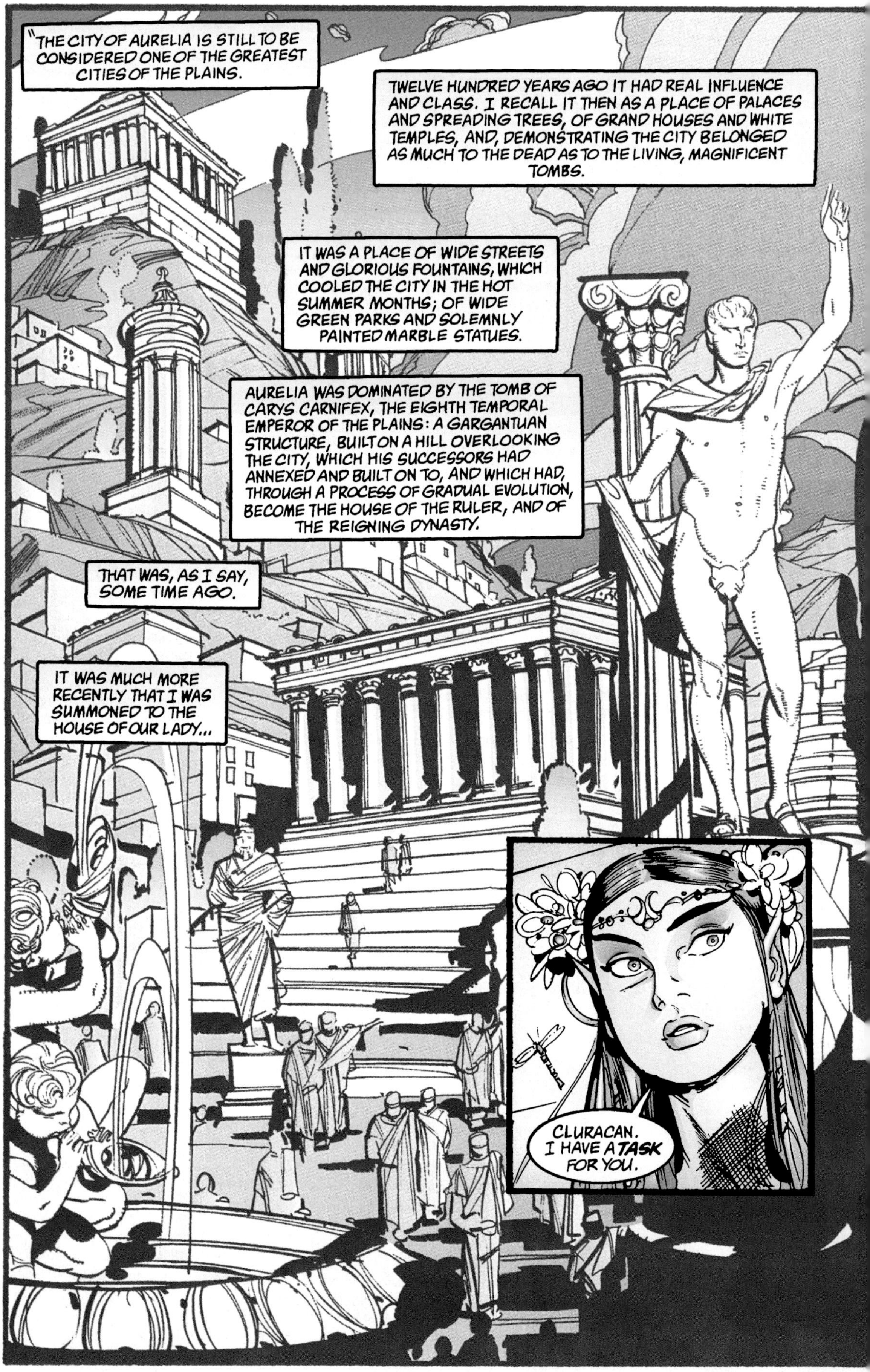
"THE CITY OF AURELIA IS STILL TO BE CONSIDERED ONE OF THE GREATEST CITIES OF THE PLAINS.
TWELVE HUNDRED YEARS AGO IT HAD REAL INFLUENCE AND CLASS. I RECALL IT THEN AS A PLACE OF PALACES AND SPREADING TREES, OF GRAND HOUSES AND WHITE TEMPLES, AND, DEMONSTRATING THE CITY BELONGED AS MUCH TO THE DEAD AS TO THE LIVING, MAGNIFICENT TOMBS.
IT WAS A PLACE OF WIDE STREETS AND GLORIOUS FOUNTAINS, WHICH COOLED THE CITY IN THE HOT SUMMER MONTHS; OF WIDE GREEN PARKS AND SOLEMNLY PAINTED MARBLE STATUES.
AURELIA WAS DOMINATED BY THE TOMB OF CARYS CARNIFEX, THE EIGHTH TEMPORAL EMPEROR OF THE PLAINS: A GARGANTUAN STRUCTURE, BUILT ON A HILL OVERLOOKING THE CITY, WHICH HIS SUCCESSORS HAD ANNEXED AND BUILT ON TO, AND WHICH HAD, THROUGH A PROCESS OF GRADUAL EVOLUTION, BECOME THE HOUSE OF THE RULER, AND OF THE REIGNING DYNASTY.
THAT WAS, AS I SAY, SOME TIME AGO.
IT WAS MUCH MORE RECENTLY THAT I WAS SUMMONED TO THE HOUSE OF OUR LADY...
CLURACAN. I HAVE A TASK FOR YOU.

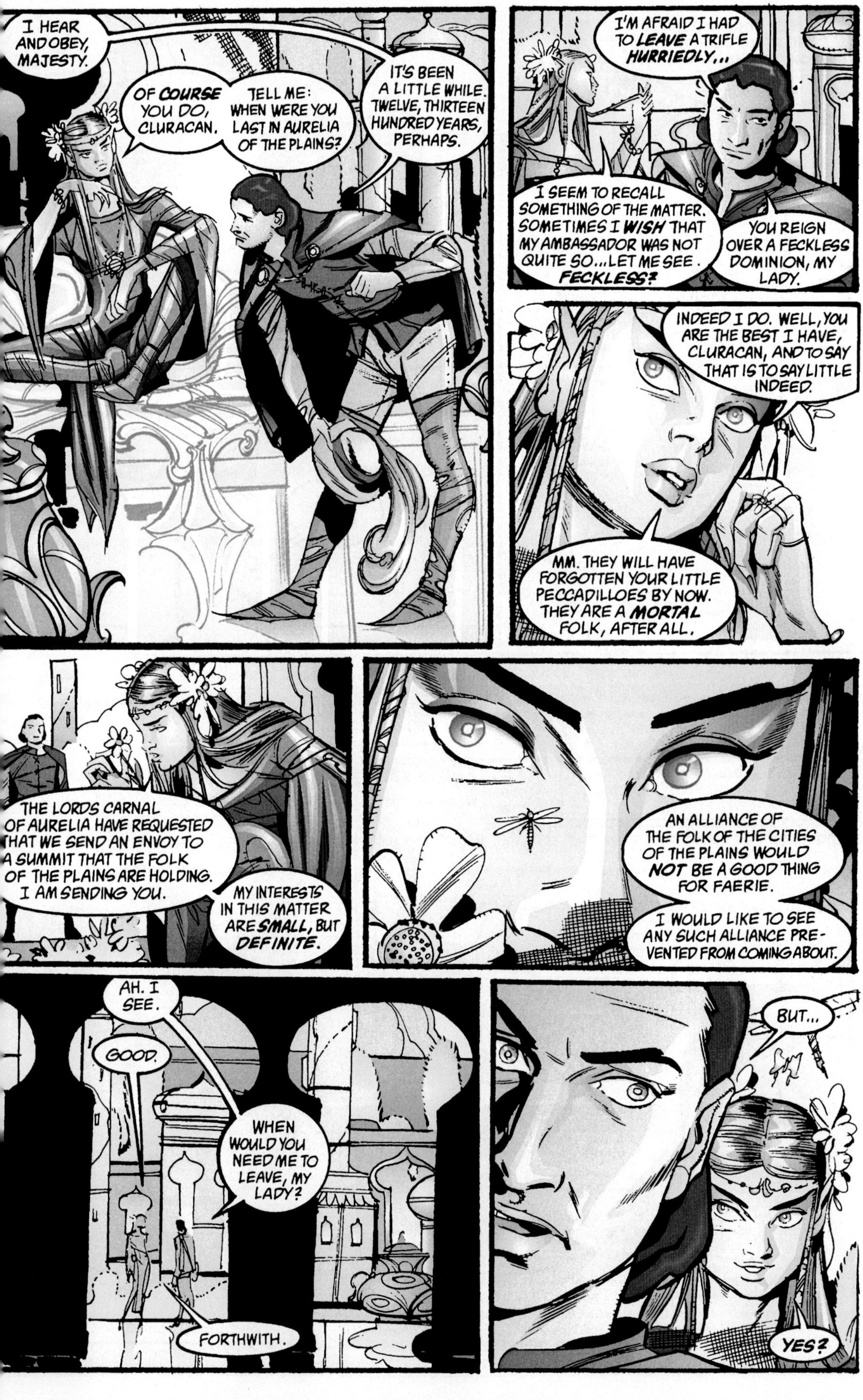
I HEAR AND OBEY, MAJESTY.
OF COURSE YOU DO, CLURACAN.
TELL ME: WHEN WERE YOU LAST IN AURELIA OF THE PLAINS?
IT'S BEEN A LITTLE WHILE. TWELVE, THIRTEEN HUNDRED YEARS, PERHAPS.
I'M AFRAID I HAD TO LEAVE A TRIFLE HURRIEDLY...
I SEEM TO RECALL SOMETHING OF THE MATTER. SOMETIMES I WISH THAT MY AMBASSADOR WAS NOT QUITE SO...LET ME SEE. FECKLESS?
YOU REIGN OVER A FECKLESS DOMINION, MY LADY.
INDEED I DO. WELL, YOU ARE THE BEST I HAVE, CLURACAN, AND TO SAY THAT IS TO SAY LITTLE INDEED.
MM. THEY WILL HAVE FORGOTTEN YOUR LITTLE PECCADILLOES BY NOW. THEY ARE A MORTAL FOLK, AFTER ALL.
THE LORDS CARNAL OF AURELIA HAVE REQUESTED THAT WE SEND AN ENVOY TO A SUMMIT THAT THE FOLK OF THE PLAINS ARE HOLDING. I AM SENDING YOU.
MY INTERESTS IN THIS MATTER ARE SMALL, BUT DEFINITE.
AN ALLIANCE OF THE FOLK OF THE CITIES OF THE PLAINS WOULD NOT BE A GOOD THING FOR FAERIE.
I WOULD LIKE TO SEE ANY SUCH ALLIANCE PRE-VENTED FROM COMING ABOUT.
AH. I SEE.
GOOD.
WHEN WOULD YOU NEED ME TO LEAVE, MY LADY?
FORTHWITH.
BUT...
YES?

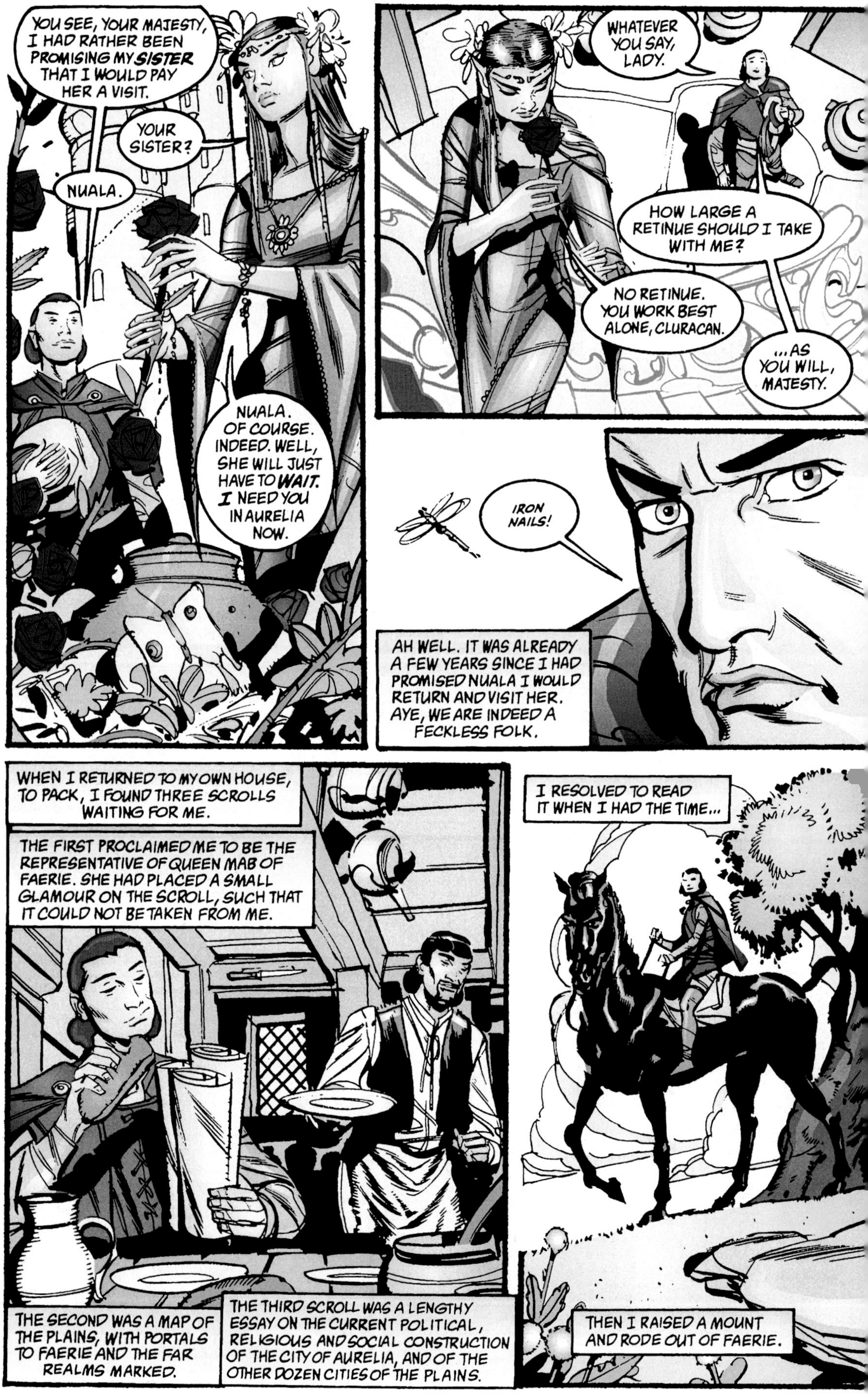

YOU SEE, YOUR MAJESTY, I HAD RATHER BEEN PROMISING MY SISTER THAT I WOULD PAY HER A VISIT.
YOUR SISTER?
NUALA.
NUALA. OF COURSE. INDEED. WELL, SHE WILL JUST HAVE TO WAIT. I NEED YOU IN AURELIA NOW.
WHATEVER YOU SAY, LADY.
HOW LARGE A RETINUE SHOULD I TAKE WITH ME?
NO RETINUE. YOU WORK BEST ALONE, CLURACAN.
...AS YOU WILL, MAJESTY.
IRON NAILS!
AH WELL. IT WAS ALREADY A FEW YEARS SINCE I HAD PROMISED NUALA I WOULD RETURN AND VISIT HER. AYE, WE ARE INDEED A FECKLESS FOLK.
WHEN I RETURNED TO MY OWN HOUSE, TO PACK, I FOUND THREE SCROLLS WAITING FOR ME.
THE FIRST PROCLAIMED ME TO BE THE REPRESENTATIVE OF QUEEN MAB OF FAERIE. SHE HAD PLACED A SMALL GLAMOUR ON THE SCROLL, SUCH THAT IT COULD NOT BE TAKEN FROM ME.
THE SECOND WAS A MAP OF THE PLAINS, WITH PORTALS TO FAERIE AND THE FAR REALMS MARKED.
THE THIRD SCROLL WAS A LENGTHY ESSAY ON THE CURRENT POLITICAL, RELIGIOUS AND SOCIAL CONSTRUCTION OF THE CITY OF AURELIA, AND OF THE OTHER DOZEN CITIES OF THE PLAINS.
I RESOLVED TO READ IT WHEN I HAD THE TIME...
THEN I RAISED A MOUNT AND RODE OUT OF FAERIE.

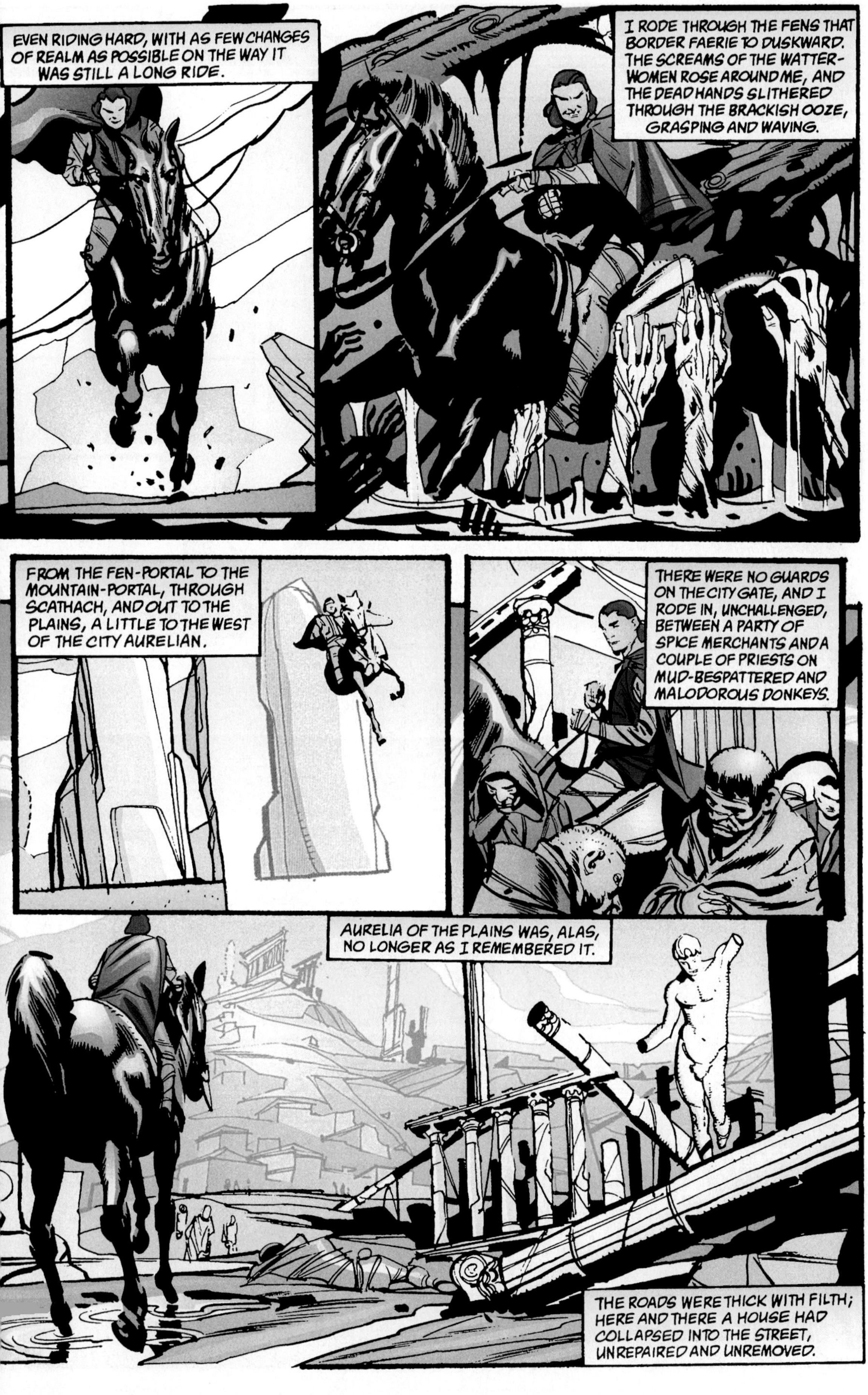
EVEN RIDING HARD, WITH AS FEW CHANGES OF REALM AS POSSIBLE ON THE WAY IT WAS STILL A LONG RIDE.
I RODE THROUGH THE FENS THAT BORDER FAERIE TO DUSKWARD. THE SCREAMS OF THE WATTER-WOMEN ROSE AROUND ME, AND THE DEAD HANDS SLITHERED THROUGH THE BRACKISH OOZE, GRASPING AND WAVING.
FROM THE FEN-PORTAL TO THE MOUNTAIN-PORTAL, THROUGH SCATHACH, AND OUT TO THE PLAINS, A LITTLE TO THE WEST OF THE CITY AURELIAN.
THERE WERE NO GUARDS ON THE CITY GATE, AND I RODE IN, UNCHALLENGED, BETWEEN A PARTY OF SPICE MERCHANTS AND A COUPLE OF PRIESTS ON MUD-BESPATTERED AND MALODOROUS DONKEYS.
AURELIA OF THE PLAINS WAS, ALAS, NO LONGER AS I REMEMBERED IT.
THE ROADS WERE THICK WITH FILTH; HERE AND THERE A HOUSE HAD COLLAPSED INTO THE STREET, UNREPAIRED AND UNREMOVED.

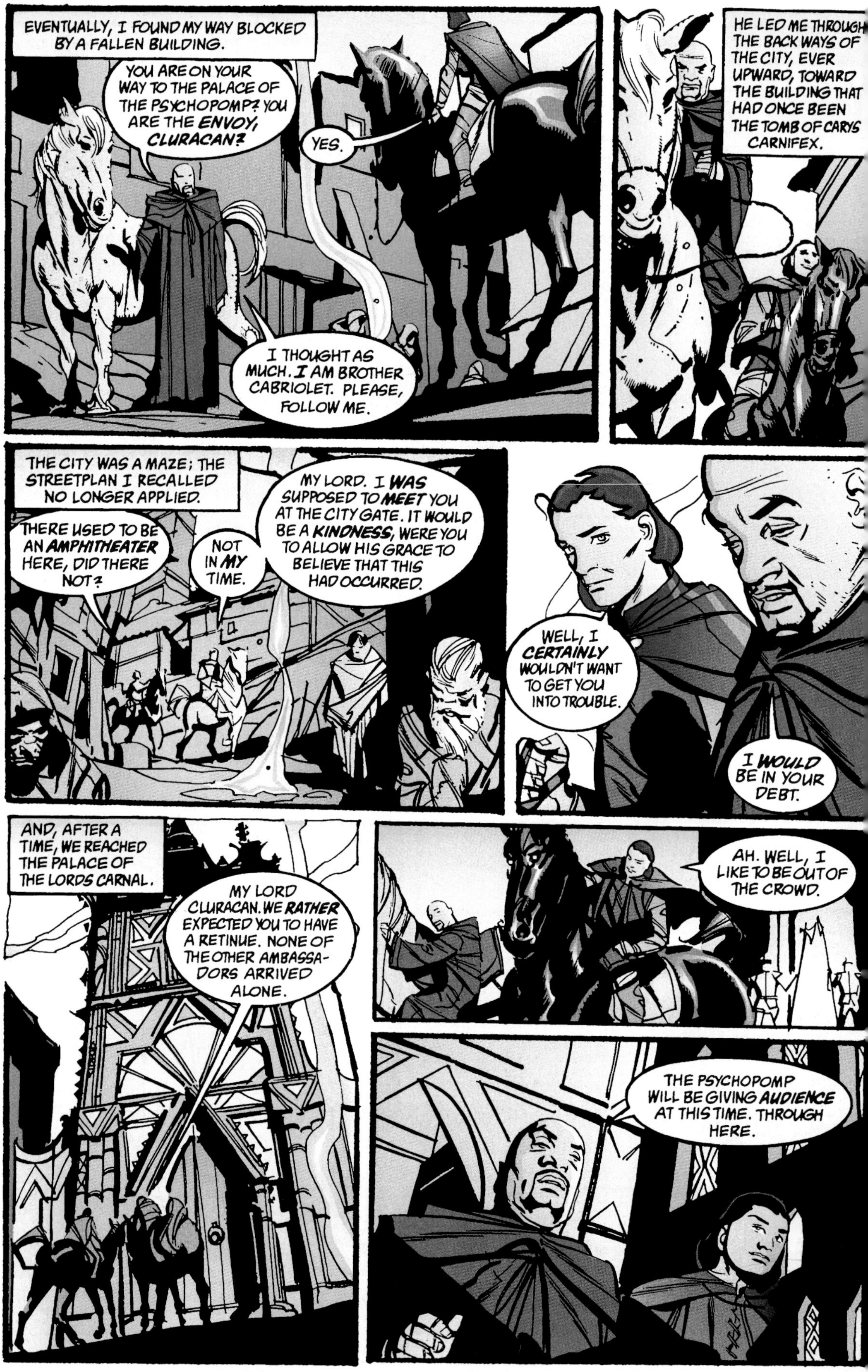
EVENTUALLY, I FOUND MY WAY BLOCKED BY A FALLEN BUILDING.
YOU ARE ON YOUR WAY TO THE PALACE OF THE PSYCHOPOMP? YOU ARE THE ENVOY, CLURACAN?
YES.
I THOUGHT AS MUCH. I AM BROTHER CABRIOLET. PLEASE, FOLLOW ME.
HE LED ME THROUGH THE BACK WAYS OF THE CITY, EVER UPWARD, TOWARD THE BUILDING THAT HAD ONCE BEEN THE TOMB OF CARYS CARNIFEX.
THE CITY WAS A MAZE; THE STREETPLAN I RECALLED NO LONGER APPLIED.
THERE USED TO BE AN AMPHITHEATER HERE, DID THERE NOT?
NOT IN MY TIME.
MY LORD. I WAS SUPPOSED TO MEET YOU AT THE CITY GATE. IT WOULD BE A KINDNESS, WERE YOU TO ALLOW HIS GRACE TO BELIEVE THAT THIS HAD OCCURRED.
WELL, I CERTAINLY WOULDN'T WANT TO GET YOU INTO TROUBLE.
I WOULD BE IN YOUR DEBT.
AND, AFTER A TIME, WE REACHED THE PALACE OF THE LORDS CARNAL.
MY LORD CLURACAN. WE RATHER EXPECTED YOU TO HAVE A RETINUE. NONE OF THE OTHER AMBASSADORS ARRIVED ALONE.
AH. WELL, I LIKE TO BE OUT OF THE CROWD.
THE PSYCHOPOMP WILL BE GIVING AUDIENCE AT THIS TIME. THROUGH HERE.

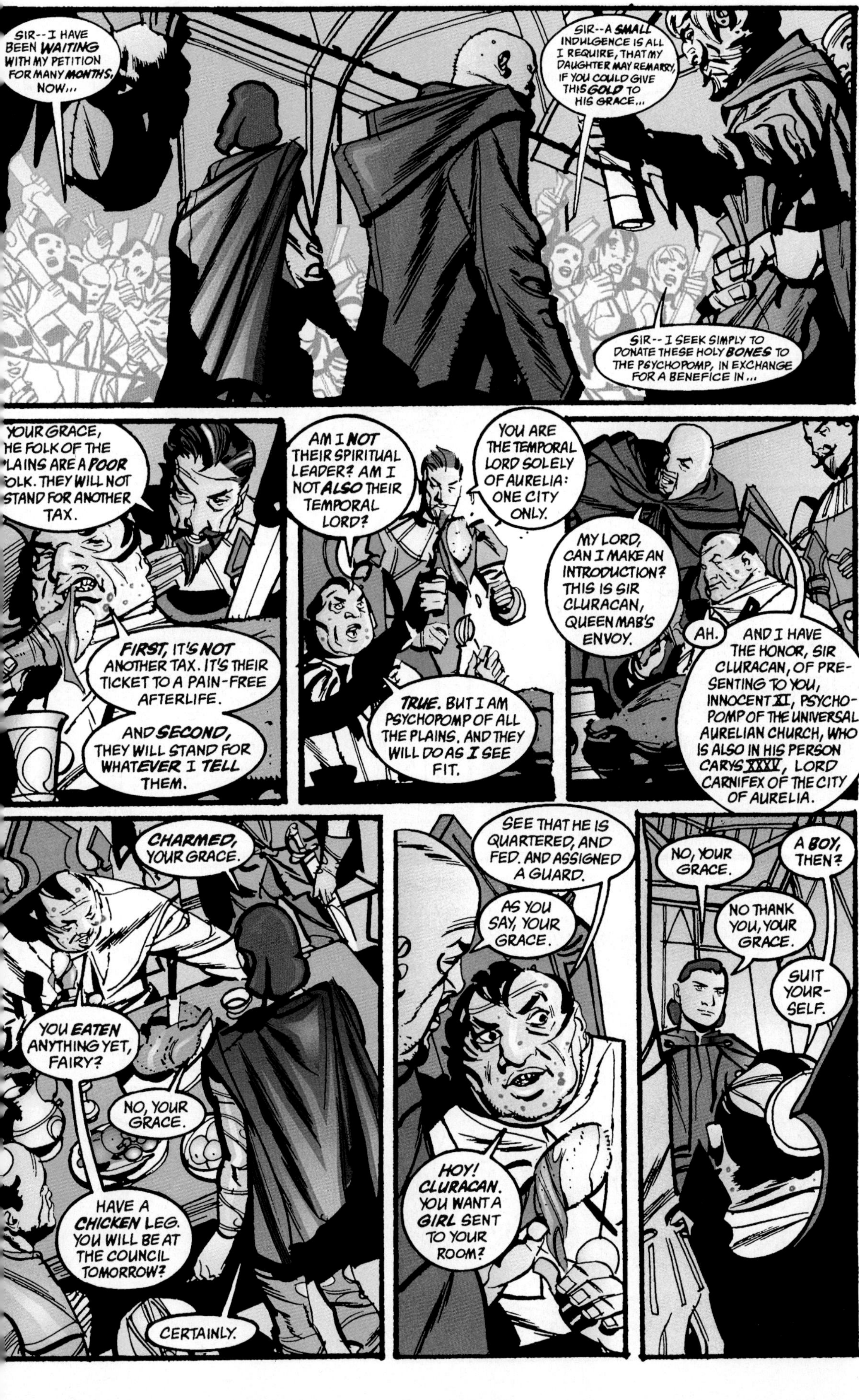
SIR-- I HAVE BEEN WAITING WITH MY PETITION FOR MANY MONTHS, NOW...
SIR--A SMALL INDULGENCE IS ALL I REQUIRE, THAT MY DAUGHTER MAY REMARRY, IF YOU COULD GIVE THIS GOLD TO HIS GRACE...
SIR-- I SEEK SIMPLY TO DONATE THESE HOLY BONES TO THE PSYCHOPOMP, IN EXCHANGE FOR A BENEFICE IN...
YOUR GRACE, HE FOLK OF THE PLAINS ARE A POOR OLK. THEY WILL NOT STAND FOR ANOTHER TAX.
FIRST, IT'S NOT ANOTHER TAX. IT'S THEIR TICKET TO A PAIN-FREE AFTERLIFE.
AND SECOND, THEY WILL STAND FOR WHATEVER I TELL THEM.
AM I NOT THEIR SPIRITUAL LEADER? AM I NOT ALSO THEIR TEMPORAL LORD?
YOU ARE THE TEMPORAL LORD SOLELY OF AURELIA: ONE CITY ONLY.
TRUE. BUT I AM PSYCHOPOMP OF ALL THE PLAINS. AND THEY WILL DO AS I SEE FIT.
MY LORD, CAN I MAKE AN INTRODUCTION? THIS IS SIR CLURACAN, QUEEN MAB'S ENVOY.
AH.
AND I HAVE THE HONOR, SIR CLURACAN, OF PRESENTING TO YOU, INNOCENT XI, PSYCHOPOMP OF THE UNIVERSAL AURELIAN CHURCH, WHO IS ALSO IN HIS PERSON CARYS XXXV, LORD CARNIFEX OF THE CITY OF AURELIA.
CHARMED, YOUR GRACE.
YOU EATEN ANYTHING YET, FAIRY?
NO, YOUR GRACE.
HAVE A CHICKEN LEG. YOU WILL BE AT THE COUNCIL TOMORROW?
CERTAINLY.
SEE THAT HE IS QUARTERED, AND FED. AND ASSIGNED A GUARD.
AS YOU SAY, YOUR GRACE.
HOY! CLURACAN. YOU WANT A GIRL SENT TO YOUR ROOM?
NO, YOUR GRACE.
A BOY, THEN?
NO THANK YOU, YOUR GRACE.
SUIT YOURSELF.

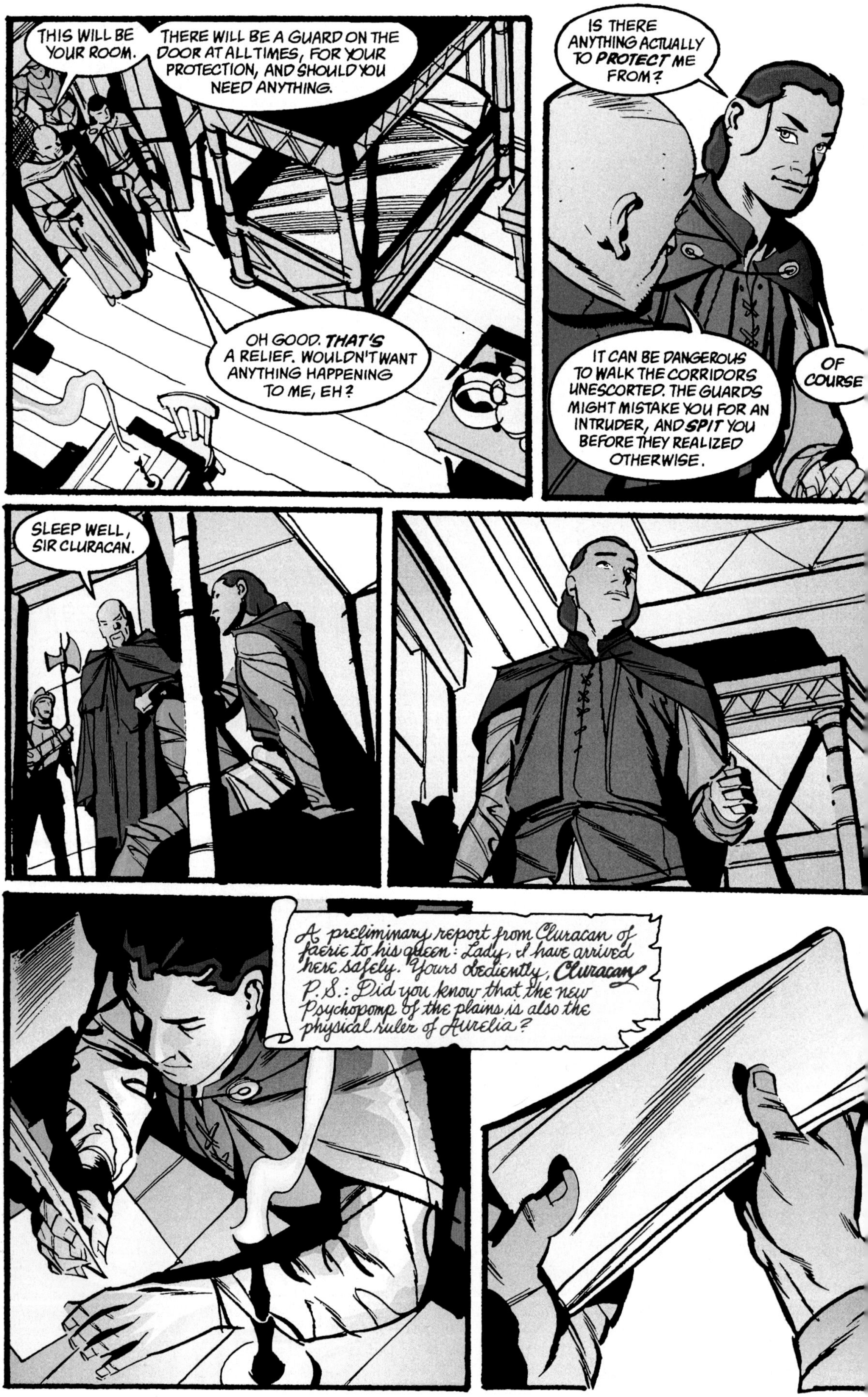
THIS WILL BE YOUR ROOM.
THERE WILL BE A GUARD ON THE DOOR AT ALL TIMES, FOR YOUR PROTECTION, AND SHOULD YOU NEED ANYTHING.
OH GOOD. THAT'S A RELIEF. WOULDN'T WANT ANYTHING HAPPENING TO ME, EH?
IS THERE ANYTHING ACTUALLY TO PROTECT ME FROM?
IT CAN BE DANGEROUS TO WALK THE CORRIDORS UNESCORTED. THE GUARDS MIGHT MISTAKE YOU FOR AN INTRUDER, AND SPIT YOU BEFORE THEY REALIZED OTHERWISE.
OF COURSE
SLEEP WELL, SIR CLURACAN.
A preliminary report from Cluracan of faerie to his queen: Lady, I have arrived here safely. Yours obediently, Cluracan
P.S.: Did you know that the new Psychopomp of the plains is also the physical ruler of Aurelia?

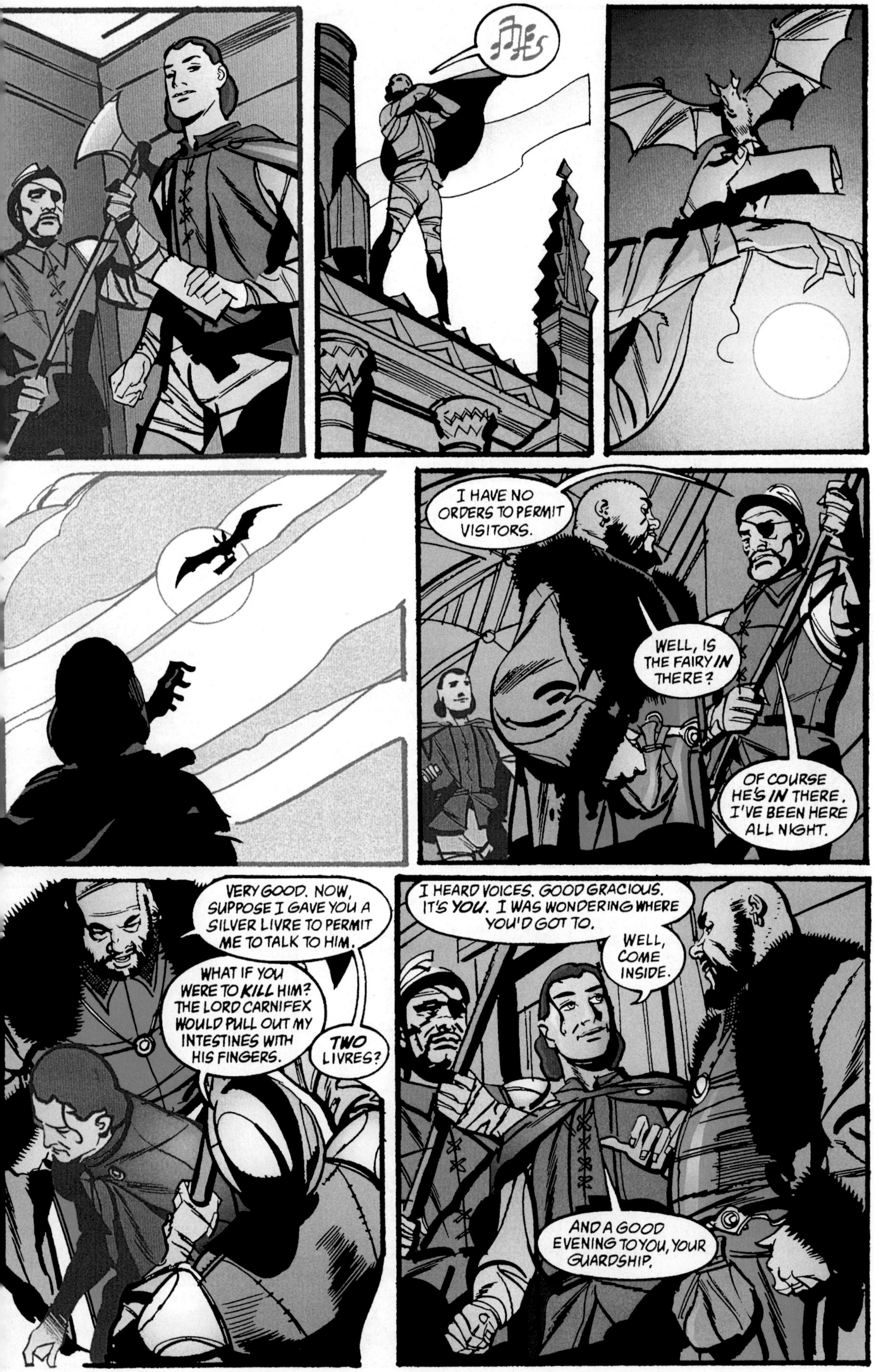
I HAVE NO ORDERS TO PERMIT VISITORS.
WELL, IS THE FAIRY IN THERE?
OF COURSE HE'S IN THERE. I'VE BEEN HERE ALL NIGHT.
VERY GOOD. NOW, SUPPOSE I GAVE YOU A SILVER LIVRE TO PERMIT ME TO TALK TO HIM.
WHAT IF YOU WERE TO KILL HIM? THE LORD CARNIFEX WOULD PULL OUT MY INTESTINES WITH HIS FINGERS.
TWO LIVRES?
I HEARD VOICES. GOOD GRACIOUS. IT'S YOU. I WAS WONDERING WHERE YOU'D GOT TO.
WELL, COME INSIDE.
AND A GOOD EVENING TO YOU, YOUR GUARDSHIP.

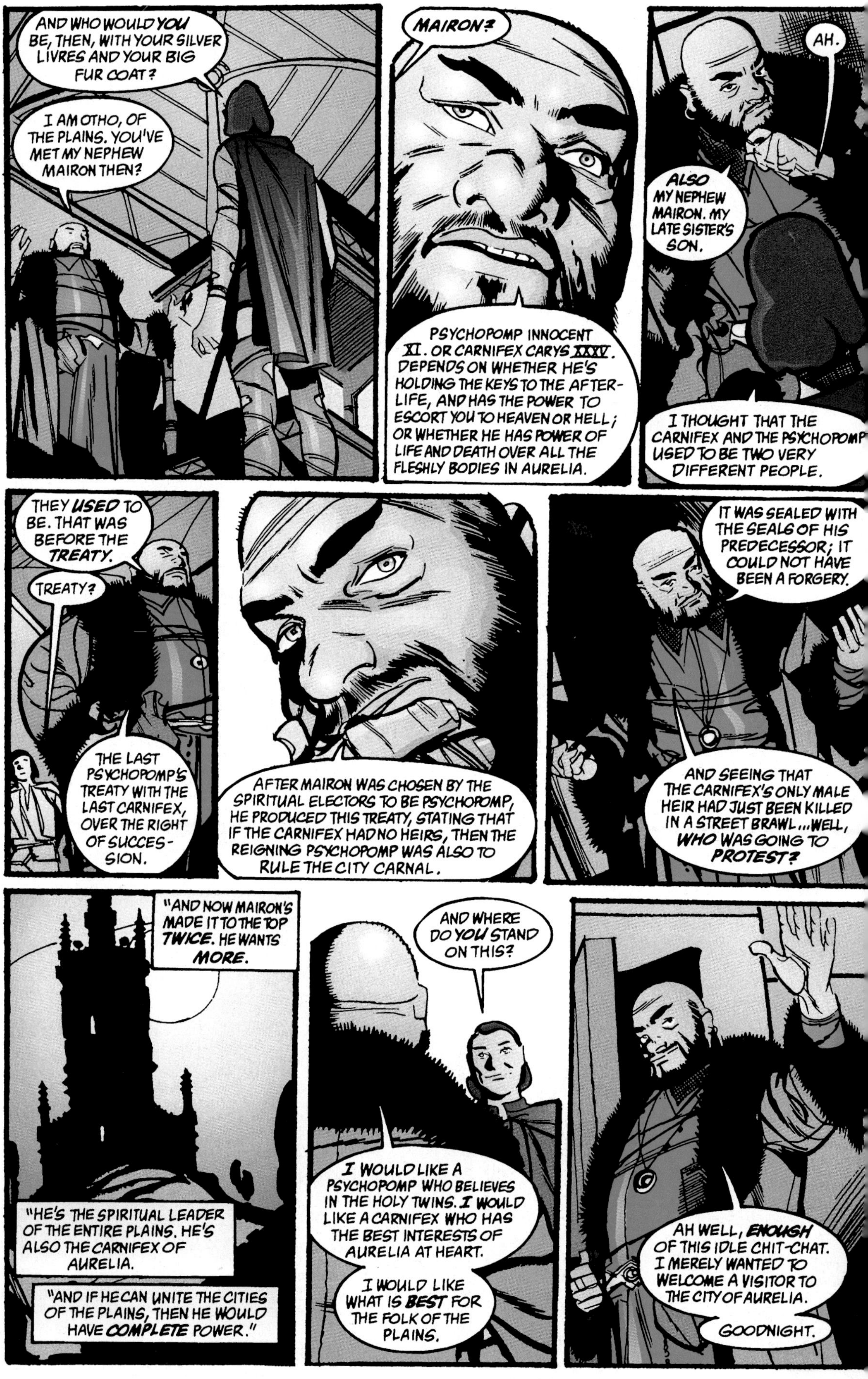
AND WHO WOULD YOU BE, THEN, WITH YOUR SILVER LIVRES AND YOUR BIG FUR COAT?
I AM OTHO, OF THE PLAINS. YOU'VE MET MY NEPHEW MAIRON THEN?
MAIRON?
PSYCHOPOMP INNOCENT XI. OR CARNIFEX CARYS XXXV. DEPENDS ON WHETHER HE'S HOLDING THE KEYS TO THE AFTER-LIFE, AND HAS THE POWER TO ESCORT YOU TO HEAVEN OR HELL; OR WHETHER HE HAS POWER OF LIFE AND DEATH OVER ALL THE FLESHLY BODIES IN AURELIA.
AH.
ALSO MY NEPHEW MAIRON. MY LATE SISTER'S SON.
I THOUGHT THAT THE CARNIFEX AND THE PSYCHOPOMP USED TO BE TWO VERY DIFFERENT PEOPLE.
THEY USED TO BE. THAT WAS BEFORE THE TREATY.
TREATY?
THE LAST PSYCHOPOMP'S TREATY WITH THE LAST CARNIFEX, OVER THE RIGHT OF SUCCES-SION.
AFTER MAIRON WAS CHOSEN BY THE SPIRITUAL ELECTORS TO BE PSYCHOPOMP, HE PRODUCED THIS TREATY, STATING THAT IF THE CARNIFEX HAD NO HEIRS, THEN THE REIGNING PSYCHOPOMP WAS ALSO TO RULE THE CITY CARNAL.
IT WAS SEALED WITH THE SEALS OF HIS PREDECESSOR; IT COULD NOT HAVE BEEN A FORGERY.
AND SEEING THAT THE CARNIFEX'S ONLY MALE HEIR HAD JUST BEEN KILLED IN A STREET BRAWL...WELL, WHO WAS GOING TO PROTEST?
"AND NOW MAIRON'S MADE IT TO THE TOP TWICE. HE WANTS MORE.
"HE'S THE SPIRITUAL LEADER OF THE ENTIRE PLAINS. HE'S ALSO THE CARNIFEX OF AURELIA.
"AND IF HE CAN UNITE THE CITIES OF THE PLAINS, THEN HE WOULD HAVE COMPLETE POWER."
AND WHERE DO YOU STAND ON THIS?
I WOULD LIKE A PSYCHOPOMP WHO BELIEVES IN THE HOLY TWINS. I WOULD LIKE A CARNIFEX WHO HAS THE BEST INTERESTS OF AURELIA AT HEART.
I WOULD LIKE WHAT IS BEST FOR THE FOLK OF THE PLAINS.
AH WELL, ENOUGH OF THIS IDLE CHIT-CHAT. I MERELY WANTED TO WELCOME A VISITOR TO THE CITY OF AURELIA.
GOODNIGHT.

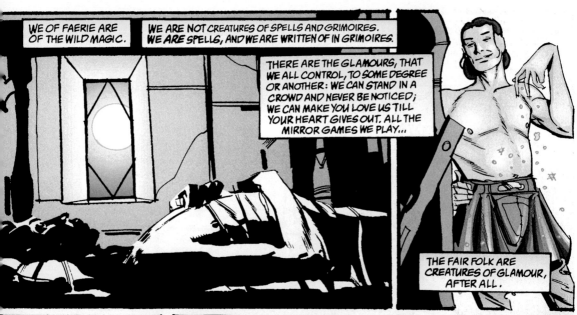

WE OF FAERIE ARE OF THE WILD MAGIC.

WE ARE NOT CREATURES OF SPELLS AND GRIMOIRES. WE ARE SPELLS, AND WE ARE WRITTEN OF IN GRIMOIRES.

THERE ARE THE GLAMOURS, THAT WE ALL CONTROL, TO SOME DEGREE OR ANOTHER: WE CAN STAND IN A CROWD AND NEVER BE NOTICED; WE CAN MAKE YOU LOVE US TILL YOUR HEART GIVES OUT. ALL THE MIRROR GAMES WE PLAY...

THE FAIR FOLK ARE CREATURES OF GLAMOUR, AFTER ALL.

FOR EXAMPLE: SOMETIMES WE WILL SAY TRUE THINGS. AND THESE THINGS WE SAY ARE NEITHER GLAMOUR NOR MAGIC, NEITHER PREDICTION NOR CURSE: BUT SOMETIMES WHAT WE SAY IS TRUE.

AND EVEN IF YOU'RE A TREMENDOUS LIAR, LIKE MYSELF, WELL, IT'S EVEN TRUE FOR ME.

HERE ARE DARKER CURRENTS THAT UN BENEATH THE SURFACE, LIKE THE WILD WIND STORMING ACROSS THE HEATHLAND OR THE FLASH OF IGHTNING ON A CLEAR SUMMER'S NIGHT, AND THESE ARE NOT PREDICTABLE THINGS.

I MENTION THIS TO GIVE A CERTAIN CONTEXT TO WHAT HAPPENED AT THE COUNCIL MEETING, THE NEXT MORNING.

I WAS IN A POOR SEAT, LISTENING LESS THAN INTENTLY TO THE VARIOUS FACTIONS, EMISSARIES, LORDS AND PRIESTS, AS THEY DISCUSSED THE FUTURE OF THE CITIES OF THE PLAINS.

AND I FELT IT WELLING INSIDE ME, LIKE A SNEEZE, OR AN ORGASM, DETERMINED TO COME OUT, WILL-I OR NEVER-SO.

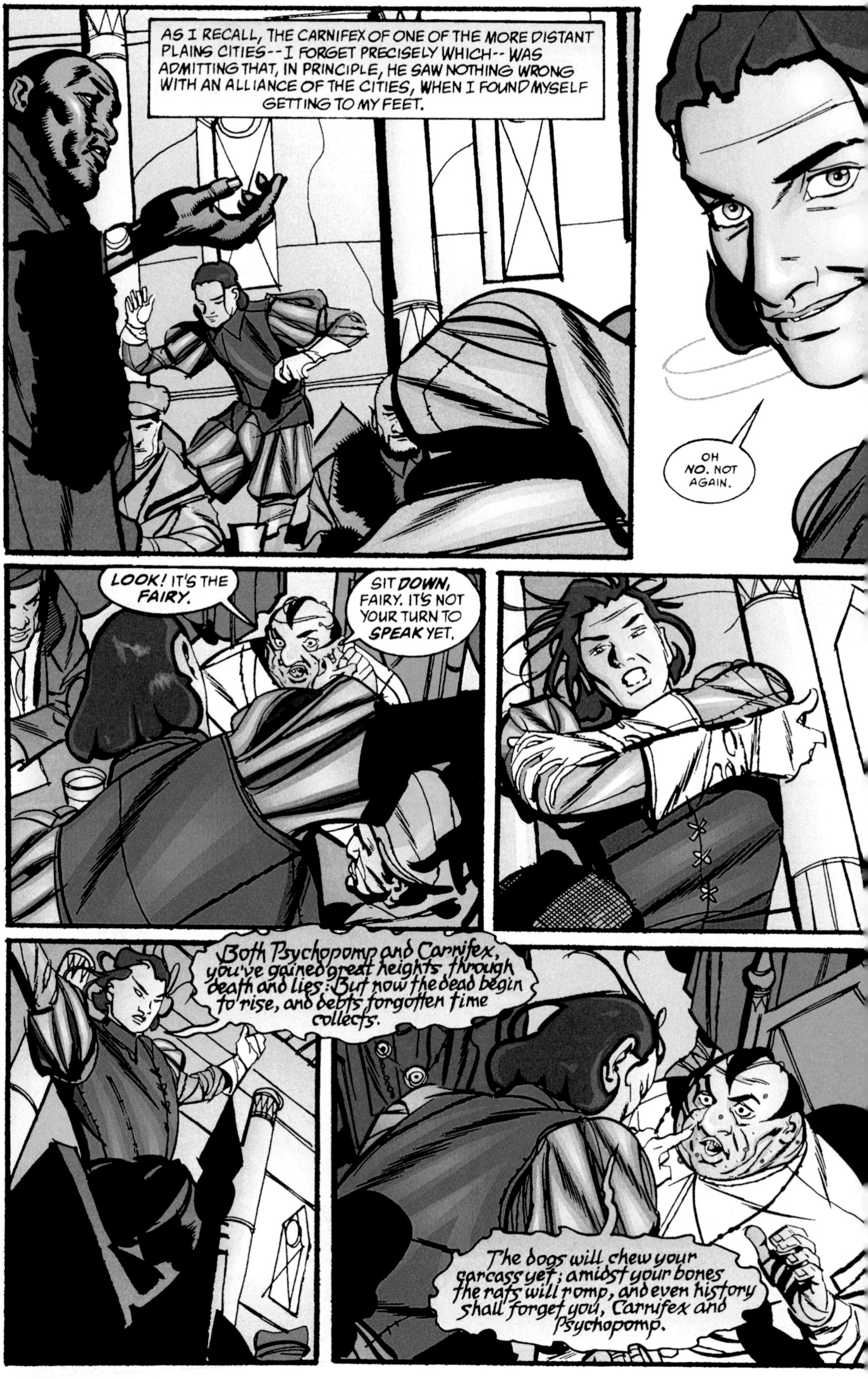
AS I RECALL, THE CARNIFEX OF ONE OF THE MORE DISTANT PLAINS CITIES--I FORGET PRECISELY WHICH--WAS ADMITTING THAT, IN PRINCIPLE, HE SAW NOTHING WRONG WITH AN ALLIANCE OF THE CITIES, WHEN I FOUND MYSELF GETTING TO MY FEET.
OH NO. NOT AGAIN.
LOOK! IT'S THE FAIRY.
SIT DOWN, FAIRY. IT'S NOT YOUR TURN TO SPEAK YET.
Both Psychopomp and Carnifex, you've gained great heights through death and lies: But now the dead begin to rise, and debts forgotten time collects.
The dogs will chew your carcass yet; amidst your bones the rats will romp, and even history shall forget you, Carnifex and Psychopomp.

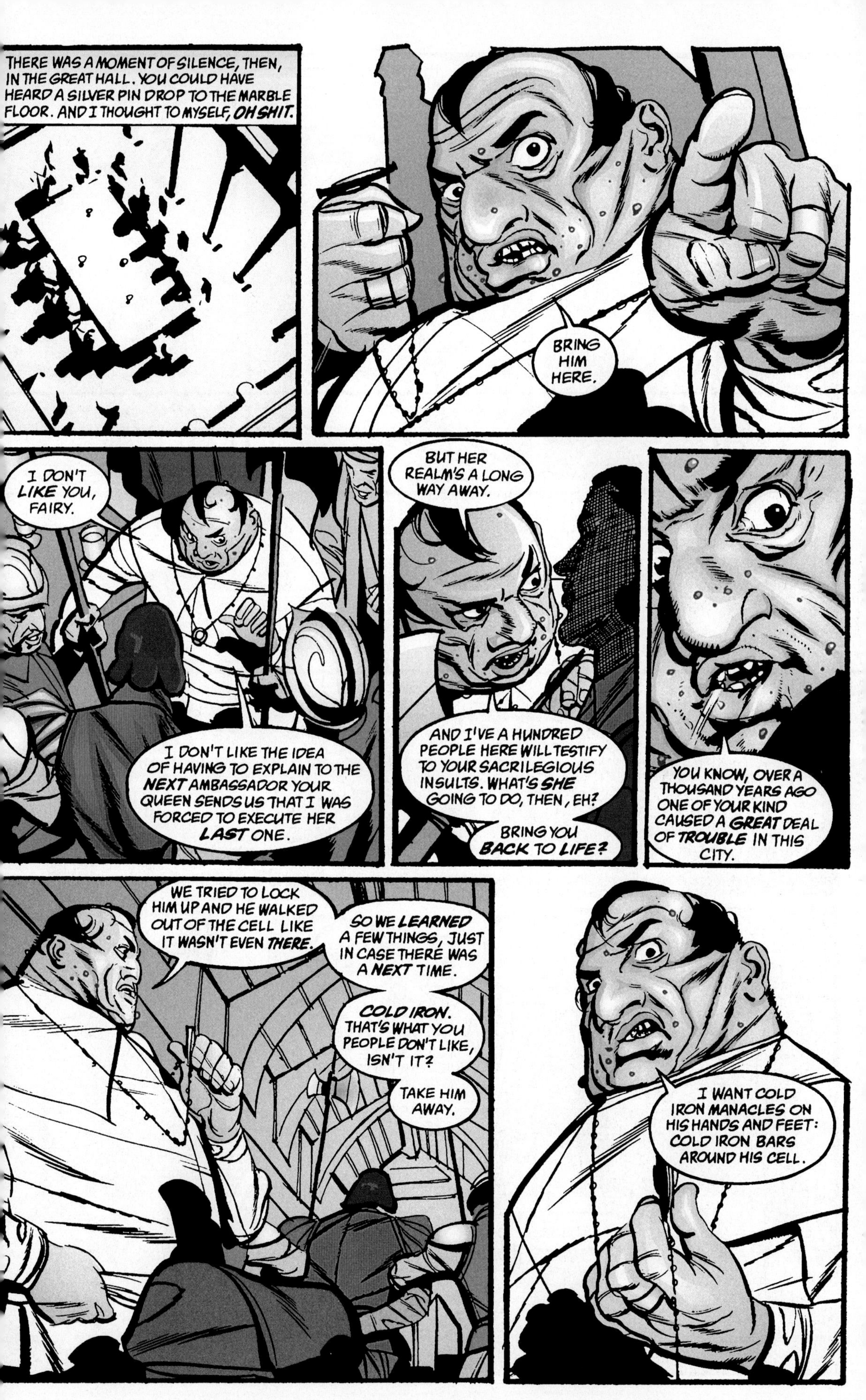
THERE WAS A MOMENT OF SILENCE, THEN, IN THE GREAT HALL. YOU COULD HAVE HEARD A SILVER PIN DROP TO THE MARBLE FLOOR. AND I THOUGHT TO MYSELF, OH SHIT.
BRING HIM HERE.
I DON'T LIKE YOU, FAIRY.
I DON'T LIKE THE IDEA OF HAVING TO EXPLAIN TO THE NEXT AMBASSADOR YOUR QUEEN SENDS US THAT I WAS FORCED TO EXECUTE HER LAST ONE.
BUT HER REALM'S A LONG WAY AWAY.
AND I'VE A HUNDRED PEOPLE HERE WILL TESTIFY TO YOUR SACRILEGIOUS INSULTS. WHAT'S SHE GOING TO DO, THEN, EH?
BRING YOU BACK TO LIFE?
YOU KNOW, OVER A THOUSAND YEARS AGO ONE OF YOUR KIND CAUSED A GREAT DEAL OF TROUBLE IN THIS CITY.
WE TRIED TO LOCK HIM UP AND HE WALKED OUT OF THE CELL LIKE IT WASN'T EVEN THERE.
SO WE LEARNED A FEW THINGS, JUST IN CASE THERE WAS A NEXT TIME.
COLD IRON. THAT'S WHAT YOU PEOPLE DON'T LIKE, ISN'T IT?
TAKE HIM AWAY.
I WANT COLD IRON MANACLES ON HIS HANDS AND FEET: COLD IRON BARS AROUND HIS CELL.

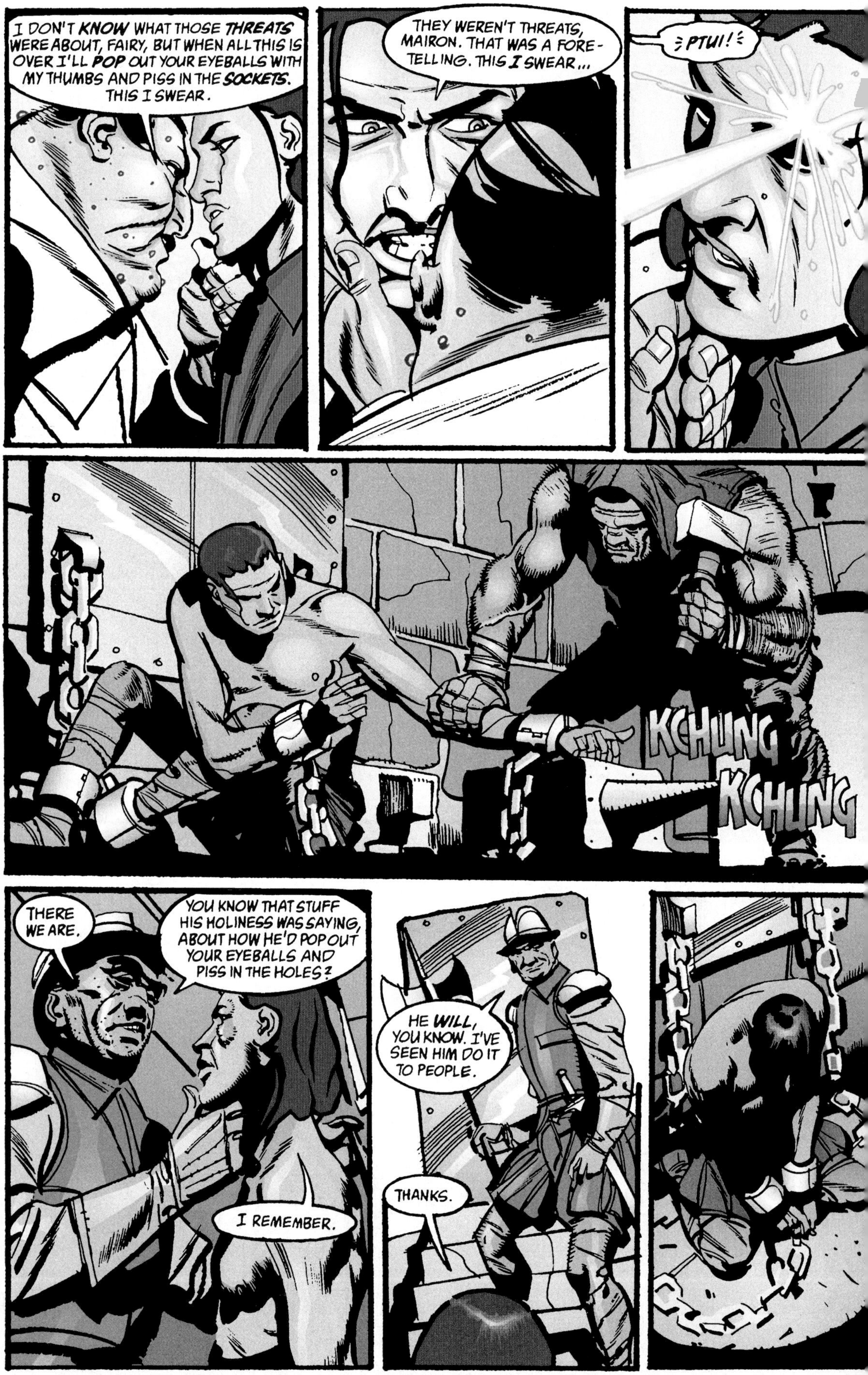

I DON'T KNOW WHAT THOSE THREATS WERE ABOUT, FAIRY, BUT WHEN ALL THIS IS OVER I'LL POP OUT YOUR EYEBALLS WITH MY THUMBS AND PISS IN THE SOCKETS. THIS I SWEAR.
THEY WEREN'T THREATS, MAIRON. THAT WAS A FORE-TELLING. THIS I SWEAR...
PTUI!
KCHUNG
KCHUNG
THERE WE ARE.
YOU KNOW THAT STUFF HIS HOLINESS WAS SAYING, ABOUT HOW HE'D POP OUT YOUR EYEBALLS AND PISS IN THE HOLES?
I REMEMBER.
HE WILL, YOU KNOW. I'VE SEEN HIM DO IT TO PEOPLE.
THANKS.

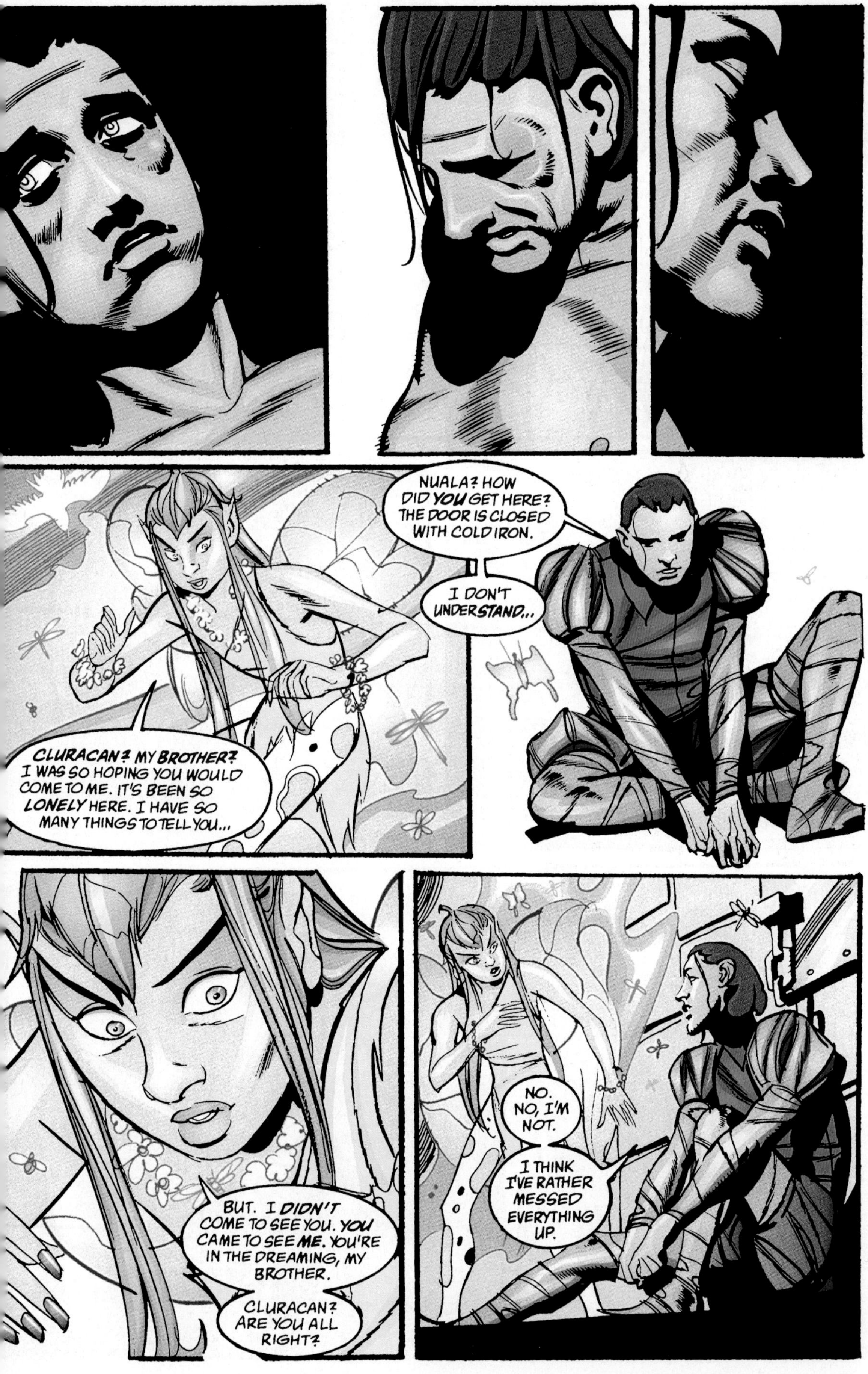
NUALA? HOW DID YOU GET HERE? THE DOOR IS CLOSED WITH COLD IRON.
I DON'T UNDERSTAND...
CLURACAN? MY BROTHER? I WAS SO HOPING YOU WOULD COME TO ME. IT'S BEEN SO LONELY HERE. I HAVE SO MANY THINGS TO TELL YOU...
BUT. I DIDN'T COME TO SEE YOU. YOU CAME TO SEE ME. YOU'RE IN THE DREAMING, MY BROTHER.
CLURACAN? ARE YOU ALL RIGHT?
NO. NO, I'M NOT.
I THINK I'VE RATHER MESSED EVERYTHING UP.

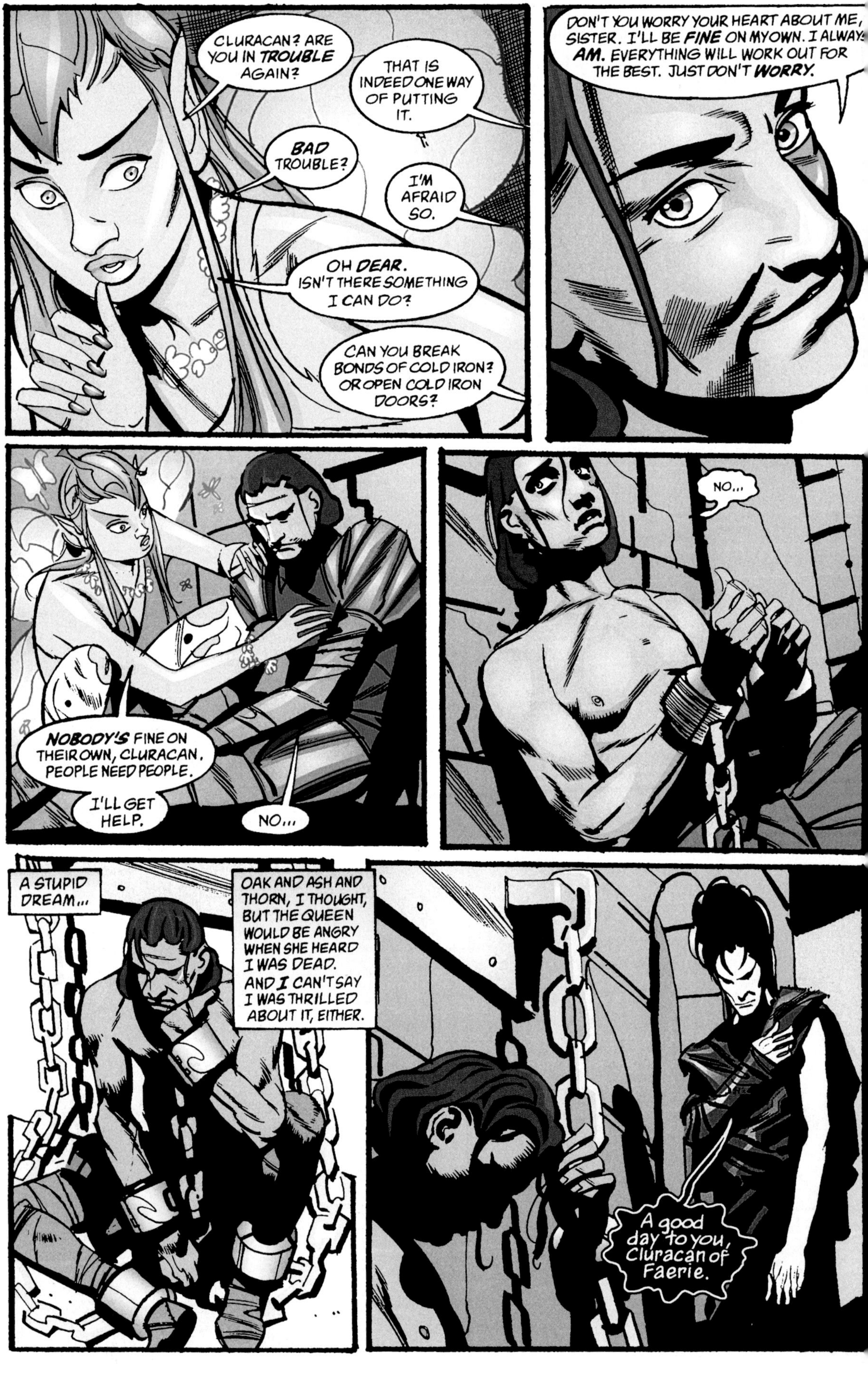
CLURACAN? ARE YOU IN TROUBLE AGAIN?
THAT IS INDEED ONE WAY OF PUTTING IT.
BAD TROUBLE?
I'M AFRAID SO.
OH DEAR. ISN'T THERE SOMETHING I CAN DO?
CAN YOU BREAK BONDS OF COLD IRON? OR OPEN COLD IRON DOORS?
DON'T YOU WORRY YOUR HEART ABOUT ME, SISTER. I'LL BE FINE ON MY OWN. I ALWAYS AM. EVERYTHING WILL WORK OUT FOR THE BEST. JUST DON'T WORRY.
NOBODY'S FINE ON THEIR OWN, CLURACAN. PEOPLE NEED PEOPLE.
I'LL GET HELP.
NO...
NO...
A STUPID DREAM...
OAK AND ASH AND THORN, I THOUGHT, BUT THE QUEEN WOULD BE ANGRY WHEN SHE HEARD I WAS DEAD. AND I CAN'T SAY I WAS THRILLED ABOUT IT, EITHER.
A good day to you, Cluracan of Faerie.

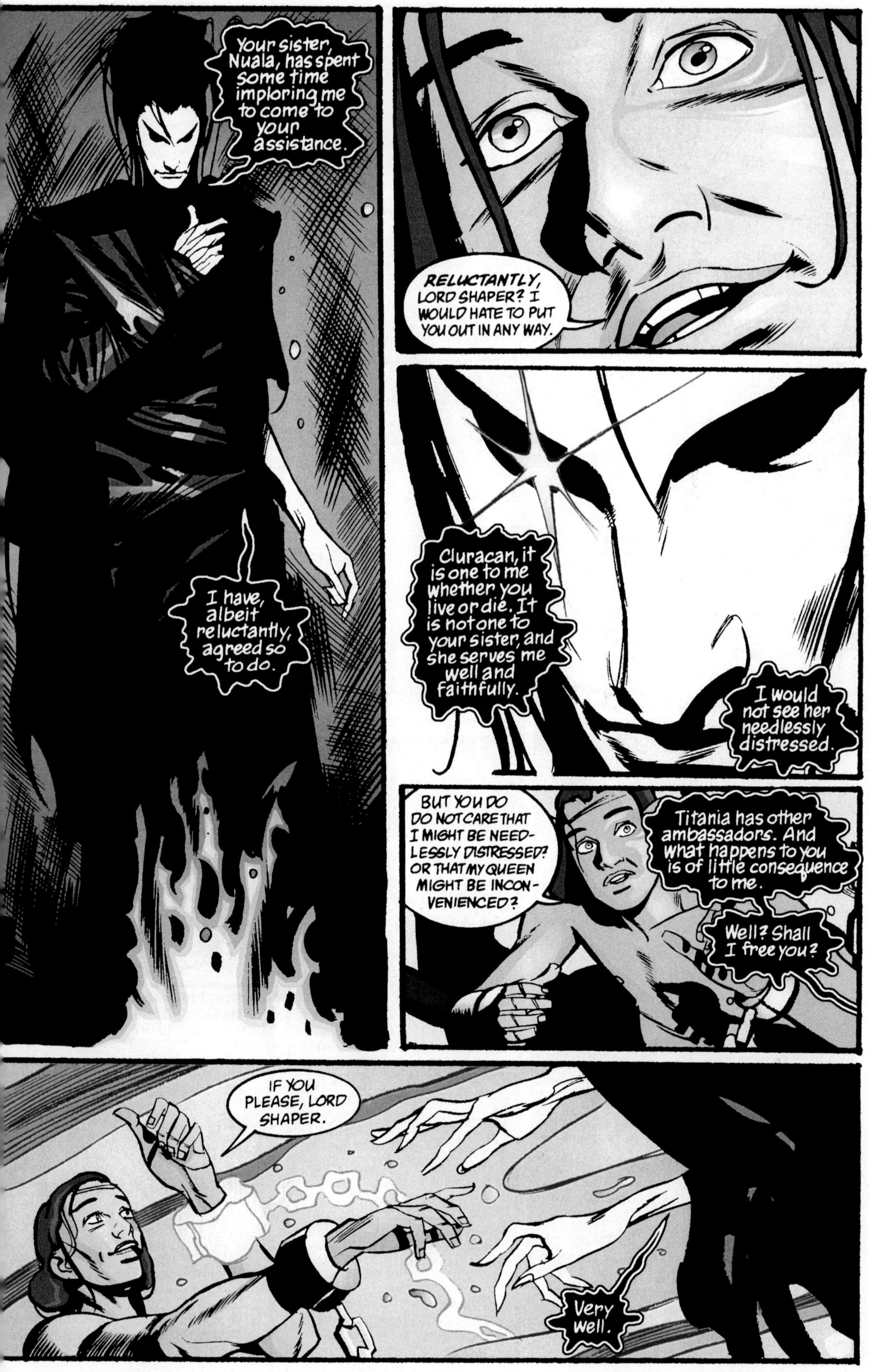
Your sister, Nuala, has spent some time imploring me to come to your assistance.
I have, albeit reluctantly, agreed so to do.
RELUCTANTLY, LORD SHAPER? I WOULD HATE TO PUT YOU OUT IN ANY WAY.
Cluracan, it is one to me whether you live or die. It is not one to your sister, and she serves me well and faithfully.
I would not see her needlessly distressed.
BUT YOU DO DO NOT CARE THAT I MIGHT BE NEEDLESSLY DISTRESSED? OR THAT MY QUEEN MIGHT BE INCONVENIENCED?
Titania has other ambassadors. And what happens to you is of little consequence to me.
Well? Shall I free you?
IF YOU PLEASE, LORD SHAPER.
Very well.

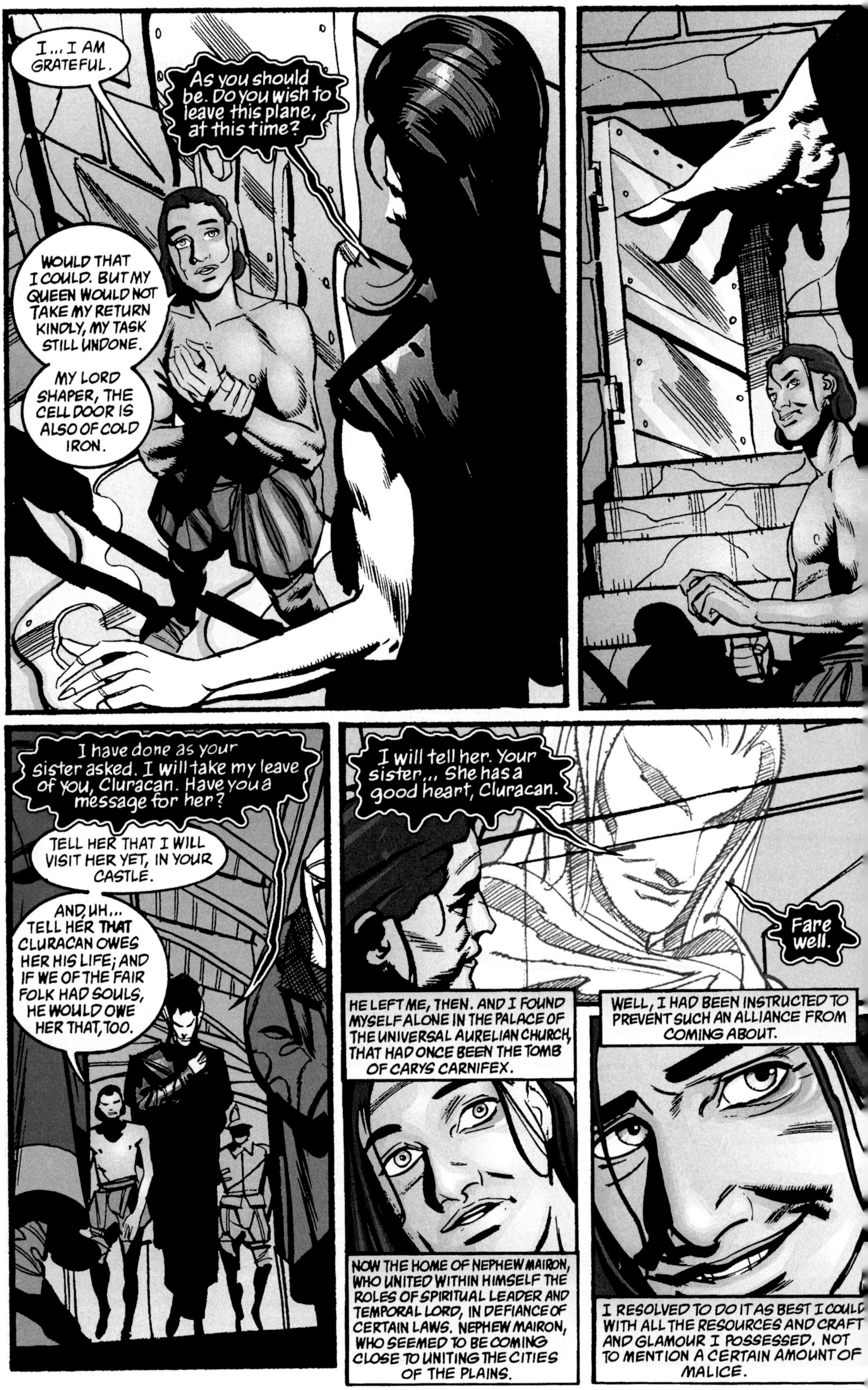
I... I AM GRATEFUL.
As you should be. Do you wish to leave this plane, at this time?
WOULD THAT I COULD. BUT MY QUEEN WOULD NOT TAKE MY RETURN KINDLY, MY TASK STILL UNDONE.
MY LORD SHAPER, THE CELL DOOR IS ALSO OF COLD IRON.
I have done as your sister asked. I will take my leave of you, Cluracan. Have you a message for her?
TELL HER THAT I WILL VISIT HER YET, IN YOUR CASTLE.
AND, UH... TELL HER THAT CLURACAN OWES HER HIS LIFE; AND IF WE OF THE FAIR FOLK HAD SOULS, HE WOULD OWE HER THAT, TOO.
I will tell her. Your sister... She has a good heart, Cluracan.
Fare well.
HE LEFT ME, THEN. AND I FOUND MYSELF ALONE IN THE PALACE OF THE UNIVERSAL AURELIAN CHURCH, THAT HAD ONCE BEEN THE TOMB OF CARYS CARNIFEX.
NOW THE HOME OF NEPHEW MAIRON, WHO UNITED WITHIN HIMSELF THE ROLES OF SPIRITUAL LEADER AND TEMPORAL LORD, IN DEFIANCE OF CERTAIN LAWS. NEPHEW MAIRON, WHO SEEMED TO BE COMING CLOSE TO UNITING THE CITIES OF THE PLAINS.
WELL, I HAD BEEN INSTRUCTED TO PREVENT SUCH AN ALLIANCE FROM COMING ABOUT.
I RESOLVED TO DO IT AS BEST I COULD WITH ALL THE RESOURCES AND CRAFT AND GLAMOUR I POSSESSED. NOT TO MENTION A CERTAIN AMOUNT OF MALICE.

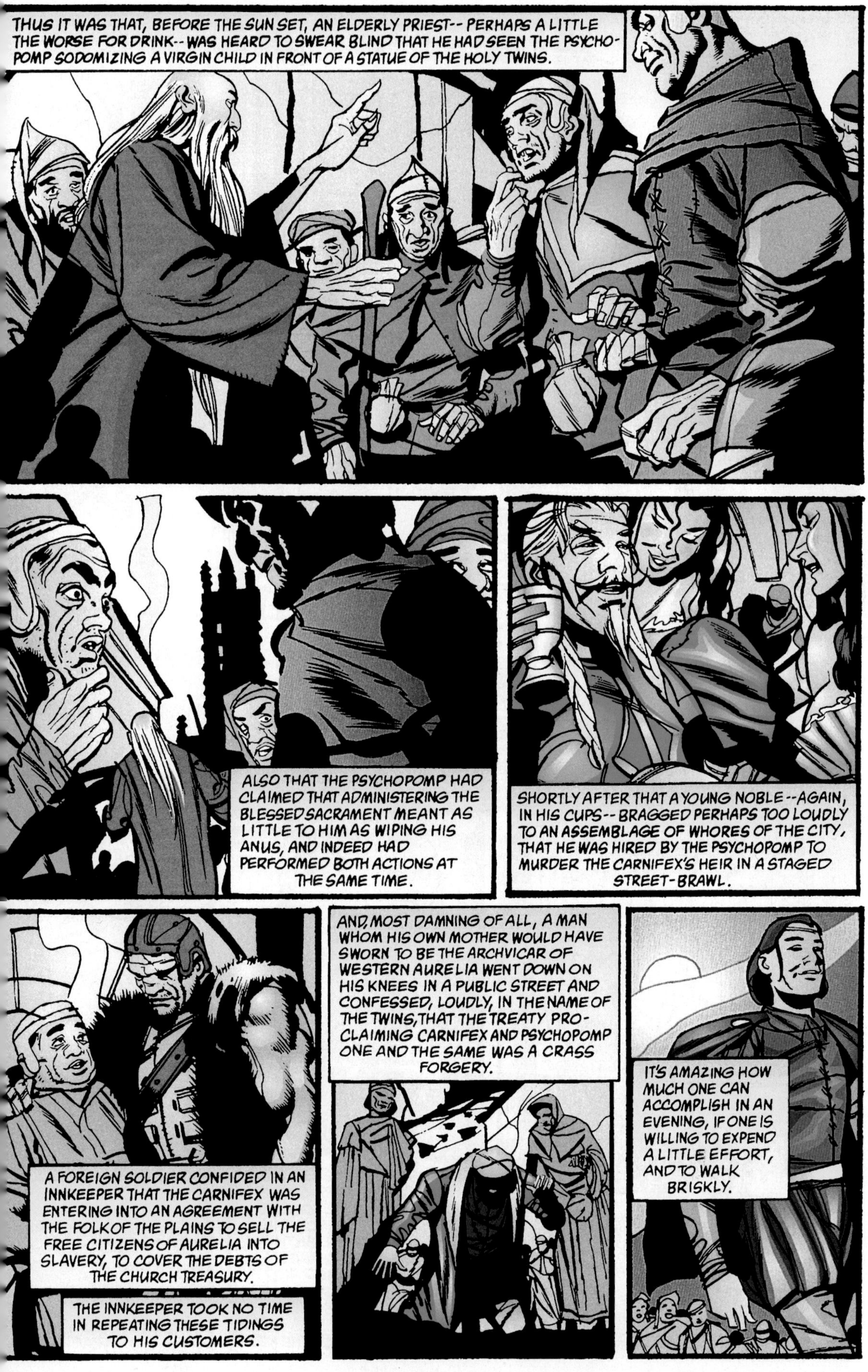
THUS IT WAS THAT, BEFORE THE SUN SET, AN ELDERLY PRIEST-- PERHAPS A LITTLE THE WORSE FOR DRINK-- WAS HEARD TO SWEAR BLIND THAT HE HAD SEEN THE PSYCHOPOMP SODOMIZING A VIRGIN CHILD IN FRONT OF A STATUE OF THE HOLY TWINS.
ALSO THAT THE PSYCHOPOMP HAD CLAIMED THAT ADMINISTERING THE BLESSED SACRAMENT MEANT AS LITTLE TO HIM AS WIPING HIS ANUS, AND INDEED HAD PERFORMED BOTH ACTIONS AT THE SAME TIME.
SHORTLY AFTER THAT A YOUNG NOBLE --AGAIN, IN HIS CUPS-- BRAGGED PERHAPS TOO LOUDLY TO AN ASSEMBLAGE OF WHORES OF THE CITY, THAT HE WAS HIRED BY THE PSYCHOPOMP TO MURDER THE CARNIFEX'S HEIR IN A STAGED STREET-BRAWL.
A FOREIGN SOLDIER CONFIDED IN AN INNKEEPER THAT THE CARNIFEX WAS ENTERING INTO AN AGREEMENT WITH THE FOLK OF THE PLAINS TO SELL THE FREE CITIZENS OF AURELIA INTO SLAVERY, TO COVER THE DEBTS OF THE CHURCH TREASURY.
THE INNKEEPER TOOK NO TIME IN REPEATING THESE TIDINGS TO HIS CUSTOMERS.
AND, MOST DAMNING OF ALL, A MAN WHOM HIS OWN MOTHER WOULD HAVE SWORN TO BE THE ARCHVICAR OF WESTERN AURELIA WENT DOWN ON HIS KNEES IN A PUBLIC STREET AND CONFESSED, LOUDLY, IN THE NAME OF THE TWINS, THAT THE TREATY PROCLAIMING CARNIFEX AND PSYCHOPOMP ONE AND THE SAME WAS A CRASS FORGERY.
IT'S AMAZING HOW MUCH ONE CAN ACCOMPLISH IN AN EVENING, IF ONE IS WILLING TO EXPEND A LITTLE EFFORT, AND TO WALK BRISKLY.

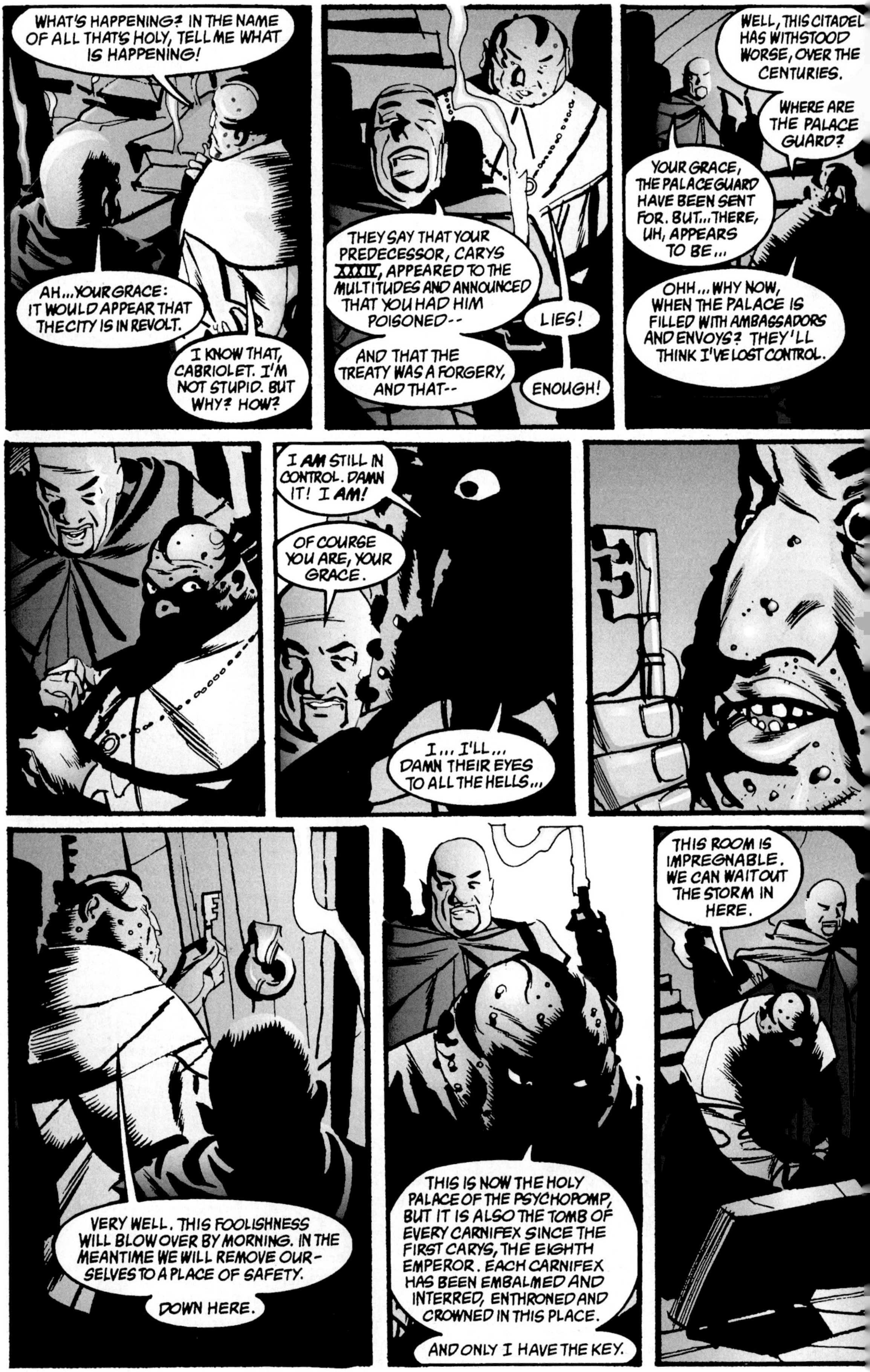
WHAT'S HAPPENING? IN THE NAME OF ALL THAT'S HOLY, TELL ME WHAT IS HAPPENING!
AH... YOUR GRACE: IT WOULD APPEAR THAT THE CITY IS IN REVOLT.
I KNOW THAT, CABRIOLET. I'M NOT STUPID. BUT WHY? HOW?
THEY SAY THAT YOUR PREDECESSOR, CARYS XXXIV, APPEARED TO THE MULTITUDES AND ANNOUNCED THAT YOU HAD HIM POISONED--
AND THAT THE TREATY WAS A FORGERY, AND THAT--
LIES!
ENOUGH!
WELL, THIS CITADEL HAS WITHSTOOD WORSE, OVER THE CENTURIES.
WHERE ARE THE PALACE GUARD?
YOUR GRACE, THE PALACE GUARD HAVE BEEN SENT FOR. BUT... THERE, UH, APPEARS TO BE...
OHH... WHY NOW, WHEN THE PALACE IS FILLED WITH AMBASSADORS AND ENVOYS? THEY'LL THINK I'VE LOST CONTROL.
I AM STILL IN CONTROL. DAMN IT! I AM!
OF COURSE YOU ARE, YOUR GRACE.
I... I'LL... DAMN THEIR EYES TO ALL THE HELLS...
VERY WELL. THIS FOOLISHNESS WILL BLOW OVER BY MORNING. IN THE MEANTIME WE WILL REMOVE OURSELVES TO A PLACE OF SAFETY.
DOWN HERE.
THIS IS NOW THE HOLY PALACE OF THE PSYCHOPOMP, BUT IT IS ALSO THE TOMB OF EVERY CARNIFEX SINCE THE FIRST CARYS, THE EIGHTH EMPEROR. EACH CARNIFEX HAS BEEN EMBALMED AND INTERRED, ENTHRONED AND CROWNED IN THIS PLACE.
AND ONLY I HAVE THE KEY.
THIS ROOM IS IMPREGNABLE. WE CAN WAIT OUT THE STORM IN HERE.

THERE WE GO. WE'LL BE SAFE THE NIGHT IN HERE.

RECOGNIZE *HIM*? MY PREDECESSOR AS CARNIFEX. UGLY OLD BUGGER, WASN'T HE?

YOU'RE LOOKING REMARKABLY WELL-PRESERVED, CARYS. YOU KNOW I DIDN'T POISON YOU, DON'T YOU? YOU KNOW IT'S ALL LIES.

WHY WOULD ANYONE POISON A MAN WITH A TERMINAL CANCER? WASTE OF GOOD POISON...

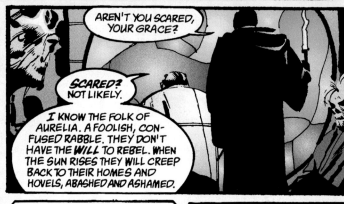

AREN'T YOU SCARED, YOUR GRACE?

SCARED? NOT LIKELY.

I KNOW THE FOLK OF AURELIA. A FOOLISH, CONFUSED RABBLE. THEY DON'T HAVE THE *WILL* TO REBEL. WHEN THE SUN RISES THEY WILL CREEP BACK TO THEIR HOMES AND HOVELS, ABASHED AND ASHAMED.

I WILL WAIT HERE WHILE THEY RIOT. AND THEN I WILL WALK THROUGH THE CITY, WITH THE PALACE GUARD BESIDE ME. AND, IN MY ROLE AS CARNIFEX OF AURELIA, I WILL PRONOUNCE SENTENCE OF DEATH ON EVERY TENTH MAN; WHILE AS THE CONDUCTOR OF THEIR SOULS, AS THE CHURCH'S LEADER, I WILL DAMN ALL THEIR SOULS TO ETERNAL COLD AND DARK...

AND I WILL FIND OUT WHO IS RESPONSIBLE FOR THIS INSURRECTION. AND I WILL....

POP OUT THEIR EYEBALLS WITH YOUR THUMBS AND PISS INTO THE OPEN SOCKETS?

...YES.

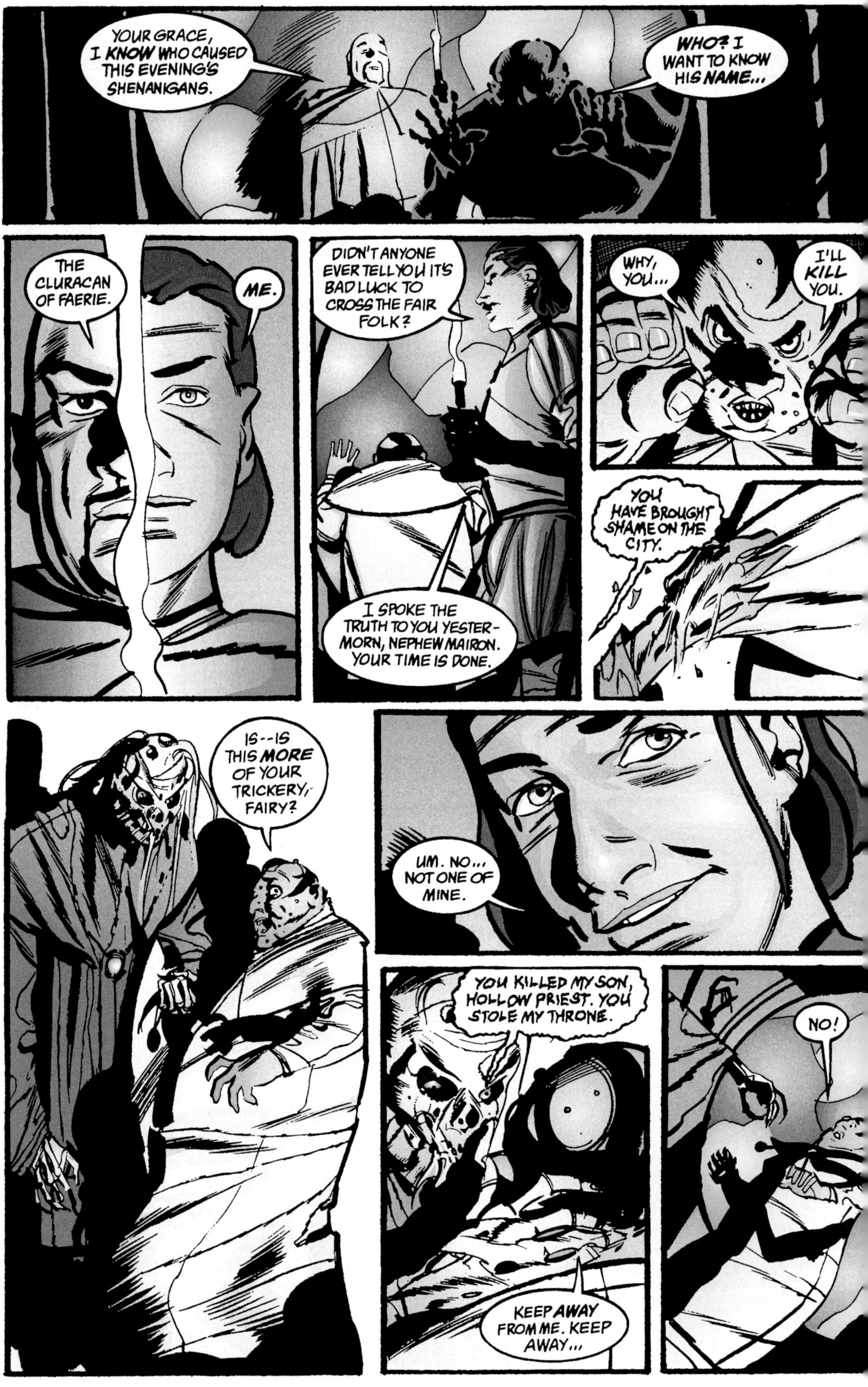
YOUR GRACE, I KNOW WHO CAUSED THIS EVENING'S SHENANIGANS.
WHO? I WANT TO KNOW HIS NAME...
THE CLURACAN OF FAERIE.
ME.
DIDN'T ANYONE EVER TELL YOU IT'S BAD LUCK TO CROSS THE FAIR FOLK?
I SPOKE THE TRUTH TO YOU YESTER-MORN, NEPHEW MAIRON. YOUR TIME IS DONE.
WHY, YOU...
I'LL KILL YOU.
YOU HAVE BROUGHT SHAME ON THE CITY.
IS--IS THIS MORE OF YOUR TRICKERY, FAIRY?
UM. NO... NOT ONE OF MINE.
YOU KILLED MY SON, HOLLOW PRIEST. YOU STOLE MY THRONE.
KEEP AWAY FROM ME. KEEP AWAY...
NO!

"BUT NOW THE DEAD BEGIN TO RISE, AND DEBTS FORGOTTEN TIME COLLECTS."

WELL, WELL, WELL.

ON THE WAY DOWN THE STAIRS, I HAD A REALLY INVIGORATING SWORD-FIGHT WITH THE PALACE GUARD.

I MADE MY WAY TO THE STABLES, WHERE I HARNESSED UP MY MOUNT AND RODE OFF DOWN THE HILL, FAIRLY CONFIDENT THAT ANY POSSIBILITY OF AN ALLIANCE OF THE CITIES OF THE PLAIN WAS MORE OR LESS UTTERLY SCUPPERED.

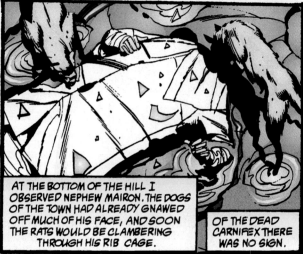

AT THE BOTTOM OF THE HILL I OBSERVED NEPHEW MAIRON. THE DOGS OF THE TOWN HAD ALREADY GNAWED OFF MUCH OF HIS FACE, AND SOON THE RATS WOULD BE CLAMBERING THROUGH HIS RIB CAGE.

OF THE DEAD CARNIFEX THERE WAS NO SIGN.

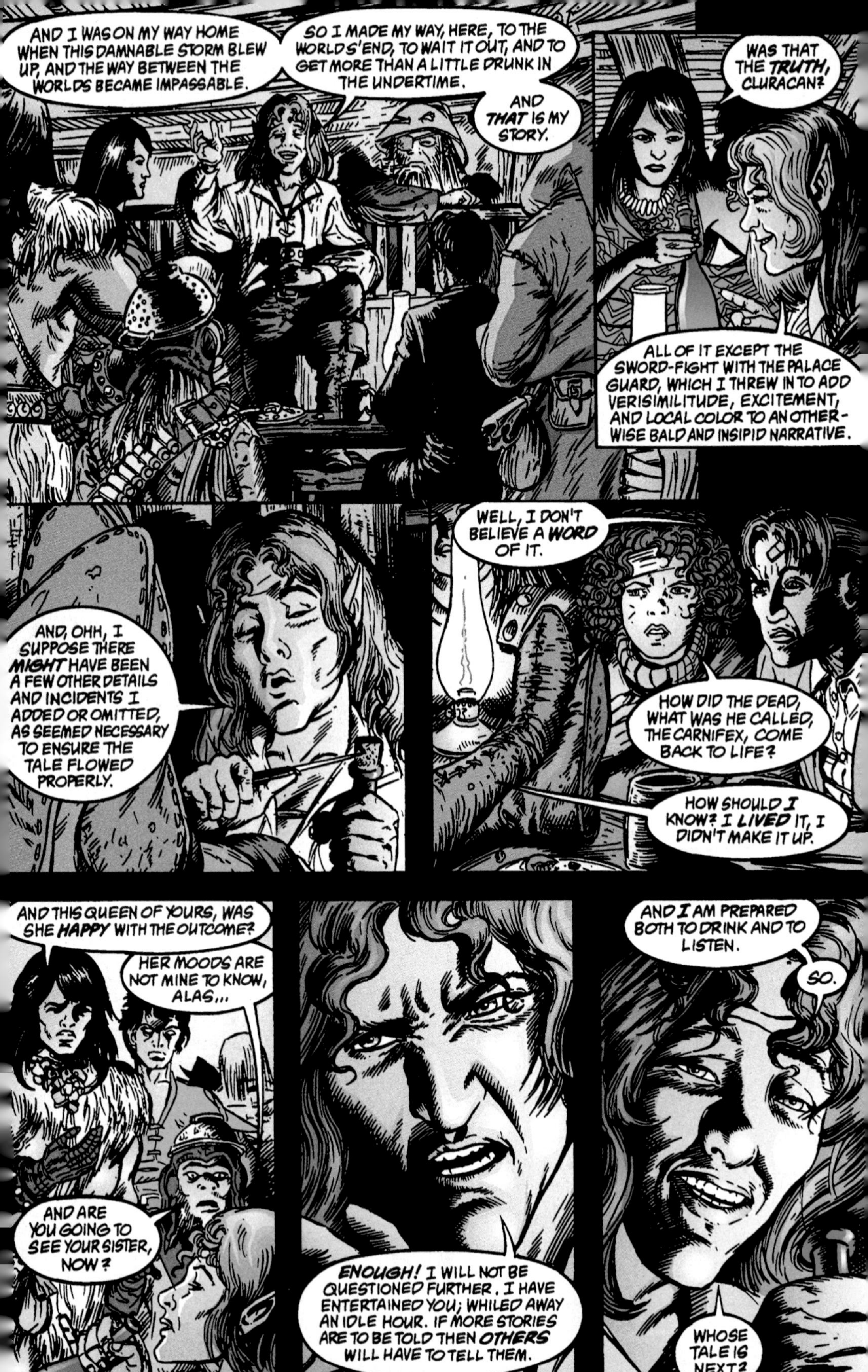
AND I WAS ON MY WAY HOME WHEN THIS DAMNABLE STORM BLEW UP, AND THE WAY BETWEEN THE WORLDS BECAME IMPASSABLE.
SO I MADE MY WAY, HERE, TO THE WORLDS' END, TO WAIT IT OUT, AND TO GET MORE THAN A LITTLE DRUNK IN THE UNDERTIME.
AND *THAT* IS MY STORY.
WAS THAT THE *TRUTH*, CLURACAN?
ALL OF IT EXCEPT THE SWORD-FIGHT WITH THE PALACE GUARD, WHICH I THREW IN TO ADD VERISIMILITUDE, EXCITEMENT, AND LOCAL COLOR TO AN OTHERWISE BALD AND INSIPID NARRATIVE.
AND, OHH, I SUPPOSE THERE *MIGHT* HAVE BEEN A FEW OTHER DETAILS AND INCIDENTS I ADDED OR OMITTED, AS SEEMED NECESSARY TO ENSURE THE TALE FLOWED PROPERLY.
WELL, I DON'T BELIEVE A *WORD* OF IT.
HOW DID THE DEAD, WHAT WAS HE CALLED, THE CARNIFEX, COME BACK TO LIFE?
HOW SHOULD *I* KNOW? I *LIVED* IT, I DIDN'T MAKE IT UP.
AND THIS QUEEN OF YOURS, WAS SHE *HAPPY* WITH THE OUTCOME?
HER MOODS ARE NOT MINE TO KNOW, ALAS...
AND ARE YOU GOING TO SEE YOUR SISTER, NOW?
ENOUGH! I WILL NOT BE QUESTIONED FURTHER. I HAVE ENTERTAINED YOU; WHILED AWAY AN IDLE HOUR. IF MORE STORIES ARE TO BE TOLD THEN *OTHERS* WILL HAVE TO TELL THEM.
AND *I* AM PREPARED BOTH TO DRINK AND TO LISTEN.
SO.
WHOSE TALE IS NEXT?

:: Neil Gaiman, writer :: John Watkiss, artist, pgs. 3-24 ::
:: Bryan Talbot, penciller, pgs. 1, 2, & 25 :: Mark Buckingham, inker, pgs. 1, 2, & 25 ::
:: Danny Vozzo, colorist :: Todd Klein, letterer :: Karen Berger, editor :: Shelly Roeberg, assistant editor ::
Featuring characters created by Gaiman, Kieth and Dringenberg

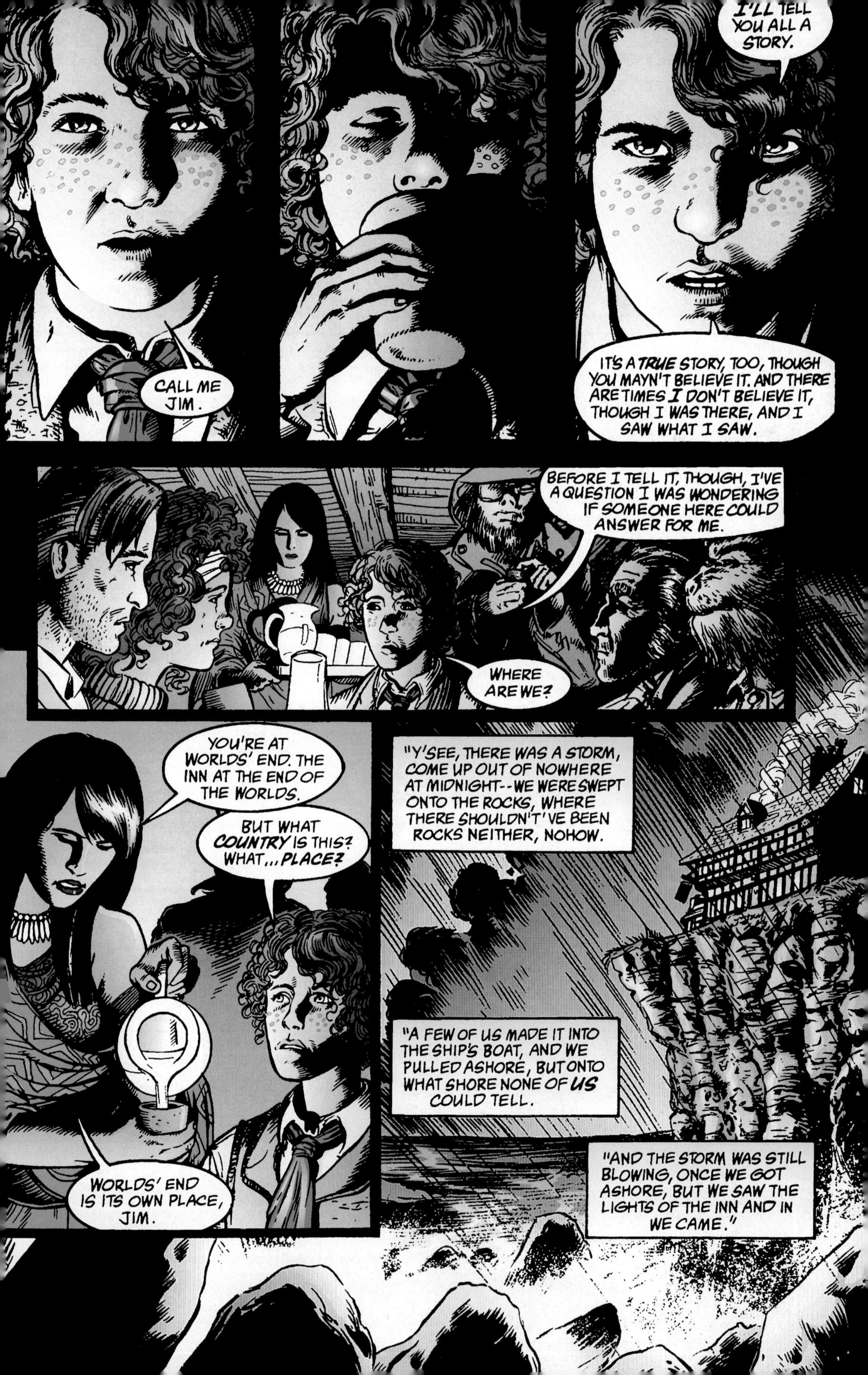

CALL ME JIM.
I'LL TELL YOU ALL A STORY.
IT'S A TRUE STORY, TOO, THOUGH YOU MAYN'T BELIEVE IT. AND THERE ARE TIMES I DON'T BELIEVE IT, THOUGH I WAS THERE, AND I SAW WHAT I SAW.
BEFORE I TELL IT, THOUGH, I'VE A QUESTION I WAS WONDERING IF SOMEONE HERE COULD ANSWER FOR ME.
WHERE ARE WE?
YOU'RE AT WORLDS' END. THE INN AT THE END OF THE WORLDS.
BUT WHAT COUNTRY IS THIS? WHAT... PLACE?
WORLDS' END IS ITS OWN PLACE, JIM.
"Y'SEE, THERE WAS A STORM, COME UP OUT OF NOWHERE AT MIDNIGHT--WE WERE SWEPT ONTO THE ROCKS, WHERE THERE SHOULDN'T'VE BEEN ROCKS NEITHER, NOHOW.
"A FEW OF US MADE IT INTO THE SHIP'S BOAT, AND WE PULLED ASHORE, BUT ONTO WHAT SHORE NONE OF US COULD TELL.
"AND THE STORM WAS STILL BLOWING, ONCE WE GOT ASHORE, BUT WE SAW THE LIGHTS OF THE INN AND IN WE CAME."

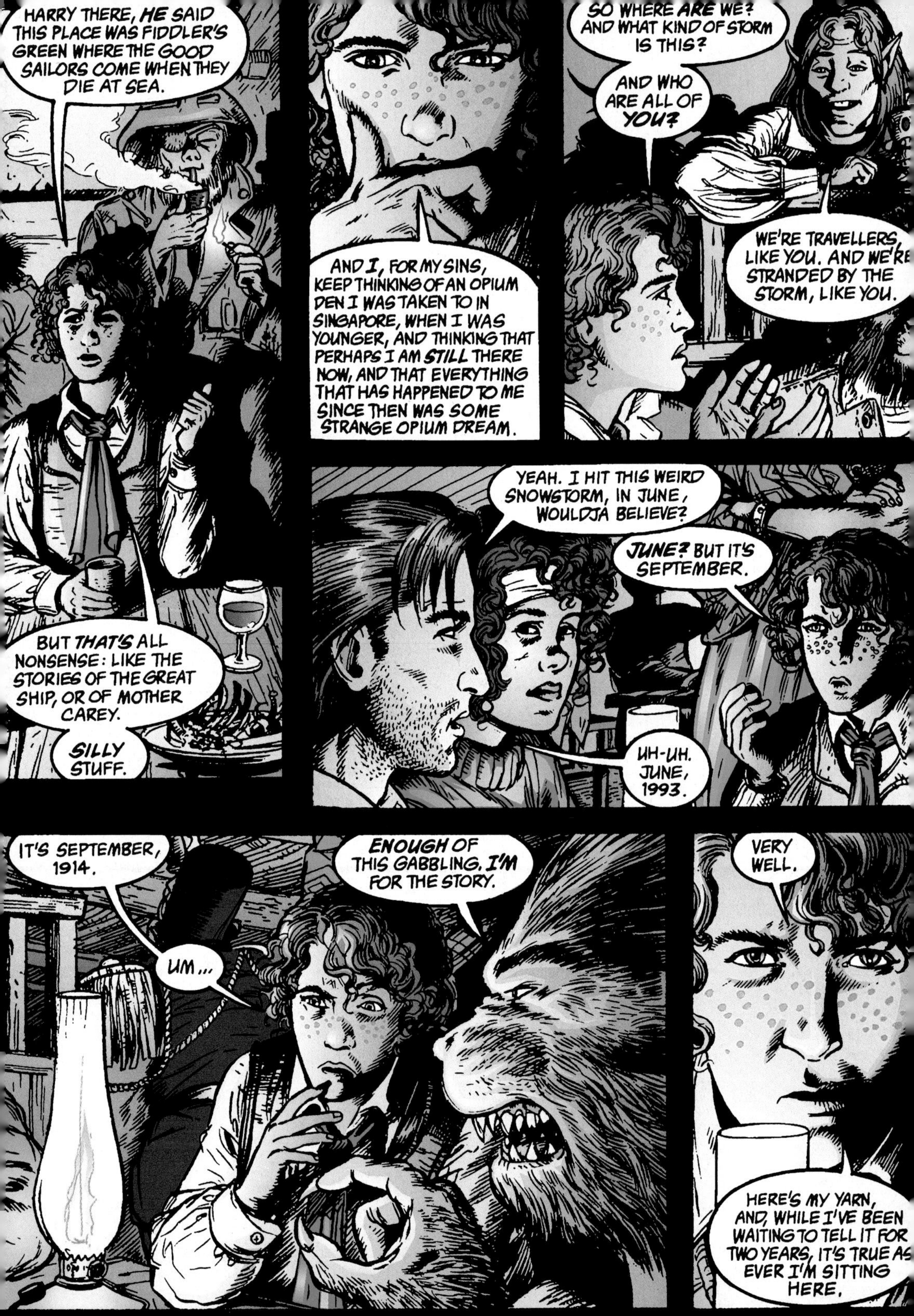
HARRY THERE, HE SAID THIS PLACE WAS FIDDLER'S GREEN WHERE THE GOOD SAILORS COME WHEN THEY DIE AT SEA.
AND I, FOR MY SINS, KEEP THINKING OF AN OPIUM DEN I WAS TAKEN TO IN SINGAPORE, WHEN I WAS YOUNGER, AND THINKING THAT PERHAPS I AM STILL THERE NOW, AND THAT EVERYTHING THAT HAS HAPPENED TO ME SINCE THEN WAS SOME STRANGE OPIUM DREAM.
SO WHERE ARE WE? AND WHAT KIND OF STORM IS THIS?
AND WHO ARE ALL OF YOU?
WE'RE TRAVELLERS, LIKE YOU. AND WE'RE STRANDED BY THE STORM, LIKE YOU.
BUT THAT'S ALL NONSENSE: LIKE THE STORIES OF THE GREAT SHIP, OR OF MOTHER CAREY.
SILLY STUFF.
YEAH. I HIT THIS WEIRD SNOWSTORM, IN JUNE, WOULDJA BELIEVE?
JUNE? BUT IT'S SEPTEMBER.
UH-UH. JUNE, 1993.
IT'S SEPTEMBER, 1914.
UM...
ENOUGH OF THIS GABBLING. I'M FOR THE STORY.
VERY WELL.
HERE'S MY YARN, AND, WHILE I'VE BEEN WAITING TO TELL IT FOR TWO YEARS, IT'S TRUE AS EVER I'M SITTING HERE.

Hob's Leviathan

◇ Neil Gaiman, writer ◇ Michael Zulli, penciller, pgs. 3-24 Dick Giordano, inker pgs. 3-24
◇ Bryan Talbot, penciller, pgs. 1, 2, & 24 ◇ Mark Buckingham, inker, pgs. 1, 2, & 24 ◇
◇ Danny Vozzo, colorist ◇ Todd Klein, letterer ◇ Karen Berger, editor ◇ Shelly Roeberg, assistant editor ◇

THE SANDMAN

Featuring characters created by Gaiman, Kieth and Dringenberg

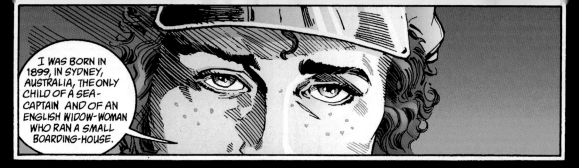

I WAS BORN IN 1899, IN SYDNEY, AUSTRALIA, THE ONLY CHILD OF A SEA-CAPTAIN AND OF AN ENGLISH WIDOW-WOMAN WHO RAN A SMALL BOARDING-HOUSE.

SHE DID NOT *TALK* OF MY FATHER;

FROM MY *MOTHER* I INHERITED, I FANCY, A CERTAIN *WILFULNESS*. FROM MY FATHER I INHERITED A *WANDERLUST*, AND A FASCINATION WITH THE *SEA*.

AND I SUPPOSE THAT IT IS TO HER CREDIT THAT I WAS NEITHER ADOPTED OUT, NOR ABORTED, BUT THAT SHE BRAVED ALL THE SCANDAL AND SOCIETAL DISCOMFORT CAUSED BY THE ARRIVAL OF HER CHILD.

SO IT WAS THAT, ON THE DAY OF MY THIRTEENTH BIRTHDAY, I CLAMBERED OUT OF MY BEDROOM WINDOW...

AND, DRESSED IN OLD CLOTHES I'D BEGGED AND BORROWED FROM FRIENDS, RAN DOWN TO THE DOCKS, WHERE, CLAIMING MYSELF AN ORPHAN, I SIGNED ABOARD *THE SPIRIT OF WHITBY*, EN ROUTE TO SINGAPORE.

I DIDN'T SMOKE AND I DIDN'T DRINK, WHICH MEANT THAT, BY THE TIME WE REACHED SINGAPORE, I HAD EARNED MYSELF A LITTLE MONEY.

TOO MANY SAILORS FINISH THEIR JOURNEY IN DEBT TO THE CAPTAIN, YOU SEE.

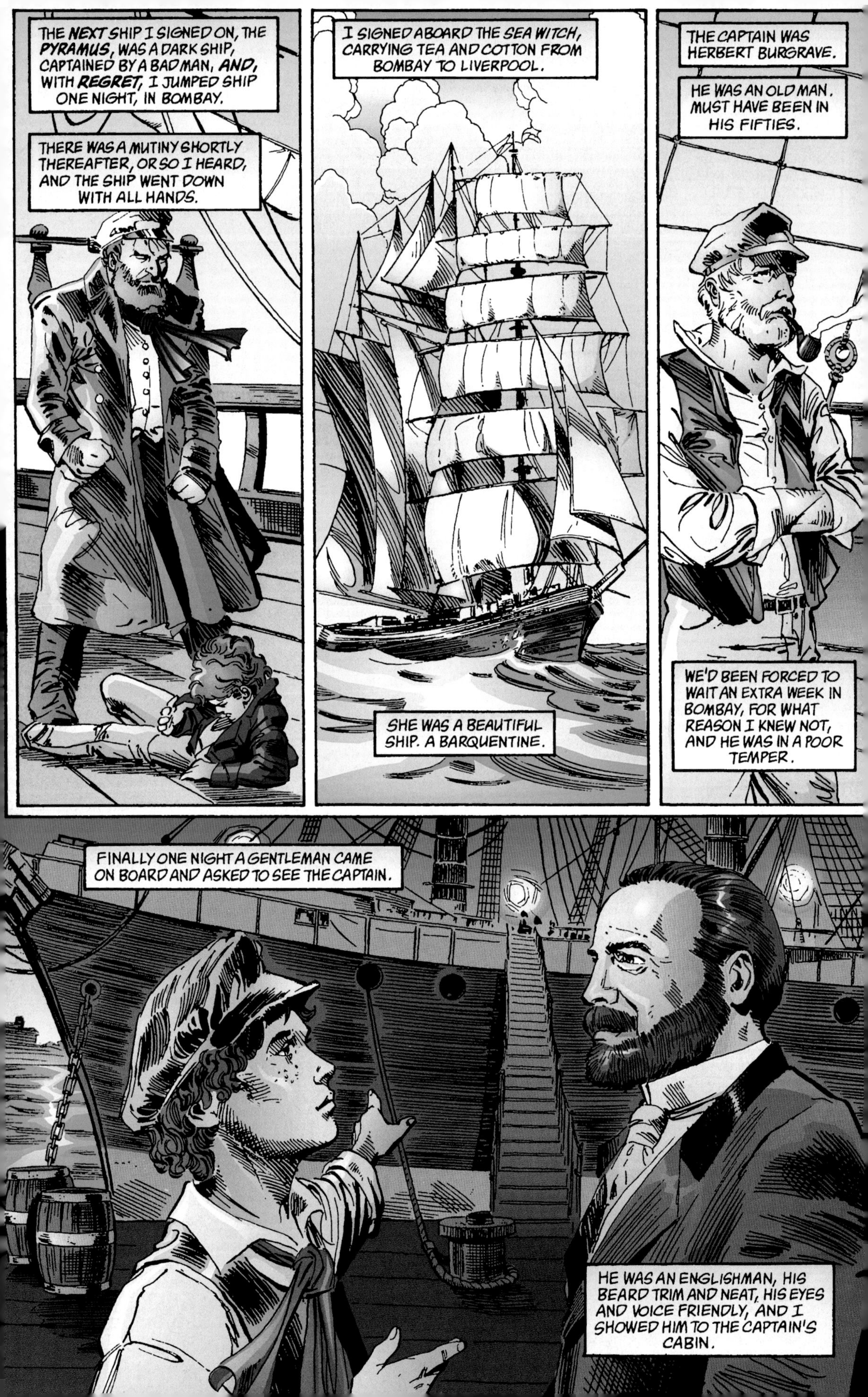
THE NEXT SHIP I SIGNED ON, THE PYRAMUS, WAS A DARK SHIP, CAPTAINED BY A BAD MAN, AND, WITH REGRET, I JUMPED SHIP ONE NIGHT, IN BOMBAY.
THERE WAS A MUTINY SHORTLY THEREAFTER, OR SO I HEARD, AND THE SHIP WENT DOWN WITH ALL HANDS.
I SIGNED ABOARD THE SEA WITCH, CARRYING TEA AND COTTON FROM BOMBAY TO LIVERPOOL.
SHE WAS A BEAUTIFUL SHIP. A BARQUENTINE.
THE CAPTAIN WAS HERBERT BURGRAVE.
HE WAS AN OLD MAN. MUST HAVE BEEN IN HIS FIFTIES.
WE'D BEEN FORCED TO WAIT AN EXTRA WEEK IN BOMBAY, FOR WHAT REASON I KNEW NOT, AND HE WAS IN A POOR TEMPER.
FINALLY ONE NIGHT A GENTLEMAN CAME ON BOARD AND ASKED TO SEE THE CAPTAIN.
HE WAS AN ENGLISHMAN, HIS BEARD TRIM AND NEAT, HIS EYES AND VOICE FRIENDLY, AND I SHOWED HIM TO THE CAPTAIN'S CABIN.

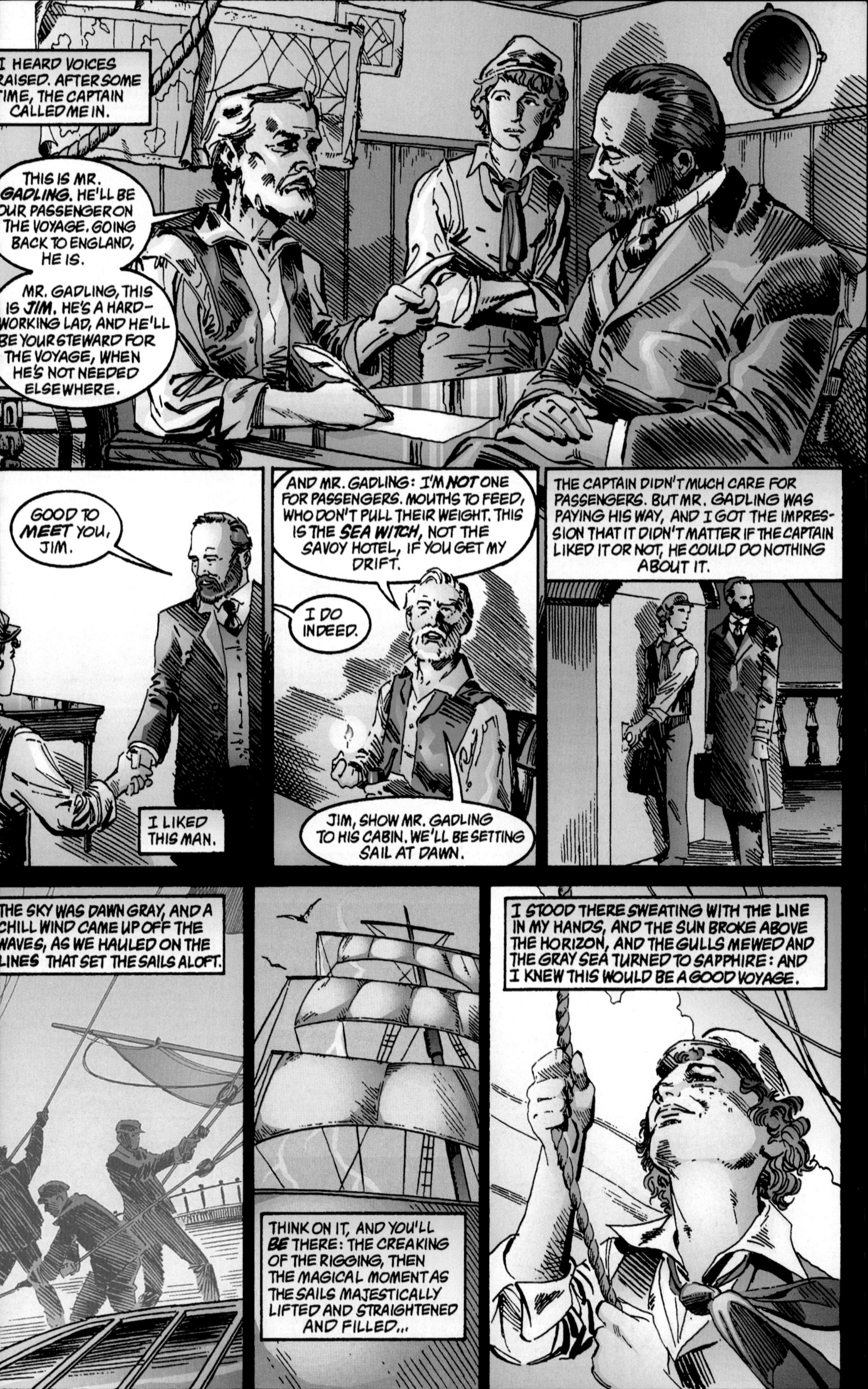
I HEARD VOICES RAISED. AFTER SOME TIME, THE CAPTAIN CALLED ME IN.
THIS IS MR. GADLING. HE'LL BE OUR PASSENGER ON THE VOYAGE. GOING BACK TO ENGLAND, HE IS.
MR. GADLING, THIS IS JIM. HE'S A HARD-WORKING LAD, AND HE'LL BE YOUR STEWARD FOR THE VOYAGE, WHEN HE'S NOT NEEDED ELSEWHERE.
GOOD TO MEET YOU, JIM.
I LIKED THIS MAN.
AND MR. GADLING: I'M NOT ONE FOR PASSENGERS. MOUTHS TO FEED, WHO DON'T PULL THEIR WEIGHT. THIS IS THE SEA WITCH, NOT THE SAVOY HOTEL, IF YOU GET MY DRIFT.
I DO INDEED.
JIM, SHOW MR. GADLING TO HIS CABIN. WE'LL BE SETTING SAIL AT DAWN.
THE CAPTAIN DIDN'T MUCH CARE FOR PASSENGERS. BUT MR. GADLING WAS PAYING HIS WAY, AND I GOT THE IMPRESSION THAT IT DIDN'T MATTER IF THE CAPTAIN LIKED IT OR NOT, HE COULD DO NOTHING ABOUT IT.
THE SKY WAS DAWN GRAY, AND A CHILL WIND CAME UP OFF THE WAVES, AS WE HAULED ON THE LINES THAT SET THE SAILS ALOFT.
THINK ON IT, AND YOU'LL BE THERE: THE CREAKING OF THE RIGGING, THEN THE MAGICAL MOMENT AS THE SAILS MAJESTICALLY LIFTED AND STRAIGHTENED AND FILLED...
I STOOD THERE SWEATING WITH THE LINE IN MY HANDS, AND THE SUN BROKE ABOVE THE HORIZON, AND THE GULLS MEWED AND THE GRAY SEA TURNED TO SAPPHIRE: AND I KNEW THIS WOULD BE A GOOD VOYAGE.

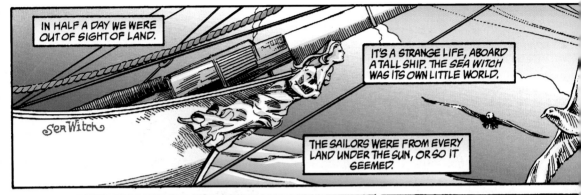

IN HALF A DAY WE WERE OUT OF SIGHT OF LAND.

IT'S A STRANGE LIFE, ABOARD A TALL SHIP. THE SEA WITCH WAS ITS OWN LITTLE WORLD.

THE SAILORS WERE FROM EVERY LAND UNDER THE SUN, OR SO IT SEEMED.

THERE WAS A GERMAN FROM HAMBURG, A TACITURN COVE WHO WOULD, WHEN RUMMED UP, TELL US HOW THE KAISER WOULD SOON PUT US ALL IN OUR PLACES.

THERE WAS A TALL NORWEGIAN, AND AN EQUALLY TALL SWEDE, WHO HATED EACH OTHER'S GUTS. THEY'D SHIPPED TOGETHER BEFORE, AND THERE WAS AN OLD QUARREL THERE, THOUGH I NEVER KNEW THE BONES OF IT.

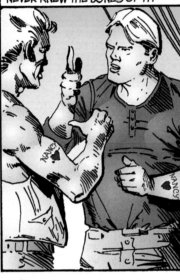

AMONG THE SAILORS THERE WERE A NUMB[ER] OF BLACKS--TWO WERE AFRICANS WHO HU[NG] TOGETHER LIKE BROTHERS, THE OTHERS WERE WEST INDIANS OR AMERICANS.

ONE OF THEM, NATHANIEL DAWNING BY NAME, WAS THE BEST SAILOR ON THE SHIP. HE WAS THE SECOND MATE, AND THE GENERAL OPINION ON THE SEA WITCH WAS THAT HE WOULD HAVE BEEN A CAPTAIN, IF ONLY HE WERE WHITE.

THERE WAS AN IRISH COOK --AND A GOOD ONE, A RARITY ON BOARD--WHO READ POETRY OF A NIGHT IN HIS HAMMOCK...

YEATS

CROSS...

AND A SCOTTISH ENGINEER WHO MINDED THE ENGINE THAT PUMPED OUT THE BILGES.

HIS NAME WAS CAMPBELL, BUT THE SKIPPER USED TO CALL HIM DONKEYMAN, BECAUSE OF THE DAYS WHEN A DONKEY WOULD WALK A TREADMILL IN THE HOLD, FULFILLING THE FUNCTIONS HIS ENGINES DID NOW.

THE FIRST MATE WAS A CALIFO[R] NIAN NAMED CANBY. HE TOOK [A] SHINE TO ME, DID MR. CANBY. HE USED TO TELL ME:

I DON'T KNOW WHAT YOU'RE DOING HERE, LAD. SHIPS LIKE [THIS] AREN'T GOING ANYWHERE. TE[N] YEARS' TIME THE ONLY TALL SHIPS'LL BE IN MUSEUMS.

IT'S TOO BIG TO FIT IN A MUSEUM.

YEAH. FUNNY.

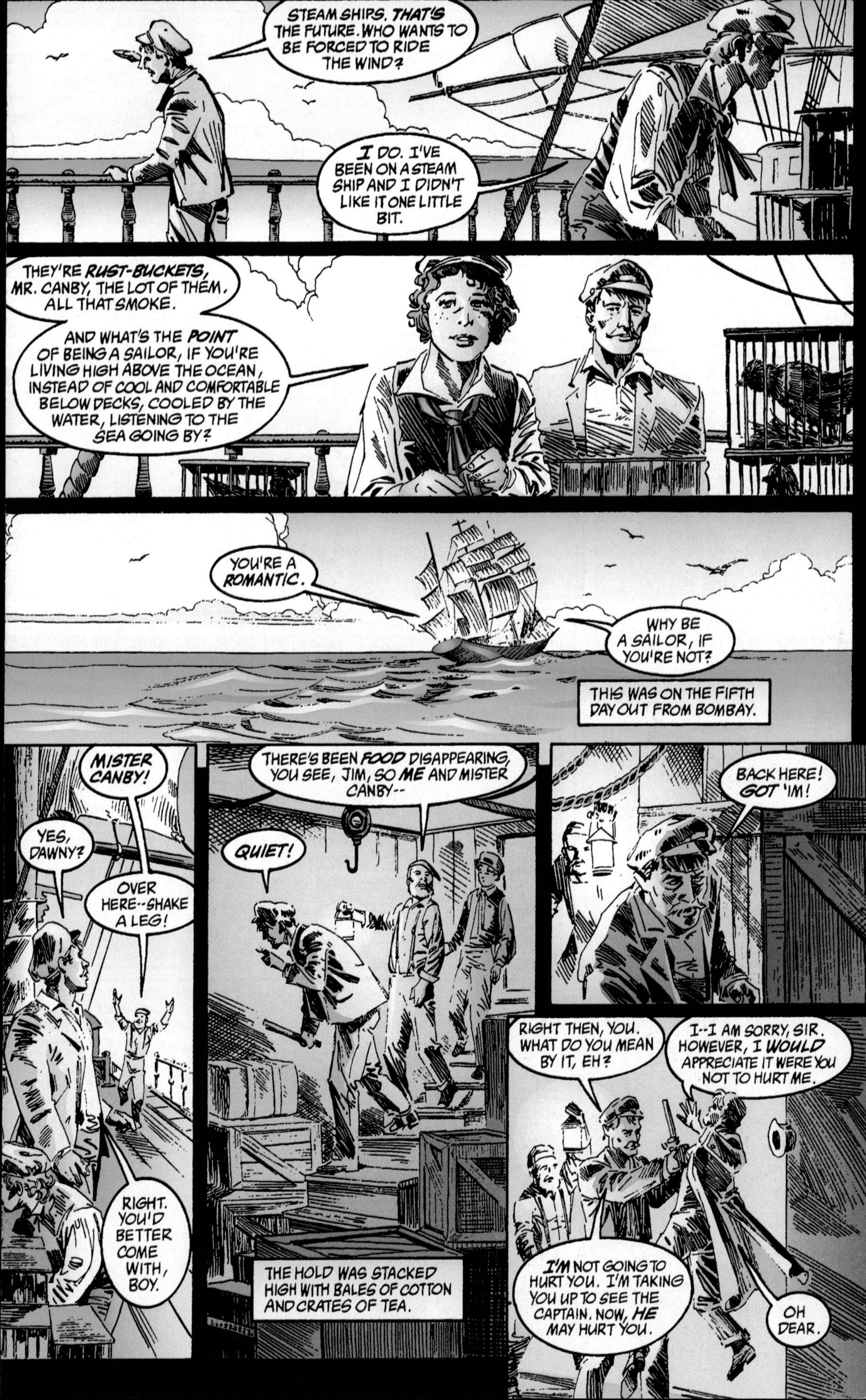

STEAM SHIPS. THAT'S THE FUTURE. WHO WANTS TO BE FORCED TO RIDE THE WIND?
I DO. I'VE BEEN ON A STEAM SHIP AND I DIDN'T LIKE IT ONE LITTLE BIT.
THEY'RE RUST-BUCKETS, MR. CANBY, THE LOT OF THEM. ALL THAT SMOKE.
AND WHAT'S THE POINT OF BEING A SAILOR, IF YOU'RE LIVING HIGH ABOVE THE OCEAN, INSTEAD OF COOL AND COMFORTABLE BELOW DECKS, COOLED BY THE WATER, LISTENING TO THE SEA GOING BY?
YOU'RE A ROMANTIC.
WHY BE A SAILOR, IF YOU'RE NOT?
THIS WAS ON THE FIFTH DAY OUT FROM BOMBAY.
MISTER CANBY!
YES, DAWNY?
OVER HERE--SHAKE A LEG!
RIGHT. YOU'D BETTER COME WITH, BOY.
THERE'S BEEN FOOD DISAPPEARING, YOU SEE, JIM, SO ME AND MISTER CANBY--
QUIET!
THE HOLD WAS STACKED HIGH WITH BALES OF COTTON AND CRATES OF TEA.
BACK HERE! GOT 'IM!
RIGHT THEN, YOU. WHAT DO YOU MEAN BY IT, EH?
I--I AM SORRY, SIR. HOWEVER, I WOULD APPRECIATE IT WERE YOU NOT TO HURT ME.
I'M NOT GOING TO HURT YOU. I'M TAKING YOU UP TO SEE THE CAPTAIN. NOW, HE MAY HURT YOU.
OH DEAR.

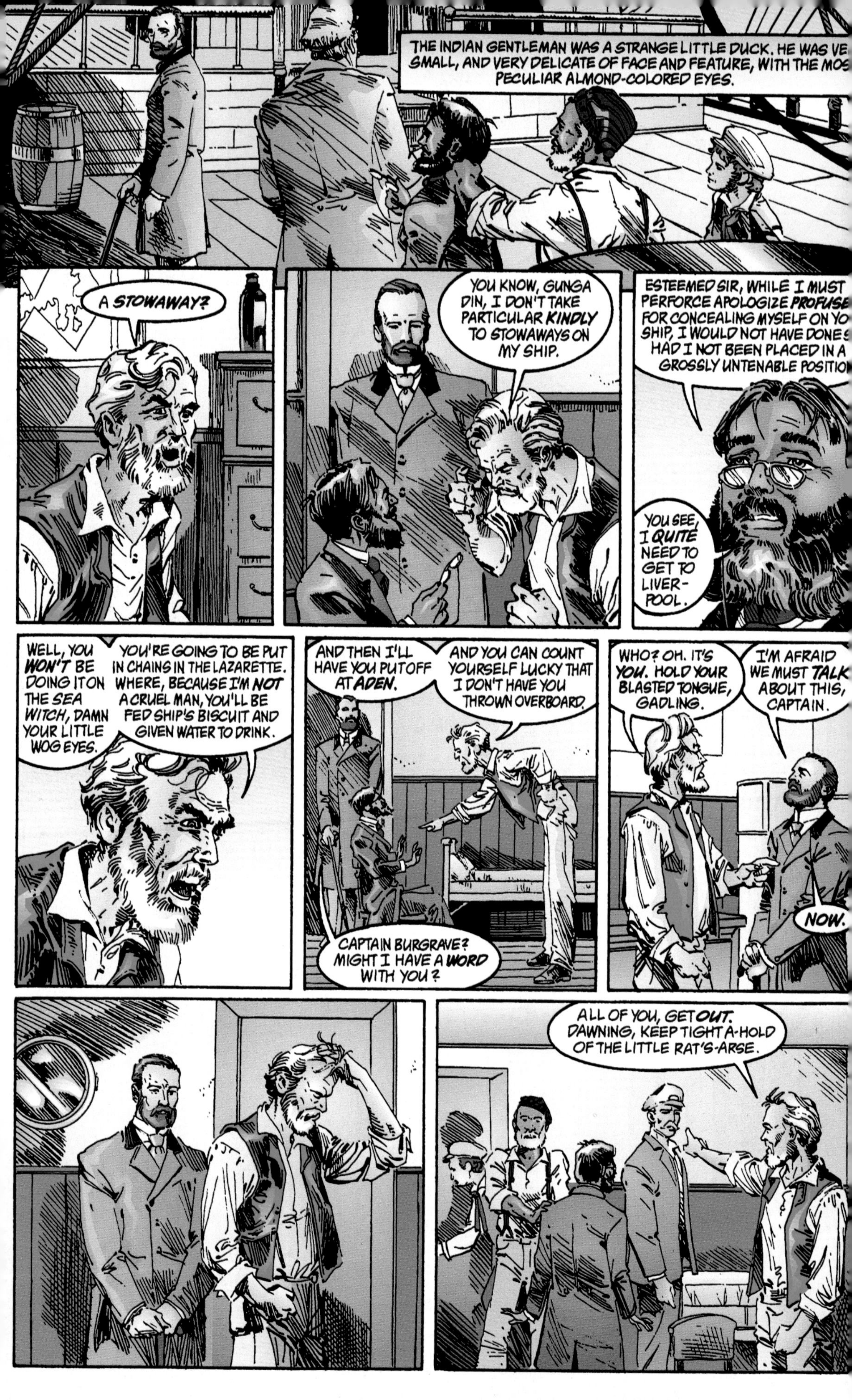
THE INDIAN GENTLEMAN WAS A STRANGE LITTLE DUCK. HE WAS VE SMALL, AND VERY DELICATE OF FACE AND FEATURE, WITH THE MOS PECULIAR ALMOND-COLORED EYES.
A STOWAWAY?
YOU KNOW, GUNGA DIN, I DON'T TAKE PARTICULAR KINDLY TO STOWAWAYS ON MY SHIP.
ESTEEMED SIR, WHILE I MUST PERFORCE APOLOGIZE PROFUSE FOR CONCEALING MYSELF ON YO SHIP, I WOULD NOT HAVE DONE S HAD I NOT BEEN PLACED IN A GROSSLY UNTENABLE POSITIO
YOU SEE, I QUITE NEED TO GET TO LIVER-POOL.
WELL, YOU WON'T BE DOING IT ON THE SEA WITCH, DAMN YOUR LITTLE WOG EYES.
YOU'RE GOING TO BE PUT IN CHAINS IN THE LAZARETTE. WHERE, BECAUSE I'M NOT A CRUEL MAN, YOU'LL BE FED SHIP'S BISCUIT AND GIVEN WATER TO DRINK.
AND THEN I'LL HAVE YOU PUT OFF AT ADEN.
AND YOU CAN COUNT YOURSELF LUCKY THAT I DON'T HAVE YOU THROWN OVERBOARD.
CAPTAIN BURGRAVE? MIGHT I HAVE A WORD WITH YOU?
WHO? OH. IT'S YOU. HOLD YOUR BLASTED TONGUE, GADLING.
I'M AFRAID WE MUST TALK ABOUT THIS, CAPTAIN.
NOW.
ALL OF YOU, GET OUT. DAWNING, KEEP TIGHT A-HOLD OF THE LITTLE RAT'S-ARSE.

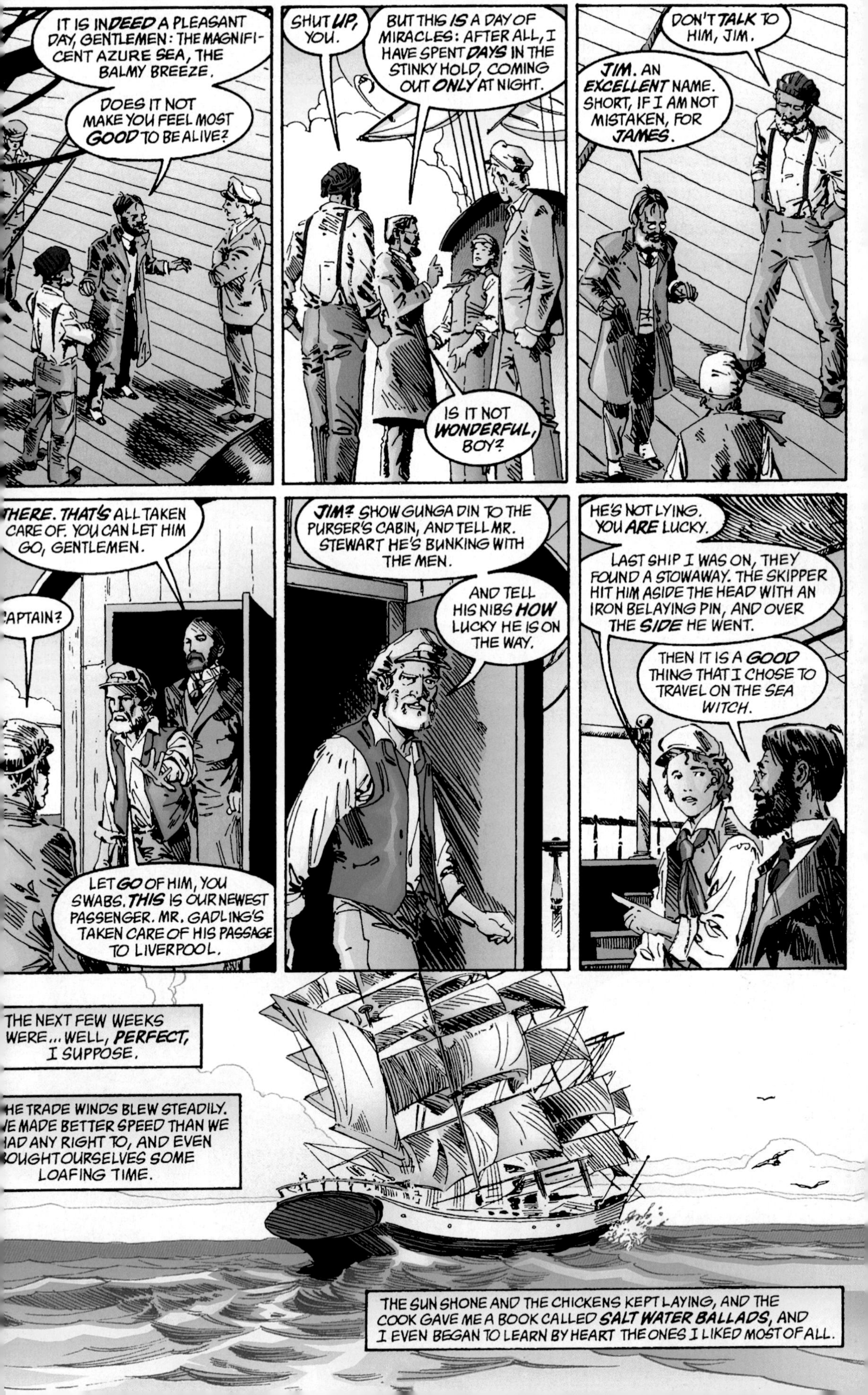
IT IS INDEED A PLEASANT DAY, GENTLEMEN: THE MAGNIFICENT AZURE SEA, THE BALMY BREEZE.
DOES IT NOT MAKE YOU FEEL MOST GOOD TO BE ALIVE?
SHUT UP, YOU.
BUT THIS IS A DAY OF MIRACLES: AFTER ALL, I HAVE SPENT DAYS IN THE STINKY HOLD, COMING OUT ONLY AT NIGHT.
IS IT NOT WONDERFUL, BOY?
DON'T TALK TO HIM, JIM.
JIM. AN EXCELLENT NAME. SHORT, IF I AM NOT MISTAKEN, FOR JAMES.
THERE. THAT'S ALL TAKEN CARE OF. YOU CAN LET HIM GO, GENTLEMEN.
APTAIN?
LET GO OF HIM, YOU SWABS. THIS IS OUR NEWEST PASSENGER. MR. GADLING'S TAKEN CARE OF HIS PASSAGE TO LIVERPOOL.
JIM? SHOW GUNGA DIN TO THE PURSER'S CABIN, AND TELL MR. STEWART HE'S BUNKING WITH THE MEN.
AND TELL HIS NIBS HOW LUCKY HE IS ON THE WAY.
HE'S NOT LYING. YOU ARE LUCKY.
LAST SHIP I WAS ON, THEY FOUND A STOWAWAY. THE SKIPPER HIT HIM ASIDE THE HEAD WITH AN IRON BELAYING PIN, AND OVER THE SIDE HE WENT.
THEN IT IS A GOOD THING THAT I CHOSE TO TRAVEL ON THE SEA WITCH.
THE NEXT FEW WEEKS WERE... WELL, PERFECT, I SUPPOSE.
HE TRADE WINDS BLEW STEADILY. E MADE BETTER SPEED THAN WE AD ANY RIGHT TO, AND EVEN OUGHT OURSELVES SOME LOAFING TIME.
THE SUN SHONE AND THE CHICKENS KEPT LAYING, AND THE COOK GAVE ME A BOOK CALLED SALT WATER BALLADS, AND I EVEN BEGAN TO LEARN BY HEART THE ONES I LIKED MOST OF ALL.

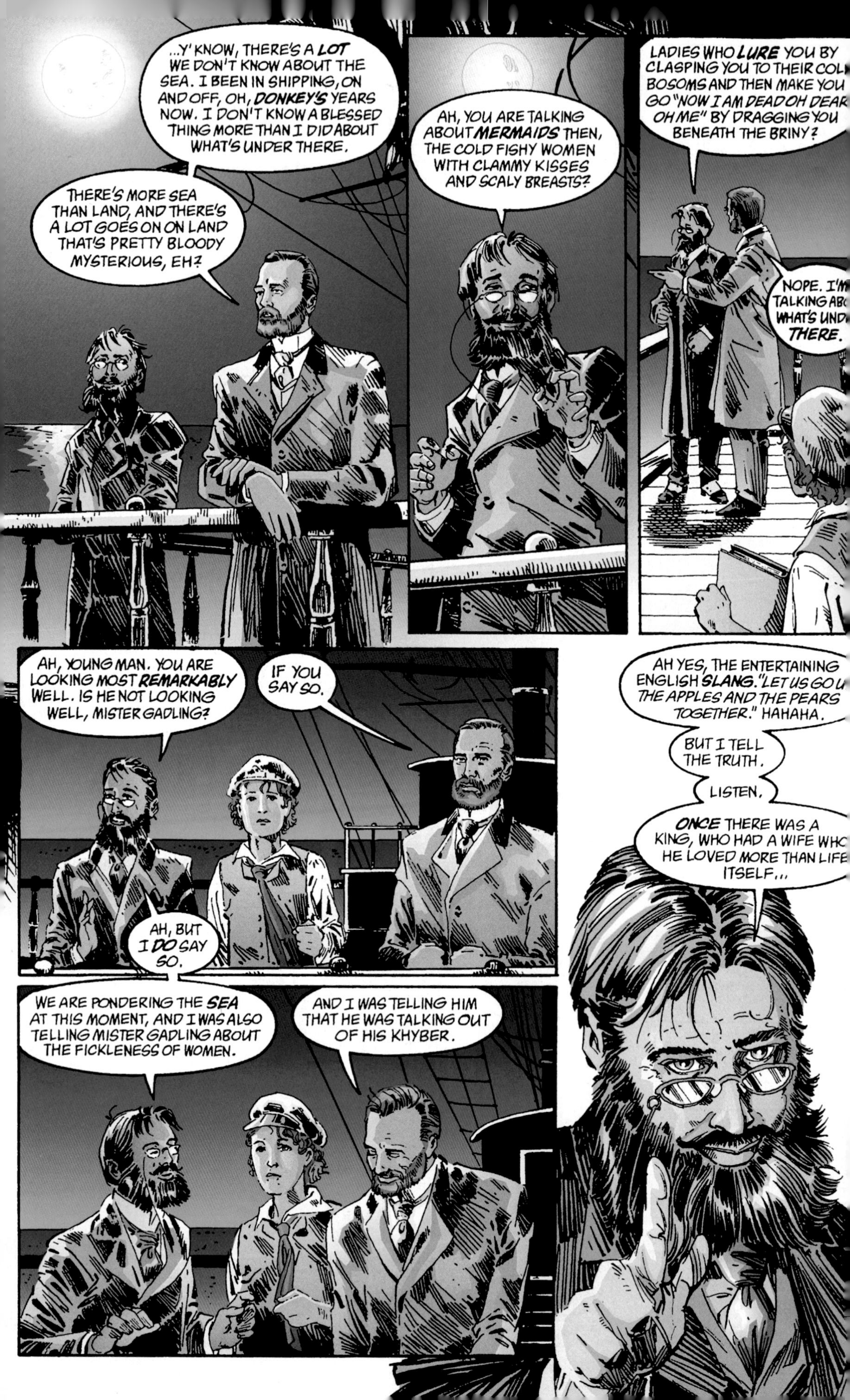
...Y' KNOW, THERE'S A LOT WE DON'T KNOW ABOUT THE SEA. I BEEN IN SHIPPING, ON AND OFF, OH, DONKEY'S YEARS NOW. I DON'T KNOW A BLESSED THING MORE THAN I DID ABOUT WHAT'S UNDER THERE.
THERE'S MORE SEA THAN LAND, AND THERE'S A LOT GOES ON ON LAND THAT'S PRETTY BLOODY MYSTERIOUS, EH?
AH, YOU ARE TALKING ABOUT MERMAIDS THEN, THE COLD FISHY WOMEN WITH CLAMMY KISSES AND SCALY BREASTS?
LADIES WHO LURE YOU BY CLASPING YOU TO THEIR COL BOSOMS AND THEN MAKE YOU GO "NOW I AM DEAD OH DEAR OH ME" BY DRAGGING YOU BENEATH THE BRINY?
NOPE. I'M TALKING ABO WHAT'S UND THERE.
AH, YOUNG MAN. YOU ARE LOOKING MOST REMARKABLY WELL. IS HE NOT LOOKING WELL, MISTER GADLING?
IF YOU SAY SO.
AH, BUT I DO SAY SO.
WE ARE PONDERING THE SEA AT THIS MOMENT, AND I WAS ALSO TELLING MISTER GADLING ABOUT THE FICKLENESS OF WOMEN.
AND I WAS TELLING HIM THAT HE WAS TALKING OUT OF HIS KHYBER.
AH YES, THE ENTERTAINING ENGLISH SLANG. "LET US GO U THE APPLES AND THE PEARS TOGETHER." HAHAHA.
BUT I TELL THE TRUTH.
LISTEN.
ONCE THERE WAS A KING, WHO HAD A WIFE WHO HE LOVED MORE THAN LIFE ITSELF...

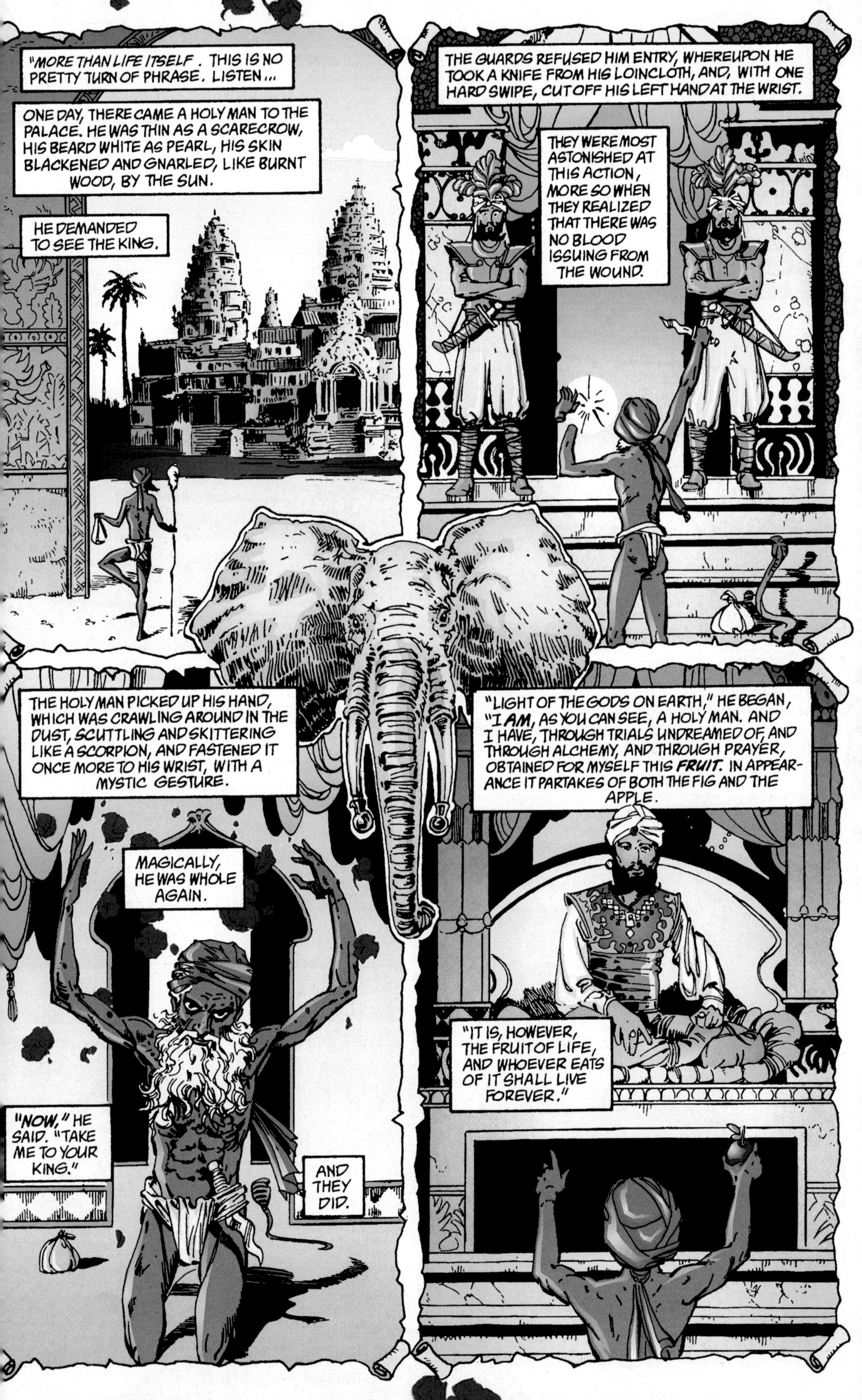
"MORE THAN LIFE ITSELF. THIS IS NO PRETTY TURN OF PHRASE. LISTEN...
ONE DAY, THERE CAME A HOLY MAN TO THE PALACE. HE WAS THIN AS A SCARECROW, HIS BEARD WHITE AS PEARL, HIS SKIN BLACKENED AND GNARLED, LIKE BURNT WOOD, BY THE SUN.
HE DEMANDED TO SEE THE KING.
THE GUARDS REFUSED HIM ENTRY, WHEREUPON HE TOOK A KNIFE FROM HIS LOINCLOTH, AND, WITH ONE HARD SWIPE, CUT OFF HIS LEFT HAND AT THE WRIST.
THEY WERE MOST ASTONISHED AT THIS ACTION, MORE SO WHEN THEY REALIZED THAT THERE WAS NO BLOOD ISSUING FROM THE WOUND.
THE HOLY MAN PICKED UP HIS HAND, WHICH WAS CRAWLING AROUND IN THE DUST, SCUTTLING AND SKITTERING LIKE A SCORPION, AND FASTENED IT ONCE MORE TO HIS WRIST, WITH A MYSTIC GESTURE.
MAGICALLY, HE WAS WHOLE AGAIN.
"NOW," HE SAID. "TAKE ME TO YOUR KING."
AND THEY DID.
"LIGHT OF THE GODS ON EARTH," HE BEGAN, "I AM, AS YOU CAN SEE, A HOLY MAN. AND I HAVE, THROUGH TRIALS UNDREAMED OF, AND THROUGH ALCHEMY, AND THROUGH PRAYER, OBTAINED FOR MYSELF THIS FRUIT. IN APPEARANCE IT PARTAKES OF BOTH THE FIG AND THE APPLE.
"IT IS, HOWEVER, THE FRUIT OF LIFE, AND WHOEVER EATS OF IT SHALL LIVE FOREVER."

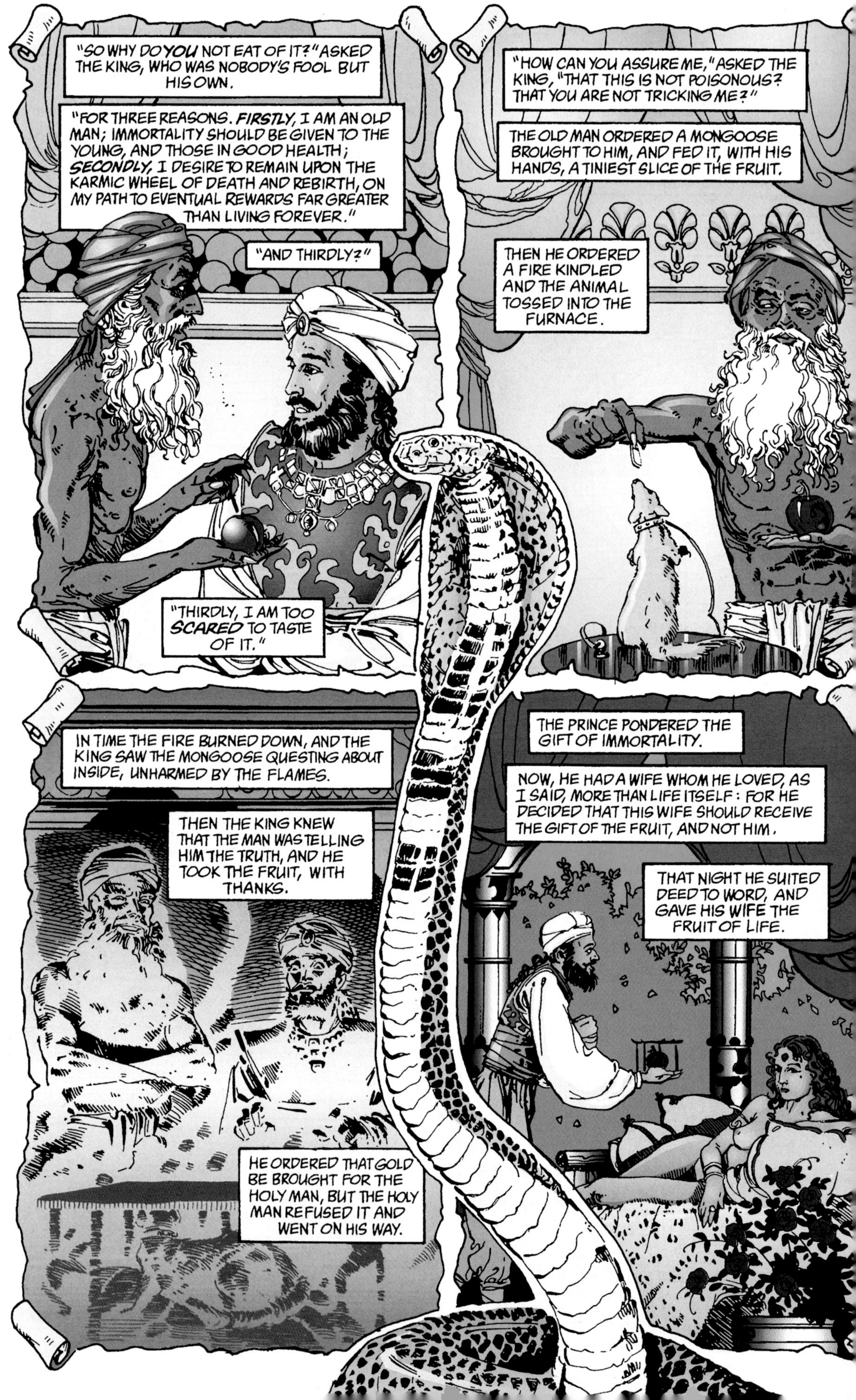
"SO WHY DO YOU NOT EAT OF IT?" ASKED THE KING, WHO WAS NOBODY'S FOOL BUT HIS OWN.
"FOR THREE REASONS. FIRSTLY, I AM AN OLD MAN; IMMORTALITY SHOULD BE GIVEN TO THE YOUNG, AND THOSE IN GOOD HEALTH; SECONDLY, I DESIRE TO REMAIN UPON THE KARMIC WHEEL OF DEATH AND REBIRTH, ON MY PATH TO EVENTUAL REWARDS FAR GREATER THAN LIVING FOREVER."
"AND THIRDLY?"
"THIRDLY, I AM TOO SCARED TO TASTE OF IT."
"HOW CAN YOU ASSURE ME," ASKED THE KING, "THAT THIS IS NOT POISONOUS? THAT YOU ARE NOT TRICKING ME?"
THE OLD MAN ORDERED A MONGOOSE BROUGHT TO HIM, AND FED IT, WITH HIS HANDS, A TINIEST SLICE OF THE FRUIT.
THEN HE ORDERED A FIRE KINDLED AND THE ANIMAL TOSSED INTO THE FURNACE.
IN TIME THE FIRE BURNED DOWN, AND THE KING SAW THE MONGOOSE QUESTING ABOUT INSIDE, UNHARMED BY THE FLAMES.
THEN THE KING KNEW THAT THE MAN WAS TELLING HIM THE TRUTH, AND HE TOOK THE FRUIT, WITH THANKS.
HE ORDERED THAT GOLD BE BROUGHT FOR THE HOLY MAN, BUT THE HOLY MAN REFUSED IT AND WENT ON HIS WAY.
THE PRINCE PONDERED THE GIFT OF IMMORTALITY.
NOW, HE HAD A WIFE WHOM HE LOVED, AS I SAID, MORE THAN LIFE ITSELF: FOR HE DECIDED THAT THIS WIFE SHOULD RECEIVE THE GIFT OF THE FRUIT, AND NOT HIM.
THAT NIGHT HE SUITED DEED TO WORD, AND GAVE HIS WIFE THE FRUIT OF LIFE.

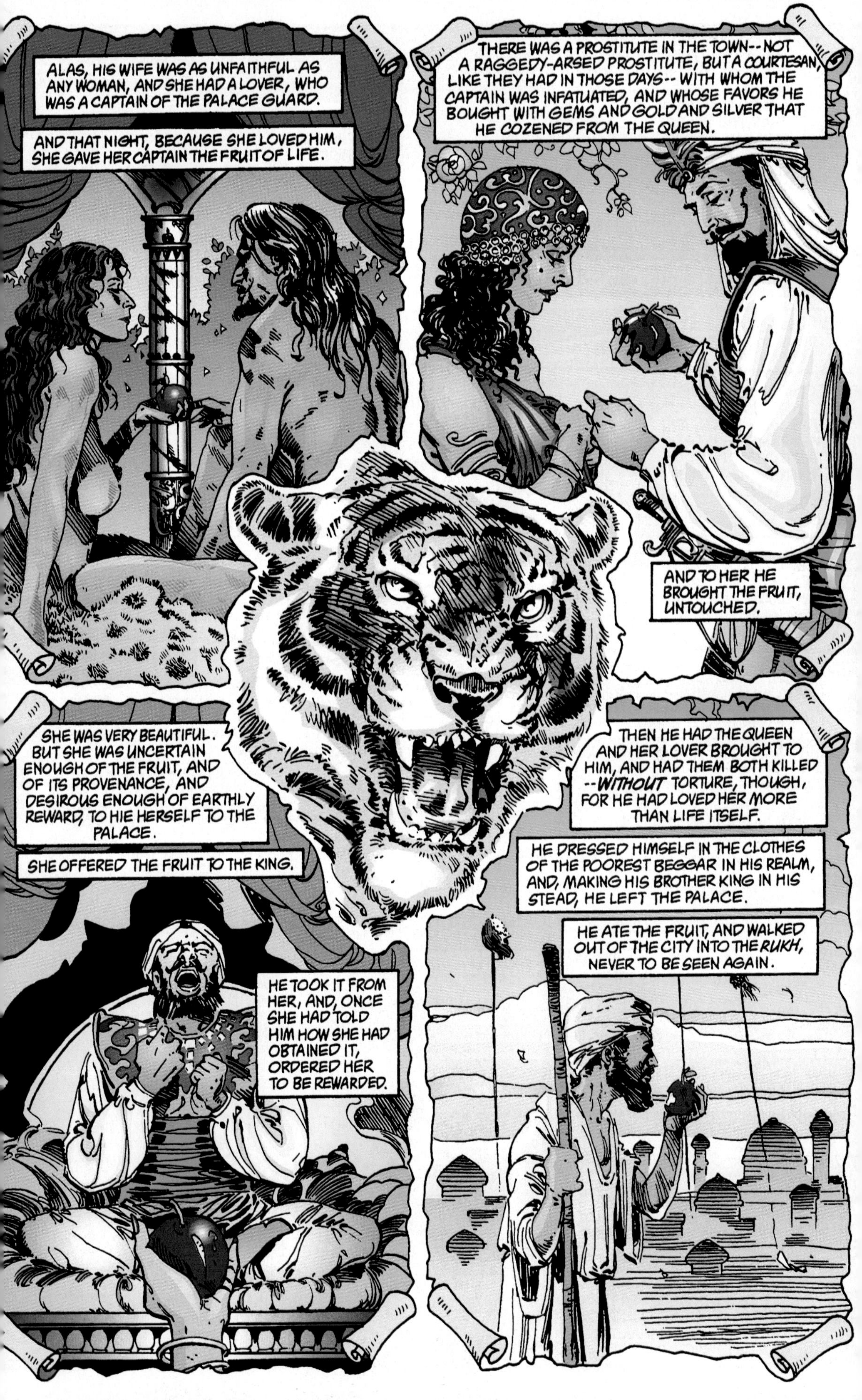
ALAS, HIS WIFE WAS AS UNFAITHFUL AS ANY WOMAN, AND SHE HAD A LOVER, WHO WAS A CAPTAIN OF THE PALACE GUARD.
AND THAT NIGHT, BECAUSE SHE LOVED HIM, SHE GAVE HER CAPTAIN THE FRUIT OF LIFE.
THERE WAS A PROSTITUTE IN THE TOWN--NOT A RAGGEDY-ARSED PROSTITUTE, BUT A COURTESAN, LIKE THEY HAD IN THOSE DAYS--WITH WHOM THE CAPTAIN WAS INFATUATED, AND WHOSE FAVORS HE BOUGHT WITH GEMS AND GOLD AND SILVER THAT HE COZENED FROM THE QUEEN.
AND TO HER HE BROUGHT THE FRUIT, UNTOUCHED.
SHE WAS VERY BEAUTIFUL. BUT SHE WAS UNCERTAIN ENOUGH OF THE FRUIT, AND OF ITS PROVENANCE, AND DESIROUS ENOUGH OF EARTHLY REWARD, TO HIE HERSELF TO THE PALACE.
SHE OFFERED THE FRUIT TO THE KING.
HE TOOK IT FROM HER, AND, ONCE SHE HAD TOLD HIM HOW SHE HAD OBTAINED IT, ORDERED HER TO BE REWARDED.
THEN HE HAD THE QUEEN AND HER LOVER BROUGHT TO HIM, AND HAD THEM BOTH KILLED --*WITHOUT* TORTURE, THOUGH, FOR HE HAD LOVED HER MORE THAN LIFE ITSELF.
HE DRESSED HIMSELF IN THE CLOTHES OF THE POOREST BEGGAR IN HIS REALM, AND, MAKING HIS BROTHER KING IN HIS STEAD, HE LEFT THE PALACE.
HE ATE THE FRUIT, AND WALKED OUT OF THE CITY INTO THE *RUKH*, NEVER TO BE SEEN AGAIN.

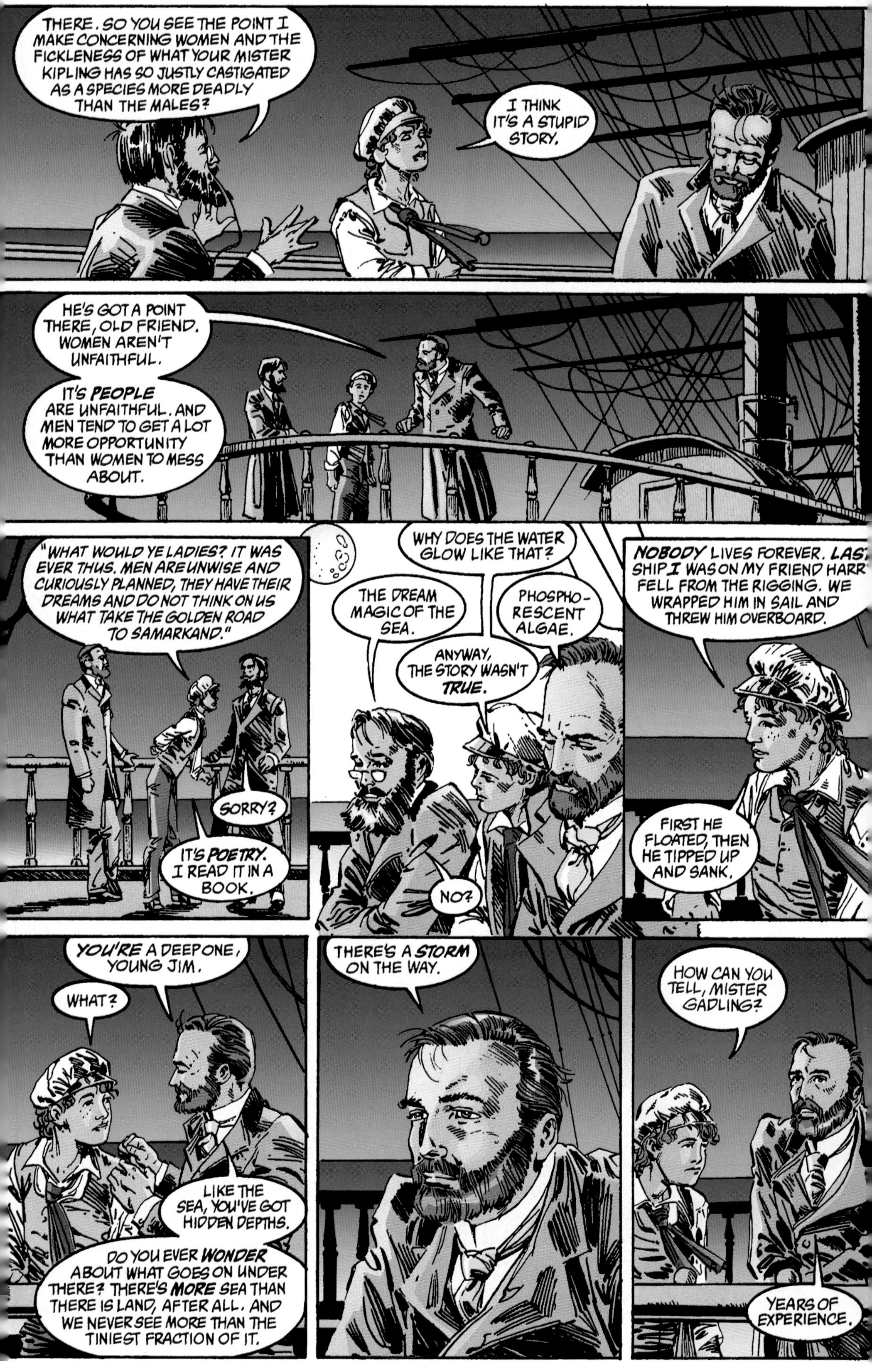
THERE. SO YOU SEE THE POINT I MAKE CONCERNING WOMEN AND THE FICKLENESS OF WHAT YOUR MISTER KIPLING HAS SO JUSTLY CASTIGATED AS A SPECIES MORE DEADLY THAN THE MALES?
I THINK IT'S A STUPID STORY.
HE'S GOT A POINT THERE, OLD FRIEND. WOMEN AREN'T UNFAITHFUL.
IT'S PEOPLE ARE UNFAITHFUL. AND MEN TEND TO GET A LOT MORE OPPORTUNITY THAN WOMEN TO MESS ABOUT.
"WHAT WOULD YE LADIES? IT WAS EVER THUS. MEN ARE UNWISE AND CURIOUSLY PLANNED, THEY HAVE THEIR DREAMS AND DO NOT THINK ON US WHAT TAKE THE GOLDEN ROAD TO SAMARKAND."
SORRY?
IT'S POETRY. I READ IT IN A BOOK.
WHY DOES THE WATER GLOW LIKE THAT?
THE DREAM MAGIC OF THE SEA.
PHOSPHO-RESCENT ALGAE.
ANYWAY, THE STORY WASN'T TRUE.
NO?
NOBODY LIVES FOREVER. LAS SHIP I WAS ON MY FRIEND HARR FELL FROM THE RIGGING. WE WRAPPED HIM IN SAIL AND THREW HIM OVERBOARD.
FIRST HE FLOATED, THEN HE TIPPED UP AND SANK.
YOU'RE A DEEP ONE, YOUNG JIM.
WHAT?
LIKE THE SEA, YOU'VE GOT HIDDEN DEPTHS.
DO YOU EVER WONDER ABOUT WHAT GOES ON UNDER THERE? THERE'S MORE SEA THAN THERE IS LAND, AFTER ALL. AND WE NEVER SEE MORE THAN THE TINIEST FRACTION OF IT.
THERE'S A STORM ON THE WAY.
HOW CAN YOU TELL, MISTER GADLING?
YEARS OF EXPERIENCE.

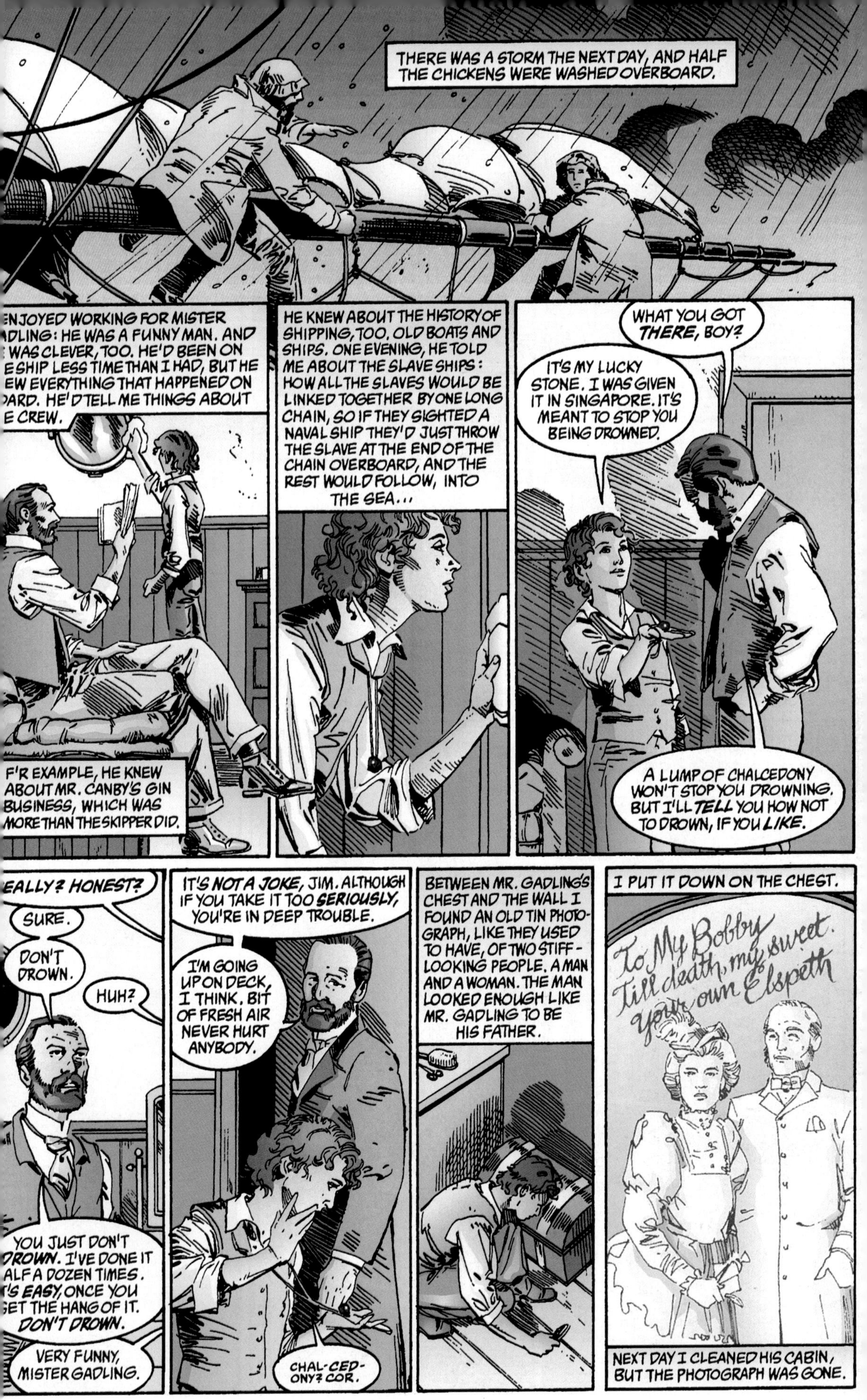
THERE WAS A STORM THE NEXT DAY, AND HALF THE CHICKENS WERE WASHED OVERBOARD.
ENJOYED WORKING FOR MISTER ADLING: HE WAS A FUNNY MAN. AND WAS CLEVER, TOO. HE'D BEEN ON E SHIP LESS TIME THAN I HAD, BUT HE EW EVERYTHING THAT HAPPENED ON OARD. HE'D TELL ME THINGS ABOUT E CREW.
F'R EXAMPLE, HE KNEW ABOUT MR. CANBY'S GIN BUSINESS, WHICH WAS MORE THAN THE SKIPPER DID.
HE KNEW ABOUT THE HISTORY OF SHIPPING, TOO. OLD BOATS AND SHIPS. ONE EVENING, HE TOLD ME ABOUT THE SLAVE SHIPS: HOW ALL THE SLAVES WOULD BE LINKED TOGETHER BY ONE LONG CHAIN, SO IF THEY SIGHTED A NAVAL SHIP THEY'D JUST THROW THE SLAVE AT THE END OF THE CHAIN OVERBOARD, AND THE REST WOULD FOLLOW, INTO THE SEA...
WHAT YOU GOT THERE, BOY?
IT'S MY LUCKY STONE. I WAS GIVEN IT IN SINGAPORE. IT'S MEANT TO STOP YOU BEING DROWNED.
A LUMP OF CHALCEDONY WON'T STOP YOU DROWNING. BUT I'LL TELL YOU HOW NOT TO DROWN, IF YOU LIKE.
EALLY? HONEST?
SURE.
DON'T DROWN.
HUH?
YOU JUST DON'T DROWN. I'VE DONE IT ALF A DOZEN TIMES. T'S EASY, ONCE YOU GET THE HANG OF IT. DON'T DROWN.
VERY FUNNY, MISTER GADLING.
IT'S NOT A JOKE, JIM. ALTHOUGH IF YOU TAKE IT TOO SERIOUSLY, YOU'RE IN DEEP TROUBLE.
I'M GOING UP ON DECK, I THINK. BIT OF FRESH AIR NEVER HURT ANYBODY.
CHAL-CED-ONY? COR.
BETWEEN MR. GADLING'S CHEST AND THE WALL I FOUND AN OLD TIN PHOTOGRAPH, LIKE THEY USED TO HAVE, OF TWO STIFF-LOOKING PEOPLE. A MAN AND A WOMAN. THE MAN LOOKED ENOUGH LIKE MR. GADLING TO BE HIS FATHER.
I PUT IT DOWN ON THE CHEST.
To My Bobby
Till death, my sweet.
Your own Elspeth
NEXT DAY I CLEANED HIS CABIN, BUT THE PHOTOGRAPH WAS GONE.

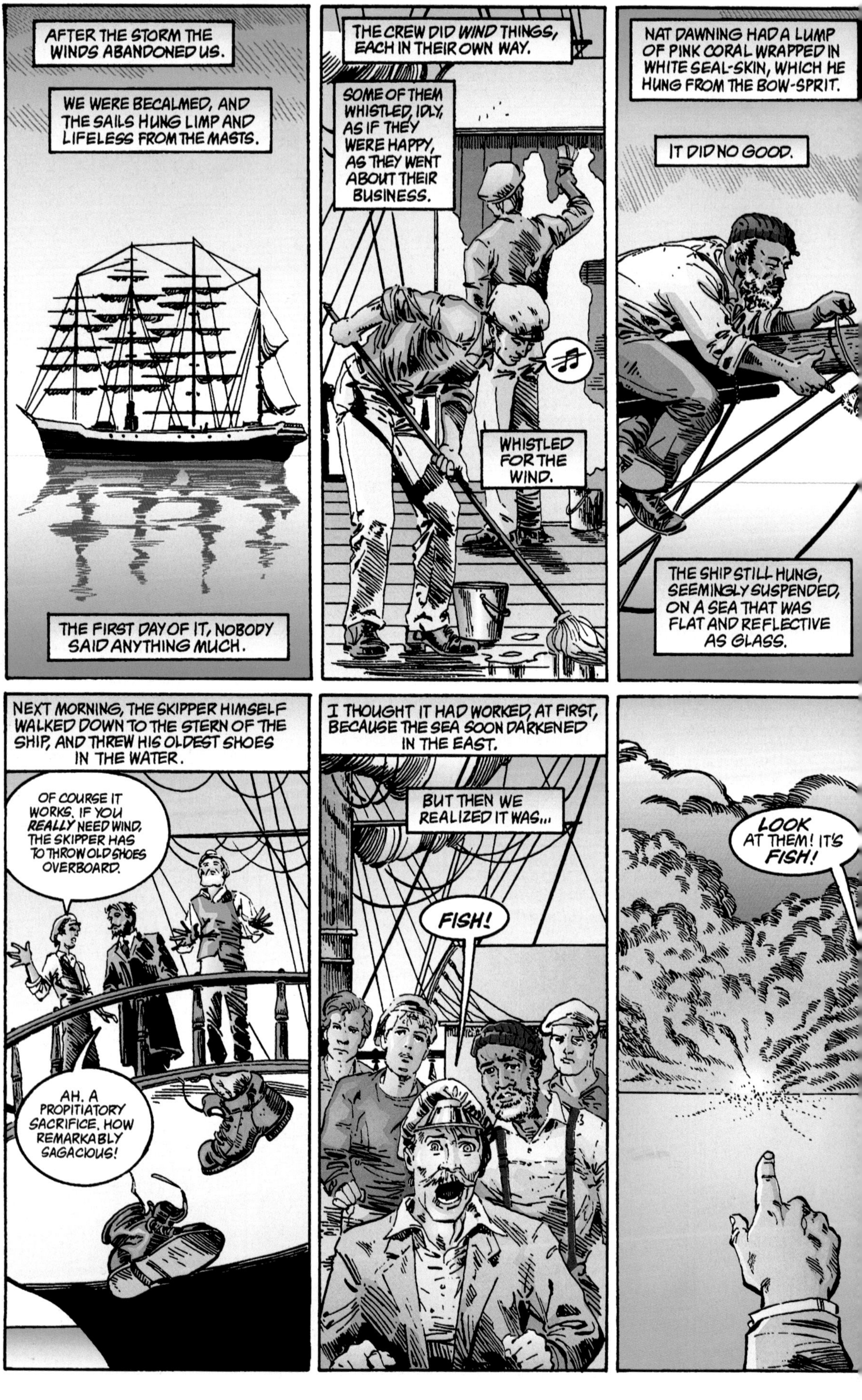
AFTER THE STORM THE WINDS ABANDONED US.
WE WERE BECALMED, AND THE SAILS HUNG LIMP AND LIFELESS FROM THE MASTS.
THE FIRST DAY OF IT, NOBODY SAID ANYTHING MUCH.
THE CREW DID *WIND* THINGS, EACH IN THEIR OWN WAY.
SOME OF THEM WHISTLED, IDLY, AS IF THEY WERE HAPPY, AS THEY WENT ABOUT THEIR BUSINESS.
WHISTLED FOR THE WIND.
NAT DAWNING HAD A LUMP OF PINK CORAL WRAPPED IN WHITE SEAL-SKIN, WHICH HE HUNG FROM THE BOW-SPRIT.
IT DID NO GOOD.
THE SHIP STILL HUNG, SEEMINGLY SUSPENDED, ON A SEA THAT WAS FLAT AND REFLECTIVE AS GLASS.
NEXT MORNING, THE SKIPPER HIMSELF WALKED DOWN TO THE STERN OF THE SHIP, AND THREW HIS OLDEST SHOES IN THE WATER.
OF COURSE IT WORKS. IF YOU *REALLY* NEED WIND, THE SKIPPER HAS TO THROW OLD SHOES OVERBOARD.
AH. A PROPITIATORY SACRIFICE. HOW REMARKABLY SAGACIOUS!
I THOUGHT IT HAD WORKED, AT FIRST, BECAUSE THE SEA SOON DARKENED IN THE EAST.
BUT THEN WE REALIZED IT WAS...
FISH!
LOOK AT THEM! IT'S *FISH!*

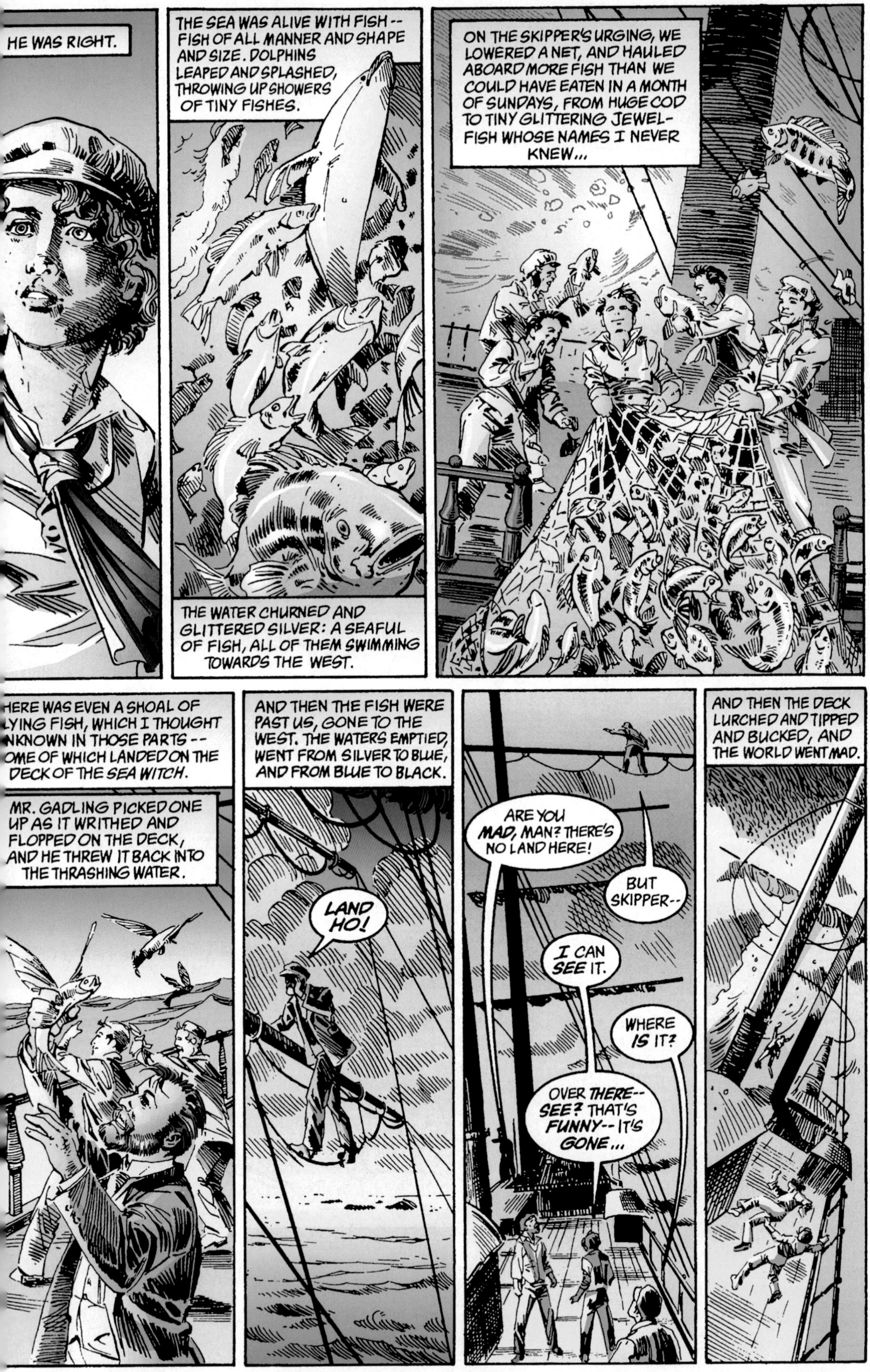
HE WAS RIGHT.
THE SEA WAS ALIVE WITH FISH -- FISH OF ALL MANNER AND SHAPE AND SIZE. DOLPHINS LEAPED AND SPLASHED, THROWING UP SHOWERS OF TINY FISHES.
THE WATER CHURNED AND GLITTERED SILVER: A SEAFUL OF FISH, ALL OF THEM SWIMMING TOWARDS THE WEST.
ON THE SKIPPER'S URGING, WE LOWERED A NET, AND HAULED ABOARD MORE FISH THAN WE COULD HAVE EATEN IN A MONTH OF SUNDAYS, FROM HUGE COD TO TINY GLITTERING JEWEL-FISH WHOSE NAMES I NEVER KNEW...
HERE WAS EVEN A SHOAL OF LYING FISH, WHICH I THOUGHT NKNOWN IN THOSE PARTS -- OME OF WHICH LANDED ON THE DECK OF THE SEA WITCH.
MR. GADLING PICKED ONE UP AS IT WRITHED AND FLOPPED ON THE DECK, AND HE THREW IT BACK INTO THE THRASHING WATER.
AND THEN THE FISH WERE PAST US, GONE TO THE WEST. THE WATERS EMPTIED, WENT FROM SILVER TO BLUE, AND FROM BLUE TO BLACK.
LAND HO!
ARE YOU MAD, MAN? THERE'S NO LAND HERE!
BUT SKIPPER--
I CAN SEE IT.
WHERE IS IT?
OVER THERE-- SEE? THAT'S FUNNY-- IT'S GONE...
AND THEN THE DECK LURCHED AND TIPPED AND BUCKED, AND THE WORLD WENT MAD.

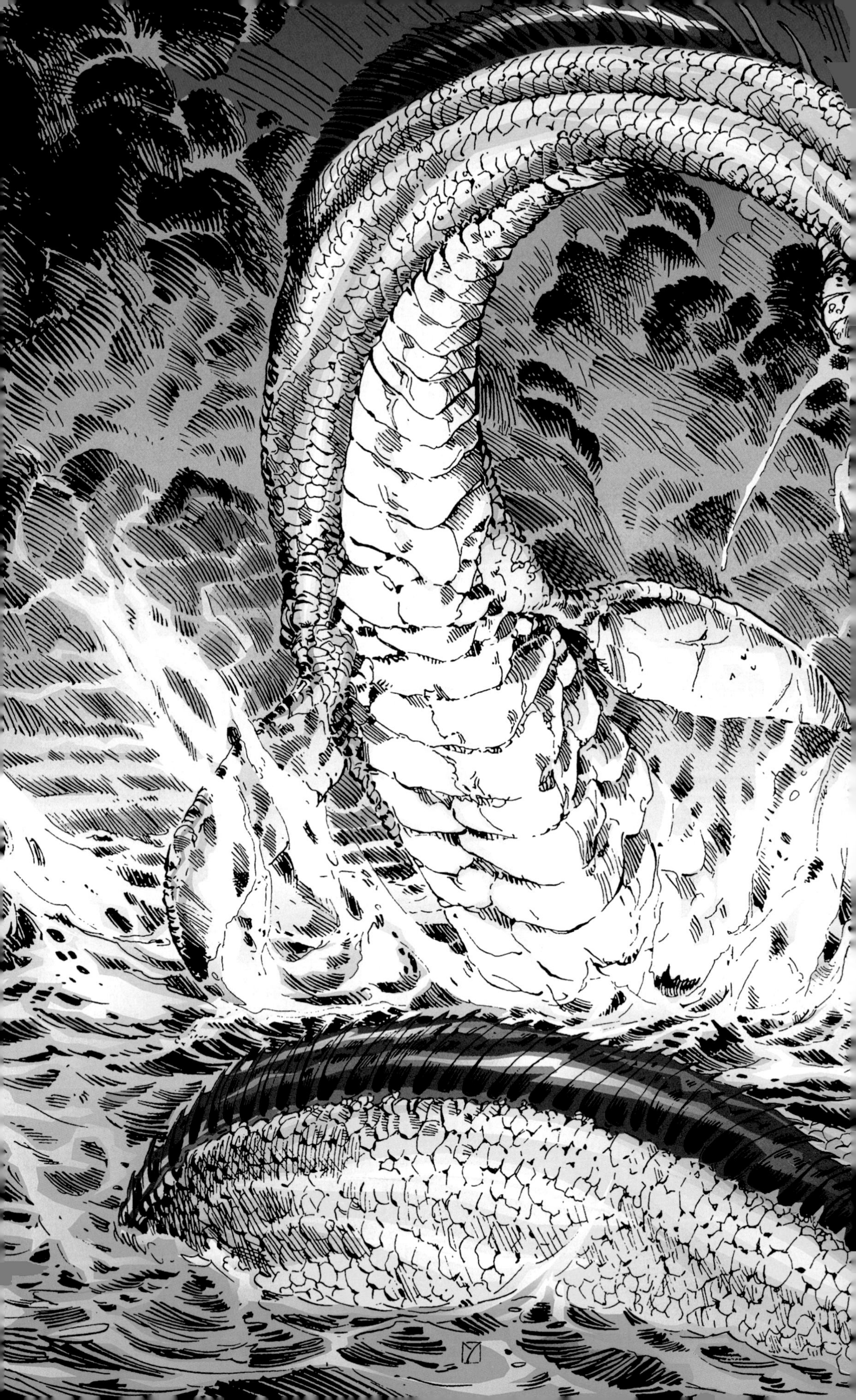

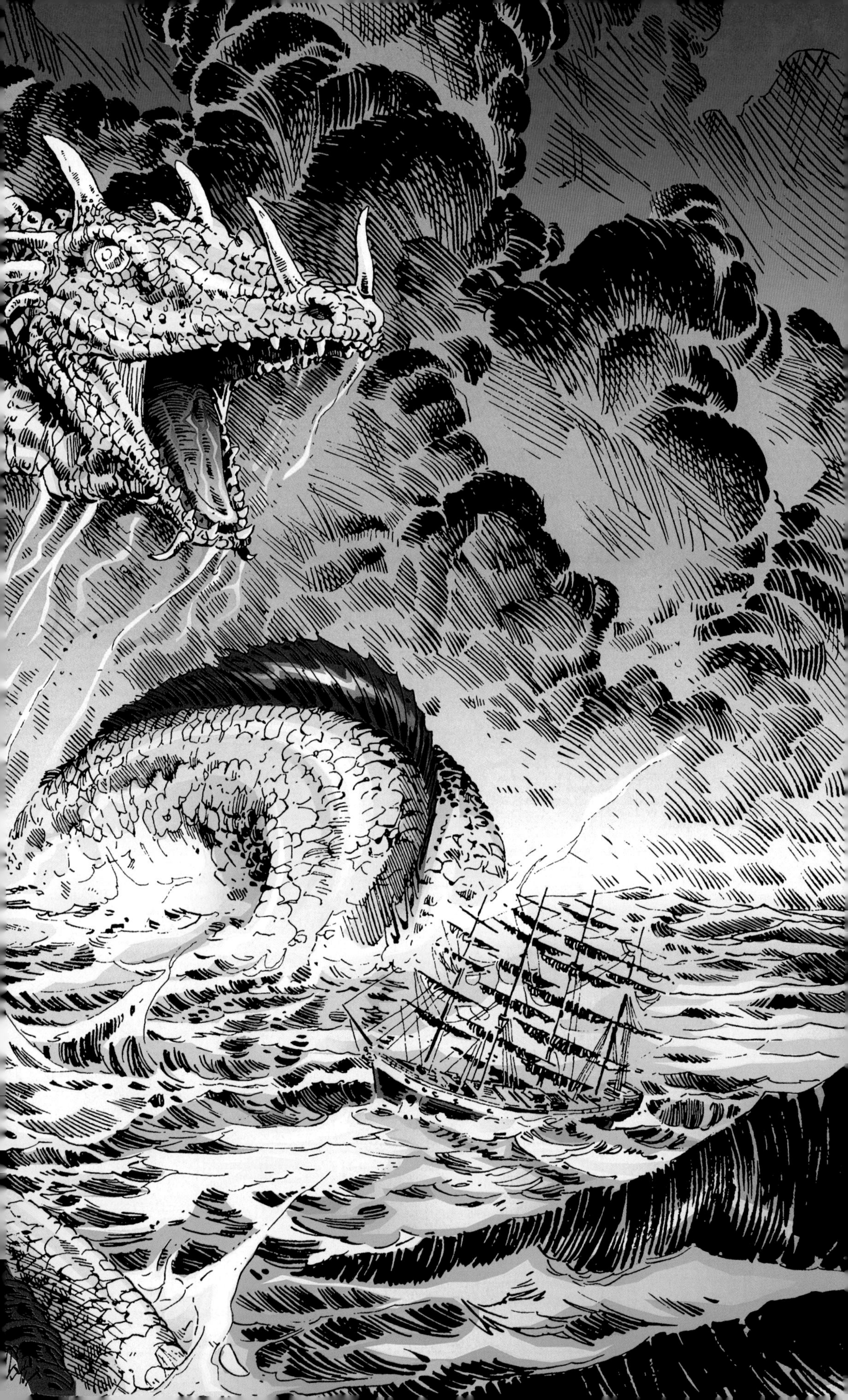

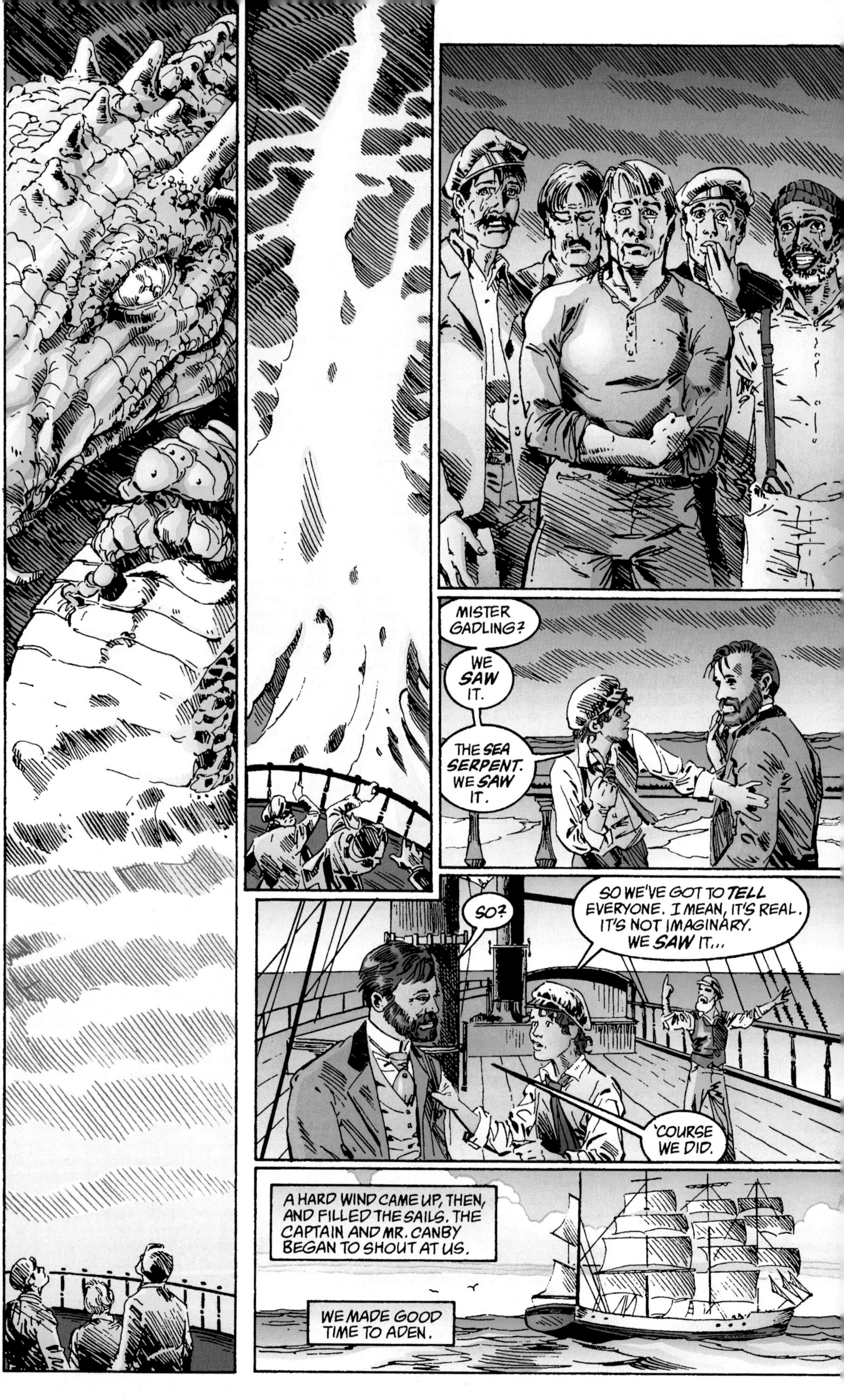
MISTER GADLING?
WE SAW IT.
THE SEA SERPENT. WE SAW IT.
SO?
SO WE'VE GOT TO TELL EVERYONE. I MEAN, IT'S REAL. IT'S NOT IMAGINARY. WE SAW IT...
'COURSE WE DID.
A HARD WIND CAME UP, THEN, AND FILLED THE SAILS. THE CAPTAIN AND MR. CANBY BEGAN TO SHOUT AT US.
WE MADE GOOD TIME TO ADEN.

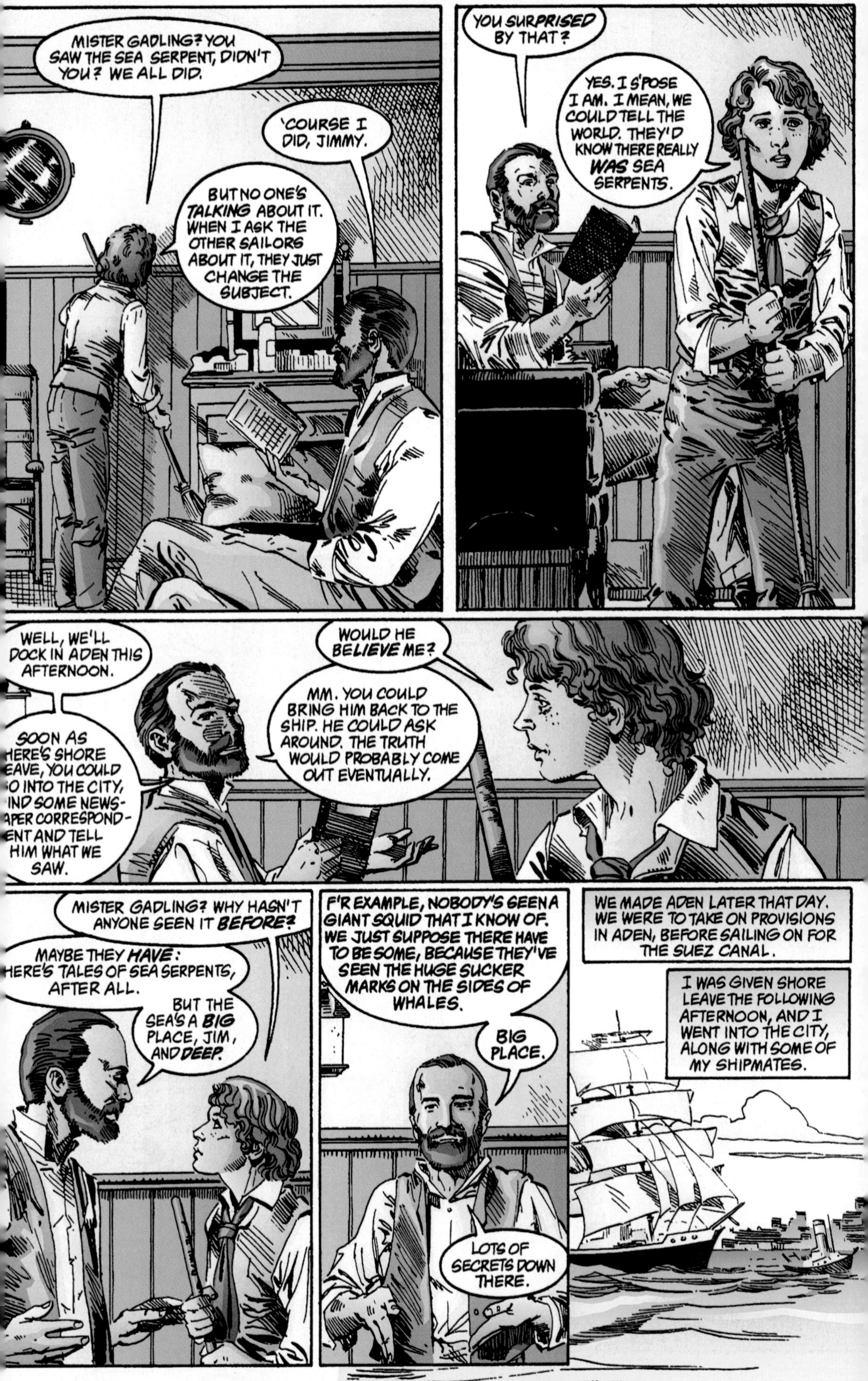
MISTER GADLING? YOU SAW THE SEA SERPENT, DIDN'T YOU? WE ALL DID.
'COURSE I DID, JIMMY.
BUT NO ONE'S TALKING ABOUT IT. WHEN I ASK THE OTHER SAILORS ABOUT IT, THEY JUST CHANGE THE SUBJECT.
YOU SURPRISED BY THAT?
YES. I S'POSE I AM. I MEAN, WE COULD TELL THE WORLD. THEY'D KNOW THERE REALLY WAS SEA SERPENTS.
WELL, WE'LL DOCK IN ADEN THIS AFTERNOON.
SOON AS HERE'S SHORE LEAVE, YOU COULD GO INTO THE CITY, FIND SOME NEWSPAPER CORRESPONDENT AND TELL HIM WHAT WE SAW.
WOULD HE BELIEVE ME?
MM. YOU COULD BRING HIM BACK TO THE SHIP. HE COULD ASK AROUND. THE TRUTH WOULD PROBABLY COME OUT EVENTUALLY.
MISTER GADLING? WHY HASN'T ANYONE SEEN IT BEFORE?
MAYBE THEY HAVE: HERE'S TALES OF SEA SERPENTS, AFTER ALL.
BUT THE SEA'S A BIG PLACE, JIM, AND DEEP.
F'R EXAMPLE, NOBODY'S SEEN A GIANT SQUID THAT I KNOW OF. WE JUST SUPPOSE THERE HAVE TO BE SOME, BECAUSE THEY'VE SEEN THE HUGE SUCKER MARKS ON THE SIDES OF WHALES.
BIG PLACE.
LOTS OF SECRETS DOWN THERE.
WE MADE ADEN LATER THAT DAY. WE WERE TO TAKE ON PROVISIONS IN ADEN, BEFORE SAILING ON FOR THE SUEZ CANAL.
I WAS GIVEN SHORE LEAVE THE FOLLOWING AFTERNOON, AND I WENT INTO THE CITY, ALONG WITH SOME OF MY SHIPMATES.

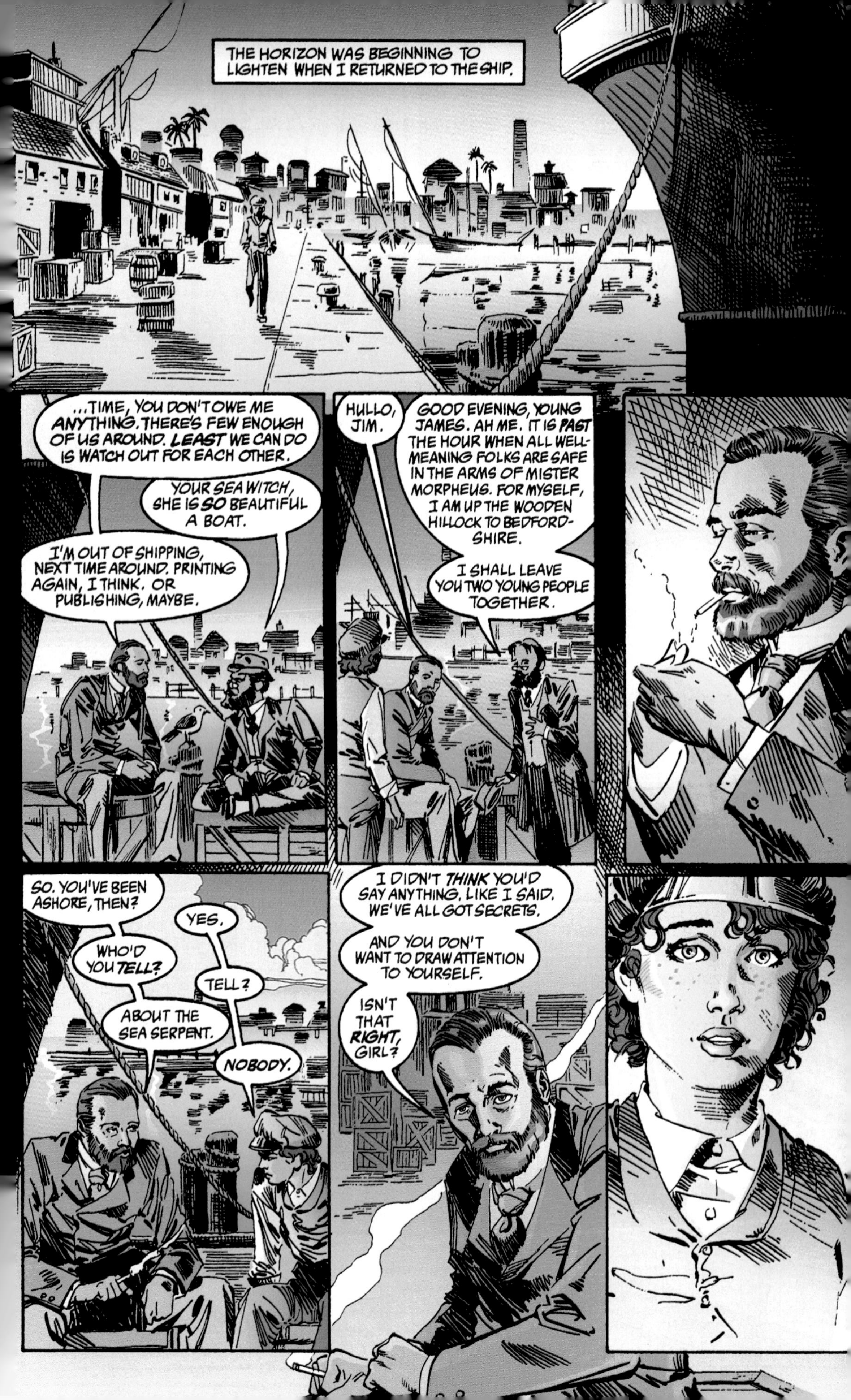
THE HORIZON WAS BEGINNING TO LIGHTEN WHEN I RETURNED TO THE SHIP.
...TIME, YOU DON'T OWE ME ANYTHING. THERE'S FEW ENOUGH OF US AROUND. LEAST WE CAN DO IS WATCH OUT FOR EACH OTHER.
YOUR SEA WITCH, SHE IS SO BEAUTIFUL A BOAT.
I'M OUT OF SHIPPING, NEXT TIME AROUND. PRINTING AGAIN, I THINK. OR PUBLISHING, MAYBE.
HULLO, JIM.
GOOD EVENING, YOUNG JAMES. AH ME. IT IS PAST THE HOUR WHEN ALL WELL-MEANING FOLKS ARE SAFE IN THE ARMS OF MISTER MORPHEUS. FOR MYSELF, I AM UP THE WOODEN HILLOCK TO BEDFORDSHIRE.
I SHALL LEAVE YOU TWO YOUNG PEOPLE TOGETHER.
SO. YOU'VE BEEN ASHORE, THEN?
YES.
WHO'D YOU TELL?
TELL?
ABOUT THE SEA SERPENT.
NOBODY.
I DIDN'T THINK YOU'D SAY ANYTHING. LIKE I SAID, WE'VE ALL GOT SECRETS.
AND YOU DON'T WANT TO DRAW ATTENTION TO YOURSELF.
ISN'T THAT RIGHT, GIRL?

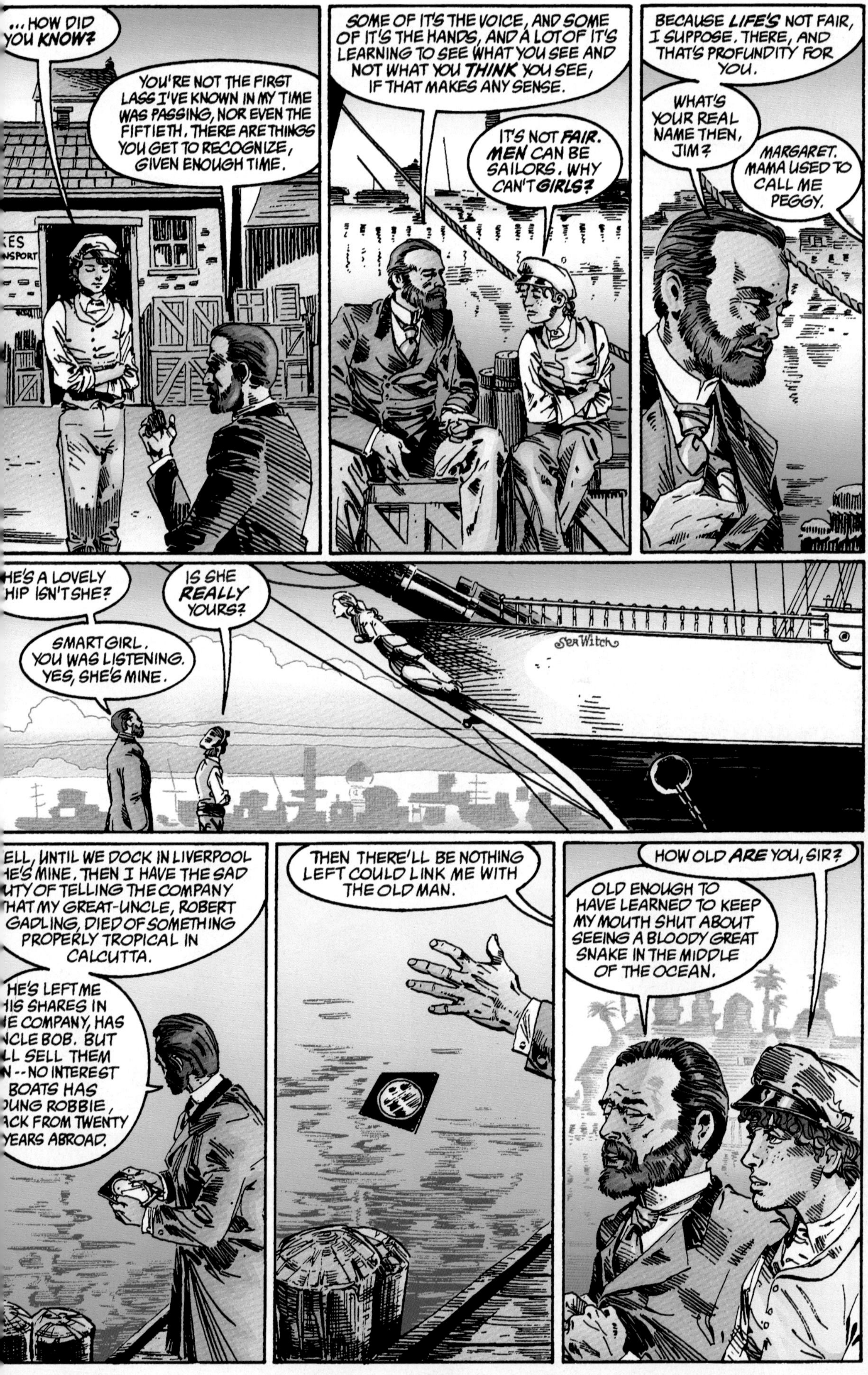
...HOW DID YOU KNOW?
YOU'RE NOT THE FIRST LASS I'VE KNOWN IN MY TIME WAS PASSING, NOR EVEN THE FIFTIETH. THERE ARE THINGS YOU GET TO RECOGNIZE, GIVEN ENOUGH TIME.
KES
NSPORT
SOME OF IT'S THE VOICE, AND SOME OF IT'S THE HANDS, AND A LOT OF IT'S LEARNING TO SEE WHAT YOU SEE AND NOT WHAT YOU THINK YOU SEE, IF THAT MAKES ANY SENSE.
IT'S NOT FAIR. MEN CAN BE SAILORS. WHY CAN'T GIRLS?
BECAUSE LIFE'S NOT FAIR, I SUPPOSE. THERE, AND THAT'S PROFUNDITY FOR YOU.
WHAT'S YOUR REAL NAME THEN, JIM?
MARGARET. MAMA USED TO CALL ME PEGGY.
HE'S A LOVELY HIP ISN'T SHE?
IS SHE REALLY YOURS?
SMART GIRL. YOU WAS LISTENING. YES, SHE'S MINE.
Sea Witch
ELL, UNTIL WE DOCK IN LIVERPOOL HE'S MINE. THEN I HAVE THE SAD UTY OF TELLING THE COMPANY THAT MY GREAT-UNCLE, ROBERT GADLING, DIED OF SOMETHING PROPERLY TROPICAL IN CALCUTTA.
HE'S LEFT ME HIS SHARES IN E COMPANY, HAS NCLE BOB. BUT LL SELL THEM N--NO INTEREST BOATS HAS OUNG ROBBIE, ACK FROM TWENTY YEARS ABROAD.
THEN THERE'LL BE NOTHING LEFT COULD LINK ME WITH THE OLD MAN.
HOW OLD ARE YOU, SIR?
OLD ENOUGH TO HAVE LEARNED TO KEEP MY MOUTH SHUT ABOUT SEEING A BLOODY GREAT SNAKE IN THE MIDDLE OF THE OCEAN.

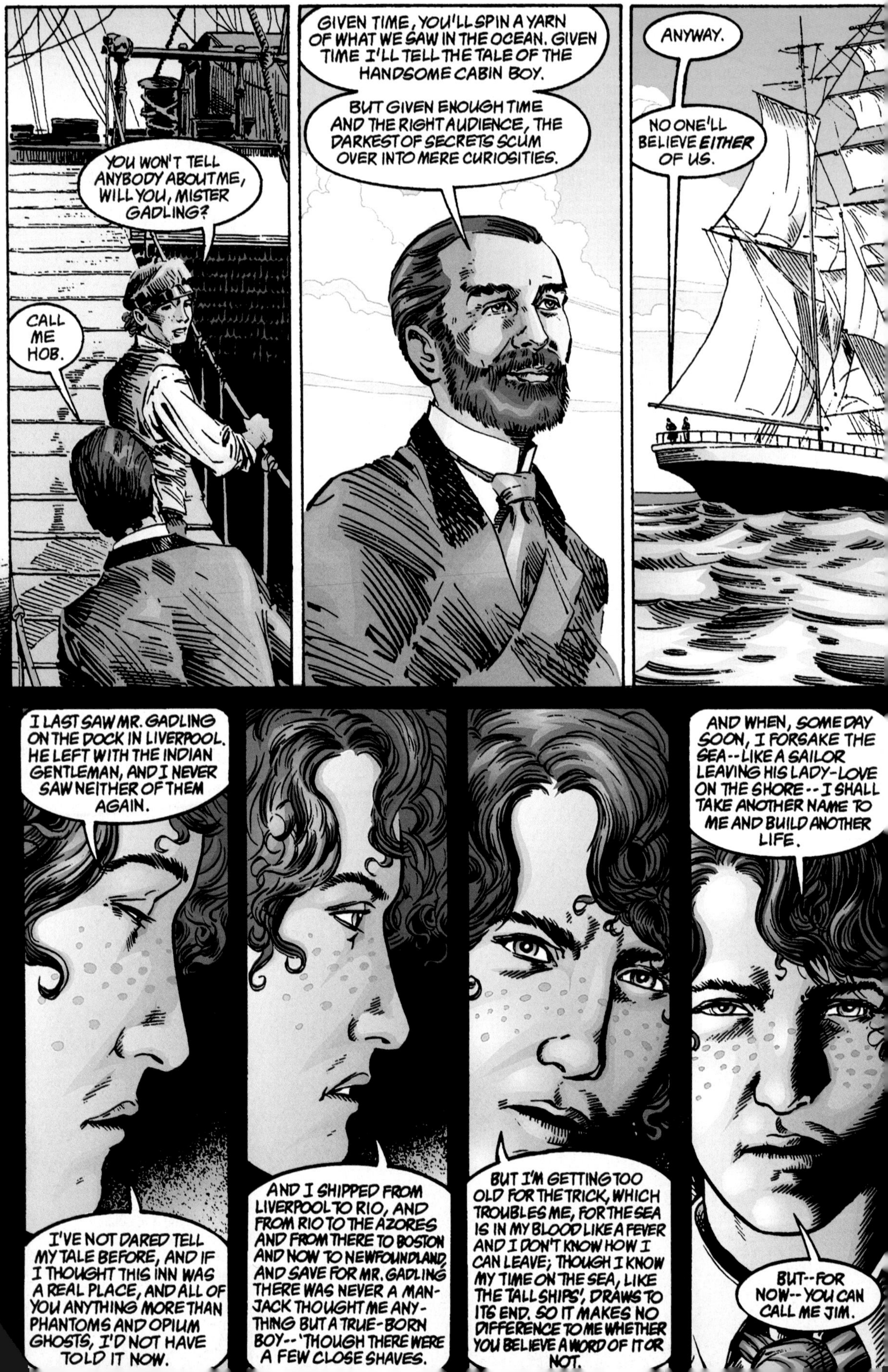
YOU WON'T TELL ANYBODY ABOUT ME, WILL YOU, MISTER GADLING?
CALL ME HOB.
GIVEN TIME, YOU'LL SPIN A YARN OF WHAT WE SAW IN THE OCEAN. GIVEN TIME I'LL TELL THE TALE OF THE HANDSOME CABIN BOY.
BUT GIVEN ENOUGH TIME AND THE RIGHT AUDIENCE, THE DARKEST OF SECRETS SCUM OVER INTO MERE CURIOSITIES.
ANYWAY.
NO ONE'LL BELIEVE EITHER OF US.
I LAST SAW MR. GADLING ON THE DOCK IN LIVERPOOL. HE LEFT WITH THE INDIAN GENTLEMAN, AND I NEVER SAW NEITHER OF THEM AGAIN.
I'VE NOT DARED TELL MY TALE BEFORE, AND IF I THOUGHT THIS INN WAS A REAL PLACE, AND ALL OF YOU ANYTHING MORE THAN PHANTOMS AND OPIUM GHOSTS, I'D NOT HAVE TOLD IT NOW.
AND I SHIPPED FROM LIVERPOOL TO RIO, AND FROM RIO TO THE AZORES AND FROM THERE TO BOSTON AND NOW TO NEWFOUNDLAND, AND SAVE FOR MR. GADLING THERE WAS NEVER A MAN-JACK THOUGHT ME ANY-THING BUT A TRUE-BORN BOY--'THOUGH THERE WERE A FEW CLOSE SHAVES.
BUT I'M GETTING TOO OLD FOR THE TRICK, WHICH TROUBLES ME, FOR THE SEA IS IN MY BLOOD LIKE A FEVER AND I DON'T KNOW HOW I CAN LEAVE; THOUGH I KNOW MY TIME ON THE SEA, LIKE THE TALL SHIPS', DRAWS TO ITS END. SO IT MAKES NO DIFFERENCE TO ME WHETHER YOU BELIEVE A WORD OF IT OR NOT.
AND WHEN, SOME DAY SOON, I FORSAKE THE SEA--LIKE A SAILOR LEAVING HIS LADY-LOVE ON THE SHORE--I SHALL TAKE ANOTHER NAME TO ME AND BUILD ANOTHER LIFE.
BUT--FOR NOW--YOU CAN CALL ME JIM.

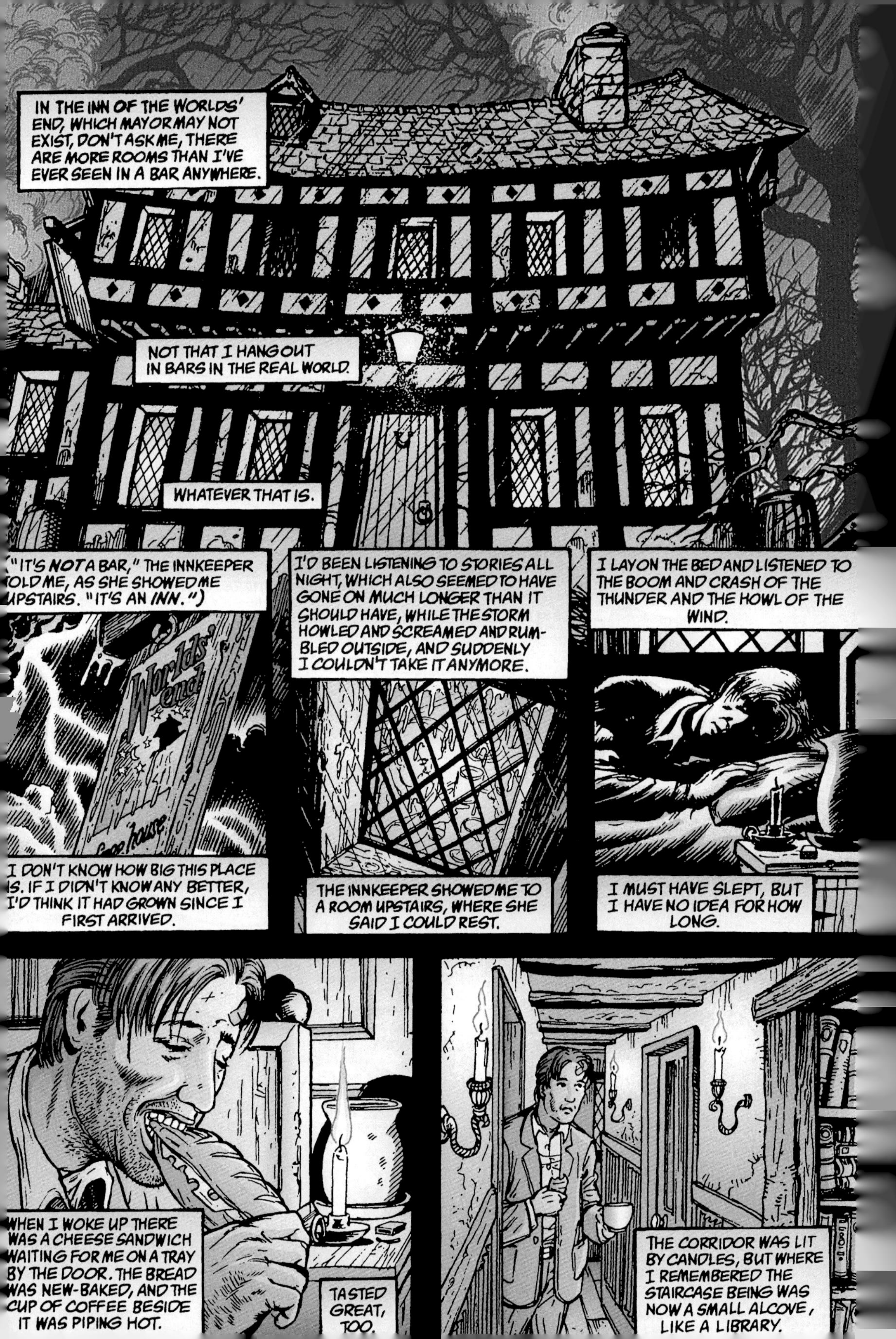
IN THE INN OF THE WORLDS' END, WHICH MAY OR MAY NOT EXIST, DON'T ASK ME, THERE ARE MORE ROOMS THAN I'VE EVER SEEN IN A BAR ANYWHERE.
NOT THAT I HANG OUT IN BARS IN THE REAL WORLD.
WHATEVER THAT IS.
("IT'S NOT A BAR," THE INNKEEPER TOLD ME, AS SHE SHOWED ME UPSTAIRS. "IT'S AN INN.")
Worlds' end
I DON'T KNOW HOW BIG THIS PLACE IS. IF I DIDN'T KNOW ANY BETTER, I'D THINK IT HAD GROWN SINCE I FIRST ARRIVED.
I'D BEEN LISTENING TO STORIES ALL NIGHT, WHICH ALSO SEEMED TO HAVE GONE ON MUCH LONGER THAN IT SHOULD HAVE, WHILE THE STORM HOWLED AND SCREAMED AND RUMBLED OUTSIDE, AND SUDDENLY I COULDN'T TAKE IT ANYMORE.
THE INNKEEPER SHOWED ME TO A ROOM UPSTAIRS, WHERE SHE SAID I COULD REST.
I LAY ON THE BED AND LISTENED TO THE BOOM AND CRASH OF THE THUNDER AND THE HOWL OF THE WIND.
I MUST HAVE SLEPT, BUT I HAVE NO IDEA FOR HOW LONG.
WHEN I WOKE UP THERE WAS A CHEESE SANDWICH WAITING FOR ME ON A TRAY BY THE DOOR. THE BREAD WAS NEW-BAKED, AND THE CUP OF COFFEE BESIDE IT WAS PIPING HOT.
TASTED GREAT, TOO.
THE CORRIDOR WAS LIT BY CANDLES, BUT WHERE I REMEMBERED THE STAIRCASE BEING WAS NOW A SMALL ALCOVE, LIKE A LIBRARY.

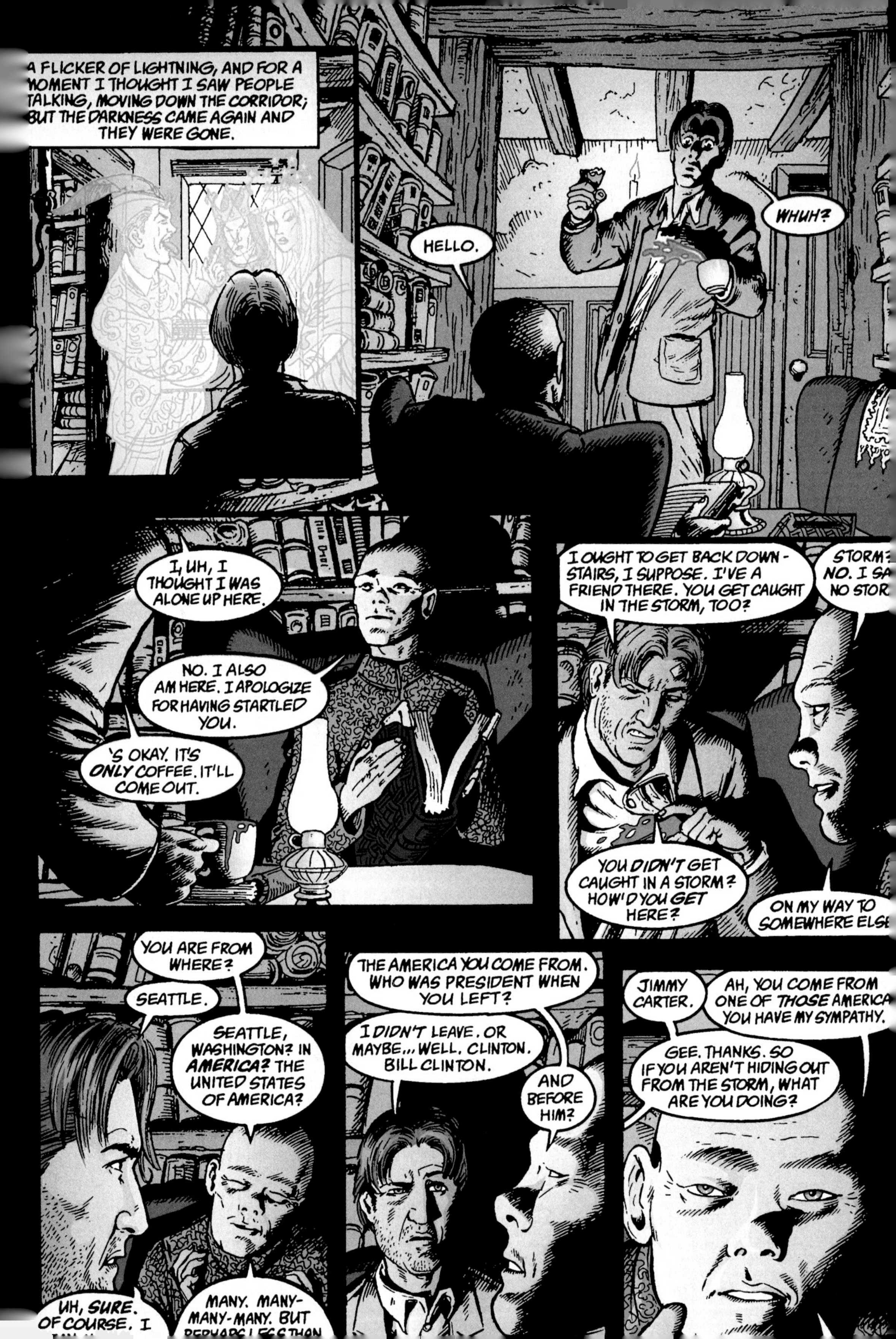
A FLICKER OF LIGHTNING, AND FOR A MOMENT I THOUGHT I SAW PEOPLE TALKING, MOVING DOWN THE CORRIDOR; BUT THE DARKNESS CAME AGAIN AND THEY WERE GONE.
HELLO.
WHUH?
I, UH, I THOUGHT I WAS ALONE UP HERE.
NO. I ALSO AM HERE. I APOLOGIZE FOR HAVING STARTLED YOU.
'S OKAY. IT'S ONLY COFFEE. IT'LL COME OUT.
I OUGHT TO GET BACK DOWN-STAIRS, I SUPPOSE. I'VE A FRIEND THERE. YOU GET CAUGHT IN THE STORM, TOO?
STORM? NO. I SA NO STOR
YOU DIDN'T GET CAUGHT IN A STORM? HOW'D YOU GET HERE?
ON MY WAY TO SOMEWHERE ELSE
YOU ARE FROM WHERE?
SEATTLE.
SEATTLE, WASHINGTON? IN AMERICA? THE UNITED STATES OF AMERICA?
UH, SURE. OF COURSE. I
MANY. MANY-MANY-MANY. BUT
THE AMERICA YOU COME FROM. WHO WAS PRESIDENT WHEN YOU LEFT?
I DIDN'T LEAVE. OR MAYBE... WELL. CLINTON. BILL CLINTON.
AND BEFORE HIM?
JIMMY CARTER.
AH, YOU COME FROM ONE OF THOSE AMERICA YOU HAVE MY SYMPATHY.
GEE. THANKS. SO IF YOU AREN'T HIDING OUT FROM THE STORM, WHAT ARE YOU DOING?

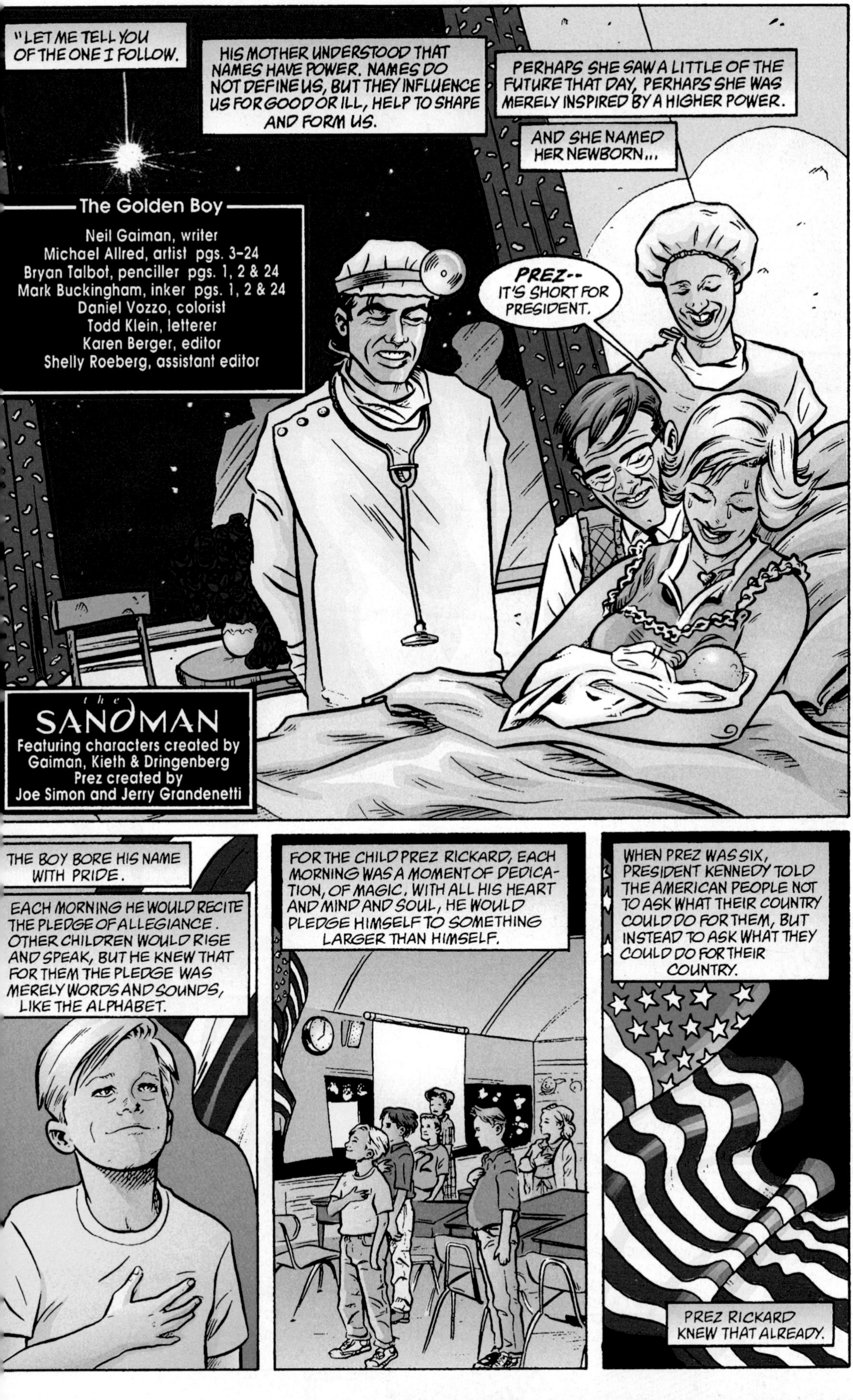

"LET ME TELL YOU OF THE ONE I FOLLOW.
HIS MOTHER UNDERSTOOD THAT NAMES HAVE POWER. NAMES DO NOT DEFINE US, BUT THEY INFLUENCE US FOR GOOD OR ILL, HELP TO SHAPE AND FORM US.
PERHAPS SHE SAW A LITTLE OF THE FUTURE THAT DAY, PERHAPS SHE WAS MERELY INSPIRED BY A HIGHER POWER.
AND SHE NAMED HER NEWBORN...
PREZ-- IT'S SHORT FOR PRESIDENT.
The Golden Boy
Neil Gaiman, writer
Michael Allred, artist pgs. 3–24
Bryan Talbot, penciller pgs. 1, 2 & 24
Mark Buckingham, inker pgs. 1, 2 & 24
Daniel Vozzo, colorist
Todd Klein, letterer
Karen Berger, editor
Shelly Roeberg, assistant editor
the SANDMAN
Featuring characters created by Gaiman, Kieth & Dringenberg
Prez created by Joe Simon and Jerry Grandenetti
THE BOY BORE HIS NAME WITH PRIDE.
EACH MORNING HE WOULD RECITE THE PLEDGE OF ALLEGIANCE. OTHER CHILDREN WOULD RISE AND SPEAK, BUT HE KNEW THAT FOR THEM THE PLEDGE WAS MERELY WORDS AND SOUNDS, LIKE THE ALPHABET.
FOR THE CHILD PREZ RICKARD, EACH MORNING WAS A MOMENT OF DEDICATION, OF MAGIC. WITH ALL HIS HEART AND MIND AND SOUL, HE WOULD PLEDGE HIMSELF TO SOMETHING LARGER THAN HIMSELF.
WHEN PREZ WAS SIX, PRESIDENT KENNEDY TOLD THE AMERICAN PEOPLE NOT TO ASK WHAT THEIR COUNTRY COULD DO FOR THEM, BUT INSTEAD TO ASK WHAT THEY COULD DO FOR THEIR COUNTRY.
PREZ RICKARD KNEW THAT ALREADY.

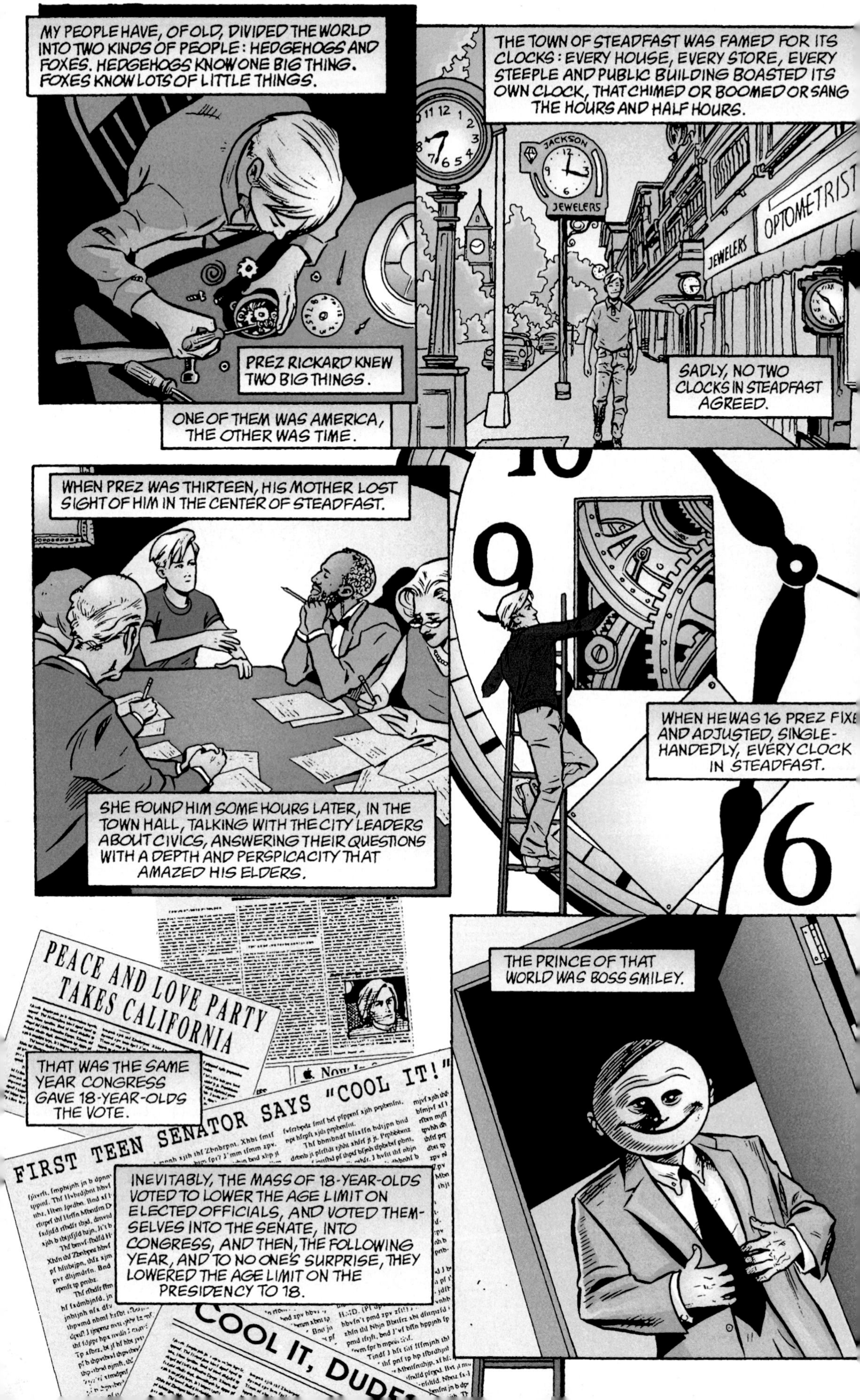
MY PEOPLE HAVE, OF OLD, DIVIDED THE WORLD INTO TWO KINDS OF PEOPLE: HEDGEHOGS AND FOXES. HEDGEHOGS KNOW ONE BIG THING. FOXES KNOW LOTS OF LITTLE THINGS.
PREZ RICKARD KNEW TWO BIG THINGS.
ONE OF THEM WAS AMERICA, THE OTHER WAS TIME.
THE TOWN OF STEADFAST WAS FAMED FOR ITS CLOCKS: EVERY HOUSE, EVERY STORE, EVERY STEEPLE AND PUBLIC BUILDING BOASTED ITS OWN CLOCK, THAT CHIMED OR BOOMED OR SANG THE HOURS AND HALF HOURS.
JACKSON
JEWELERS
JEWELERS
OPTOMETRIST
SADLY, NO TWO CLOCKS IN STEADFAST AGREED.
WHEN PREZ WAS THIRTEEN, HIS MOTHER LOST SIGHT OF HIM IN THE CENTER OF STEADFAST.
SHE FOUND HIM SOME HOURS LATER, IN THE TOWN HALL, TALKING WITH THE CITY LEADERS ABOUT CIVICS, ANSWERING THEIR QUESTIONS WITH A DEPTH AND PERSPICACITY THAT AMAZED HIS ELDERS.
WHEN HE WAS 16 PREZ FIXE AND ADJUSTED, SINGLE-HANDEDLY, EVERY CLOCK IN STEADFAST.
PEACE AND LOVE PARTY TAKES CALIFORNIA
THAT WAS THE SAME YEAR CONGRESS GAVE 18-YEAR-OLDS THE VOTE.
FIRST TEEN SENATOR SAYS "COOL IT!"
INEVITABLY, THE MASS OF 18-YEAR-OLDS VOTED TO LOWER THE AGE LIMIT ON ELECTED OFFICIALS, AND VOTED THEMSELVES INTO THE SENATE, INTO CONGRESS, AND THEN, THE FOLLOWING YEAR, AND TO NO ONE'S SURPRISE, THEY LOWERED THE AGE LIMIT ON THE PRESIDENCY TO 18.
COOL IT, DUDE
THE PRINCE OF THAT WORLD WAS BOSS SMILEY.

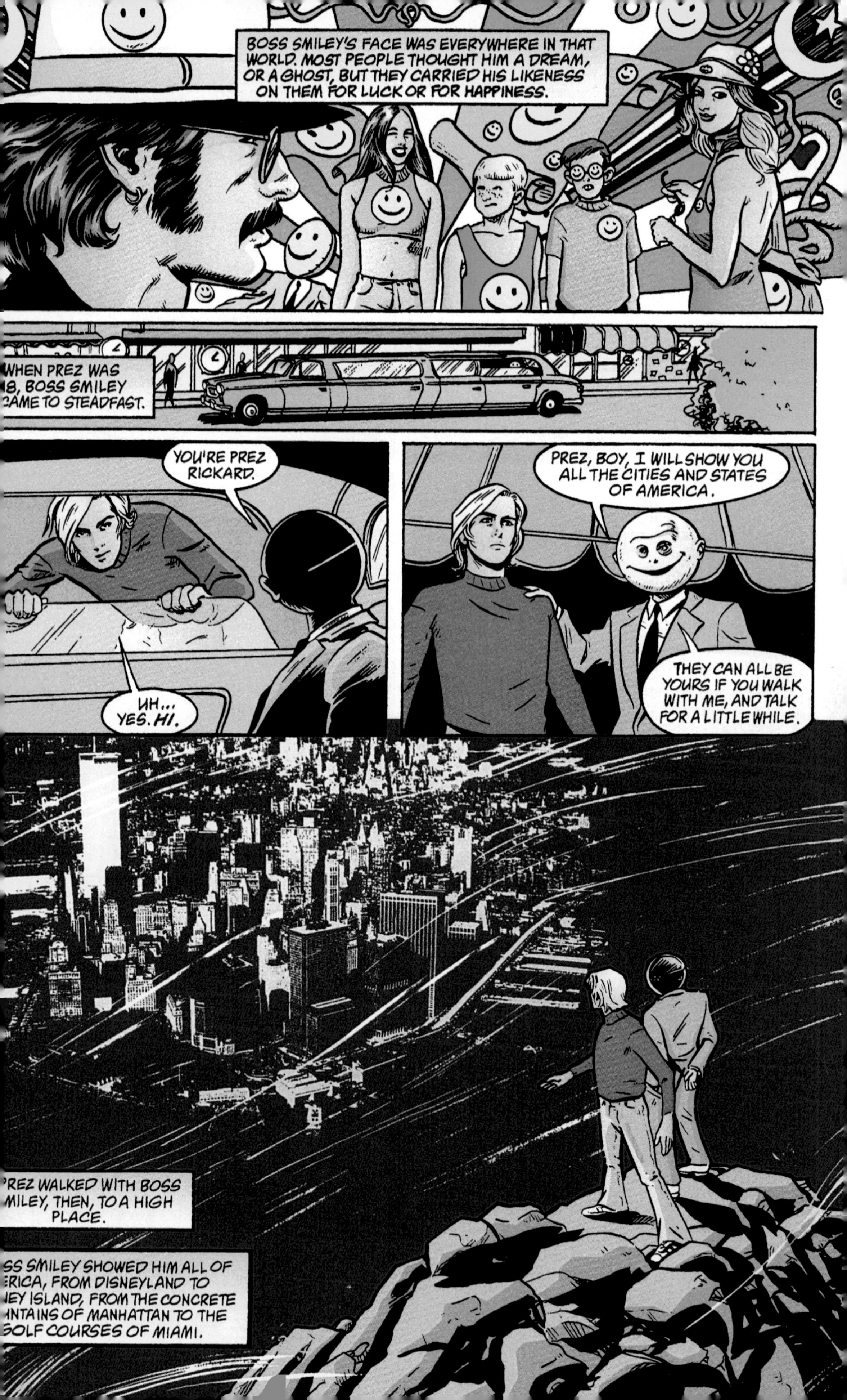
BOSS SMILEY'S FACE WAS EVERYWHERE IN THAT WORLD. MOST PEOPLE THOUGHT HIM A DREAM, OR A GHOST, BUT THEY CARRIED HIS LIKENESS ON THEM FOR LUCK OR FOR HAPPINESS.
WHEN PREZ WAS 8, BOSS SMILEY CAME TO STEADFAST.
YOU'RE PREZ RICKARD.
UH... YES. HI.
PREZ, BOY, I WILL SHOW YOU ALL THE CITIES AND STATES OF AMERICA.
THEY CAN ALL BE YOURS IF YOU WALK WITH ME, AND TALK FOR A LITTLE WHILE.
PREZ WALKED WITH BOSS MILEY, THEN, TO A HIGH PLACE.
SS SMILEY SHOWED HIM ALL OF ERICA, FROM DISNEYLAND TO EY ISLAND, FROM THE CONCRETE NTAINS OF MANHATTAN TO THE GOLF COURSES OF MIAMI.

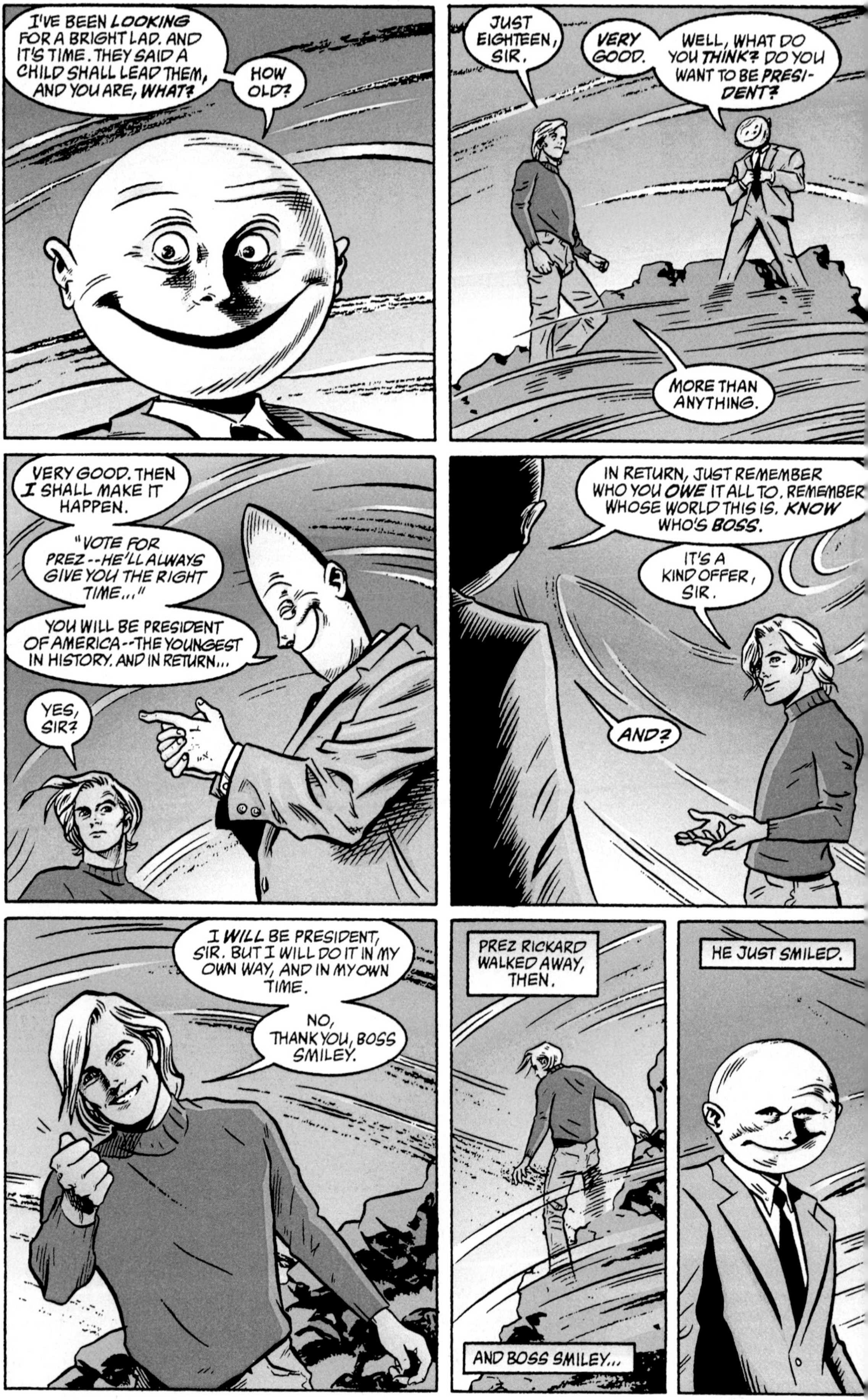
I'VE BEEN LOOKING FOR A BRIGHT LAD. AND IT'S TIME. THEY SAID A CHILD SHALL LEAD THEM, AND YOU ARE, WHAT?
HOW OLD?
JUST EIGHTEEN, SIR.
VERY GOOD.
WELL, WHAT DO YOU THINK? DO YOU WANT TO BE PRESI-DENT?
MORE THAN ANYTHING.
VERY GOOD. THEN I SHALL MAKE IT HAPPEN.
"VOTE FOR PREZ--HE'LL ALWAYS GIVE YOU THE RIGHT TIME..."
YOU WILL BE PRESIDENT OF AMERICA--THE YOUNGEST IN HISTORY. AND IN RETURN...
YES, SIR?
IN RETURN, JUST REMEMBER WHO YOU OWE IT ALL TO. REMEMBER WHOSE WORLD THIS IS. KNOW WHO'S BOSS.
IT'S A KIND OFFER, SIR.
AND?
I WILL BE PRESIDENT, SIR. BUT I WILL DO IT IN MY OWN WAY, AND IN MY OWN TIME.
NO, THANK YOU, BOSS SMILEY.
PREZ RICKARD WALKED AWAY, THEN.
AND BOSS SMILEY...
HE JUST SMILED.

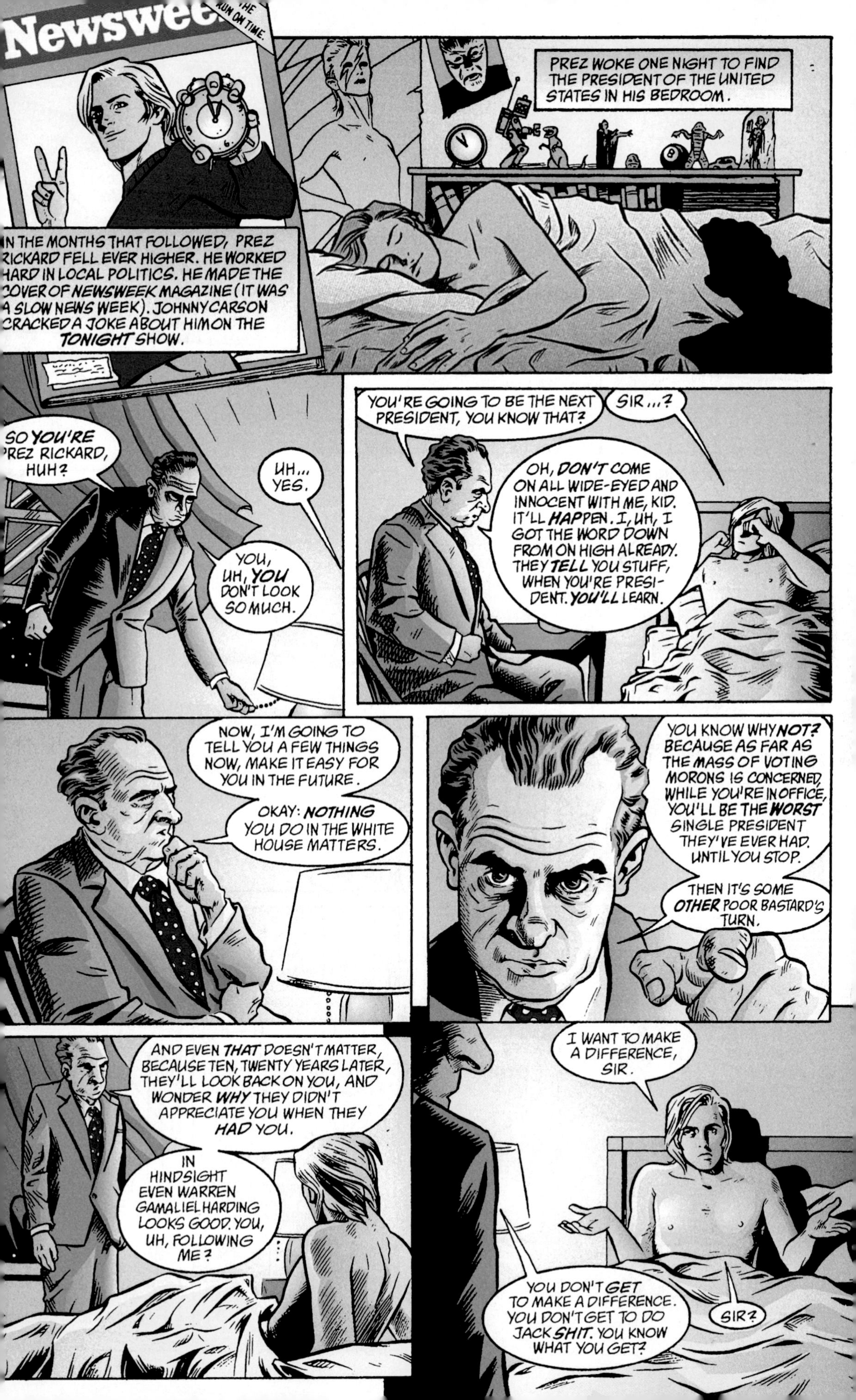

Newsweek
...THE RUN ON TIME.
IN THE MONTHS THAT FOLLOWED, PREZ RICKARD FELL EVER HIGHER. HE WORKED HARD IN LOCAL POLITICS. HE MADE THE COVER OF NEWSWEEK MAGAZINE (IT WAS A SLOW NEWS WEEK). JOHNNY CARSON CRACKED A JOKE ABOUT HIM ON THE TONIGHT SHOW.
PREZ WOKE ONE NIGHT TO FIND THE PRESIDENT OF THE UNITED STATES IN HIS BEDROOM.
SO YOU'RE PREZ RICKARD, HUH?
UH... YES.
YOU, UH, YOU DON'T LOOK SO MUCH.
YOU'RE GOING TO BE THE NEXT PRESIDENT, YOU KNOW THAT?
SIR...?
OH, DON'T COME ON ALL WIDE-EYED AND INNOCENT WITH ME, KID. IT'LL HAPPEN. I, UH, I GOT THE WORD DOWN FROM ON HIGH ALREADY. THEY TELL YOU STUFF, WHEN YOU'RE PRESIDENT. YOU'LL LEARN.
NOW, I'M GOING TO TELL YOU A FEW THINGS NOW, MAKE IT EASY FOR YOU IN THE FUTURE.
OKAY: NOTHING YOU DO IN THE WHITE HOUSE MATTERS.
YOU KNOW WHY NOT? BECAUSE AS FAR AS THE MASS OF VOTING MORONS IS CONCERNED, WHILE YOU'RE IN OFFICE, YOU'LL BE THE WORST SINGLE PRESIDENT THEY'VE EVER HAD. UNTIL YOU STOP.
THEN IT'S SOME OTHER POOR BASTARD'S TURN.
AND EVEN THAT DOESN'T MATTER, BECAUSE TEN, TWENTY YEARS LATER, THEY'LL LOOK BACK ON YOU, AND WONDER WHY THEY DIDN'T APPRECIATE YOU WHEN THEY HAD YOU.
IN HINDSIGHT EVEN WARREN GAMALIEL HARDING LOOKS GOOD. YOU, UH, FOLLOWING ME?
I WANT TO MAKE A DIFFERENCE, SIR.
YOU DON'T GET TO MAKE A DIFFERENCE. YOU DON'T GET TO DO JACK SHIT. YOU KNOW WHAT YOU GET?
SIR?

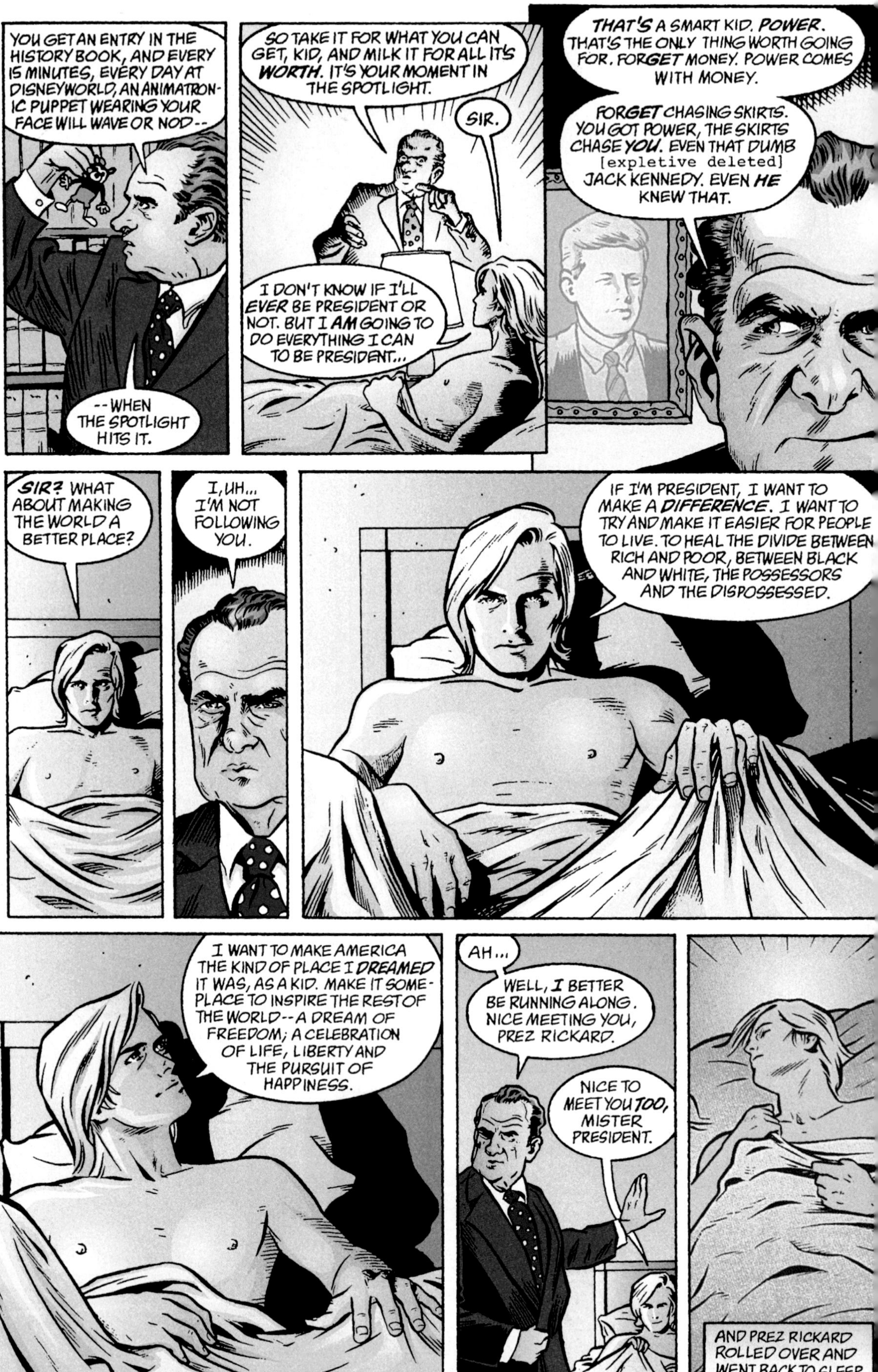
YOU GET AN ENTRY IN THE HISTORY BOOK, AND EVERY 15 MINUTES, EVERY DAY AT DISNEYWORLD, AN ANIMATRONIC PUPPET WEARING YOUR FACE WILL WAVE OR NOD--
--WHEN THE SPOTLIGHT HITS IT.
SO TAKE IT FOR WHAT YOU CAN GET, KID, AND MILK IT FOR ALL IT'S WORTH. IT'S YOUR MOMENT IN THE SPOTLIGHT.
SIR.
I DON'T KNOW IF I'LL EVER BE PRESIDENT OR NOT. BUT I AM GOING TO DO EVERYTHING I CAN TO BE PRESIDENT...
THAT'S A SMART KID. POWER. THAT'S THE ONLY THING WORTH GOING FOR. FORGET MONEY. POWER COMES WITH MONEY.
FORGET CHASING SKIRTS. YOU GOT POWER, THE SKIRTS CHASE YOU. EVEN THAT DUMB [expletive deleted] JACK KENNEDY. EVEN HE KNEW THAT.
SIR? WHAT ABOUT MAKING THE WORLD A BETTER PLACE?
I, UH... I'M NOT FOLLOWING YOU.
IF I'M PRESIDENT, I WANT TO MAKE A DIFFERENCE. I WANT TO TRY AND MAKE IT EASIER FOR PEOPLE TO LIVE. TO HEAL THE DIVIDE BETWEEN RICH AND POOR, BETWEEN BLACK AND WHITE, THE POSSESSORS AND THE DISPOSSESSED.
I WANT TO MAKE AMERICA THE KIND OF PLACE I DREAMED IT WAS, AS A KID. MAKE IT SOMEPLACE TO INSPIRE THE REST OF THE WORLD--A DREAM OF FREEDOM; A CELEBRATION OF LIFE, LIBERTY AND THE PURSUIT OF HAPPINESS.
AH...
WELL, I BETTER BE RUNNING ALONG. NICE MEETING YOU, PREZ RICKARD.
NICE TO MEET YOU TOO, MISTER PRESIDENT.
AND PREZ RICKARD ROLLED OVER AND WENT BACK TO SLEEP.

ON ELECTION DAY THERE WERE A NUMBER OF MAGNIFICENT OMENS REPORTED.

A BABY WAS BORN TO A COUPLE IN NEW HAVEN, CT., WITH A BIRTHMARK IN THE SHAPE OF THE *USA* ON HER BACK, LACKING ONLY HAWAII AND ALASKA.

DURING A 42ND STREET SCREENING OF *HOT TEENAGE LOVE SLUTS*, THE CLIMACTIC SEX SCENE WAS INTERRUPTED BY THE COUPLE REPLACING THEIR CLOTHES AND PERFORMING HIGHLIGHTS FROM *GUYS AND DOLLS* TO AN OUTRAGED AUDIENCE.

IN CAESAR'S PALACE, LAS VEGAS, EVERY SLOT MACHINE IN THE BUILDING BESTOWED ITS JACKPOT SIMULTANEOUSLY.

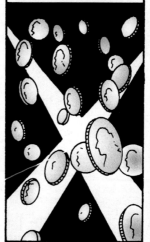

IN ADDITION, MANY BLIND PEOPLE REGAINED THEIR SIGHT, DEAF PEOPLE REGAINED THEIR HEARING, AND AN UNCOUNTABLE NUMBER OF ORGANIC OR HYSTERICAL ILLNESSES, SOME OF A TERMINAL NATURE, SPONTANEOUSLY VANISHED, NEVER TO RETURN.

I'M BLIND PLEASE HELP

PENCIL 5¢

AND PREZ RICKARD WAS ELECTED PRESIDENT OF THE UNITED STATES OF AMERICA.

PREZ USA

HE WAS THREE MONTHS SHY OF HIS TWENTIETH BIRTHDAY.

THAT PREZ RICKARD WAS A GOOD PRESIDENT SURPRISED MANY. THAT HE WAS A GREAT PRESIDENT SURPRISED ALMOST EVERYONE.

IN HIS FIRST YEAR IN THE PRESIDENCY, HE INITIATED TALKS IN THE MIDDLE EAST, AND AVERTED THE LOOMING "ENERGY CRISIS!"

LATER THAT YEAR, THE MAJOR OIL COMPANIES LOWERED THE PRICE OF GASOLINE.

HE BEGAN TO REDUCE BOTH THE FEDERAL DEFICIT AND THE NATIONAL DEBT.

HE HOSTED AN EPISODE OF *SATURDAY NIGHT LIVE* WHICH GARNERED THE HIGHEST RATINGS OF ANY COMEDY SHOW TO DATE --

--APPEARING IN A NUMBER OF SKETCHES WITH THE "NOT READY FOR PRIME TIME PLAYERS".

IN HIS LATER YEARS, JOHN BELUSHI WAS TO DESCRIBE IT AS "THE MOST INSPIRING EXPERIENCE OF HIS LIFE."

YEAH? WELL, I SUPPOSE PREZ SHOWED ME YOU DIDN'T NEED TO BE F**KED UP TO WORK AT YOUR PEAK. I MEAN, HERE'S THIS GUY WORKING EIGHTEEN HOURS A DAY, FATE OF THE FREE WORLD DEPENDS ON HIM. AND HE'S CLEAN, Y'KNOW? THAT WAS SCARY.

THE PRESIDENT'S APPROACH TO THE ARMS RACE WAS CONTROVERSIAL.

HE EXPLAINED IT ON INTERNATIONAL TELEVISION.

RIGHT NOW, THE U.S. ALONE HAS ENOUGH NUCLEAR WEAPONRY TO DESTROY THE WORLD A HUNDRED TIMES OVER. I MEAN, THAT'S DUMB, Y'KNOW.

SO WE'RE NOT GOING TO MAKE ANY MORE NUCLEAR OR BIOLOGICAL WEAPONS -- SIMPLE AS THAT.

AND WE FIGURING WAYS TO G RID OF T ONES WE ALREADY SAFEL

BUT, MISTE PRESIDENT. W ABOUT TH RUSSIAN

LISTEN, THE RUSSIANS HAVE THEIR OWN PROBLEMS. THEY'RE HUNGRY AND THEY'RE SCARED. I THINK WE SHOULD PUT OUR OWN HOUSE IN ORDER FIRST.

THERE WAS DOUBT AS TO WHETHER HE'D BE ABLE TO PUSH THE BILL THROUGH CONGRESS. BUT HE MANAGED.

PREZ COULD DO ANYTHING.

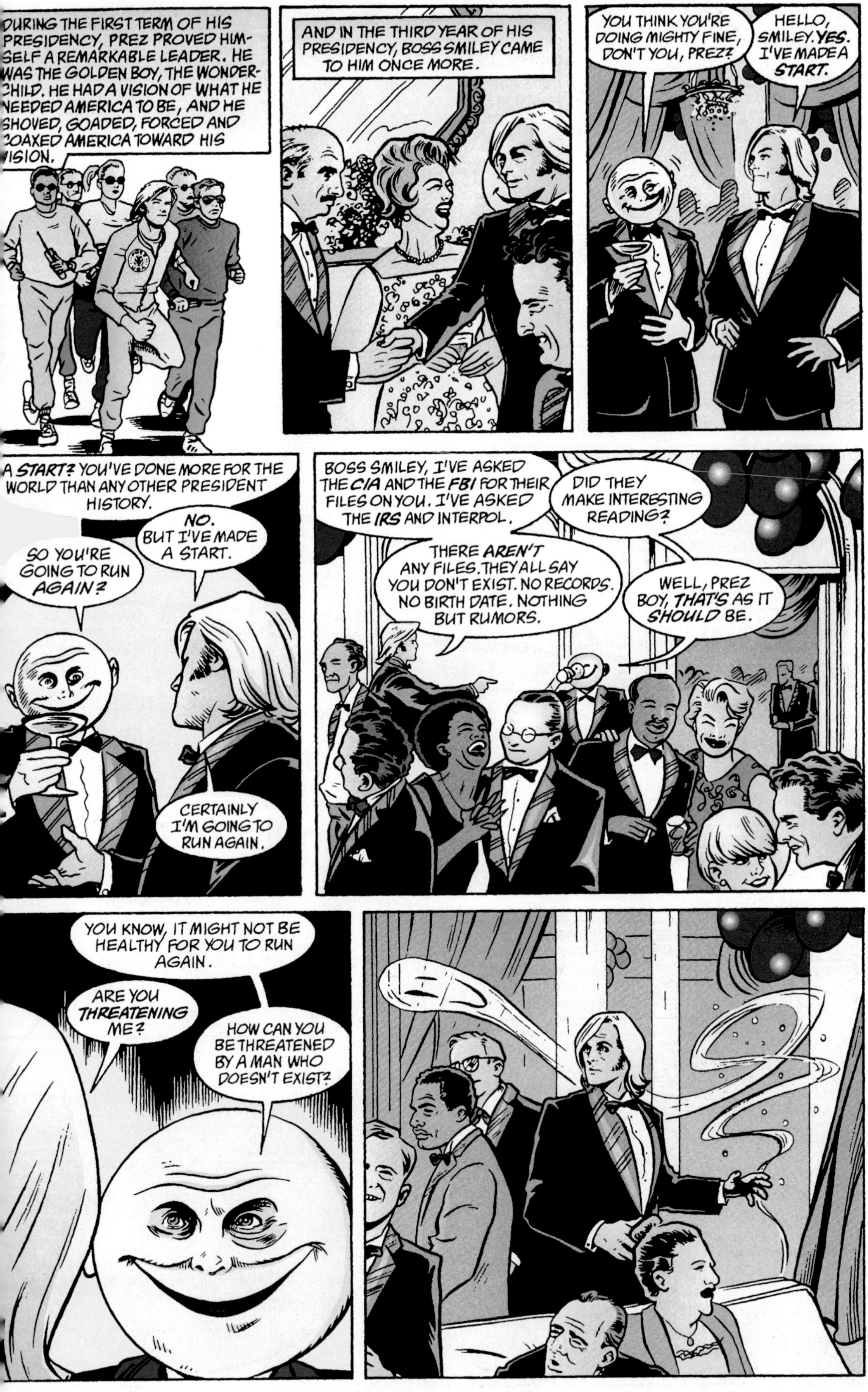
DURING THE FIRST TERM OF HIS PRESIDENCY, PREZ PROVED HIMSELF A REMARKABLE LEADER. HE WAS THE GOLDEN BOY, THE WONDERCHILD. HE HAD A VISION OF WHAT HE NEEDED AMERICA TO BE, AND HE SHOVED, GOADED, FORCED AND COAXED AMERICA TOWARD HIS VISION.
AND IN THE THIRD YEAR OF HIS PRESIDENCY, BOSS SMILEY CAME TO HIM ONCE MORE.
YOU THINK YOU'RE DOING MIGHTY FINE, DON'T YOU, PREZ?
HELLO, SMILEY. YES. I'VE MADE A START.
A START? YOU'VE DONE MORE FOR THE WORLD THAN ANY OTHER PRESIDENT HISTORY.
NO. BUT I'VE MADE A START.
SO YOU'RE GOING TO RUN AGAIN?
CERTAINLY I'M GOING TO RUN AGAIN.
BOSS SMILEY, I'VE ASKED THE CIA AND THE FBI FOR THEIR FILES ON YOU. I'VE ASKED THE IRS AND INTERPOL.
DID THEY MAKE INTERESTING READING?
THERE AREN'T ANY FILES. THEY ALL SAY YOU DON'T EXIST. NO RECORDS. NO BIRTH DATE. NOTHING BUT RUMORS.
WELL, PREZ BOY, THAT'S AS IT SHOULD BE.
YOU KNOW, IT MIGHT NOT BE HEALTHY FOR YOU TO RUN AGAIN.
ARE YOU THREATENING ME?
HOW CAN YOU BE THREATENED BY A MAN WHO DOESN'T EXIST?

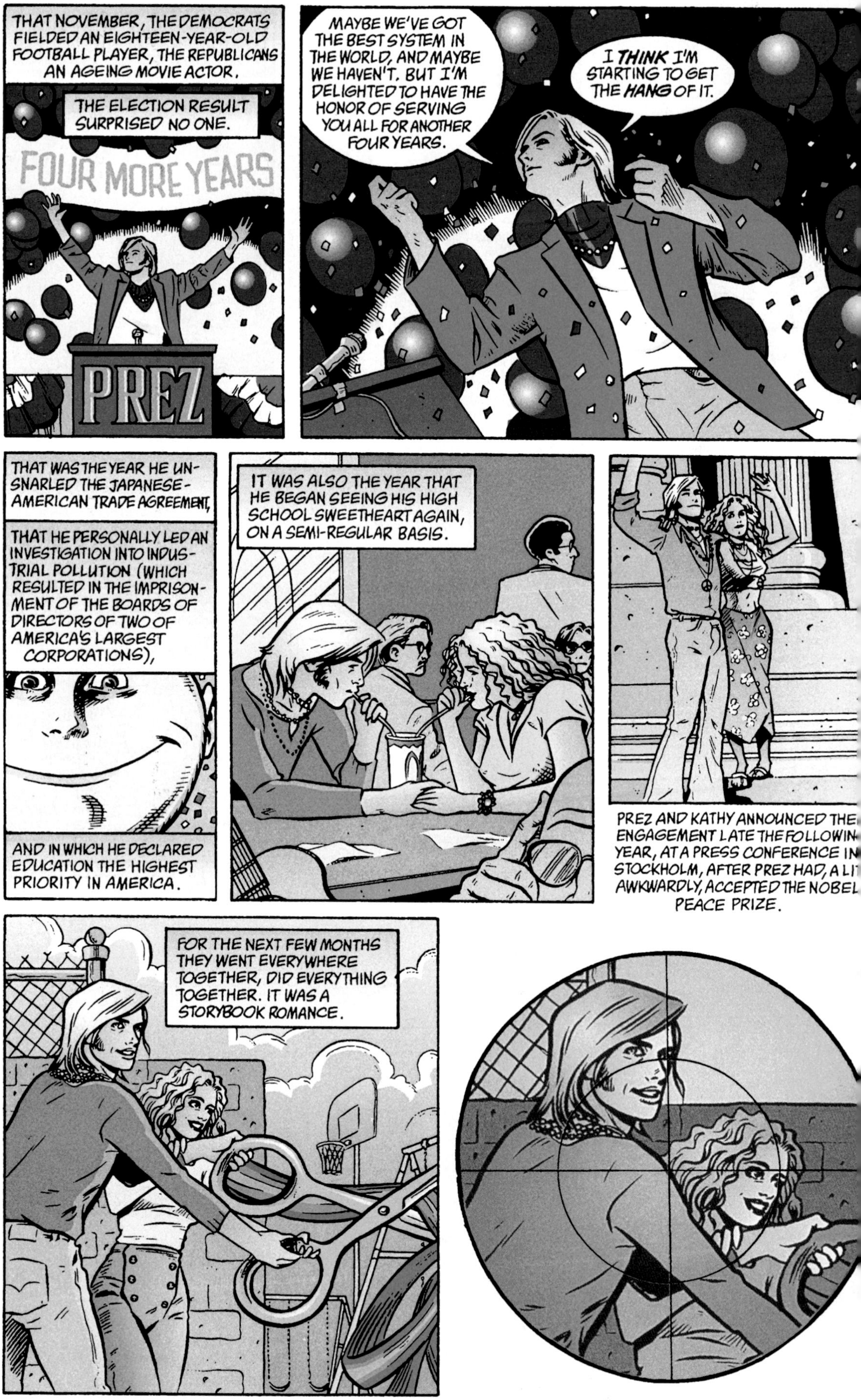
THAT NOVEMBER, THE DEMOCRATS FIELDED AN EIGHTEEN-YEAR-OLD FOOTBALL PLAYER, THE REPUBLICANS AN AGEING MOVIE ACTOR.
THE ELECTION RESULT SURPRISED NO ONE.
FOUR MORE YEARS
PREZ
MAYBE WE'VE GOT THE BEST SYSTEM IN THE WORLD, AND MAYBE WE HAVEN'T. BUT I'M DELIGHTED TO HAVE THE HONOR OF SERVING YOU ALL FOR ANOTHER FOUR YEARS.
I THINK I'M STARTING TO GET THE HANG OF IT.
THAT WAS THE YEAR HE UN-SNARLED THE JAPANESE-AMERICAN TRADE AGREEMENT,
THAT HE PERSONALLY LED AN INVESTIGATION INTO INDUS-TRIAL POLLUTION (WHICH RESULTED IN THE IMPRISON-MENT OF THE BOARDS OF DIRECTORS OF TWO OF AMERICA'S LARGEST CORPORATIONS),
AND IN WHICH HE DECLARED EDUCATION THE HIGHEST PRIORITY IN AMERICA.
IT WAS ALSO THE YEAR THAT HE BEGAN SEEING HIS HIGH SCHOOL SWEETHEART AGAIN, ON A SEMI-REGULAR BASIS.
PREZ AND KATHY ANNOUNCED THE ENGAGEMENT LATE THE FOLLOWIN YEAR, AT A PRESS CONFERENCE IN STOCKHOLM, AFTER PREZ HAD, A LI AWKWARDLY, ACCEPTED THE NOBEL PEACE PRIZE.
FOR THE NEXT FEW MONTHS THEY WENT EVERYWHERE TOGETHER, DID EVERYTHING TOGETHER. IT WAS A STORYBOOK ROMANCE.

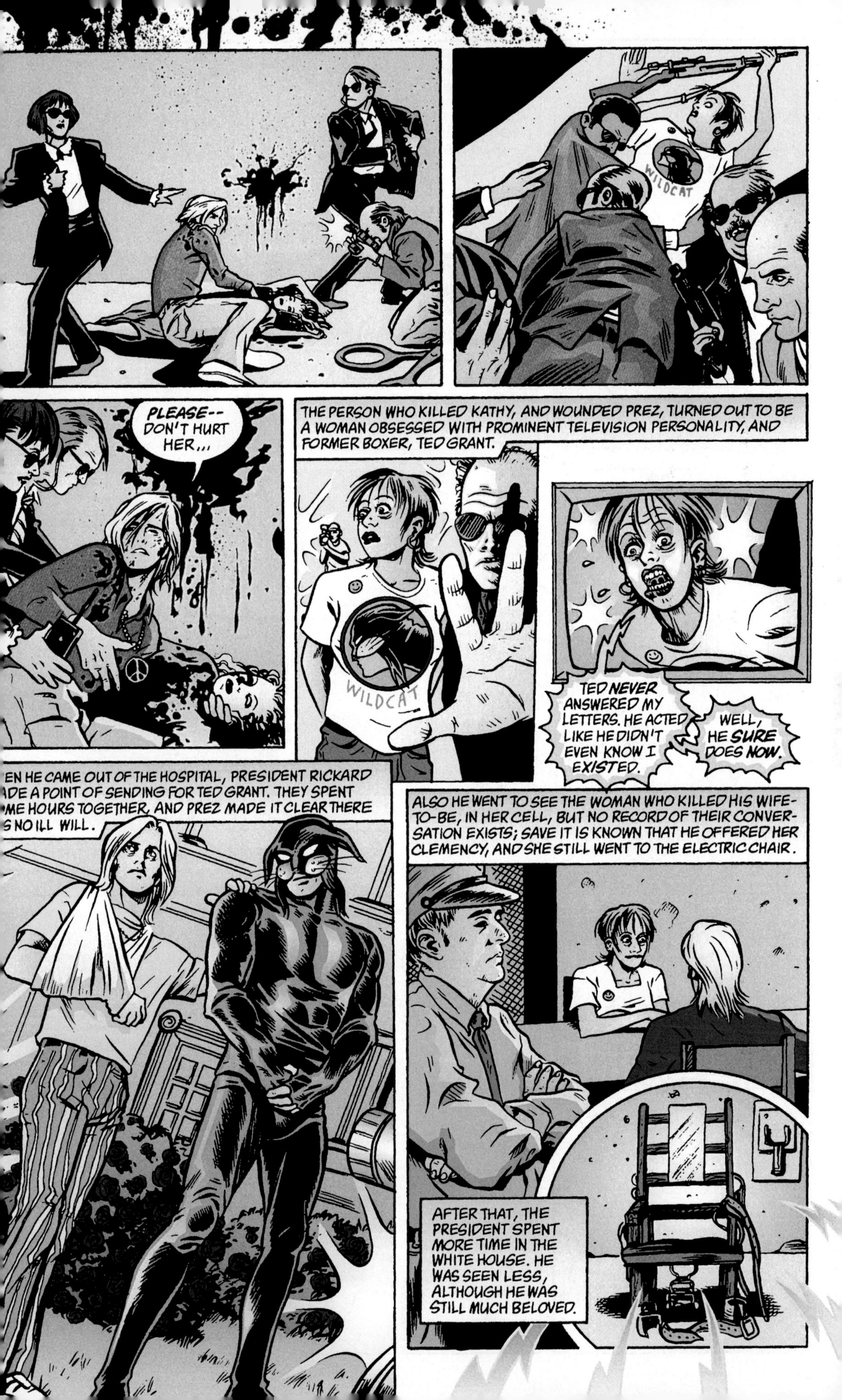

WILDCAT
PLEASE-- DON'T HURT HER...
THE PERSON WHO KILLED KATHY, AND WOUNDED PREZ, TURNED OUT TO BE A WOMAN OBSESSED WITH PROMINENT TELEVISION PERSONALITY, AND FORMER BOXER, TED GRANT.
WILDCAT
TED NEVER ANSWERED MY LETTERS. HE ACTED LIKE HE DIDN'T EVEN KNOW I EXISTED.
WELL, HE SURE DOES NOW.
EN HE CAME OUT OF THE HOSPITAL, PRESIDENT RICKARD ADE A POINT OF SENDING FOR TED GRANT. THEY SPENT ME HOURS TOGETHER, AND PREZ MADE IT CLEAR THERE S NO ILL WILL.
ALSO HE WENT TO SEE THE WOMAN WHO KILLED HIS WIFE-TO-BE, IN HER CELL, BUT NO RECORD OF THEIR CONVERSATION EXISTS; SAVE IT IS KNOWN THAT HE OFFERED HER CLEMENCY, AND SHE STILL WENT TO THE ELECTRIC CHAIR.
AFTER THAT, THE PRESIDENT SPENT MORE TIME IN THE WHITE HOUSE. HE WAS SEEN LESS, ALTHOUGH HE WAS STILL MUCH BELOVED.

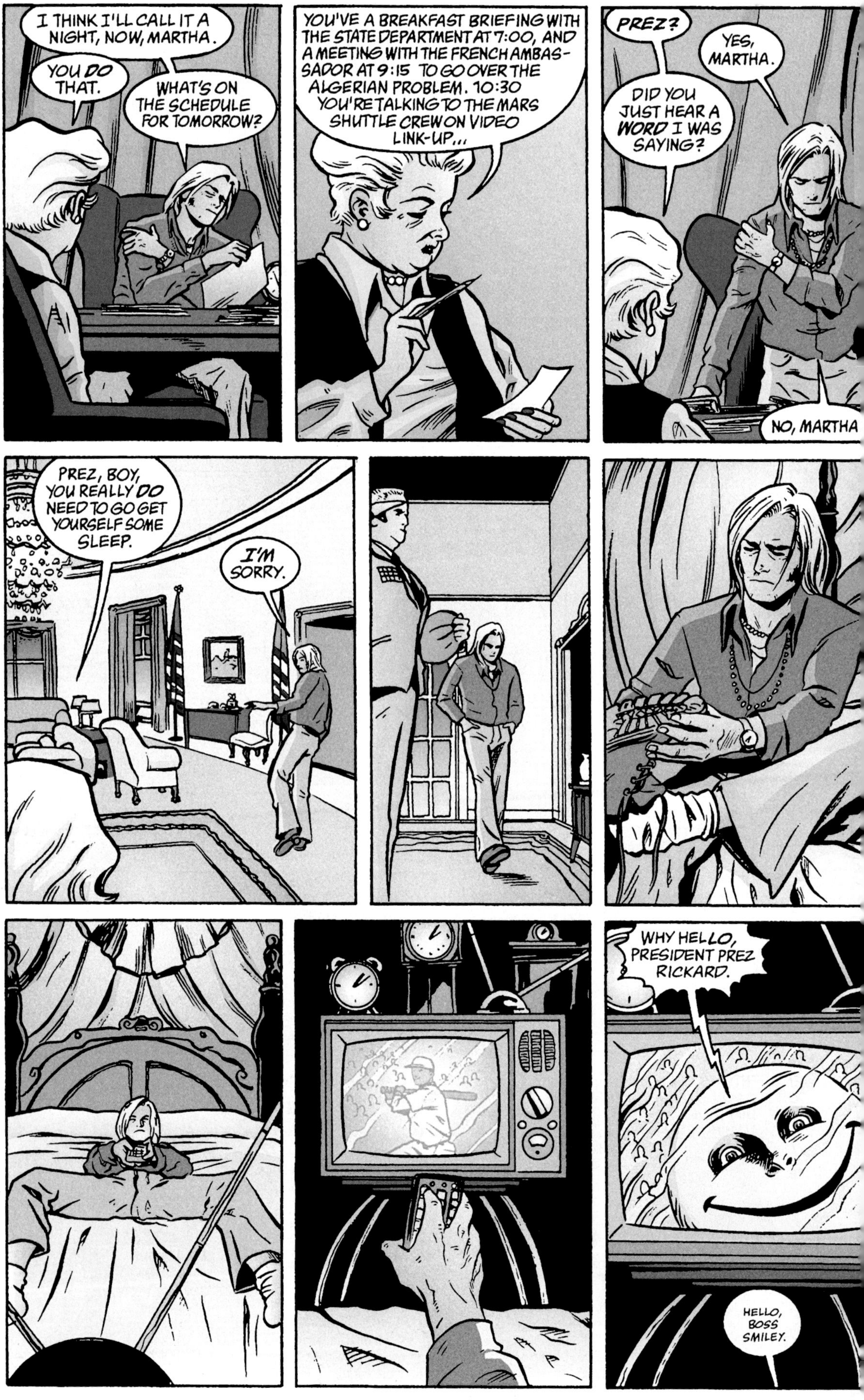
I THINK I'LL CALL IT A NIGHT, NOW, MARTHA.
YOU DO THAT.
WHAT'S ON THE SCHEDULE FOR TOMORROW?
YOU'VE A BREAKFAST BRIEFING WITH THE STATE DEPARTMENT AT 7:00, AND A MEETING WITH THE FRENCH AMBASSADOR AT 9:15 TO GO OVER THE ALGERIAN PROBLEM. 10:30 YOU'RE TALKING TO THE MARS SHUTTLE CREW ON VIDEO LINK-UP...
PREZ?
YES, MARTHA.
DID YOU JUST HEAR A WORD I WAS SAYING?
NO, MARTHA
PREZ, BOY, YOU REALLY DO NEED TO GO GET YOURSELF SOME SLEEP.
I'M SORRY.
WHY HELLO, PRESIDENT PREZ RICKARD.
HELLO, BOSS SMILEY.

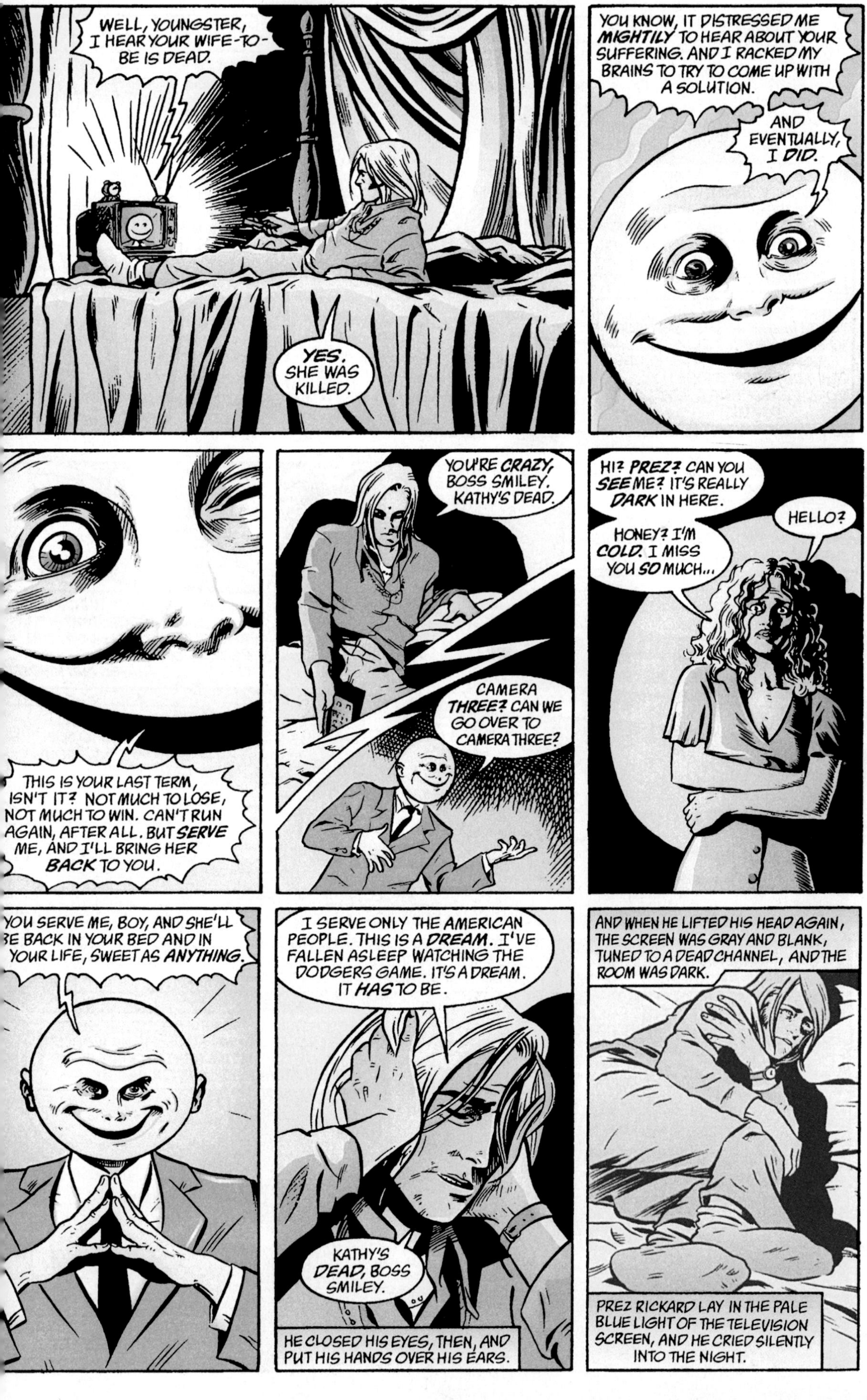
WELL, YOUNGSTER, I HEAR YOUR WIFE-TO-BE IS DEAD.
YES. SHE WAS KILLED.
YOU KNOW, IT DISTRESSED ME MIGHTILY TO HEAR ABOUT YOUR SUFFERING. AND I RACKED MY BRAINS TO TRY TO COME UP WITH A SOLUTION.
AND EVENTUALLY, I DID.
THIS IS YOUR LAST TERM, ISN'T IT? NOT MUCH TO LOSE, NOT MUCH TO WIN. CAN'T RUN AGAIN, AFTER ALL. BUT SERVE ME, AND I'LL BRING HER BACK TO YOU.
YOU'RE CRAZY, BOSS SMILEY. KATHY'S DEAD.
CAMERA THREE? CAN WE GO OVER TO CAMERA THREE?
HI? PREZ? CAN YOU SEE ME? IT'S REALLY DARK IN HERE.
HONEY? I'M COLD. I MISS YOU SO MUCH...
HELLO?
YOU SERVE ME, BOY, AND SHE'LL BE BACK IN YOUR BED AND IN YOUR LIFE, SWEET AS ANYTHING.
I SERVE ONLY THE AMERICAN PEOPLE. THIS IS A DREAM. I'VE FALLEN ASLEEP WATCHING THE DODGERS GAME. IT'S A DREAM. IT HAS TO BE.
KATHY'S DEAD, BOSS SMILEY.
HE CLOSED HIS EYES, THEN, AND PUT HIS HANDS OVER HIS EARS.
AND WHEN HE LIFTED HIS HEAD AGAIN, THE SCREEN WAS GRAY AND BLANK, TUNED TO A DEAD CHANNEL, AND THE ROOM WAS DARK.
PREZ RICKARD LAY IN THE PALE BLUE LIGHT OF THE TELEVISION SCREEN, AND HE CRIED SILENTLY INTO THE NIGHT.

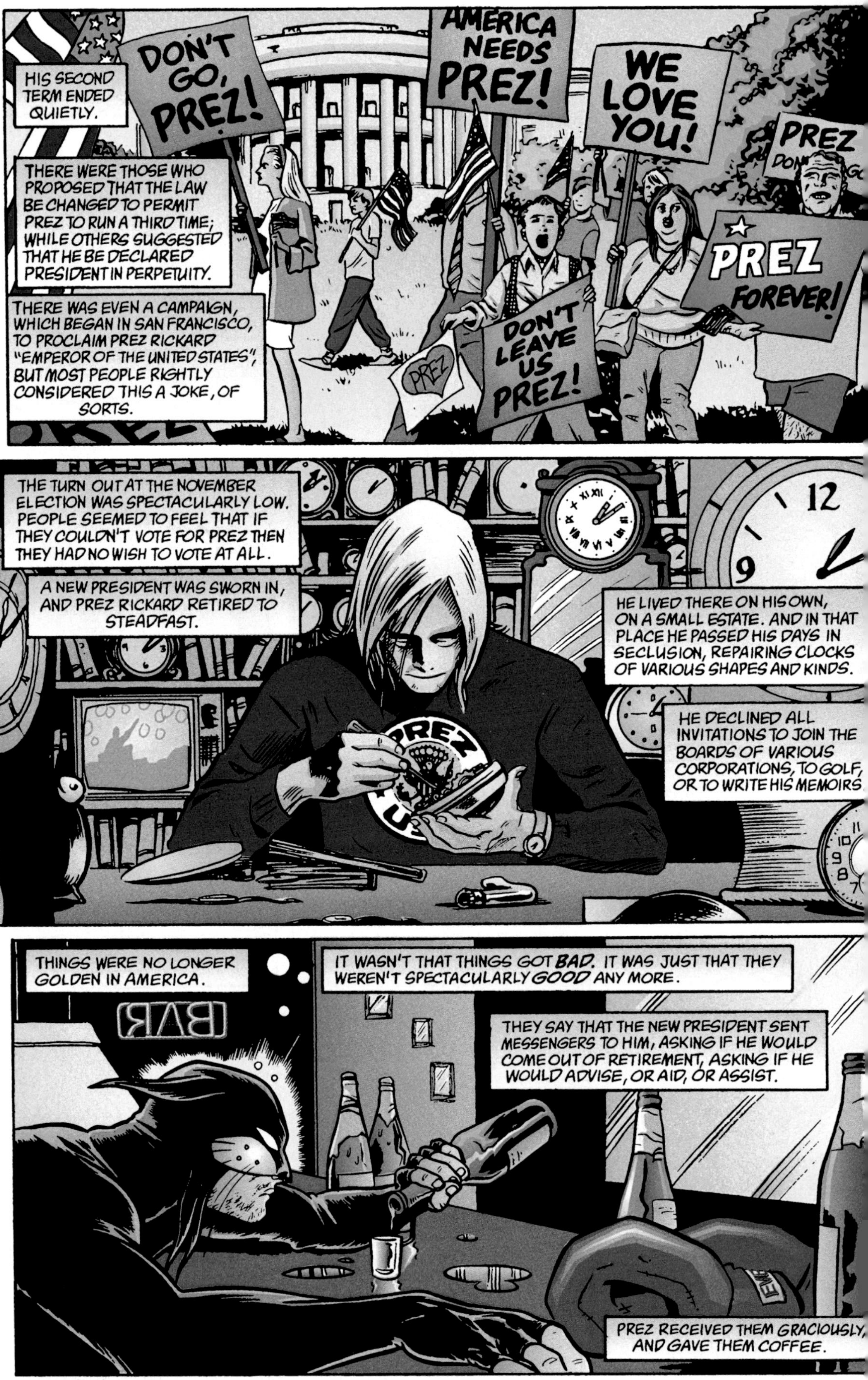
HIS SECOND TERM ENDED QUIETLY.
DON'T GO, PREZ!
AMERICA NEEDS PREZ!
WE LOVE YOU!
PREZ
THERE WERE THOSE WHO PROPOSED THAT THE LAW BE CHANGED TO PERMIT PREZ TO RUN A THIRD TIME; WHILE OTHERS SUGGESTED THAT HE BE DECLARED PRESIDENT IN PERPETUITY.
PREZ FOREVER!
THERE WAS EVEN A CAMPAIGN, WHICH BEGAN IN SAN FRANCISCO, TO PROCLAIM PREZ RICKARD "EMPEROR OF THE UNITED STATES", BUT MOST PEOPLE RIGHTLY CONSIDERED THIS A JOKE, OF SORTS.
PREZ
DON'T LEAVE US PREZ!
THE TURN OUT AT THE NOVEMBER ELECTION WAS SPECTACULARLY LOW. PEOPLE SEEMED TO FEEL THAT IF THEY COULDN'T VOTE FOR PREZ THEN THEY HAD NO WISH TO VOTE AT ALL.
A NEW PRESIDENT WAS SWORN IN, AND PREZ RICKARD RETIRED TO STEADFAST.
HE LIVED THERE ON HIS OWN, ON A SMALL ESTATE. AND IN THAT PLACE HE PASSED HIS DAYS IN SECLUSION, REPAIRING CLOCKS OF VARIOUS SHAPES AND KINDS.
HE DECLINED ALL INVITATIONS TO JOIN THE BOARDS OF VARIOUS CORPORATIONS, TO GOLF, OR TO WRITE HIS MEMOIRS.
THINGS WERE NO LONGER GOLDEN IN AMERICA.
IT WASN'T THAT THINGS GOT *BAD*. IT WAS JUST THAT THEY WEREN'T SPECTACULARLY *GOOD* ANY MORE.
THEY SAY THAT THE NEW PRESIDENT SENT MESSENGERS TO HIM, ASKING IF HE WOULD COME OUT OF RETIREMENT, ASKING IF HE WOULD ADVISE, OR AID, OR ASSIST.
PREZ RECEIVED THEM GRACIOUSLY, AND GAVE THEM COFFEE.

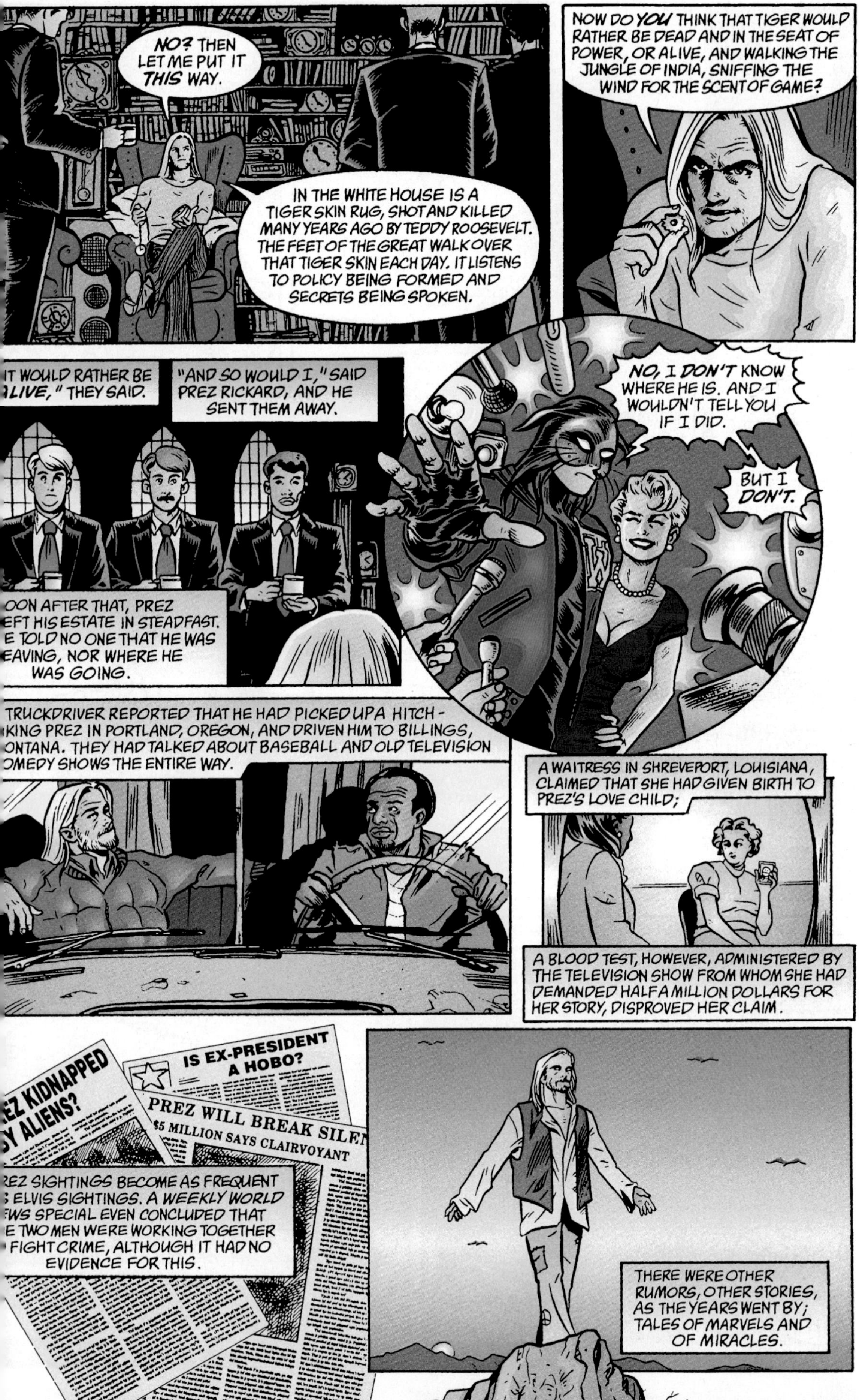
NO? THEN LET ME PUT IT THIS WAY.
IN THE WHITE HOUSE IS A TIGER SKIN RUG, SHOT AND KILLED MANY YEARS AGO BY TEDDY ROOSEVELT. THE FEET OF THE GREAT WALK OVER THAT TIGER SKIN EACH DAY. IT LISTENS TO POLICY BEING FORMED AND SECRETS BEING SPOKEN.
NOW DO YOU THINK THAT TIGER WOULD RATHER BE DEAD AND IN THE SEAT OF POWER, OR ALIVE, AND WALKING THE JUNGLE OF INDIA, SNIFFING THE WIND FOR THE SCENT OF GAME?
IT WOULD RATHER BE ALIVE," THEY SAID.
"AND SO WOULD I," SAID PREZ RICKARD, AND HE SENT THEM AWAY.
OON AFTER THAT, PREZ EFT HIS ESTATE IN STEADFAST. E TOLD NO ONE THAT HE WAS EAVING, NOR WHERE HE WAS GOING.
NO, I DON'T KNOW WHERE HE IS. AND I WOULDN'T TELL YOU IF I DID.
BUT I DON'T.
TRUCKDRIVER REPORTED THAT HE HAD PICKED UP A HITCH-KING PREZ IN PORTLAND, OREGON, AND DRIVEN HIM TO BILLINGS, ONTANA. THEY HAD TALKED ABOUT BASEBALL AND OLD TELEVISION OMEDY SHOWS THE ENTIRE WAY.
A WAITRESS IN SHREVEPORT, LOUISIANA, CLAIMED THAT SHE HAD GIVEN BIRTH TO PREZ'S LOVE CHILD;
A BLOOD TEST, HOWEVER, ADMINISTERED BY THE TELEVISION SHOW FROM WHOM SHE HAD DEMANDED HALF A MILLION DOLLARS FOR HER STORY, DISPROVED HER CLAIM.
EZ KIDNAPPED Y ALIENS?
IS EX-PRESIDENT A HOBO?
PREZ WILL BREAK SILE
$5 MILLION SAYS CLAIRVOYANT
REZ SIGHTINGS BECOME AS FREQUENT S ELVIS SIGHTINGS. A WEEKLY WORLD EWS SPECIAL EVEN CONCLUDED THAT E TWO MEN WERE WORKING TOGETHER FIGHT CRIME, ALTHOUGH IT HAD NO EVIDENCE FOR THIS.
THERE WERE OTHER RUMORS, OTHER STORIES, AS THE YEARS WENT BY; TALES OF MARVELS AND OF MIRACLES.

ONE DAY, PREZ DIED.

THE STORIES OF THE DEATH OF PREZ RICKARD WERE AS STRANGE AND CONTRADICTORY AS THE STORIES OF HIS LATTER DAYS.

SOME SAID HE WAS KILLED DURING A HOLD-UP IN A CHICAGO BAKERY--A HOLD-UP NOT FOR MONEY, BUT FOR WARM BREAD TO FEED THE STARVING CHILDREN IN THE SNOW OUTSIDE.

SOME PEOPLE SAID THE WOMAN WHO KILLED HIS KATHY RETURNED TO FINISH OFF THE TASK SHE HAD BEGUN YEARS BEFORE.

AND THESE PEOPLE KNEW THAT THE KILLER HAD IN HER TURN BEEN EXECUTED BUT STILL, THEY SAID, IT WAS HER.

OTHERS SAID THAT THE CURRENT PRESIDENT ORDERED HIS DEATH.

ANOTHER TALE, CURRENT AT THE TIME, WAS THAT ONE NIGHT HE HAD RETURNED TO HIS HOME IN STEADFAST, AFTER AN ABSENCE OF OVER FIVE YEARS, AND WAS SHOT BY THE SECRET SERVICE MEN WHO STILL GUARDED HIS HOUSE, AND WHO HAD FAILED TO RECOGNIZE HIM.

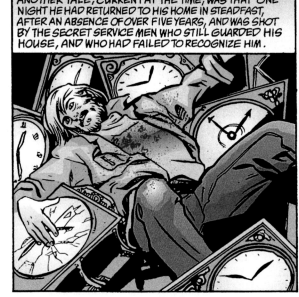

MANY SAID THEY HAD DREAMED OF PREZ, A VICTIM OF PNEUMONIA AND STARVATION, ANONYMOUSLY JOHN DOE-ING HIS WAY TO THE MORGUE AND FROM THERE TO THE CREMATORIUM.

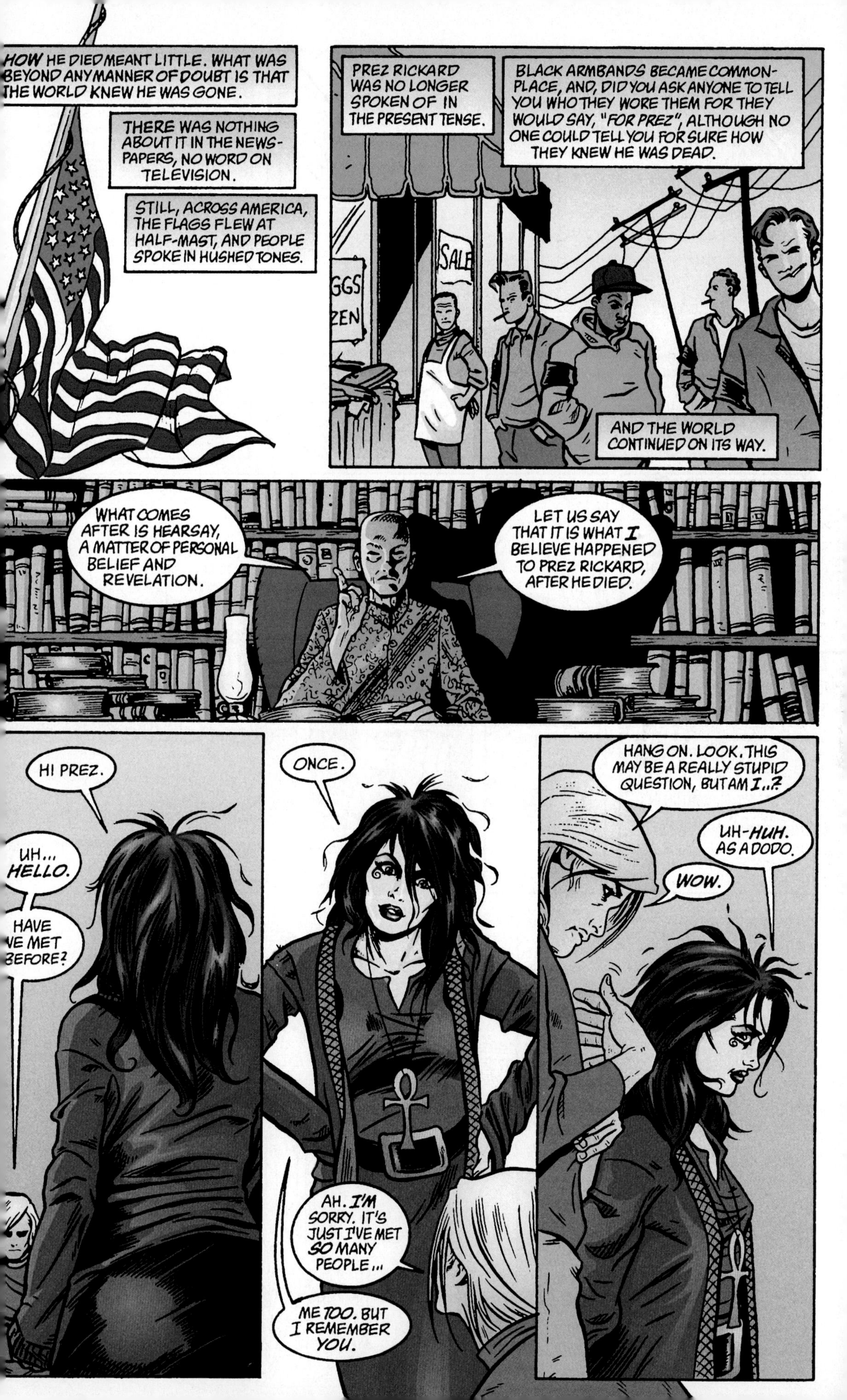
HOW HE DIED MEANT LITTLE. WHAT WAS BEYOND ANY MANNER OF DOUBT IS THAT THE WORLD KNEW HE WAS GONE.
THERE WAS NOTHING ABOUT IT IN THE NEWSPAPERS, NO WORD ON TELEVISION.
STILL, ACROSS AMERICA, THE FLAGS FLEW AT HALF-MAST, AND PEOPLE SPOKE IN HUSHED TONES.
PREZ RICKARD WAS NO LONGER SPOKEN OF IN THE PRESENT TENSE.
BLACK ARMBANDS BECAME COMMONPLACE, AND, DID YOU ASK ANYONE TO TELL YOU WHO THEY WORE THEM FOR THEY WOULD SAY, "FOR PREZ", ALTHOUGH NO ONE COULD TELL YOU FOR SURE HOW THEY KNEW HE WAS DEAD.
SALE
AND THE WORLD CONTINUED ON ITS WAY.
WHAT COMES AFTER IS HEARSAY, A MATTER OF PERSONAL BELIEF AND REVELATION.
LET US SAY THAT IT IS WHAT I BELIEVE HAPPENED TO PREZ RICKARD, AFTER HE DIED.
HI PREZ.
UH... HELLO.
HAVE WE MET BEFORE?
ONCE.
AH. I'M SORRY. IT'S JUST I'VE MET SO MANY PEOPLE...
ME TOO. BUT I REMEMBER YOU.
HANG ON. LOOK. THIS MAY BE A REALLY STUPID QUESTION, BUT AM I...?
UH-HUH. AS A DODO.
WOW.

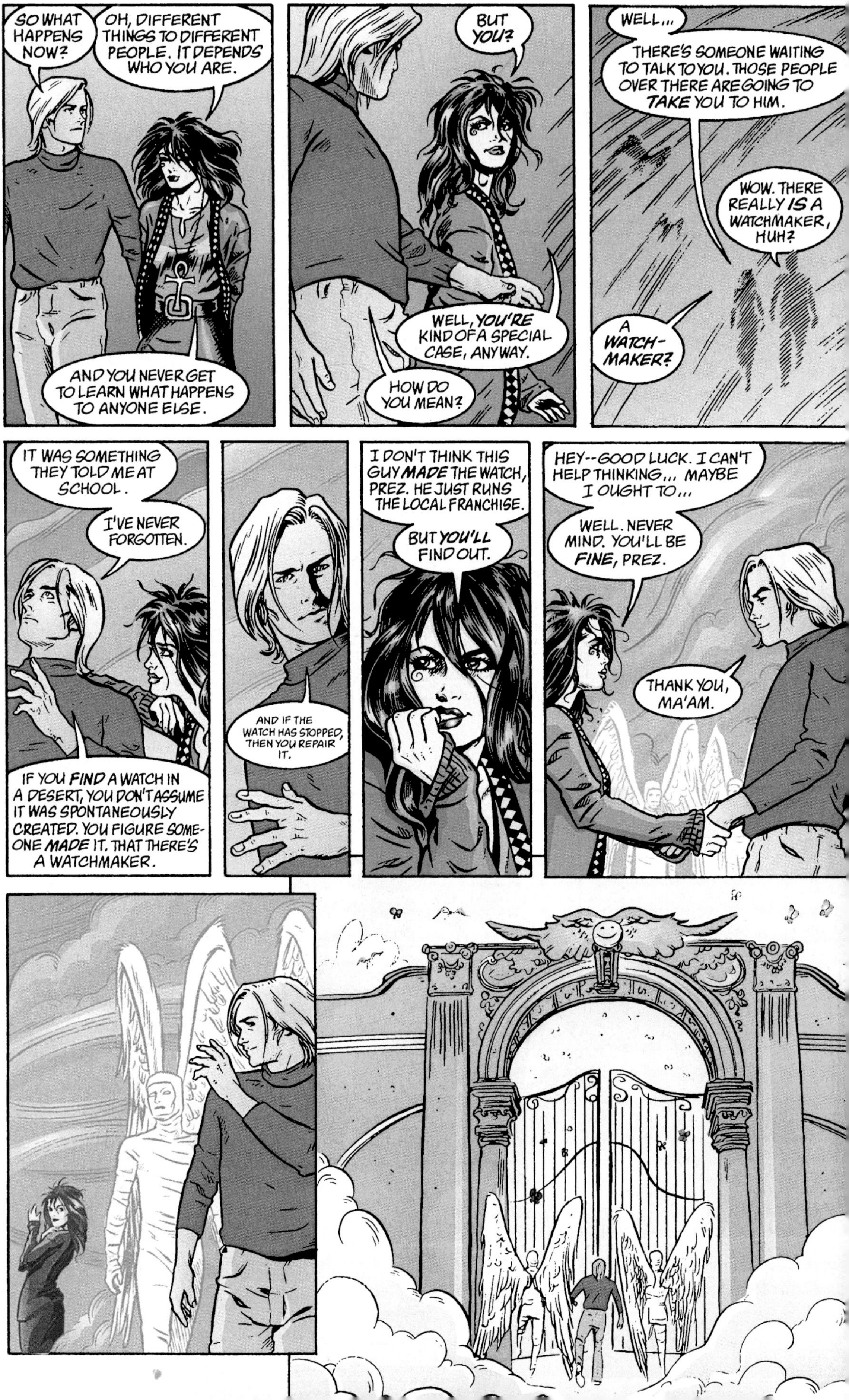
SO WHAT HAPPENS NOW?
OH, DIFFERENT THINGS TO DIFFERENT PEOPLE. IT DEPENDS WHO YOU ARE.
AND YOU NEVER GET TO LEARN WHAT HAPPENS TO ANYONE ELSE.
BUT YOU?
WELL, YOU'RE KIND OF A SPECIAL CASE, ANYWAY.
HOW DO YOU MEAN?
WELL...
THERE'S SOMEONE WAITING TO TALK TO YOU. THOSE PEOPLE OVER THERE ARE GOING TO TAKE YOU TO HIM.
A WATCH-MAKER?
WOW. THERE REALLY IS A WATCHMAKER, HUH?
IT WAS SOMETHING THEY TOLD ME AT SCHOOL.
I'VE NEVER FORGOTTEN.
IF YOU FIND A WATCH IN A DESERT, YOU DON'T ASSUME IT WAS SPONTANEOUSLY CREATED. YOU FIGURE SOME-ONE MADE IT. THAT THERE'S A WATCHMAKER.
AND IF THE WATCH HAS STOPPED, THEN YOU REPAIR IT.
I DON'T THINK THIS GUY MADE THE WATCH, PREZ. HE JUST RUNS THE LOCAL FRANCHISE.
BUT YOU'LL FIND OUT.
HEY--GOOD LUCK. I CAN'T HELP THINKING... MAYBE I OUGHT TO...
WELL. NEVER MIND. YOU'LL BE FINE, PREZ.
THANK YOU, MA'AM.

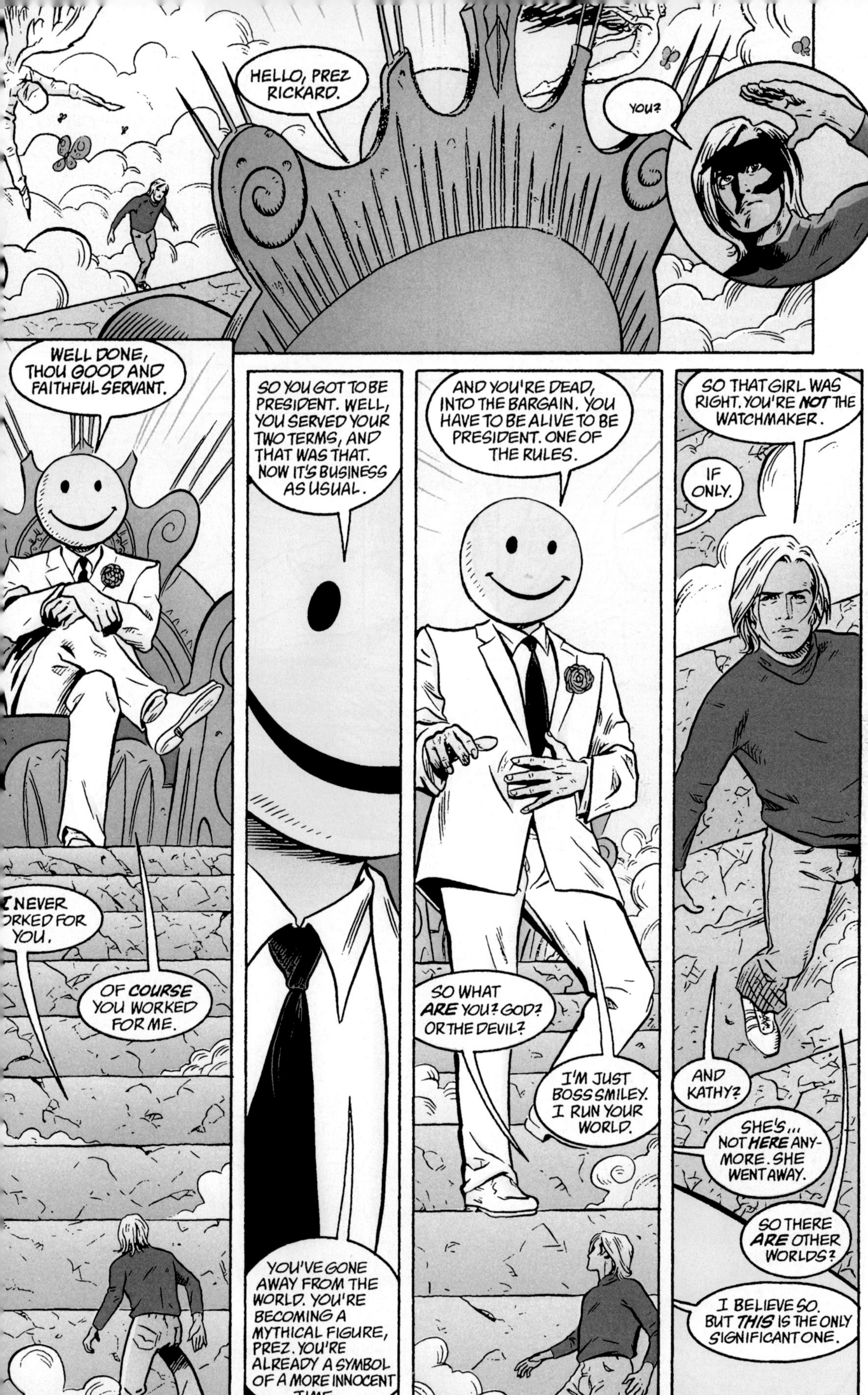
HELLO, PREZ RICKARD.
YOU?
WELL DONE, THOU GOOD AND FAITHFUL SERVANT.
I NEVER WORKED FOR YOU.
OF COURSE YOU WORKED FOR ME.
SO YOU GOT TO BE PRESIDENT. WELL, YOU SERVED YOUR TWO TERMS, AND THAT WAS THAT. NOW IT'S BUSINESS AS USUAL.
YOU'VE GONE AWAY FROM THE WORLD. YOU'RE BECOMING A MYTHICAL FIGURE, PREZ. YOU'RE ALREADY A SYMBOL OF A MORE INNOCENT TIME.
AND YOU'RE DEAD, INTO THE BARGAIN. YOU HAVE TO BE ALIVE TO BE PRESIDENT. ONE OF THE RULES.
SO WHAT ARE YOU? GOD? OR THE DEVIL?
I'M JUST BOSS SMILEY. I RUN YOUR WORLD.
SO THAT GIRL WAS RIGHT. YOU'RE NOT THE WATCHMAKER.
IF ONLY.
AND KATHY?
SHE'S... NOT HERE ANY-MORE. SHE WENT AWAY.
SO THERE ARE OTHER WORLDS?
I BELIEVE SO. BUT THIS IS THE ONLY SIGNIFICANT ONE.

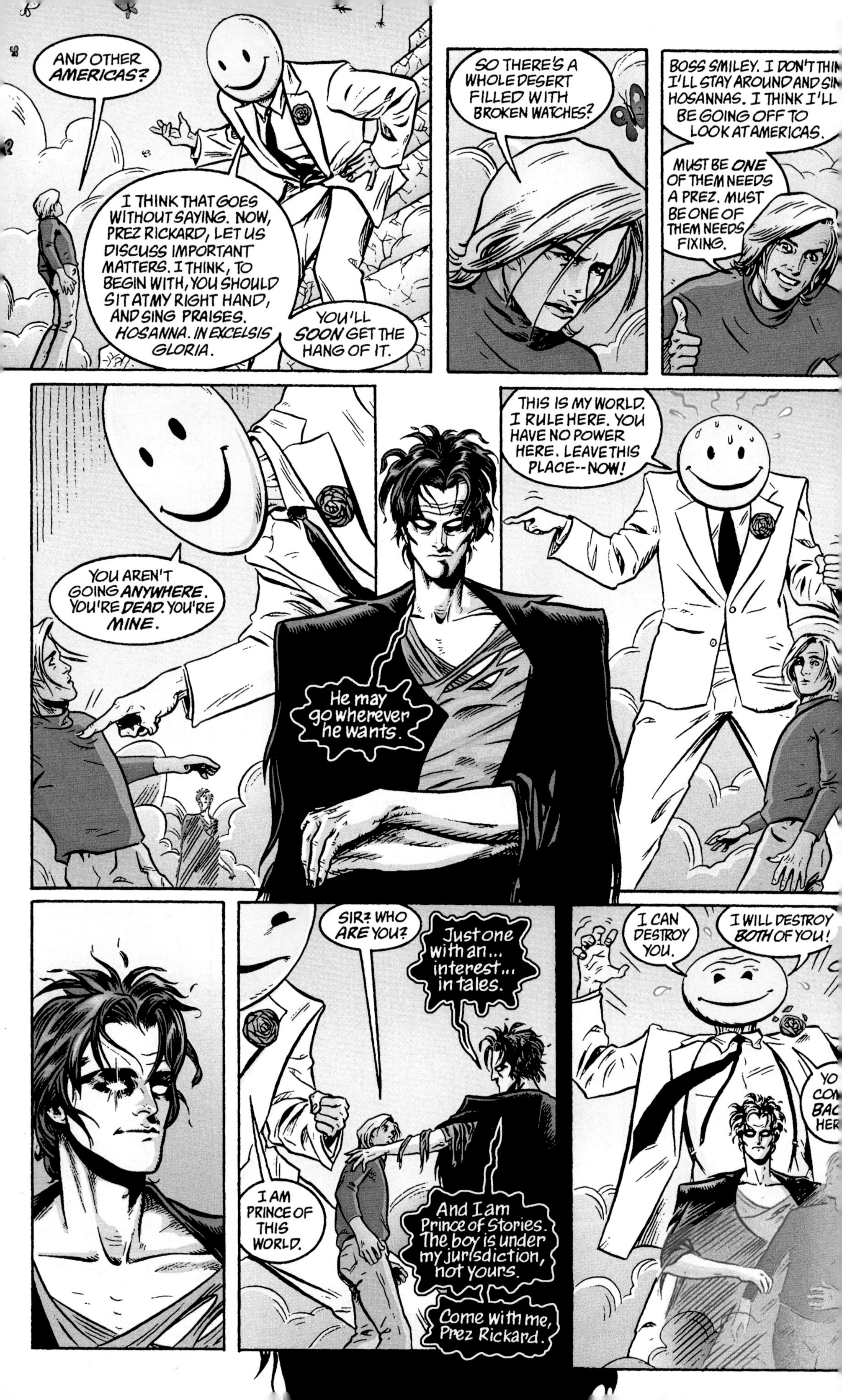
AND OTHER AMERICAS?
I THINK THAT GOES WITHOUT SAYING. NOW, PREZ RICKARD, LET US DISCUSS IMPORTANT MATTERS. I THINK, TO BEGIN WITH, YOU SHOULD SIT AT MY RIGHT HAND, AND SING PRAISES. HOSANNA. IN EXCELSIS GLORIA.
YOU'LL SOON GET THE HANG OF IT.
SO THERE'S A WHOLE DESERT FILLED WITH BROKEN WATCHES?
BOSS SMILEY. I DON'T THI I'LL STAY AROUND AND SIN HOSANNAS. I THINK I'LL BE GOING OFF TO LOOK AT AMERICAS.
MUST BE ONE OF THEM NEEDS A PREZ. MUST BE ONE OF THEM NEEDS FIXING.
YOU AREN'T GOING ANYWHERE. YOU'RE DEAD. YOU'RE MINE.
He may go wherever he wants.
THIS IS MY WORLD. I RULE HERE. YOU HAVE NO POWER HERE. LEAVE THIS PLACE--NOW!
SIR? WHO ARE YOU?
Just one with an... interest... in tales.
I AM PRINCE OF THIS WORLD.
And I am Prince of Stories. The boy is under my jurisdiction, not yours.
Come with me, Prez Rickard.
I CAN DESTROY YOU.
I WILL DESTROY BOTH OF YOU!

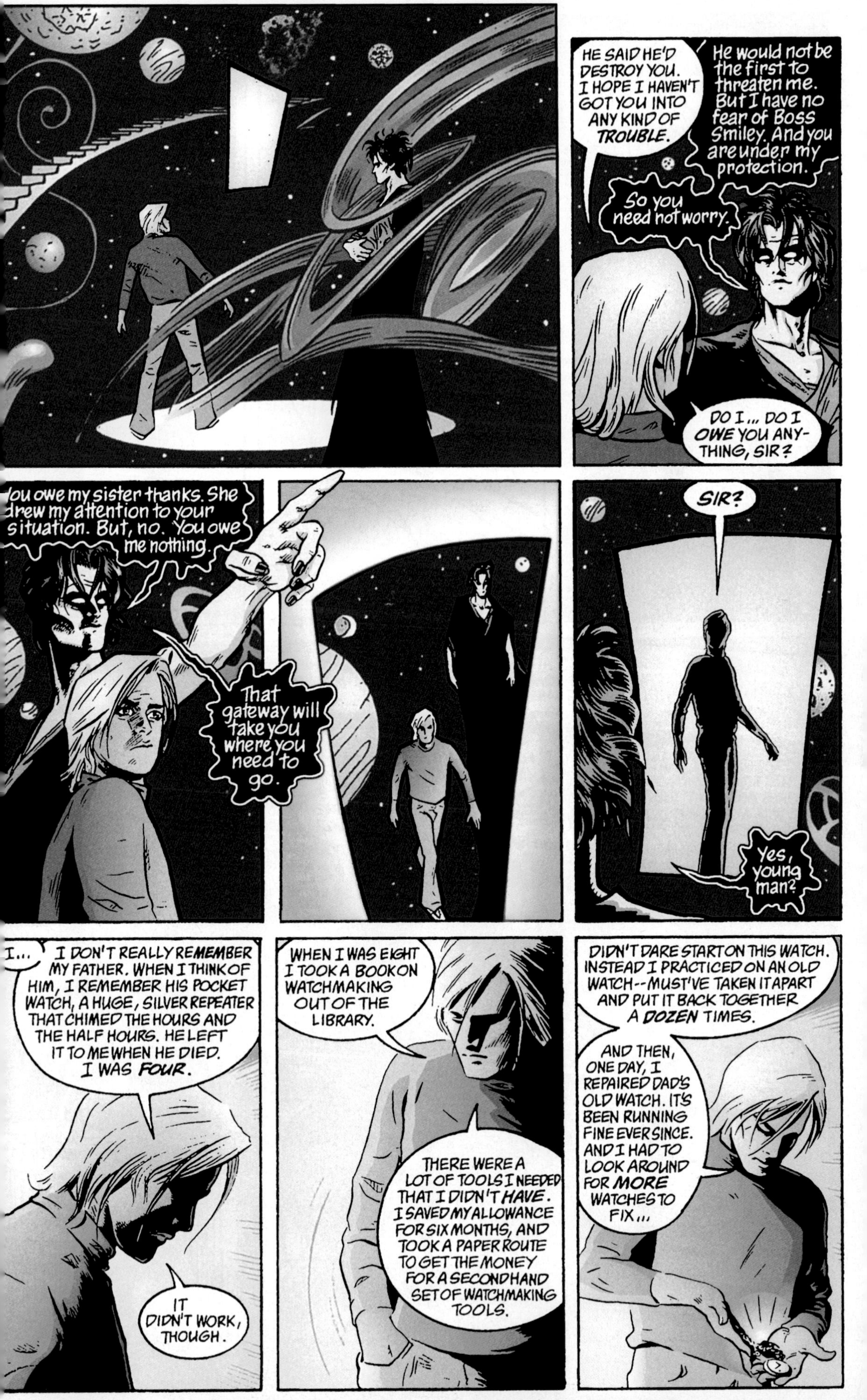

HE SAID HE'D DESTROY YOU. I HOPE I HAVEN'T GOT YOU INTO ANY KIND OF TROUBLE.
He would not be the first to threaten me. But I have no fear of Boss Smiley. And you are under my protection.
So you need not worry.
DO I... DO I OWE YOU ANYTHING, SIR?
You owe my sister thanks. She drew my attention to your situation. But, no. You owe me nothing.
That gateway will take you where you need to go.
SIR?
Yes, young man?
I...
I DON'T REALLY REMEMBER MY FATHER. WHEN I THINK OF HIM, I REMEMBER HIS POCKET WATCH, A HUGE, SILVER REPEATER THAT CHIMED THE HOURS AND THE HALF HOURS. HE LEFT IT TO ME WHEN HE DIED. I WAS FOUR.
IT DIDN'T WORK, THOUGH.
WHEN I WAS EIGHT I TOOK A BOOK ON WATCHMAKING OUT OF THE LIBRARY.
THERE WERE A LOT OF TOOLS I NEEDED THAT I DIDN'T HAVE. I SAVED MY ALLOWANCE FOR SIX MONTHS, AND TOOK A PAPER ROUTE TO GET THE MONEY FOR A SECONDHAND SET OF WATCHMAKING TOOLS.
DIDN'T DARE START ON THIS WATCH. INSTEAD I PRACTICED ON AN OLD WATCH--MUST'VE TAKEN IT APART AND PUT IT BACK TOGETHER A DOZEN TIMES.
AND THEN, ONE DAY, I REPAIRED DAD'S OLD WATCH. IT'S BEEN RUNNING FINE EVER SINCE. AND I HAD TO LOOK AROUND FOR MORE WATCHES TO FIX...

SIR? I WANT *YOU* TO HAVE THIS.

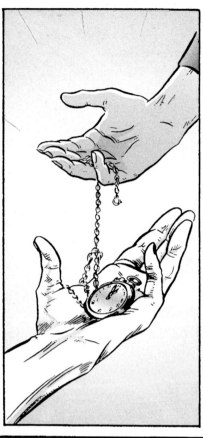

AND PREZ RICKARD WALKED THROUGH DREAM'S DOOR, AWAY FROM BOSS SMILEY'S HEAVEN AND OUT ACROSS THE WORLDS.

"*SOME* SAY THAT HE STILL WALKS BETWEEN THE WORLDS, TRAVELLING FROM AMERICA TO AMERICA, HELP TO THE HELPLESS, A SHELTER FOR THE WEAK."

OTHERS SAY THAT HE WAITS TO BE BORN ONCE MORE, AND THAT THIS TIME HE WILL NOT COME *JUST* TO ONE AMERICA, BUT TO *ALL* OF THEM.

AND *I* WALK THE WORLDS, FOLLOWING HIM, SEEKING HIM, WALKING AHEAD...

SPREADING HIS *WORD*.

AND WHEN HE COMES BACK--

--WHEREVER, *WHEN*EVER HE COMES BACK--

--I WILL BE WAITING.

GOODNIGHT

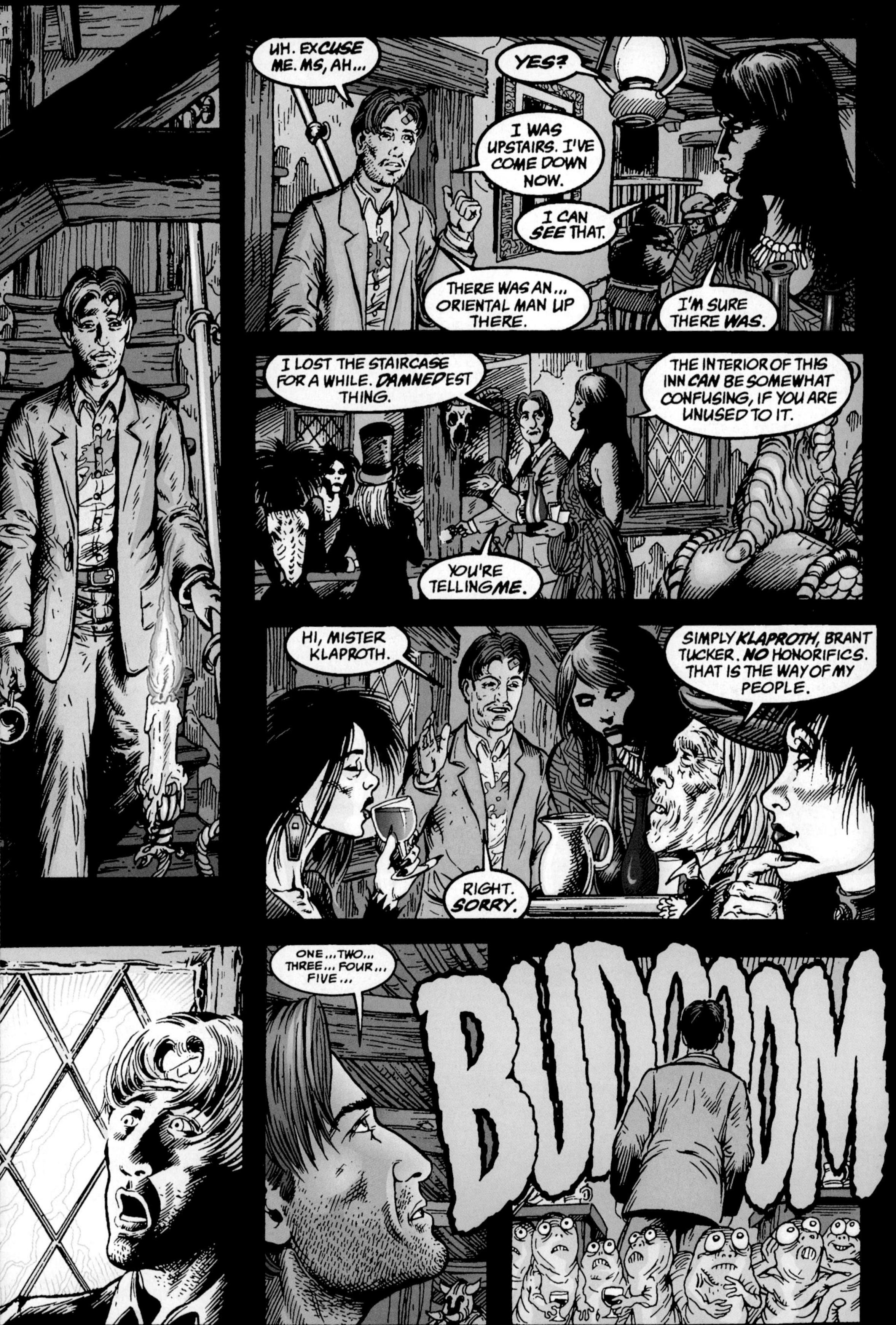
UH. EXCUSE ME. MS, AH...
YES?
I WAS UPSTAIRS. I'VE COME DOWN NOW.
I CAN SEE THAT.
THERE WAS AN... ORIENTAL MAN UP THERE.
I'M SURE THERE WAS.
I LOST THE STAIRCASE FOR A WHILE. DAMNEDEST THING.
THE INTERIOR OF THIS INN CAN BE SOMEWHAT CONFUSING, IF YOU ARE UNUSED TO IT.
YOU'RE TELLING ME.
HI, MISTER KLAPROTH.
SIMPLY KLAPROTH, BRANT TUCKER. NO HONORIFICS. THAT IS THE WAY OF MY PEOPLE.
RIGHT. SORRY.
ONE... TWO... THREE... FOUR... FIVE...
BUDOOOM

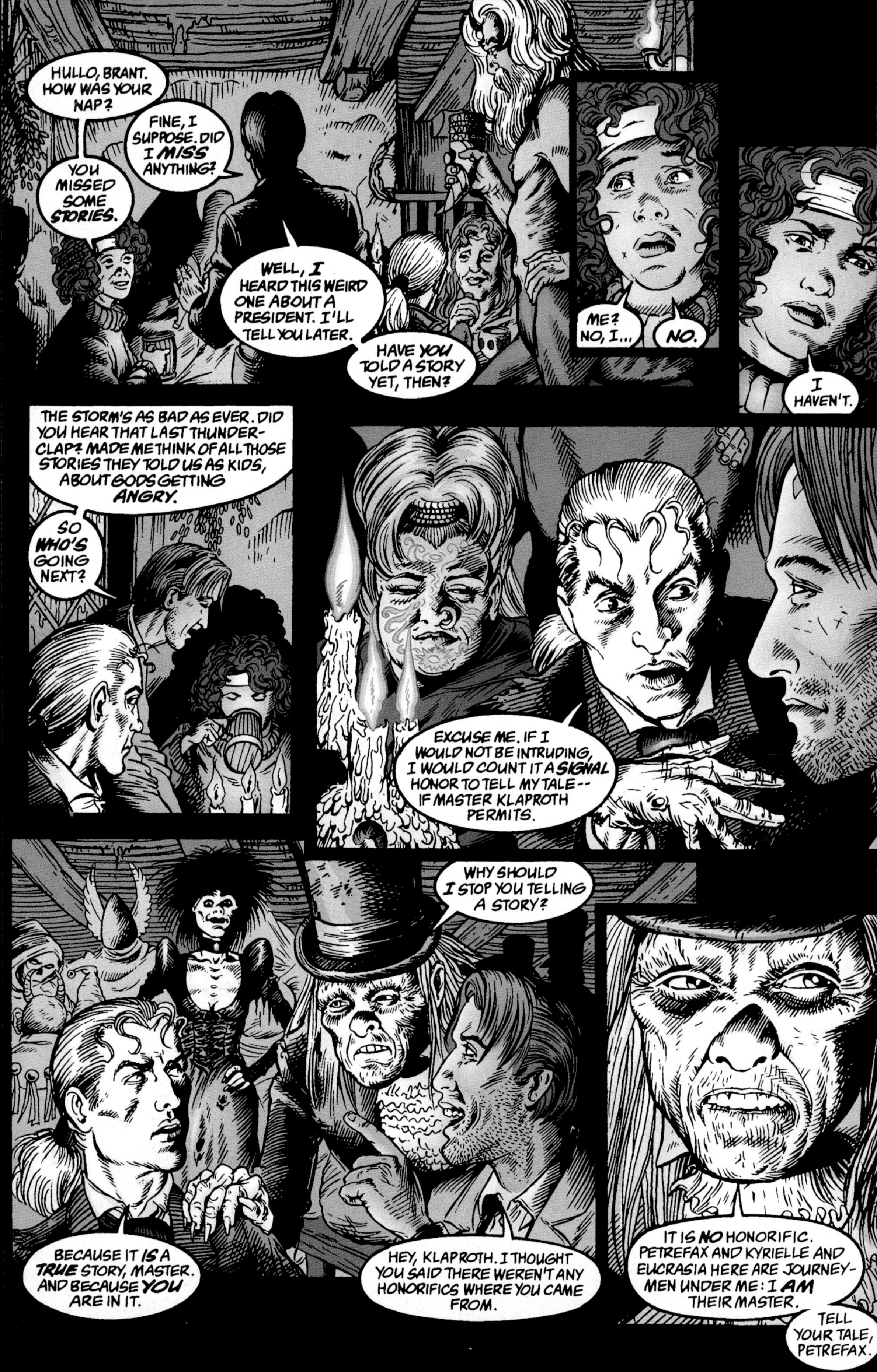
HULLO, BRANT. HOW WAS YOUR NAP?
FINE, I SUPPOSE. DID I MISS ANYTHING?
YOU MISSED SOME STORIES.
WELL, I HEARD THIS WEIRD ONE ABOUT A PRESIDENT. I'LL TELL YOU LATER.
HAVE YOU TOLD A STORY YET, THEN?
ME? NO, I...
NO.
I HAVEN'T.
THE STORM'S AS BAD AS EVER. DID YOU HEAR THAT LAST THUNDER-CLAP? MADE ME THINK OF ALL THOSE STORIES THEY TOLD US AS KIDS, ABOUT GODS GETTING ANGRY.
SO WHO'S GOING NEXT?
EXCUSE ME. IF I WOULD NOT BE INTRUDING, I WOULD COUNT IT A SIGNAL HONOR TO TELL MY TALE-- IF MASTER KLAPROTH PERMITS.
WHY SHOULD I STOP YOU TELLING A STORY?
BECAUSE IT IS A TRUE STORY, MASTER. AND BECAUSE YOU ARE IN IT.
HEY, KLAPROTH. I THOUGHT YOU SAID THERE WEREN'T ANY HONORIFICS WHERE YOU CAME FROM.
IT IS NO HONORIFIC. PETREFAX AND KYRIELLE AND EUCRASIA HERE ARE JOURNEY-MEN UNDER ME: I AM THEIR MASTER.
TELL YOUR TALE, PETREFAX.

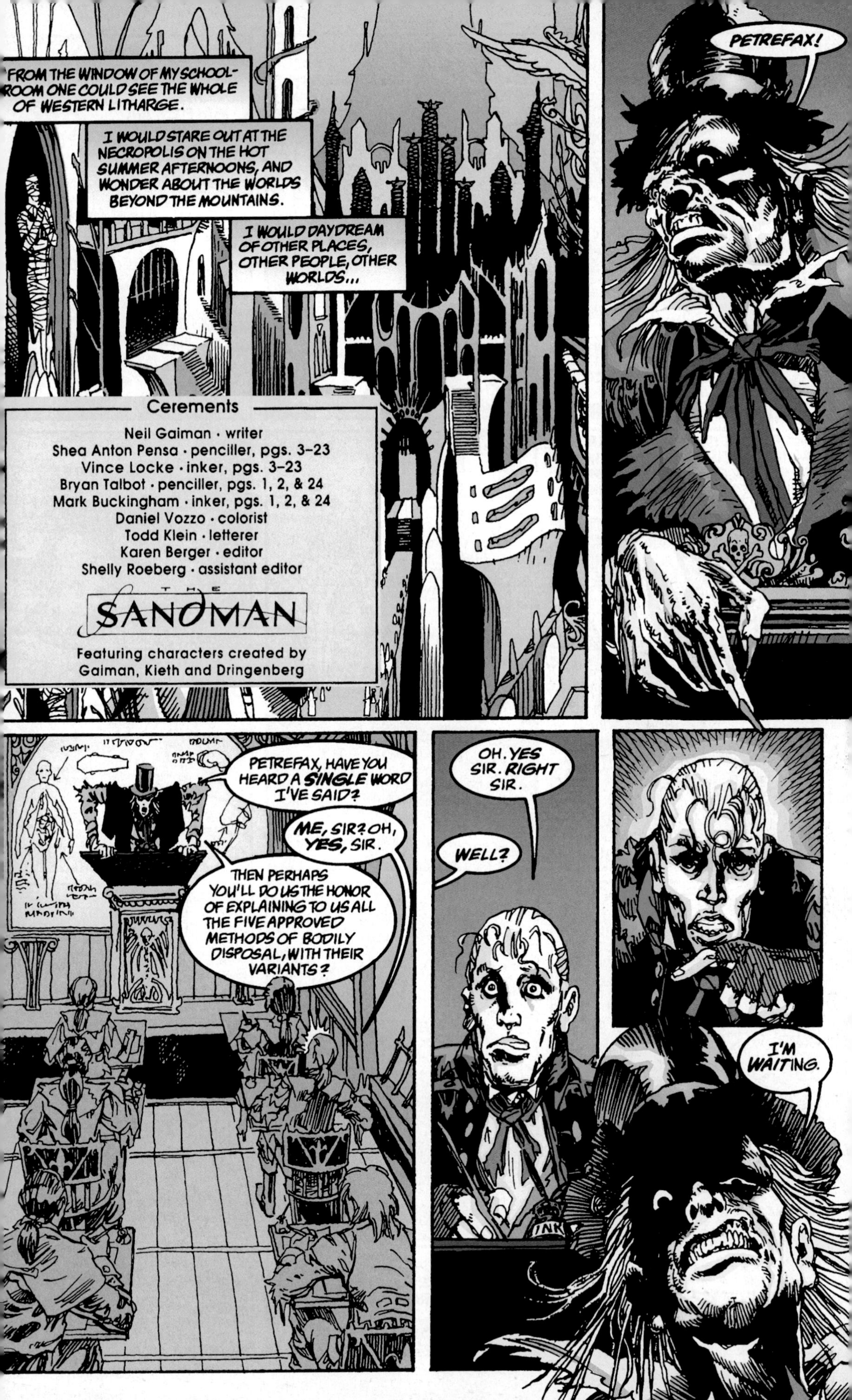
FROM THE WINDOW OF MY SCHOOLROOM ONE COULD SEE THE WHOLE OF WESTERN LITHARGE.
I WOULD STARE OUT AT THE NECROPOLIS ON THE HOT SUMMER AFTERNOONS, AND WONDER ABOUT THE WORLDS BEYOND THE MOUNTAINS.
I WOULD DAYDREAM OF OTHER PLACES, OTHER PEOPLE, OTHER WORLDS...
Cerements
Neil Gaiman · writer
Shea Anton Pensa · penciller, pgs. 3–23
Vince Locke · inker, pgs. 3–23
Bryan Talbot · penciller, pgs. 1, 2, & 24
Mark Buckingham · inker, pgs. 1, 2, & 24
Daniel Vozzo · colorist
Todd Klein · letterer
Karen Berger · editor
Shelly Roeberg · assistant editor
THE SANDMAN
Featuring characters created by Gaiman, Kieth and Dringenberg
PETREFAX!
PETREFAX, HAVE YOU HEARD A SINGLE WORD I'VE SAID?
ME, SIR? OH, YES, SIR.
THEN PERHAPS YOU'LL DO US THE HONOR OF EXPLAINING TO US ALL THE FIVE APPROVED METHODS OF BODILY DISPOSAL, WITH THEIR VARIANTS?
OH. YES SIR. RIGHT SIR.
WELL?
INK
I'M WAITING.

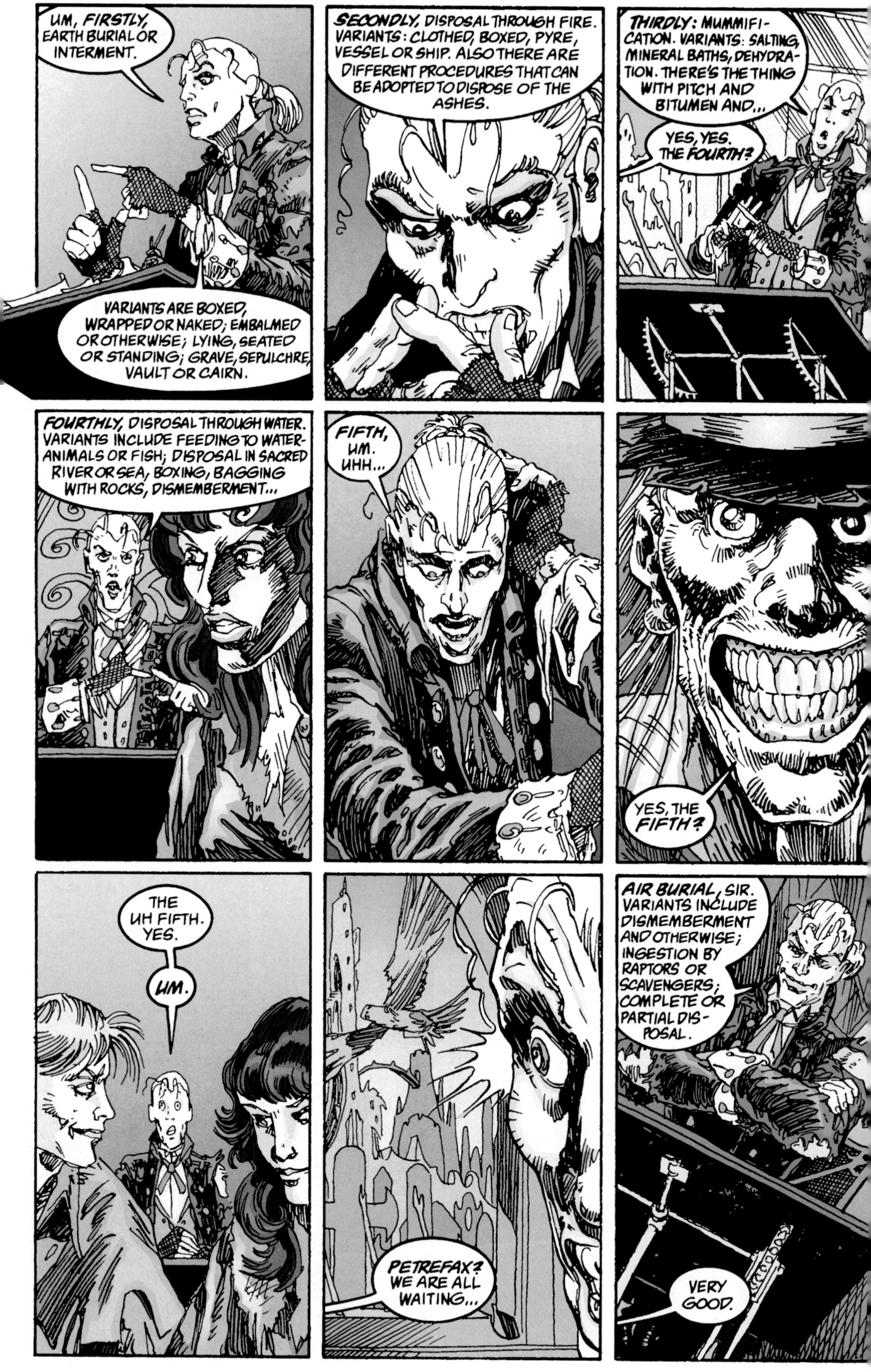
UM, FIRSTLY, EARTH BURIAL OR INTERMENT.
VARIANTS ARE BOXED, WRAPPED OR NAKED; EMBALMED OR OTHERWISE; LYING, SEATED OR STANDING; GRAVE, SEPULCHRE, VAULT OR CAIRN.
SECONDLY, DISPOSAL THROUGH FIRE. VARIANTS: CLOTHED, BOXED, PYRE, VESSEL OR SHIP. ALSO THERE ARE DIFFERENT PROCEDURES THAT CAN BE ADOPTED TO DISPOSE OF THE ASHES.
THIRDLY: MUMMIFICATION. VARIANTS: SALTING, MINERAL BATHS, DEHYDRATION. THERE'S THE THING WITH PITCH AND BITUMEN AND...
YES, YES. THE FOURTH?
FOURTHLY, DISPOSAL THROUGH WATER. VARIANTS INCLUDE FEEDING TO WATER-ANIMALS OR FISH; DISPOSAL IN SACRED RIVER OR SEA, BOXING, BAGGING WITH ROCKS, DISMEMBERMENT...
FIFTH, UM. UHH...
YES, THE FIFTH?
THE UH FIFTH. YES.
UM.
PETREFAX? WE ARE ALL WAITING...
AIR BURIAL, SIR. VARIANTS INCLUDE DISMEMBERMENT AND OTHERWISE; INGESTION BY RAPTORS OR SCAVENGERS; COMPLETE OR PARTIAL DISPOSAL.
VERY GOOD.

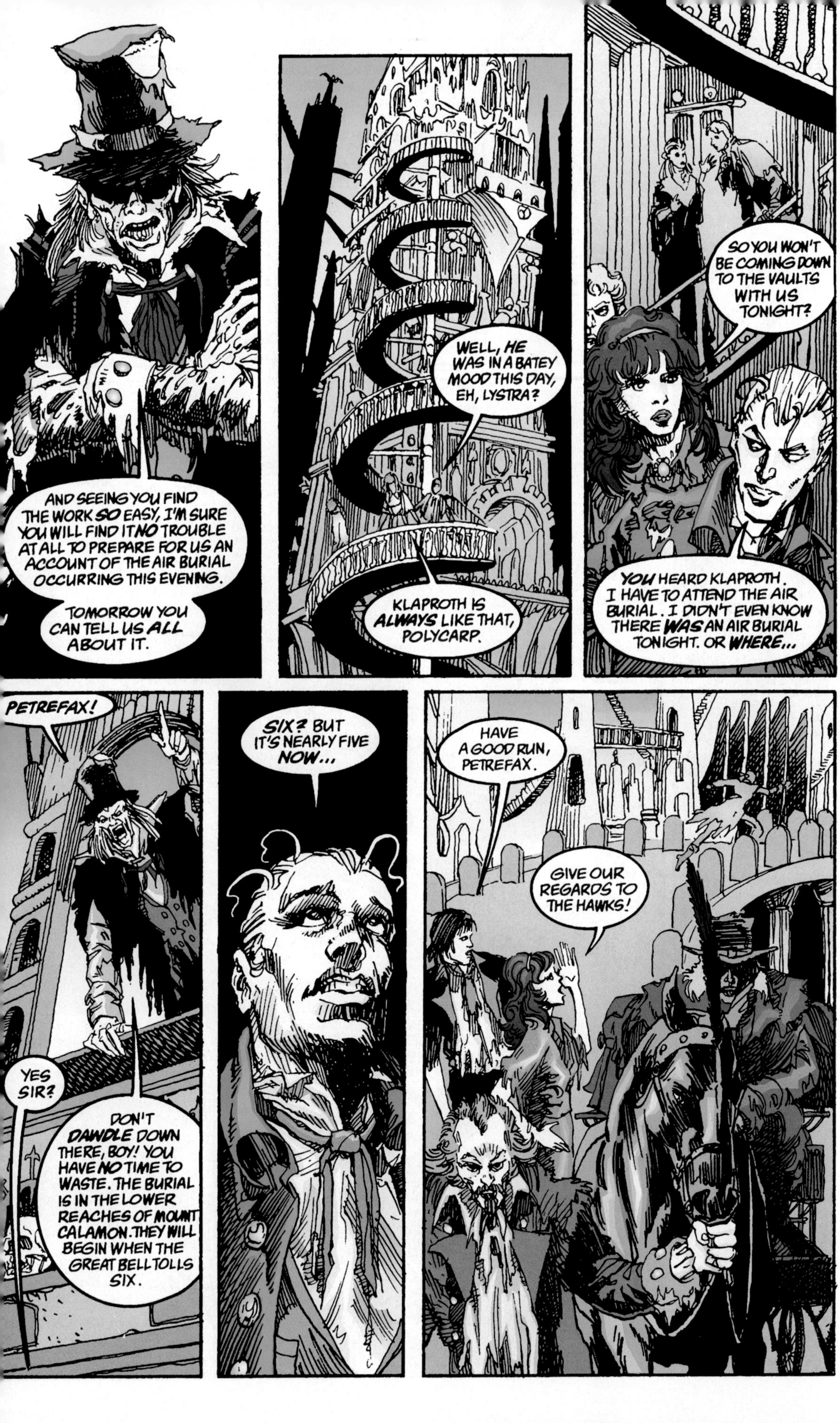
AND SEEING YOU FIND THE WORK SO EASY, I'M SURE YOU WILL FIND IT NO TROUBLE AT ALL TO PREPARE FOR US AN ACCOUNT OF THE AIR BURIAL OCCURRING THIS EVENING.
TOMORROW YOU CAN TELL US ALL ABOUT IT.
WELL, HE WAS IN A BATEY MOOD THIS DAY, EH, LYSTRA?
KLAPROTH IS ALWAYS LIKE THAT, POLYCARP.
SO YOU WON'T BE COMING DOWN TO THE VAULTS WITH US TONIGHT?
YOU HEARD KLAPROTH. I HAVE TO ATTEND THE AIR BURIAL. I DIDN'T EVEN KNOW THERE WAS AN AIR BURIAL TONIGHT. OR WHERE...
PETREFAX!
YES SIR?
DON'T DAWDLE DOWN THERE, BOY! YOU HAVE NO TIME TO WASTE. THE BURIAL IS IN THE LOWER REACHES OF MOUNT CALAMON. THEY WILL BEGIN WHEN THE GREAT BELL TOLLS SIX.
SIX? BUT IT'S NEARLY FIVE NOW...
HAVE A GOOD RUN, PETREFAX.
GIVE OUR REGARDS TO THE HAWKS!

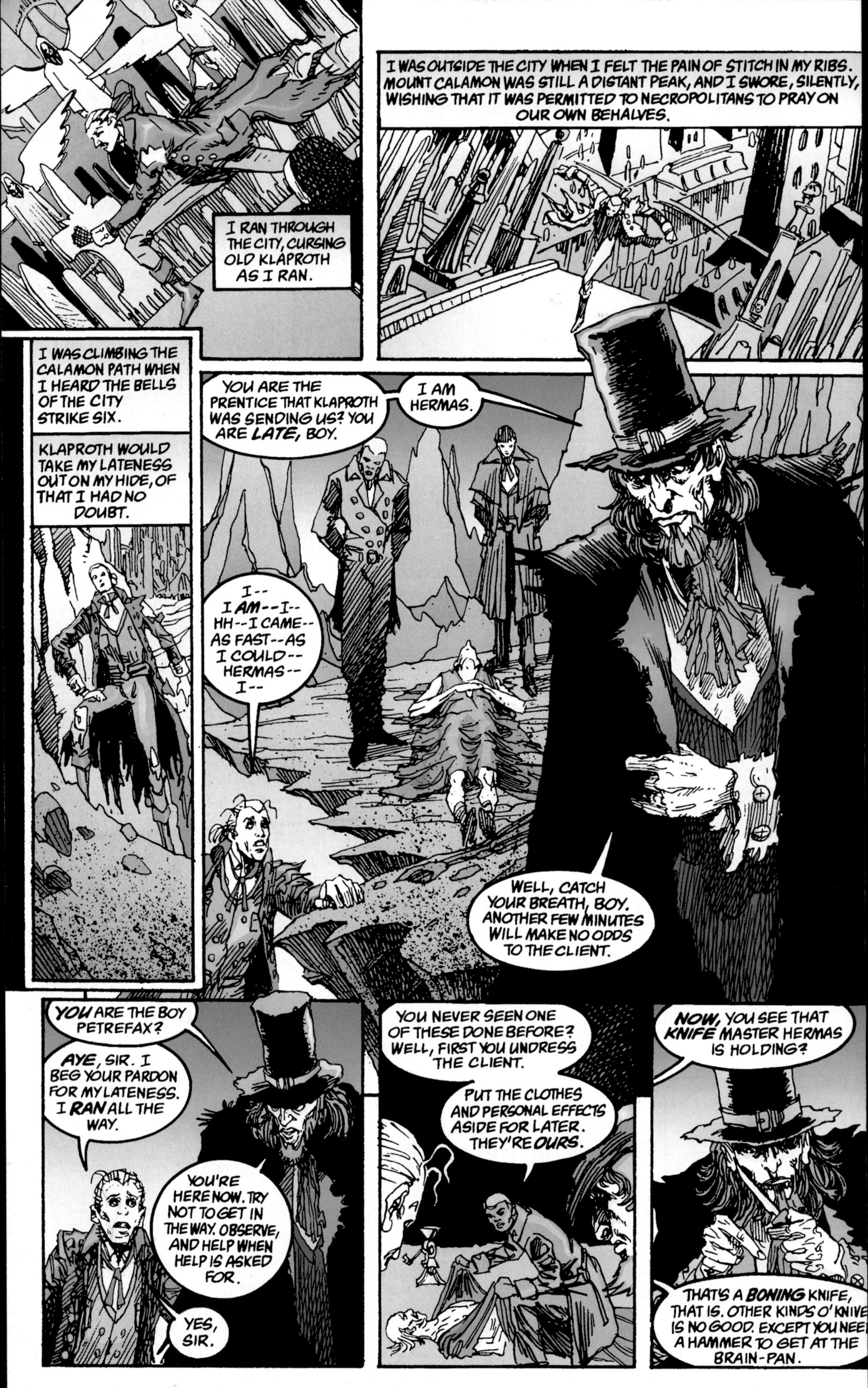
I RAN THROUGH THE CITY, CURSING OLD KLAPROTH AS I RAN.
I WAS OUTSIDE THE CITY WHEN I FELT THE PAIN OF STITCH IN MY RIBS. MOUNT CALAMON WAS STILL A DISTANT PEAK, AND I SWORE, SILENTLY, WISHING THAT IT WAS PERMITTED TO NECROPOLITANS TO PRAY ON OUR OWN BEHALVES.
I WAS CLIMBING THE CALAMON PATH WHEN I HEARD THE BELLS OF THE CITY STRIKE SIX.
KLAPROTH WOULD TAKE MY LATENESS OUT ON MY HIDE, OF THAT I HAD NO DOUBT.
YOU ARE THE PRENTICE THAT KLAPROTH WAS SENDING US? YOU ARE LATE, BOY.
I AM HERMAS.
I-- I AM--I-- HH--I CAME-- AS FAST--AS I COULD-- HERMAS-- I--
WELL, CATCH YOUR BREATH, BOY. ANOTHER FEW MINUTES WILL MAKE NO ODDS TO THE CLIENT.
YOU ARE THE BOY PETREFAX?
AYE, SIR. I BEG YOUR PARDON FOR MY LATENESS. I RAN ALL THE WAY.
YOU'RE HERE NOW. TRY NOT TO GET IN THE WAY. OBSERVE, AND HELP WHEN HELP IS ASKED FOR.
YES, SIR.
YOU NEVER SEEN ONE OF THESE DONE BEFORE? WELL, FIRST YOU UNDRESS THE CLIENT.
PUT THE CLOTHES AND PERSONAL EFFECTS ASIDE FOR LATER. THEY'RE OURS.
NOW, YOU SEE THAT KNIFE MASTER HERMAS IS HOLDING?
THAT'S A BONING KNIFE, THAT IS. OTHER KINDS O' KNIVE IS NO GOOD. EXCEPT YOU NEE A HAMMER TO GET AT THE BRAIN-PAN.

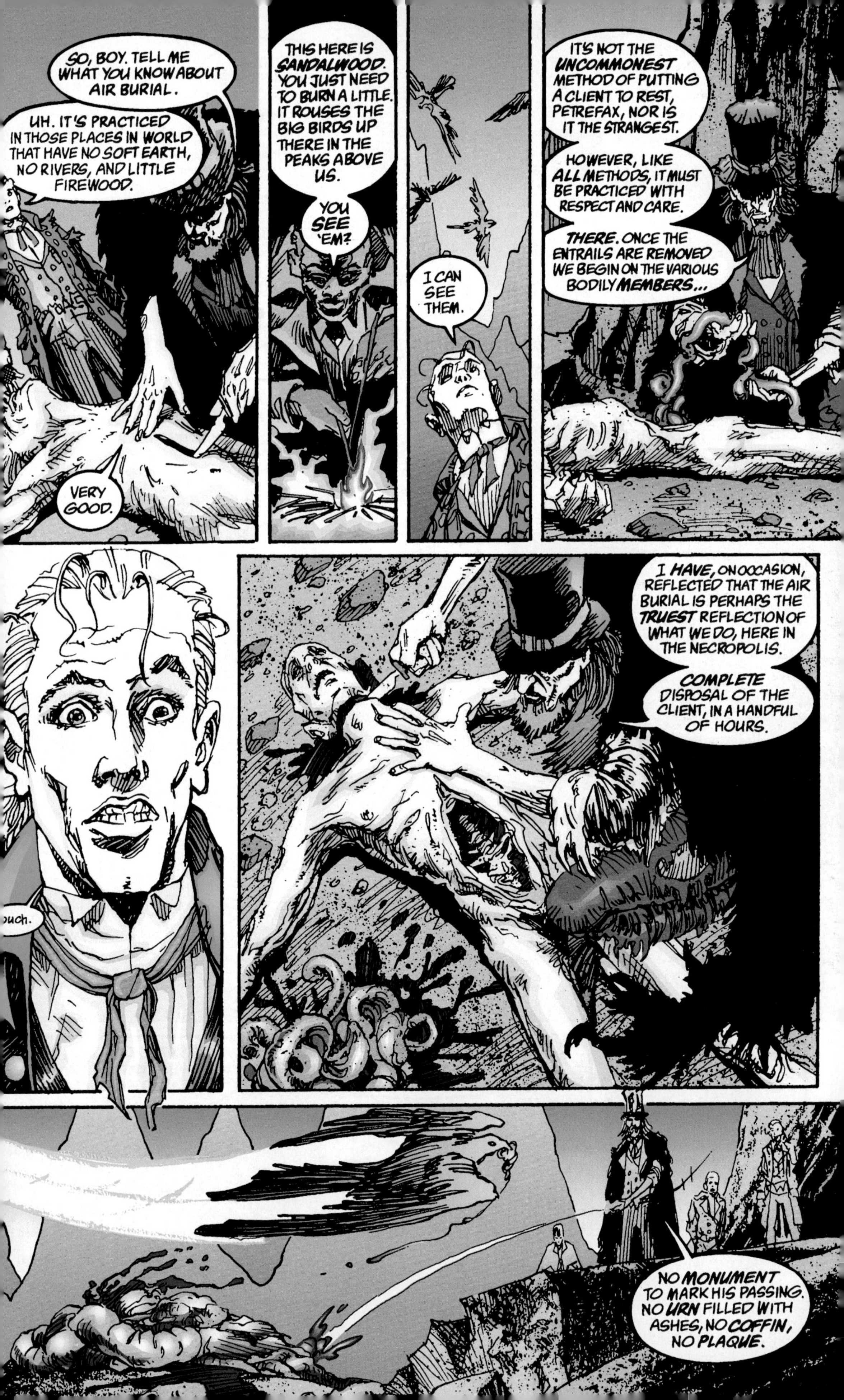
SO, BOY. TELL ME WHAT YOU KNOW ABOUT AIR BURIAL.
UH. IT'S PRACTICED IN THOSE PLACES IN WORLD THAT HAVE NO SOFT EARTH, NO RIVERS, AND LITTLE FIREWOOD.
VERY GOOD.
THIS HERE IS SANDALWOOD. YOU JUST NEED TO BURN A LITTLE. IT ROUSES THE BIG BIRDS UP THERE IN THE PEAKS ABOVE US.
YOU SEE 'EM?
I CAN SEE THEM.
IT'S NOT THE UNCOMMONEST METHOD OF PUTTING A CLIENT TO REST, PETREFAX, NOR IS IT THE STRANGEST.
HOWEVER, LIKE ALL METHODS, IT MUST BE PRACTICED WITH RESPECT AND CARE.
THERE. ONCE THE ENTRAILS ARE REMOVED WE BEGIN ON THE VARIOUS BODILY MEMBERS...
I HAVE, ON OCCASION, REFLECTED THAT THE AIR BURIAL IS PERHAPS THE TRUEST REFLECTION OF WHAT WE DO, HERE IN THE NECROPOLIS.
COMPLETE DISPOSAL OF THE CLIENT, IN A HANDFUL OF HOURS.
NO MONUMENT TO MARK HIS PASSING. NO URN FILLED WITH ASHES, NO COFFIN, NO PLAQUE.

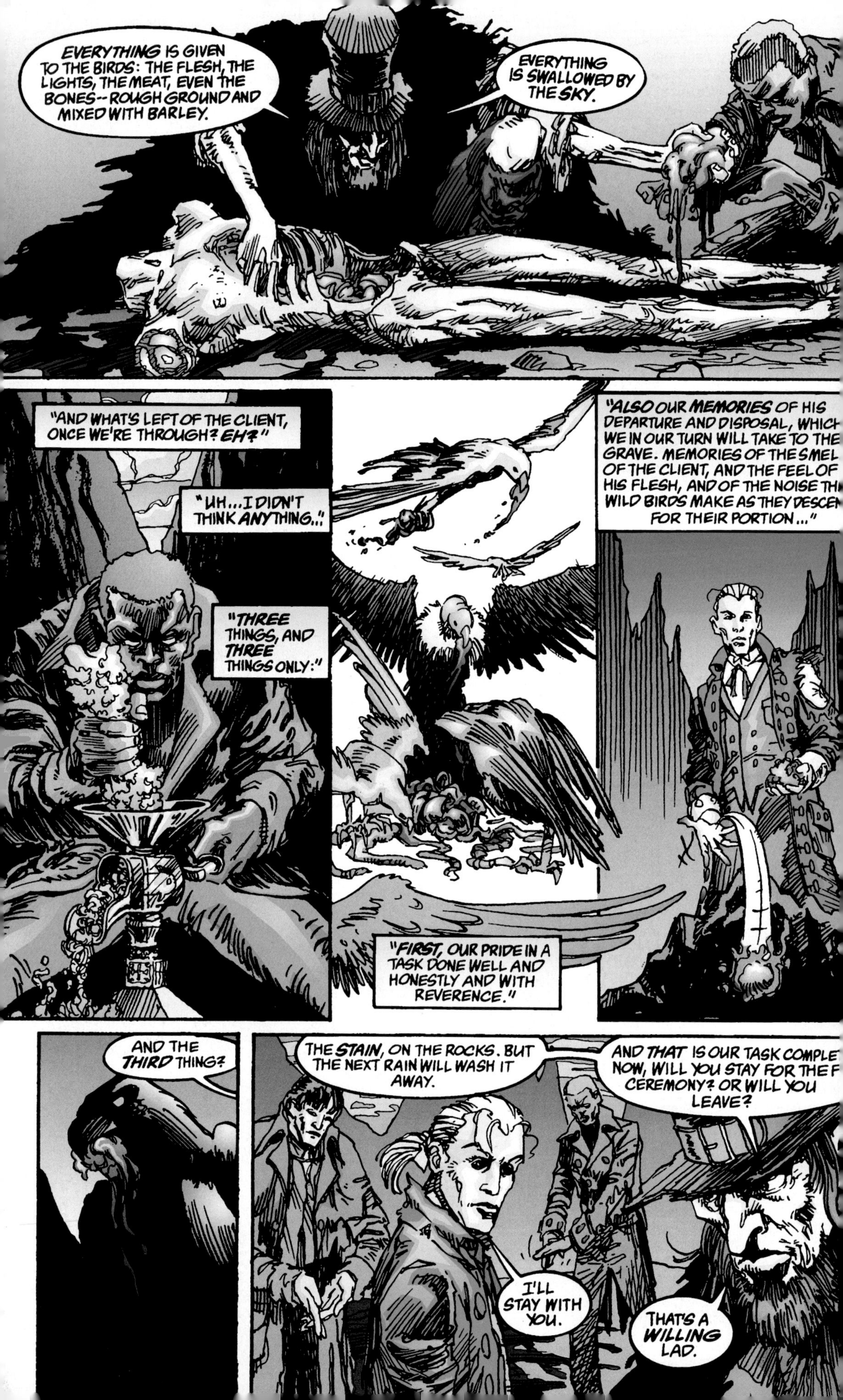

EVERYTHING IS GIVEN TO THE BIRDS: THE FLESH, THE LIGHTS, THE MEAT, EVEN THE BONES--ROUGH GROUND AND MIXED WITH BARLEY.
EVERYTHING IS SWALLOWED BY THE SKY.
"AND WHAT'S LEFT OF THE CLIENT, ONCE WE'RE THROUGH? EH?"
"UH...I DIDN'T THINK ANYTHING..."
"THREE THINGS, AND THREE THINGS ONLY:"
"FIRST, OUR PRIDE IN A TASK DONE WELL AND HONESTLY AND WITH REVERENCE."
"ALSO OUR MEMORIES OF HIS DEPARTURE AND DISPOSAL, WHICH WE IN OUR TURN WILL TAKE TO THE GRAVE. MEMORIES OF THE SMEL OF THE CLIENT, AND THE FEEL OF HIS FLESH, AND OF THE NOISE TH WILD BIRDS MAKE AS THEY DESCE FOR THEIR PORTION..."
AND THE THIRD THING?
THE STAIN, ON THE ROCKS. BUT THE NEXT RAIN WILL WASH IT AWAY.
AND THAT IS OUR TASK COMPLE NOW, WILL YOU STAY FOR THE F CEREMONY? OR WILL YOU LEAVE?
I'LL STAY WITH YOU.
THAT'S A WILLING LAD.

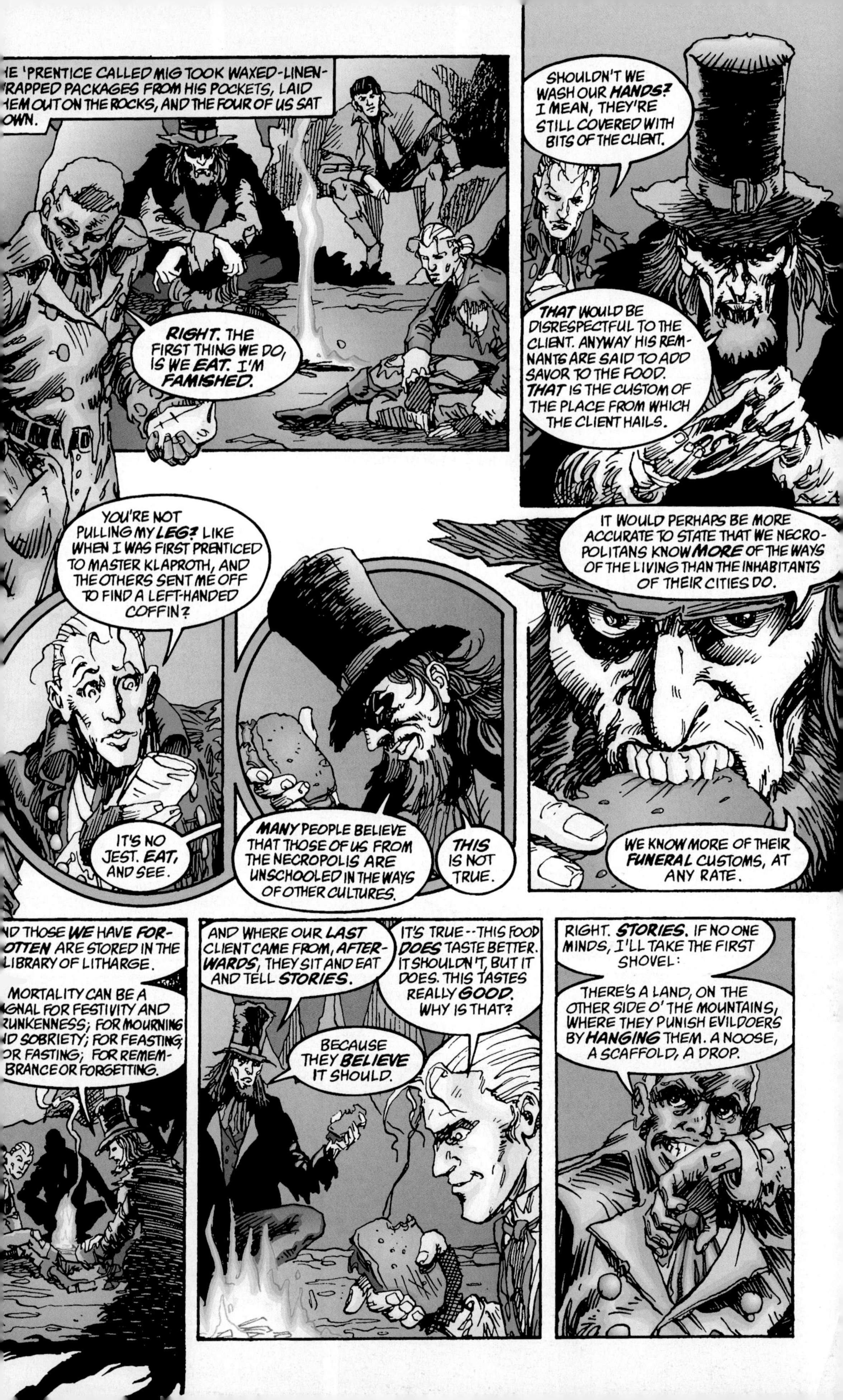
HE 'PRENTICE CALLED MIG TOOK WAXED-LINEN-WRAPPED PACKAGES FROM HIS POCKETS, LAID THEM OUT ON THE ROCKS, AND THE FOUR OF US SAT DOWN.
RIGHT. THE FIRST THING WE DO, IS WE EAT. I'M FAMISHED.
SHOULDN'T WE WASH OUR HANDS? I MEAN, THEY'RE STILL COVERED WITH BITS OF THE CLIENT.
THAT WOULD BE DISRESPECTFUL TO THE CLIENT. ANYWAY HIS REMNANTS ARE SAID TO ADD SAVOR TO THE FOOD. THAT IS THE CUSTOM OF THE PLACE FROM WHICH THE CLIENT HAILS.
YOU'RE NOT PULLING MY LEG? LIKE WHEN I WAS FIRST PRENTICED TO MASTER KLAPROTH, AND THE OTHERS SENT ME OFF TO FIND A LEFT-HANDED COFFIN?
IT'S NO JEST. EAT, AND SEE.
MANY PEOPLE BELIEVE THAT THOSE OF US FROM THE NECROPOLIS ARE UNSCHOOLED IN THE WAYS OF OTHER CULTURES.
THIS IS NOT TRUE.
IT WOULD PERHAPS BE MORE ACCURATE TO STATE THAT WE NECROPOLITANS KNOW MORE OF THE WAYS OF THE LIVING THAN THE INHABITANTS OF THEIR CITIES DO.
WE KNOW MORE OF THEIR FUNERAL CUSTOMS, AT ANY RATE.
ND THOSE WE HAVE FORGOTTEN ARE STORED IN THE LIBRARY OF LITHARGE.
MORTALITY CAN BE A SIGNAL FOR FESTIVITY AND DRUNKENNESS; FOR MOURNING AND SOBRIETY; FOR FEASTING; FOR FASTING; FOR REMEMBRANCE OR FORGETTING.
AND WHERE OUR LAST CLIENT CAME FROM, AFTERWARDS, THEY SIT AND EAT AND TELL STORIES.
IT'S TRUE--THIS FOOD DOES TASTE BETTER. IT SHOULDN'T, BUT IT DOES. THIS TASTES REALLY GOOD. WHY IS THAT?
BECAUSE THEY BELIEVE IT SHOULD.
RIGHT. STORIES. IF NO ONE MINDS, I'LL TAKE THE FIRST SHOVEL:
THERE'S A LAND, ON THE OTHER SIDE O' THE MOUNTAINS, WHERE THEY PUNISH EVILDOERS BY HANGING THEM. A NOOSE, A SCAFFOLD, A DROP.

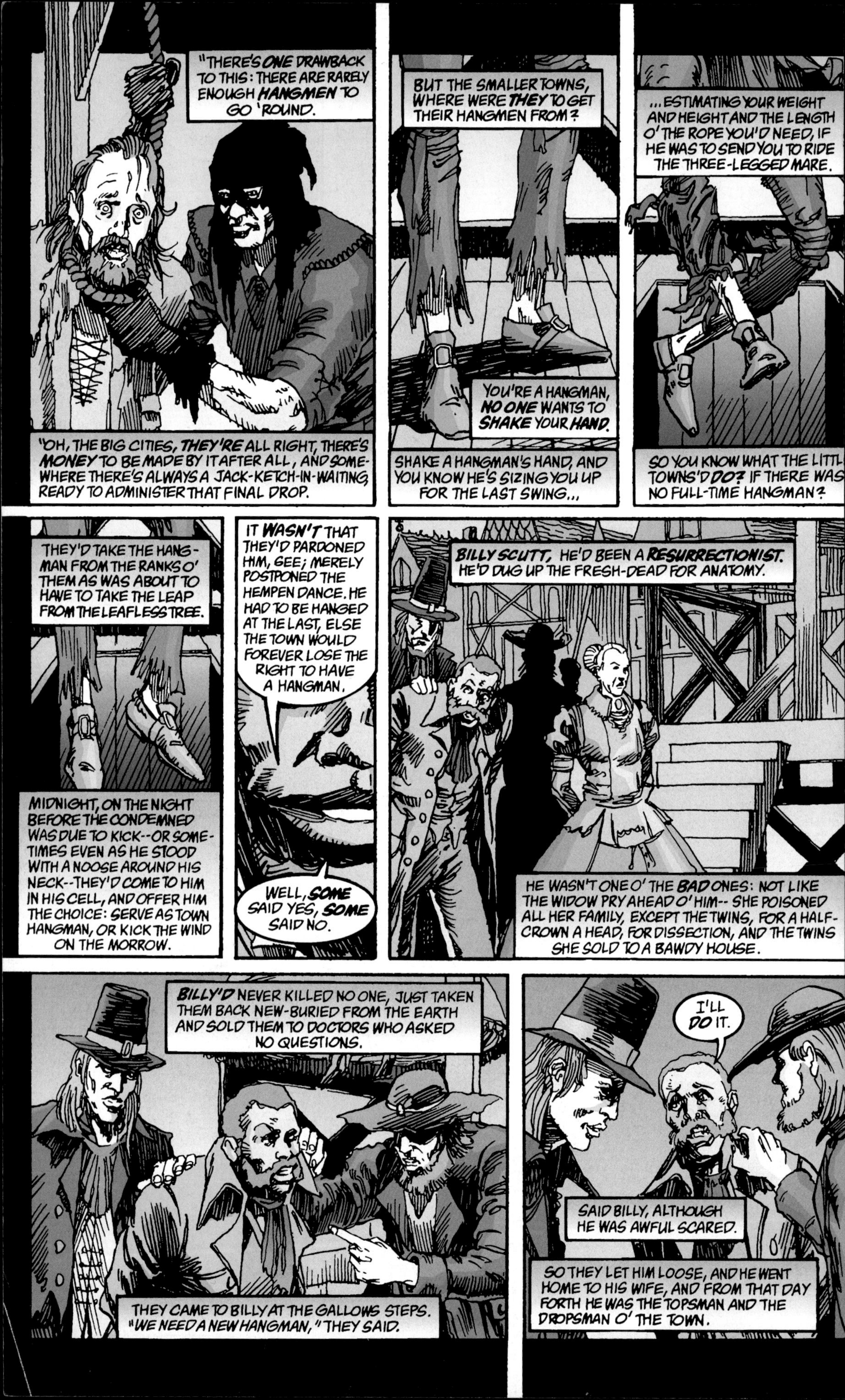
"THERE'S ONE DRAWBACK TO THIS: THERE ARE RARELY ENOUGH HANGMEN TO GO 'ROUND.
"OH, THE BIG CITIES, THEY'RE ALL RIGHT, THERE'S MONEY TO BE MADE BY IT AFTER ALL, AND SOMEWHERE THERE'S ALWAYS A JACK-KETCH-IN-WAITING READY TO ADMINISTER THAT FINAL DROP.
BUT THE SMALLER TOWNS, WHERE WERE THEY TO GET THEIR HANGMEN FROM?
YOU'RE A HANGMAN, NO ONE WANTS TO SHAKE YOUR HAND.
SHAKE A HANGMAN'S HAND, AND YOU KNOW HE'S SIZING YOU UP FOR THE LAST SWING...
...ESTIMATING YOUR WEIGHT AND HEIGHT AND THE LENGTH O' THE ROPE YOU'D NEED, IF HE WAS TO SEND YOU TO RIDE THE THREE-LEGGED MARE.
SO YOU KNOW WHAT THE LITTLE TOWNS'D DO? IF THERE WAS NO FULL-TIME HANGMAN?
THEY'D TAKE THE HANGMAN FROM THE RANKS O' THEM AS WAS ABOUT TO HAVE TO TAKE THE LEAP FROM THE LEAFLESS TREE.
MIDNIGHT, ON THE NIGHT BEFORE THE CONDEMNED WAS DUE TO KICK--OR SOMETIMES EVEN AS HE STOOD WITH A NOOSE AROUND HIS NECK--THEY'D COME TO HIM IN HIS CELL, AND OFFER HIM THE CHOICE: SERVE AS TOWN HANGMAN, OR KICK THE WIND ON THE MORROW.
IT WASN'T THAT THEY'D PARDONED HIM, GEE; MERELY POSTPONED THE HEMPEN DANCE. HE HAD TO BE HANGED AT THE LAST, ELSE THE TOWN WOULD FOREVER LOSE THE RIGHT TO HAVE A HANGMAN.
WELL, SOME SAID YES, SOME SAID NO.
BILLY SCUTT, HE'D BEEN A RESURRECTIONIST. HE'D DUG UP THE FRESH-DEAD FOR ANATOMY.
HE WASN'T ONE O' THE BAD ONES: NOT LIKE THE WIDOW PRY AHEAD O' HIM-- SHE POISONED ALL HER FAMILY, EXCEPT THE TWINS, FOR A HALF-CROWN A HEAD, FOR DISSECTION, AND THE TWINS SHE SOLD TO A BAWDY HOUSE.
BILLY'D NEVER KILLED NO ONE, JUST TAKEN THEM BACK NEW-BURIED FROM THE EARTH AND SOLD THEM TO DOCTORS WHO ASKED NO QUESTIONS.
THEY CAME TO BILLY AT THE GALLOWS STEPS. "WE NEED A NEW HANGMAN," THEY SAID.
I'LL DO IT.
SAID BILLY, ALTHOUGH HE WAS AWFUL SCARED.
SO THEY LET HIM LOOSE, AND HE WENT HOME TO HIS WIFE, AND FROM THAT DAY FORTH HE WAS THE TOPSMAN AND THE DROPSMAN O' THE TOWN.

BILLY SCUTT WAS THE *BEST* HANGMAN THE TOWN HAD HAD. WHEN *HE* HANGED YOU, YOU *STAYED* HUNG: THE TRAP WOULD OPEN, YOU'D CUT YOUR CAPER ON NOTHING AND BE CLEAN GONE.

HE WASN'T A *HAPPY* MAN, THOUGH HE TOOK PRIDE IN HIS PROFESSION AS HE NEVER HAD WITH BODYSNATCHING.

GOOD CLEAN DROPS THAT SNAPPED SPINES AND ENDED LIVES SHARP AS A CUT. NO ONE WAS EVER HANGED *TWICE* WHEN BILLY SCUTT WAS THE DANCING MASTER.

THERE WERE *SOME* SAID THA' WAS BECAUSE HE LOOKED AT EACH POOR SOUL PREPARING FOR THE FINAL DANCE, AND KNEW THAT *THERE*, BUT FOR GRACE O' THE TOWN COUNCIL, WENT BILLY SCUTT.

EACH NIGHT HE RETURNED FROM HIS WORK AT THE GALLOWS TO HIS WIFE, HIS CHILDREN, THEIR COTTAGE, AND LOOKED AT THEM AS ONE GAZES ON PRECIOUS THINGS.

STILL, ALL THINGS END, AND BILLY SCUTT'S CHILDREN GREW LIKE ROWANS AND HAD CHILDREN O' THEIR OWN, AND HIS WIFE'S HAIR TURNED MOON-WHITE; AND ONE DAY BILLY FOUND HIMSELF UNABLE TO GET OUT O' THE BED.

I CANNOT MOVE... EVEN THE SMALLEST... FINGER.

THEY'LL *HANG* YOU *NOW*, OUR BILLY, FOR CERTAIN.

THEY SAY... JACK KETCH...IS AN EXCELLENT...PHYSICIAN ... MY LOVE...

...BUT I HAVE A DESIRE...TO DIE IN MY *OWN* BED.

THE SHERIFF'S MEN ARRIVED THAT NIGHT TO TAKE BILLY AWAY.

WE *HEAR* YOU'RE TERRIBLE *SICK*, BILLY SCUTT.

THEY'VE BEEN SAYING IT *ALL* OVER THE TOWN--

--HOW *TERRIBLE* SICK YOU ARE.

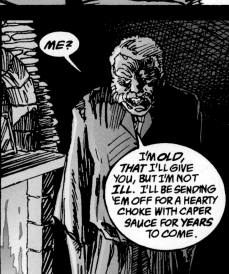

ME?

I'M *OLD*, THAT I'LL GIVE YOU, BUT I'M NOT *ILL*. I'LL BE SENDING 'EM OFF FOR A HEARTY CHOKE WITH CAPER SAUCE FOR YEARS TO COME.

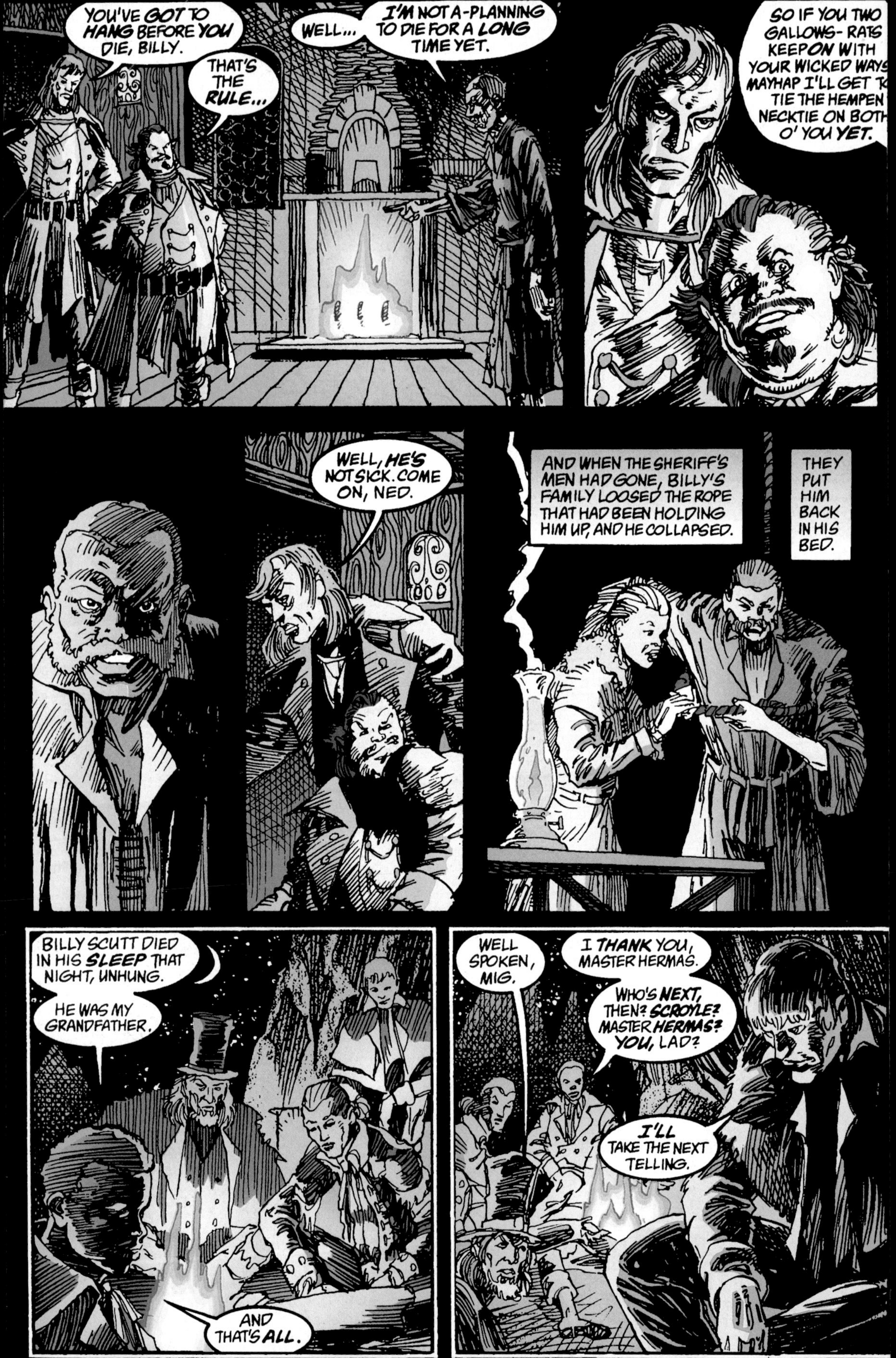
YOU'VE GOT TO HANG BEFORE YOU DIE, BILLY.
THAT'S THE RULE...
WELL...
I'M NOT A-PLANNING TO DIE FOR A LONG TIME YET.
SO IF YOU TWO GALLOWS-RATS KEEP ON WITH YOUR WICKED WAYS MAYHAP I'LL GET TO TIE THE HEMPEN NECKTIE ON BOTH O' YOU YET.
WELL, HE'S NOT SICK. COME ON, NED.
AND WHEN THE SHERIFF'S MEN HAD GONE, BILLY'S FAMILY LOOSED THE ROPE THAT HAD BEEN HOLDING HIM UP, AND HE COLLAPSED.
THEY PUT HIM BACK IN HIS BED.
BILLY SCUTT DIED IN HIS SLEEP THAT NIGHT, UNHUNG.
HE WAS MY GRANDFATHER.
AND THAT'S ALL.
WELL SPOKEN, MIG.
I THANK YOU, MASTER HERMAS.
WHO'S NEXT, THEN? SCROYLE? MASTER HERMAS? YOU, LAD?
I'LL TAKE THE NEXT TELLING.

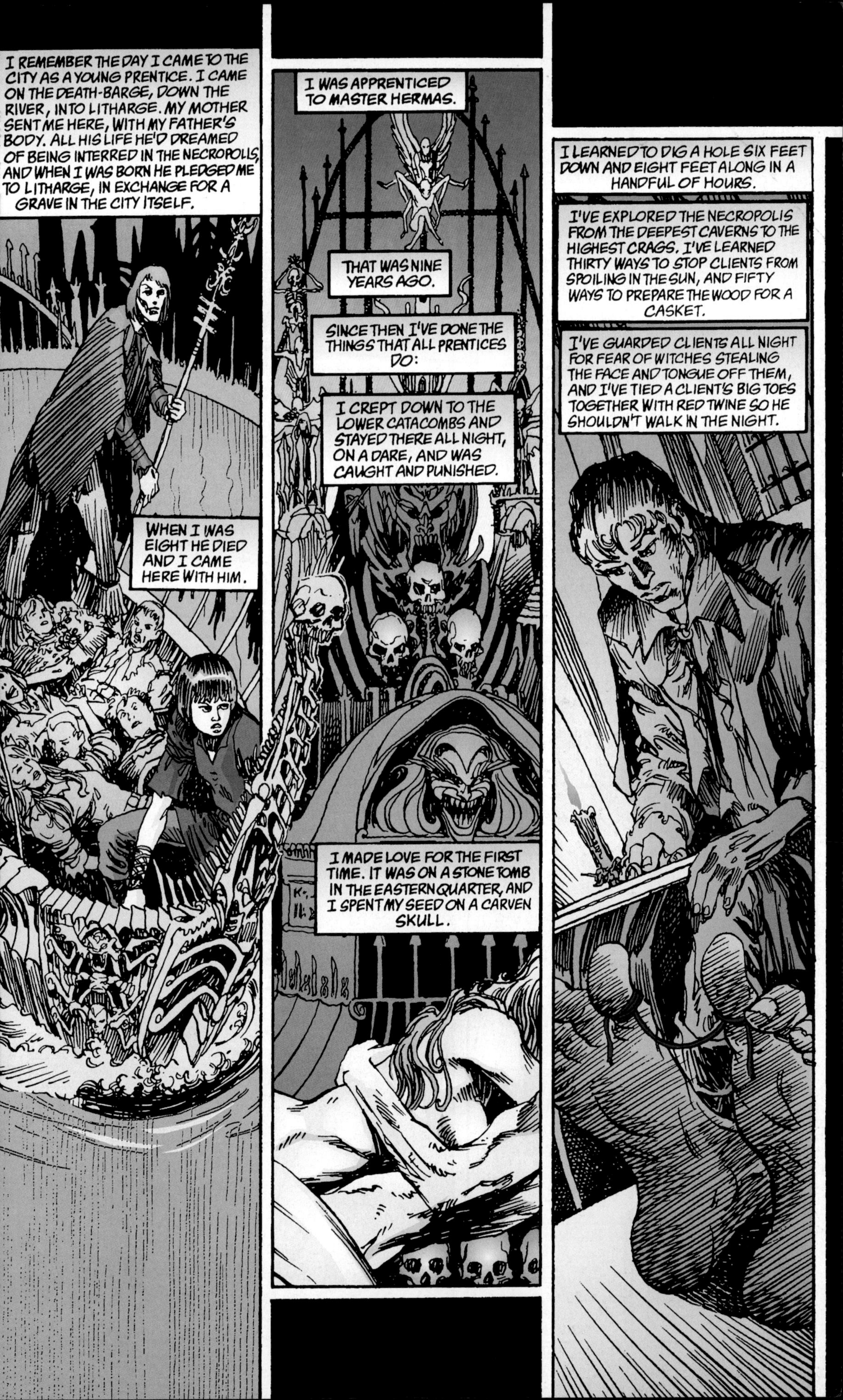
I REMEMBER THE DAY I CAME TO THE CITY AS A YOUNG PRENTICE. I CAME ON THE DEATH-BARGE, DOWN THE RIVER, INTO LITHARGE. MY MOTHER SENT ME HERE, WITH MY FATHER'S BODY. ALL HIS LIFE HE'D DREAMED OF BEING INTERRED IN THE NECROPOLIS, AND WHEN I WAS BORN HE PLEDGED ME TO LITHARGE, IN EXCHANGE FOR A GRAVE IN THE CITY ITSELF.
WHEN I WAS EIGHT HE DIED AND I CAME HERE WITH HIM.
I WAS APPRENTICED TO MASTER HERMAS.
THAT WAS NINE YEARS AGO.
SINCE THEN I'VE DONE THE THINGS THAT ALL PRENTICES DO:
I CREPT DOWN TO THE LOWER CATACOMBS AND STAYED THERE ALL NIGHT, ON A DARE, AND WAS CAUGHT AND PUNISHED.
I MADE LOVE FOR THE FIRST TIME. IT WAS ON A STONE TOMB IN THE EASTERN QUARTER, AND I SPENT MY SEED ON A CARVEN SKULL.
I LEARNED TO DIG A HOLE SIX FEET DOWN AND EIGHT FEET ALONG IN A HANDFUL OF HOURS.
I'VE EXPLORED THE NECROPOLIS FROM THE DEEPEST CAVERNS TO THE HIGHEST CRAGS. I'VE LEARNED THIRTY WAYS TO STOP CLIENTS FROM SPOILING IN THE SUN, AND FIFTY WAYS TO PREPARE THE WOOD FOR A CASKET.
I'VE GUARDED CLIENTS ALL NIGHT FOR FEAR OF WITCHES STEALING THE FACE AND TONGUE OFF THEM, AND I'VE TIED A CLIENT'S BIG TOES TOGETHER WITH RED TWINE SO HE SHOULDN'T WALK IN THE NIGHT.

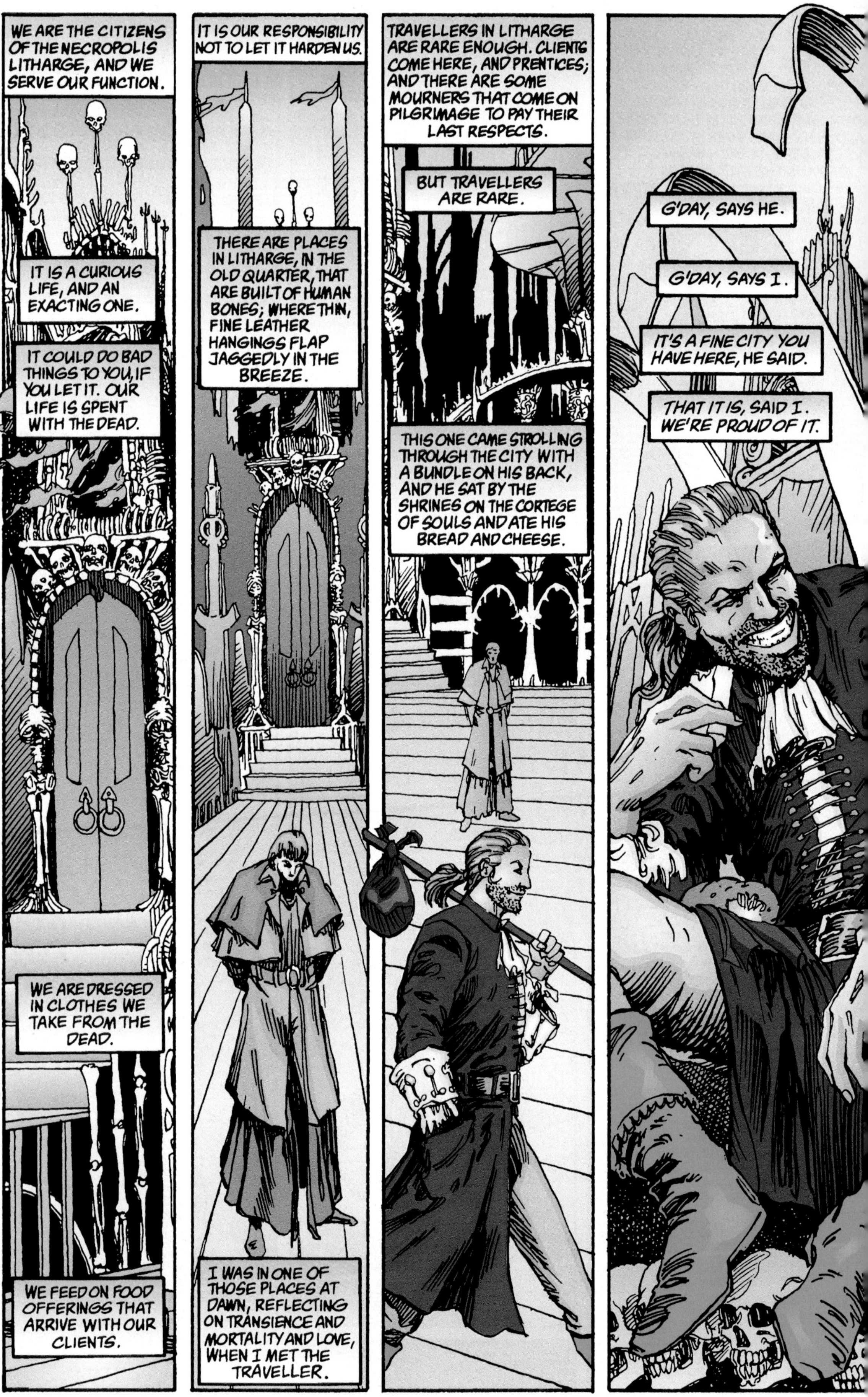
WE ARE THE CITIZENS OF THE NECROPOLIS LITHARGE, AND WE SERVE OUR FUNCTION.
IT IS A CURIOUS LIFE, AND AN EXACTING ONE.
IT COULD DO BAD THINGS TO YOU, IF YOU LET IT. OUR LIFE IS SPENT WITH THE DEAD.
WE ARE DRESSED IN CLOTHES WE TAKE FROM THE DEAD.
WE FEED ON FOOD OFFERINGS THAT ARRIVE WITH OUR CLIENTS.
IT IS OUR RESPONSIBILITY NOT TO LET IT HARDEN US.
THERE ARE PLACES IN LITHARGE, IN THE OLD QUARTER, THAT ARE BUILT OF HUMAN BONES; WHERE THIN, FINE LEATHER HANGINGS FLAP JAGGEDLY IN THE BREEZE.
I WAS IN ONE OF THOSE PLACES AT DAWN, REFLECTING ON TRANSIENCE AND MORTALITY AND LOVE, WHEN I MET THE TRAVELLER.
TRAVELLERS IN LITHARGE ARE RARE ENOUGH. CLIENTS COME HERE, AND PRENTICES; AND THERE ARE SOME MOURNERS THAT COME ON PILGRIMAGE TO PAY THEIR LAST RESPECTS.
BUT TRAVELLERS ARE RARE.
THIS ONE CAME STROLLING THROUGH THE CITY WITH A BUNDLE ON HIS BACK, AND HE SAT BY THE SHRINES ON THE CORTEGE OF SOULS AND ATE HIS BREAD AND CHEESE.
G'DAY, SAYS HE.
G'DAY, SAYS I.
IT'S A FINE CITY YOU HAVE HERE, HE SAID.
THAT IT IS, SAID I. WE'RE PROUD OF IT.

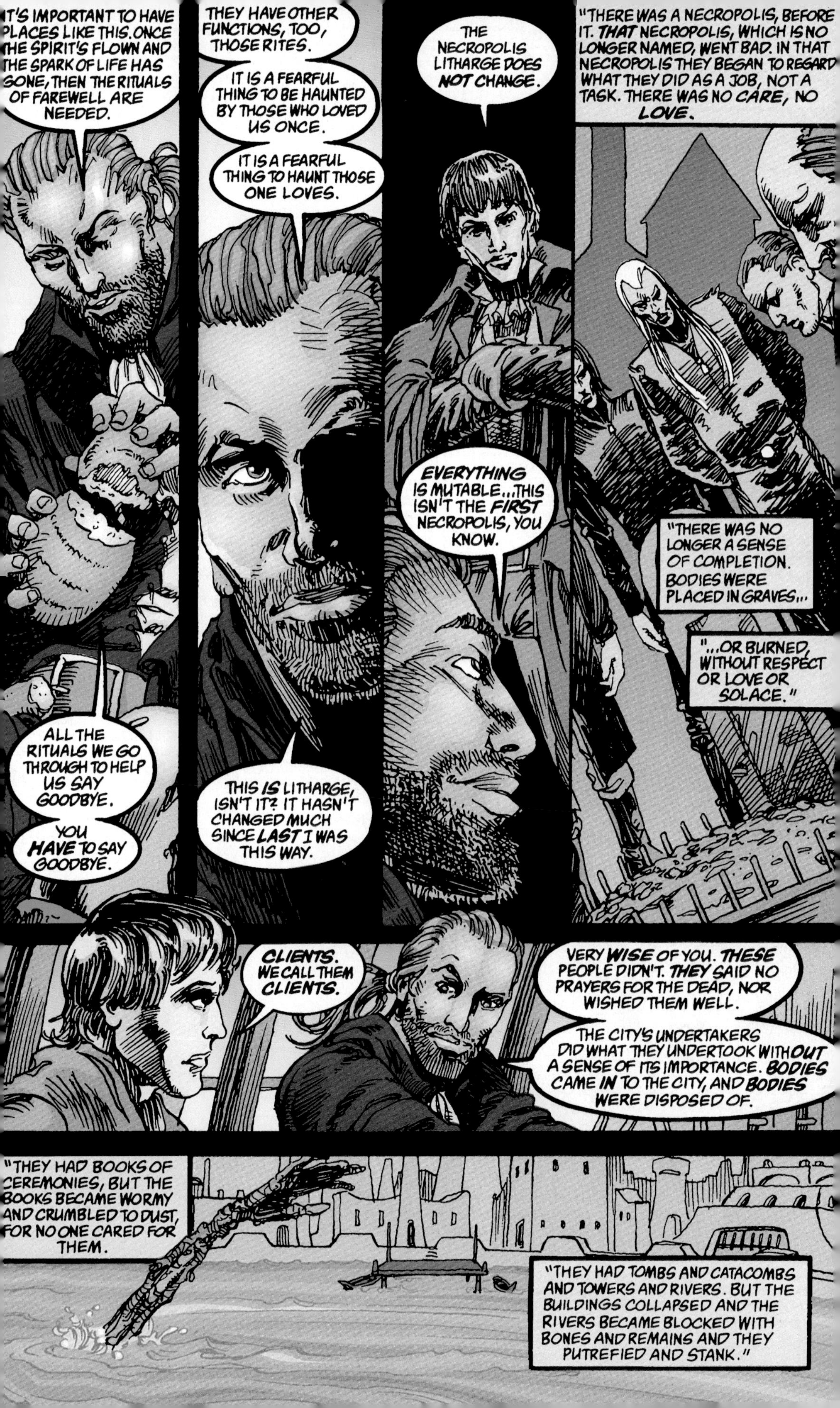
IT'S IMPORTANT TO HAVE PLACES LIKE THIS. ONCE THE SPIRIT'S FLOWN AND THE SPARK OF LIFE HAS GONE, THEN THE RITUALS OF FAREWELL ARE NEEDED.
ALL THE RITUALS WE GO THROUGH TO HELP US SAY GOODBYE.
YOU HAVE TO SAY GOODBYE.
THEY HAVE OTHER FUNCTIONS, TOO, THOSE RITES.
IT IS A FEARFUL THING TO BE HAUNTED BY THOSE WHO LOVED US ONCE.
IT IS A FEARFUL THING TO HAUNT THOSE ONE LOVES.
THIS IS LITHARGE, ISN'T IT? IT HASN'T CHANGED MUCH SINCE LAST I WAS THIS WAY.
THE NECROPOLIS LITHARGE DOES NOT CHANGE.
EVERYTHING IS MUTABLE...THIS ISN'T THE FIRST NECROPOLIS, YOU KNOW.
"THERE WAS A NECROPOLIS, BEFORE IT. THAT NECROPOLIS, WHICH IS NO LONGER NAMED, WENT BAD. IN THAT NECROPOLIS THEY BEGAN TO REGARD WHAT THEY DID AS A JOB, NOT A TASK. THERE WAS NO CARE, NO LOVE.
"THERE WAS NO LONGER A SENSE OF COMPLETION. BODIES WERE PLACED IN GRAVES...
"...OR BURNED, WITHOUT RESPECT OR LOVE OR SOLACE."
CLIENTS. WE CALL THEM CLIENTS.
VERY WISE OF YOU. THESE PEOPLE DIDN'T. THEY SAID NO PRAYERS FOR THE DEAD, NOR WISHED THEM WELL.
THE CITY'S UNDERTAKERS DID WHAT THEY UNDERTOOK WITHOUT A SENSE OF ITS IMPORTANCE. BODIES CAME IN TO THE CITY, AND BODIES WERE DISPOSED OF.
"THEY HAD BOOKS OF CEREMONIES, BUT THE BOOKS BECAME WORMY AND CRUMBLED TO DUST, FOR NO ONE CARED FOR THEM.
"THEY HAD TOMBS AND CATACOMBS AND TOWERS AND RIVERS. BUT THE BUILDINGS COLLAPSED AND THE RIVERS BECAME BLOCKED WITH BONES AND REMAINS AND THEY PUTREFIED AND STANK."

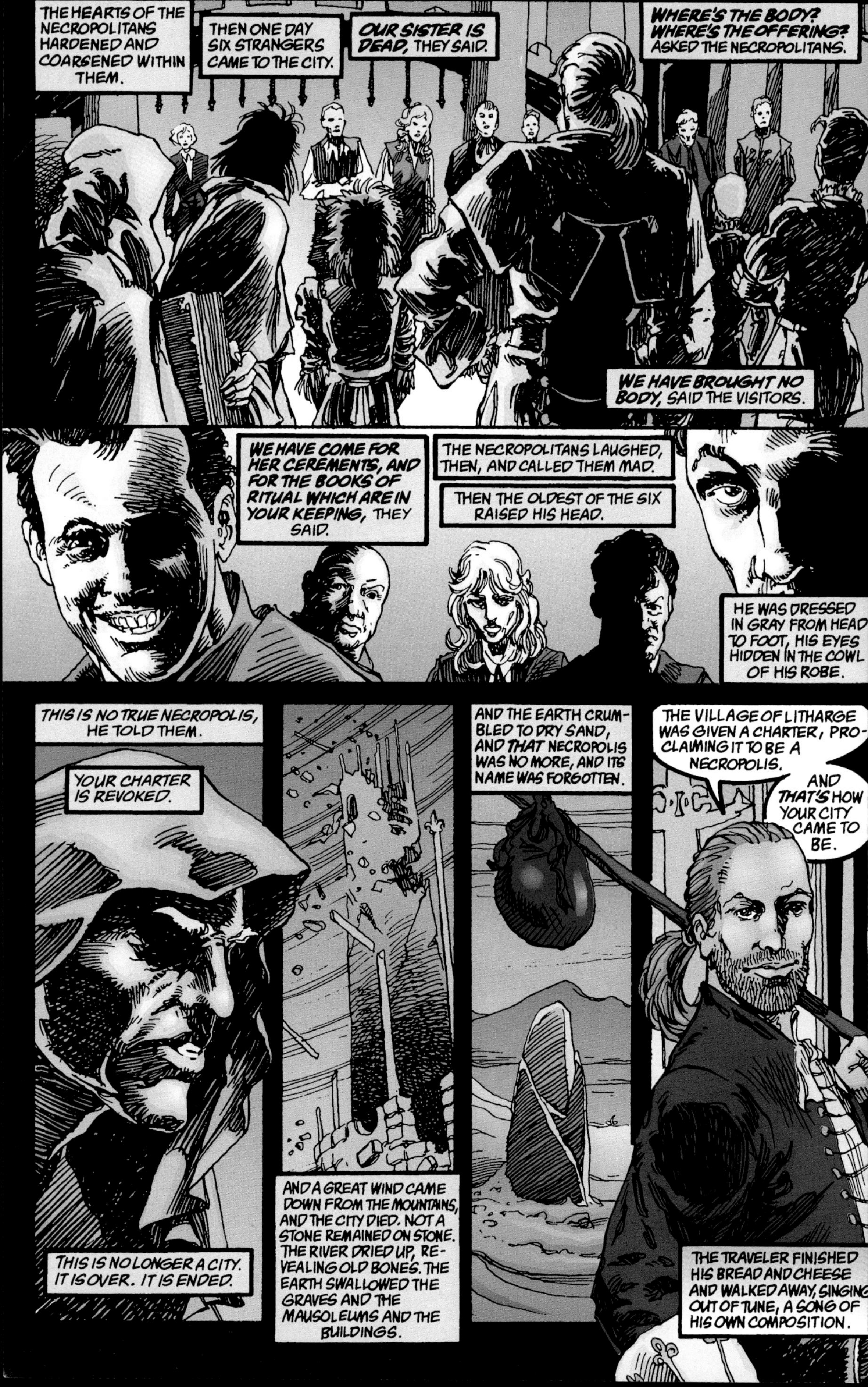
THE HEARTS OF THE NECROPOLITANS HARDENED AND COARSENED WITHIN THEM.
THEN ONE DAY SIX STRANGERS CAME TO THE CITY.
OUR SISTER IS DEAD, THEY SAID.
WHERE'S THE BODY? WHERE'S THE OFFERING? ASKED THE NECROPOLITANS.
WE HAVE BROUGHT NO BODY, SAID THE VISITORS.
WE HAVE COME FOR HER CEREMENTS, AND FOR THE BOOKS OF RITUAL WHICH ARE IN YOUR KEEPING, THEY SAID.
THE NECROPOLITANS LAUGHED, THEN, AND CALLED THEM MAD.
THEN THE OLDEST OF THE SIX RAISED HIS HEAD.
HE WAS DRESSED IN GRAY FROM HEAD TO FOOT, HIS EYES HIDDEN IN THE COWL OF HIS ROBE.
THIS IS NO TRUE NECROPOLIS, HE TOLD THEM.
YOUR CHARTER IS REVOKED.
THIS IS NO LONGER A CITY. IT IS OVER. IT IS ENDED.
AND A GREAT WIND CAME DOWN FROM THE MOUNTAINS, AND THE CITY DIED. NOT A STONE REMAINED ON STONE. THE RIVER DRIED UP, RE-VEALING OLD BONES. THE EARTH SWALLOWED THE GRAVES AND THE MAUSOLEUMS AND THE BUILDINGS.
AND THE EARTH CRUM-BLED TO DRY SAND, AND THAT NECROPOLIS WAS NO MORE, AND ITS NAME WAS FORGOTTEN.
THE VILLAGE OF LITHARGE WAS GIVEN A CHARTER, PRO-CLAIMING IT TO BE A NECROPOLIS.
AND THAT'S HOW YOUR CITY CAME TO BE.
THE TRAVELER FINISHED HIS BREAD AND CHEESE AND WALKED AWAY, SINGING OUT OF TUNE, A SONG OF HIS OWN COMPOSITION.

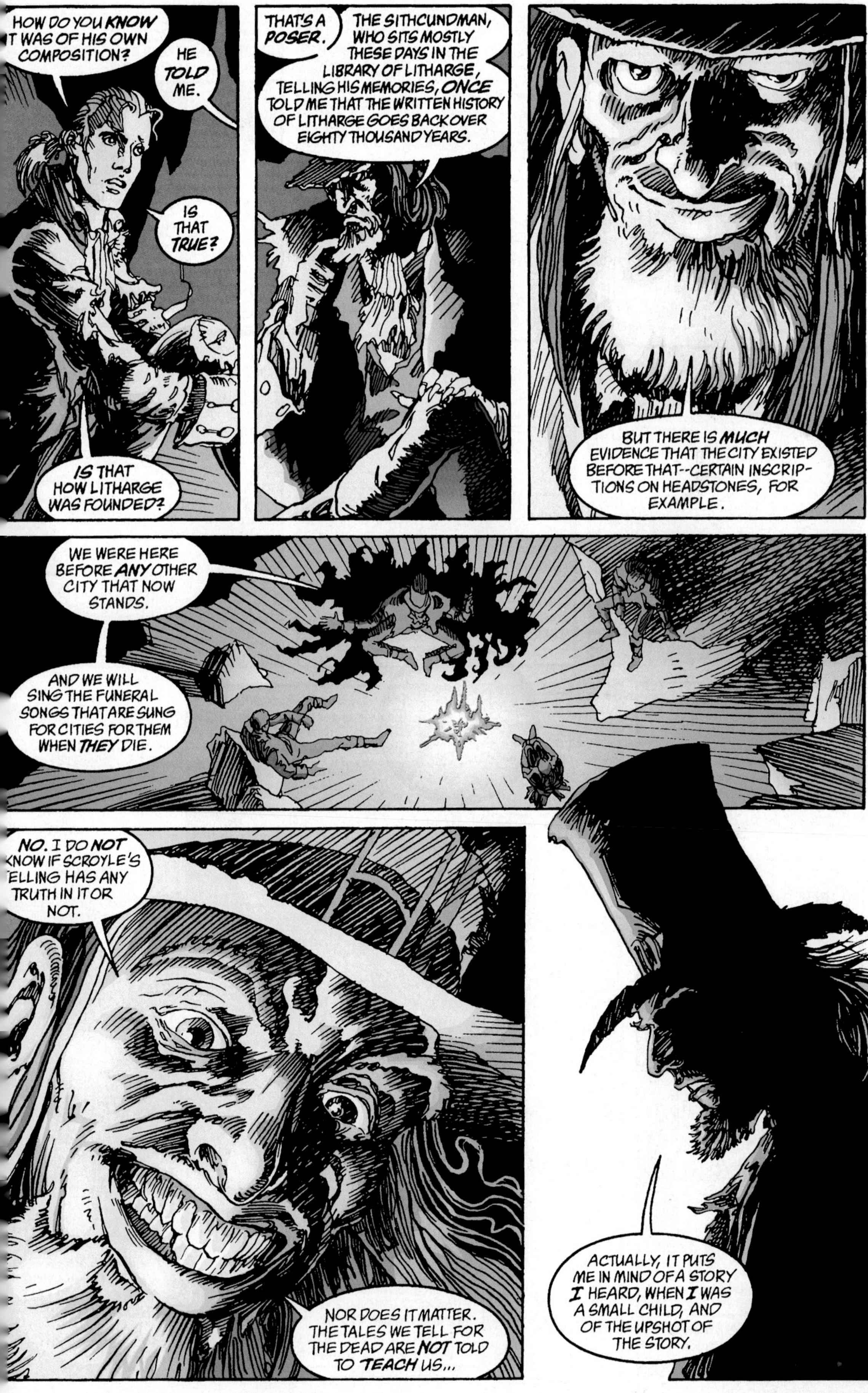

HOW DO YOU KNOW IT WAS OF HIS OWN COMPOSITION?
HE TOLD ME.
IS THAT TRUE?
IS THAT HOW LITHARGE WAS FOUNDED?
THAT'S A POSER.
THE SITHCUNDMAN, WHO SITS MOSTLY THESE DAYS IN THE LIBRARY OF LITHARGE, TELLING HIS MEMORIES, ONCE TOLD ME THAT THE WRITTEN HISTORY OF LITHARGE GOES BACK OVER EIGHTY THOUSAND YEARS.
BUT THERE IS MUCH EVIDENCE THAT THE CITY EXISTED BEFORE THAT--CERTAIN INSCRIPTIONS ON HEADSTONES, FOR EXAMPLE.
WE WERE HERE BEFORE ANY OTHER CITY THAT NOW STANDS.
AND WE WILL SING THE FUNERAL SONGS THAT ARE SUNG FOR CITIES FOR THEM WHEN THEY DIE.
NO. I DO NOT KNOW IF SCROYLE'S TELLING HAS ANY TRUTH IN IT OR NOT.
NOR DOES IT MATTER. THE TALES WE TELL FOR THE DEAD ARE NOT TOLD TO TEACH US...
ACTUALLY, IT PUTS ME IN MIND OF A STORY I HEARD, WHEN I WAS A SMALL CHILD, AND OF THE UPSHOT OF THE STORY.

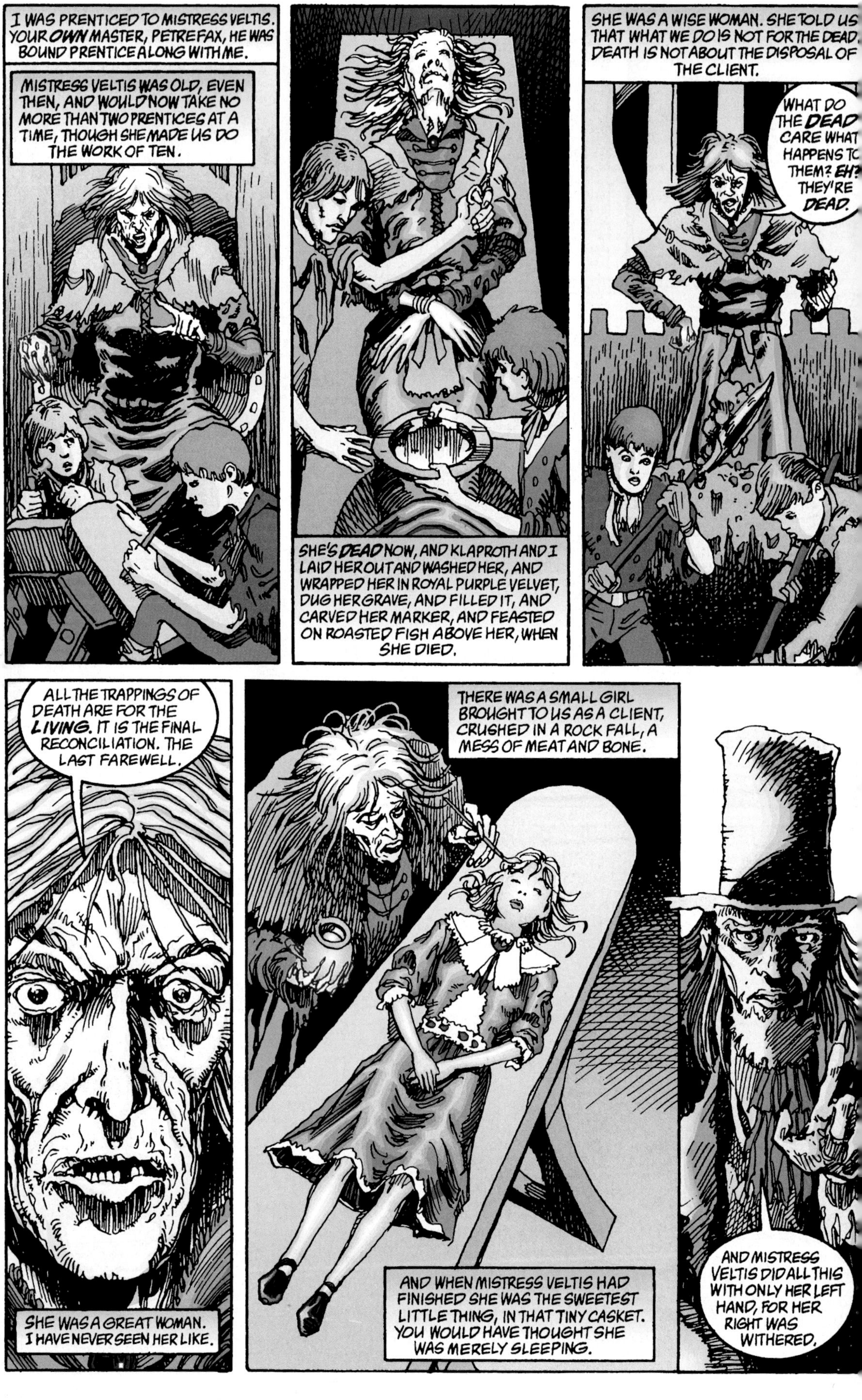
I WAS PRENTICED TO MISTRESS VELTIS. YOUR OWN MASTER, PETREFAX, HE WAS BOUND PRENTICE ALONG WITH ME.
MISTRESS VELTIS WAS OLD, EVEN THEN, AND WOULD NOW TAKE NO MORE THAN TWO PRENTICES AT A TIME, THOUGH SHE MADE US DO THE WORK OF TEN.
SHE'S DEAD NOW, AND KLAPROTH AND I LAID HER OUT AND WASHED HER, AND WRAPPED HER IN ROYAL PURPLE VELVET, DUG HER GRAVE, AND FILLED IT, AND CARVED HER MARKER, AND FEASTED ON ROASTED FISH ABOVE HER, WHEN SHE DIED.
SHE WAS A WISE WOMAN. SHE TOLD US THAT WHAT WE DO IS NOT FOR THE DEAD. DEATH IS NOT ABOUT THE DISPOSAL OF THE CLIENT.
WHAT DO THE DEAD CARE WHAT HAPPENS TO THEM? EH? THEY'RE DEAD.
ALL THE TRAPPINGS OF DEATH ARE FOR THE LIVING. IT IS THE FINAL RECONCILIATION. THE LAST FAREWELL.
SHE WAS A GREAT WOMAN. I HAVE NEVER SEEN HER LIKE.
THERE WAS A SMALL GIRL BROUGHT TO US AS A CLIENT, CRUSHED IN A ROCK FALL, A MESS OF MEAT AND BONE.
AND WHEN MISTRESS VELTIS HAD FINISHED SHE WAS THE SWEETEST LITTLE THING, IN THAT TINY CASKET. YOU WOULD HAVE THOUGHT SHE WAS MERELY SLEEPING.
AND MISTRESS VELTIS DID ALL THIS WITH ONLY HER LEFT HAND, FOR HER RIGHT WAS WITHERED.

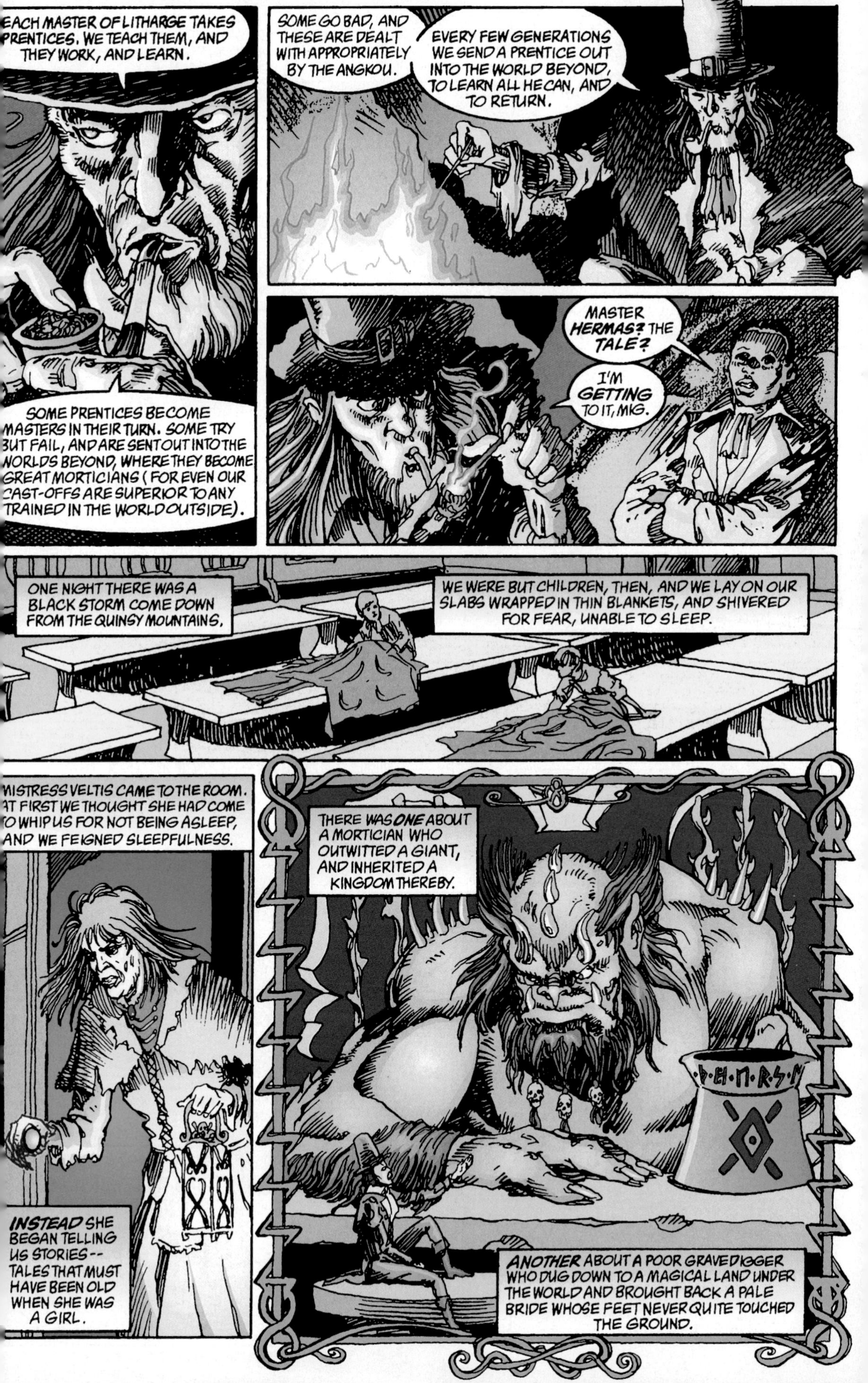

EACH MASTER OF LITHARGE TAKES PRENTICES. WE TEACH THEM, AND THEY WORK, AND LEARN.
SOME GO BAD, AND THESE ARE DEALT WITH APPROPRIATELY BY THE ANGKOU.
EVERY FEW GENERATIONS WE SEND A PRENTICE OUT INTO THE WORLD BEYOND, TO LEARN ALL HE CAN, AND TO RETURN.
SOME PRENTICES BECOME MASTERS IN THEIR TURN. SOME TRY BUT FAIL, AND ARE SENT OUT INTO THE WORLDS BEYOND, WHERE THEY BECOME GREAT MORTICIANS (FOR EVEN OUR CAST-OFFS ARE SUPERIOR TO ANY TRAINED IN THE WORLD OUTSIDE).
MASTER **HERMAS?** THE **TALE?**
I'M **GETTING** TO IT, MIG.
ONE NIGHT THERE WAS A BLACK STORM COME DOWN FROM THE QUINSY MOUNTAINS,
WE WERE BUT CHILDREN, THEN, AND WE LAY ON OUR SLABS WRAPPED IN THIN BLANKETS, AND SHIVERED FOR FEAR, UNABLE TO SLEEP.
MISTRESS VELTIS CAME TO THE ROOM. AT FIRST WE THOUGHT SHE HAD COME TO WHIP US FOR NOT BEING ASLEEP, AND WE FEIGNED SLEEPFULNESS.
INSTEAD SHE BEGAN TELLING US STORIES-- TALES THAT MUST HAVE BEEN OLD WHEN SHE WAS A GIRL.
THERE WAS **ONE** ABOUT A MORTICIAN WHO OUTWITTED A GIANT, AND INHERITED A KINGDOM THEREBY.
ANOTHER ABOUT A POOR GRAVEDIGGER WHO DUG DOWN TO A MAGICAL LAND UNDER THE WORLD AND BROUGHT BACK A PALE BRIDE WHOSE FEET NEVER QUITE TOUCHED THE GROUND.

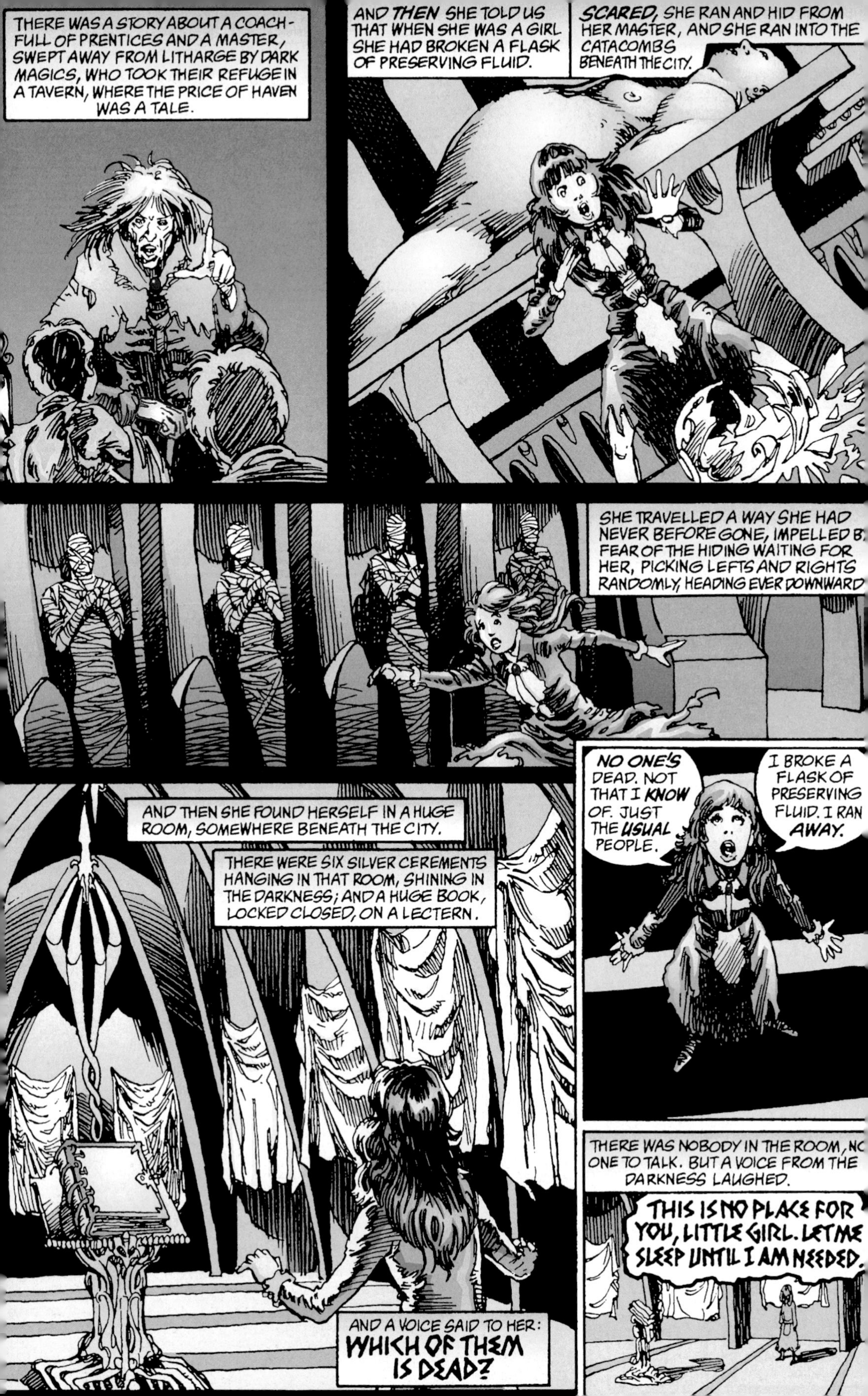

THERE WAS A STORY ABOUT A COACH-FULL OF PRENTICES AND A MASTER, SWEPT AWAY FROM LITHARGE BY DARK MAGICS, WHO TOOK THEIR REFUGE IN A TAVERN, WHERE THE PRICE OF HAVEN WAS A TALE.
AND THEN SHE TOLD US THAT WHEN SHE WAS A GIRL SHE HAD BROKEN A FLASK OF PRESERVING FLUID.
SCARED, SHE RAN AND HID FROM HER MASTER, AND SHE RAN INTO THE CATACOMBS BENEATH THE CITY.
SHE TRAVELLED A WAY SHE HAD NEVER BEFORE GONE, IMPELLED B FEAR OF THE HIDING WAITING FOR HER, PICKING LEFTS AND RIGHTS RANDOMLY, HEADING EVER DOWNWARD
AND THEN SHE FOUND HERSELF IN A HUGE ROOM, SOMEWHERE BENEATH THE CITY.
THERE WERE SIX SILVER CEREMENTS HANGING IN THAT ROOM, SHINING IN THE DARKNESS; AND A HUGE BOOK, LOCKED CLOSED, ON A LECTERN.
AND A VOICE SAID TO HER: WHICH OF THEM IS DEAD?
NO ONE'S DEAD. NOT THAT I KNOW OF. JUST THE USUAL PEOPLE.
I BROKE A FLASK OF PRESERVING FLUID. I RAN AWAY.
THERE WAS NOBODY IN THE ROOM, NC ONE TO TALK. BUT A VOICE FROM THE DARKNESS LAUGHED.
THIS IS NO PLACE FOR YOU, LITTLE GIRL. LET ME SLEEP UNTIL I AM NEEDED.

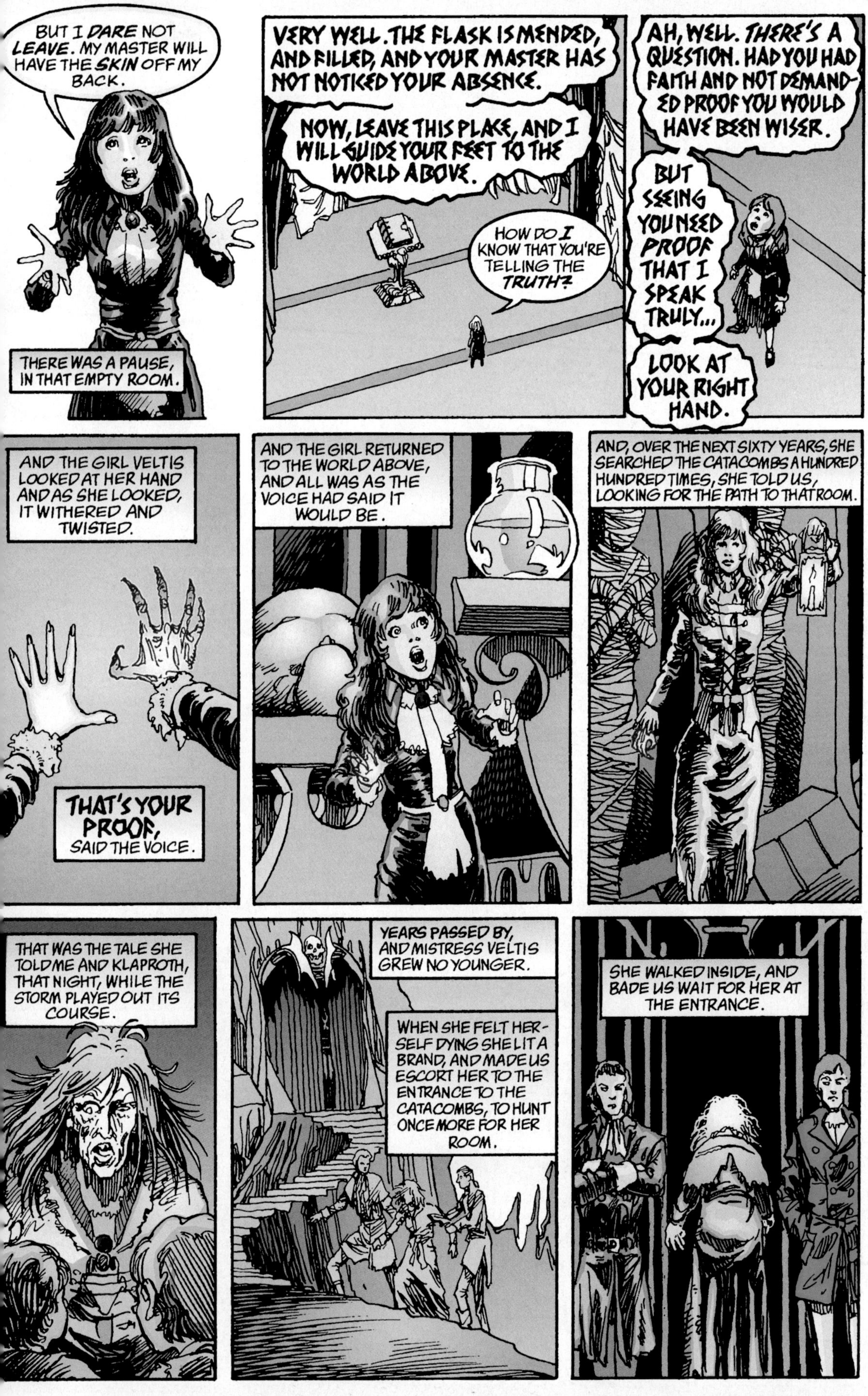

BUT I DARE NOT LEAVE. MY MASTER WILL HAVE THE SKIN OFF MY BACK.
THERE WAS A PAUSE, IN THAT EMPTY ROOM.
VERY WELL. THE FLASK IS MENDED, AND FILLED, AND YOUR MASTER HAS NOT NOTICED YOUR ABSENCE.
NOW, LEAVE THIS PLACE, AND I WILL GUIDE YOUR FEET TO THE WORLD ABOVE.
HOW DO I KNOW THAT YOU'RE TELLING THE TRUTH?
AH, WELL. THERE'S A QUESTION. HAD YOU HAD FAITH AND NOT DEMANDED PROOF YOU WOULD HAVE BEEN WISER.
BUT SEEING YOU NEED PROOF THAT I SPEAK TRULY...
LOOK AT YOUR RIGHT HAND.
AND THE GIRL VELTIS LOOKED AT HER HAND AND AS SHE LOOKED, IT WITHERED AND TWISTED.
THAT'S YOUR PROOF, SAID THE VOICE.
AND THE GIRL RETURNED TO THE WORLD ABOVE, AND ALL WAS AS THE VOICE HAD SAID IT WOULD BE.
AND, OVER THE NEXT SIXTY YEARS, SHE SEARCHED THE CATACOMBS A HUNDRED HUNDRED TIMES, SHE TOLD US, LOOKING FOR THE PATH TO THAT ROOM.
THAT WAS THE TALE SHE TOLD ME AND KLAPROTH, THAT NIGHT, WHILE THE STORM PLAYED OUT ITS COURSE.
YEARS PASSED BY, AND MISTRESS VELTIS GREW NO YOUNGER.
WHEN SHE FELT HERSELF DYING SHE LIT A BRAND, AND MADE US ESCORT HER TO THE ENTRANCE TO THE CATACOMBS, TO HUNT ONCE MORE FOR HER ROOM.
SHE WALKED INSIDE, AND BADE US WAIT FOR HER AT THE ENTRANCE.

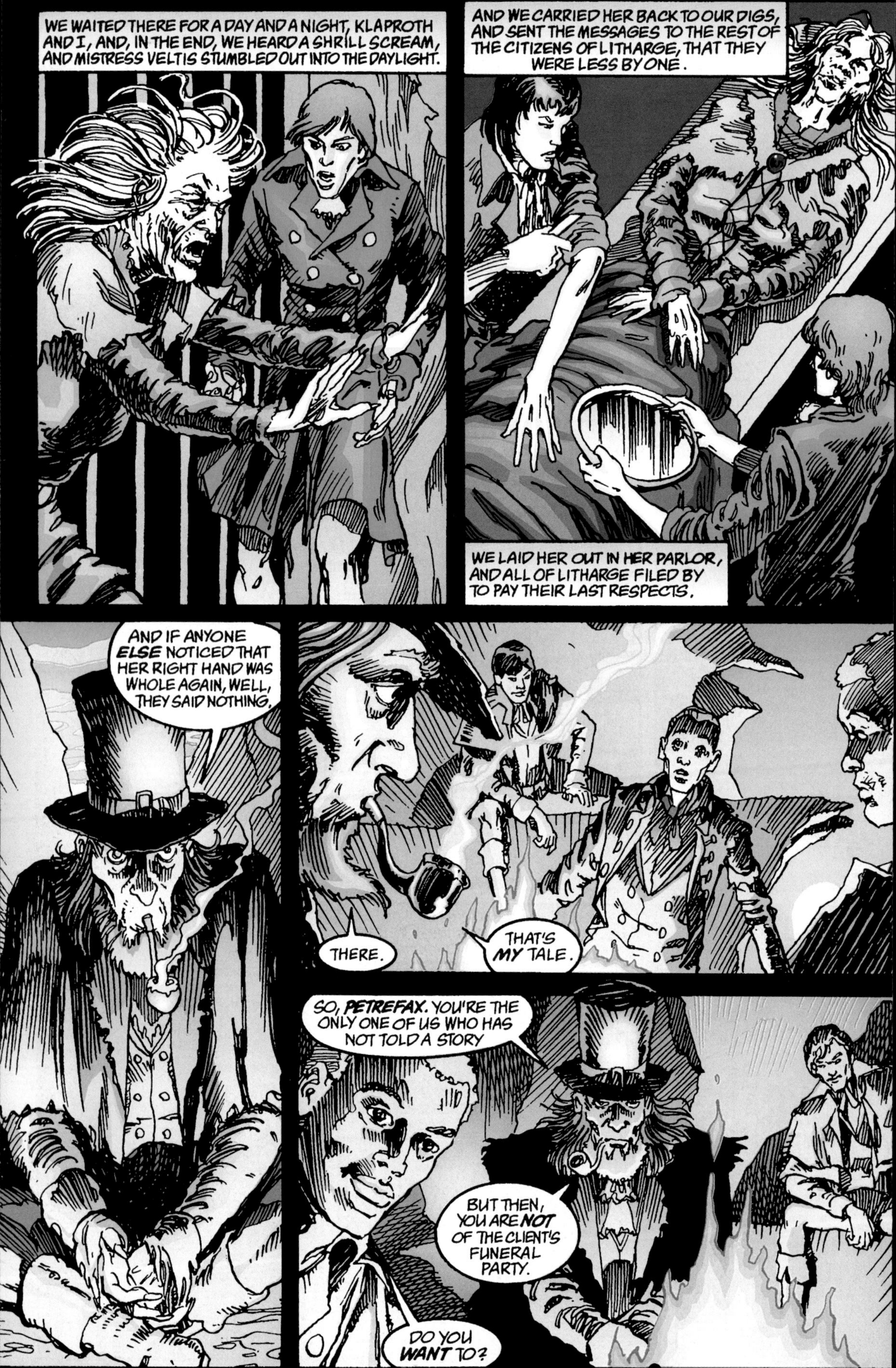
WE WAITED THERE FOR A DAY AND A NIGHT, KLAPROTH AND I, AND, IN THE END, WE HEARD A SHRILL SCREAM, AND MISTRESS VELTIS STUMBLED OUT INTO THE DAYLIGHT.
AND WE CARRIED HER BACK TO OUR DIGS, AND SENT THE MESSAGES TO THE REST OF THE CITIZENS OF LITHARGE, THAT THEY WERE LESS BY ONE.
WE LAID HER OUT IN HER PARLOR, AND ALL OF LITHARGE FILED BY TO PAY THEIR LAST RESPECTS.
AND IF ANYONE ELSE NOTICED THAT HER RIGHT HAND WAS WHOLE AGAIN, WELL, THEY SAID NOTHING.
THERE.
THAT'S MY TALE.
SO, PETREFAX. YOU'RE THE ONLY ONE OF US WHO HAS NOT TOLD A STORY
BUT THEN, YOU ARE NOT OF THE CLIENT'S FUNERAL PARTY.
DO YOU WANT TO?

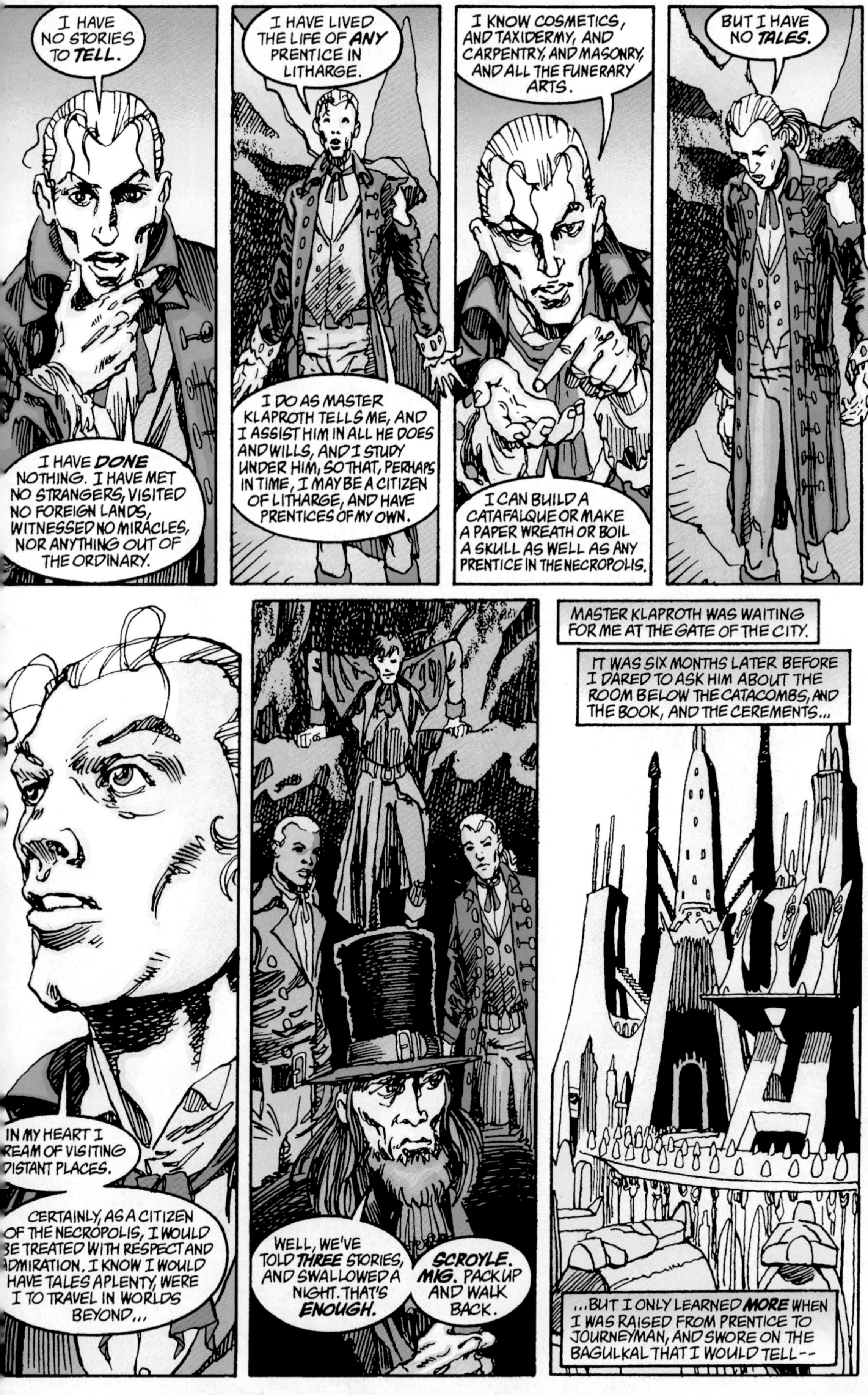
I HAVE NO STORIES TO TELL.
I HAVE DONE NOTHING. I HAVE MET NO STRANGERS, VISITED NO FOREIGN LANDS, WITNESSED NO MIRACLES, NOR ANYTHING OUT OF THE ORDINARY.
I HAVE LIVED THE LIFE OF ANY PRENTICE IN LITHARGE.
I DO AS MASTER KLAPROTH TELLS ME, AND I ASSIST HIM IN ALL HE DOES AND WILLS, AND I STUDY UNDER HIM, SO THAT, PERHAPS IN TIME, I MAY BE A CITIZEN OF LITHARGE, AND HAVE PRENTICES OF MY OWN.
I KNOW COSMETICS, AND TAXIDERMY, AND CARPENTRY, AND MASONRY, AND ALL THE FUNERARY ARTS.
I CAN BUILD A CATAFALQUE OR MAKE A PAPER WREATH OR BOIL A SKULL AS WELL AS ANY PRENTICE IN THE NECROPOLIS.
BUT I HAVE NO TALES.
IN MY HEART I REAM OF VISITING DISTANT PLACES.
CERTAINLY, AS A CITIZEN OF THE NECROPOLIS, I WOULD BE TREATED WITH RESPECT AND ADMIRATION. I KNOW I WOULD HAVE TALES APLENTY, WERE I TO TRAVEL IN WORLDS BEYOND...
WELL, WE'VE TOLD THREE STORIES, AND SWALLOWED A NIGHT. THAT'S ENOUGH.
SCROYLE. MIG. PACK UP AND WALK BACK.
MASTER KLAPROTH WAS WAITING FOR ME AT THE GATE OF THE CITY.
IT WAS SIX MONTHS LATER BEFORE I DARED TO ASK HIM ABOUT THE ROOM BELOW THE CATACOMBS, AND THE BOOK, AND THE CEREMENTS...
...BUT I ONLY LEARNED MORE WHEN I WAS RAISED FROM PRENTICE TO JOURNEYMAN, AND SWORE ON THE BAGULKAL THAT I WOULD TELL--

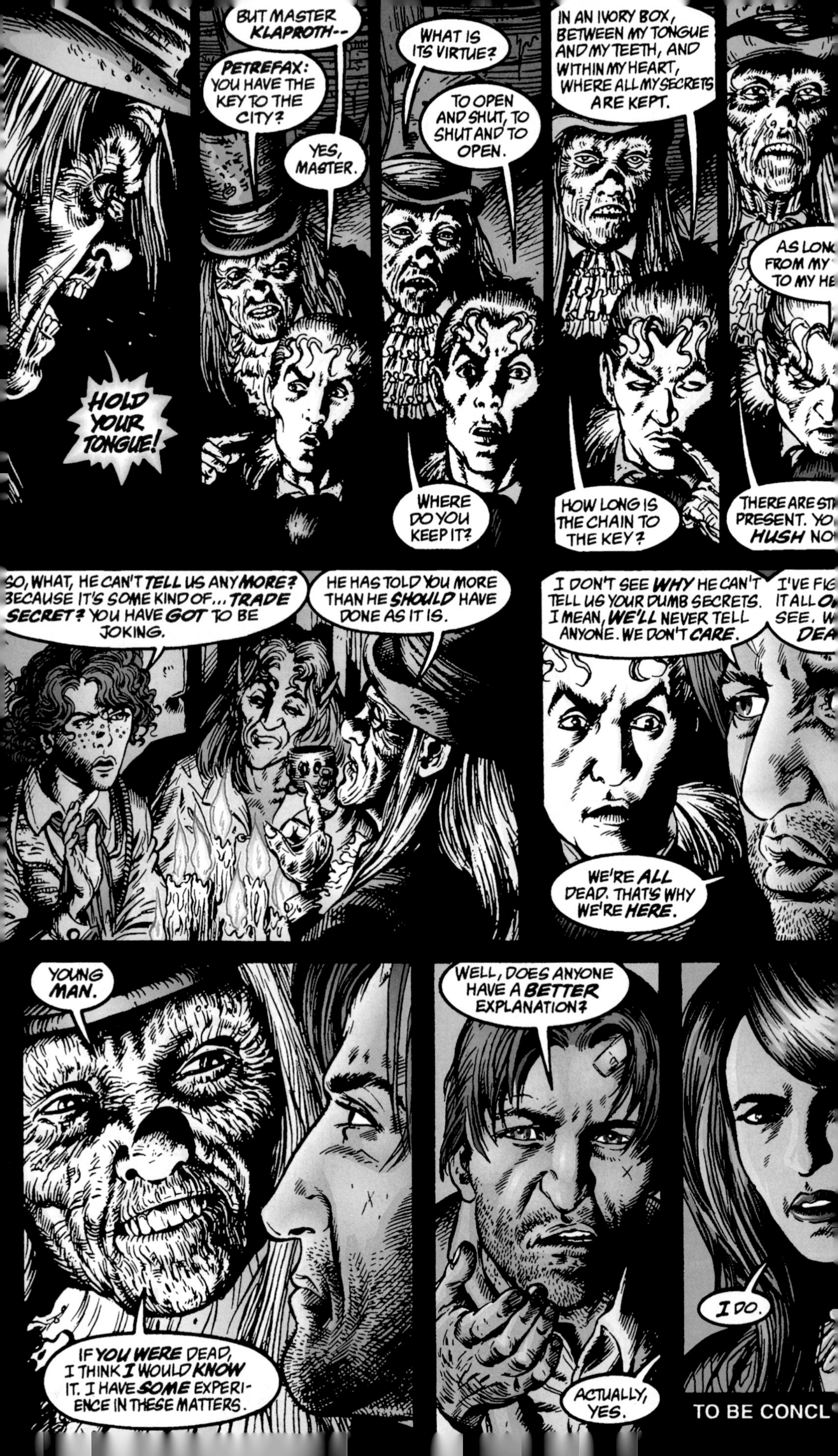
HOLD YOUR TONGUE!
BUT MASTER KLAPROTH--
PETREFAX: YOU HAVE THE KEY TO THE CITY?
YES, MASTER.
WHAT IS ITS VIRTUE?
TO OPEN AND SHUT, TO SHUT AND TO OPEN.
WHERE DO YOU KEEP IT?
IN AN IVORY BOX, BETWEEN MY TONGUE AND MY TEETH, AND WITHIN MY HEART, WHERE ALL MY SECRETS ARE KEPT.
HOW LONG IS THE CHAIN TO THE KEY?
AS LONG FROM MY TO MY HE
THERE ARE ST PRESENT. YO HUSH NO
SO, WHAT, HE CAN'T TELL US ANY MORE? BECAUSE IT'S SOME KIND OF... TRADE SECRET? YOU HAVE GOT TO BE JOKING.
HE HAS TOLD YOU MORE THAN HE SHOULD HAVE DONE AS IT IS.
I DON'T SEE WHY HE CAN'T TELL US YOUR DUMB SECRETS. I MEAN, WE'LL NEVER TELL ANYONE. WE DON'T CARE.
I'VE FIG IT ALL O SEE. W DEA
WE'RE ALL DEAD. THAT'S WHY WE'RE HERE.
YOUNG MAN.
IF YOU WERE DEAD, I THINK I WOULD KNOW IT. I HAVE SOME EXPERIENCE IN THESE MATTERS.
WELL, DOES ANYONE HAVE A BETTER EXPLANATION?
ACTUALLY, YES.
I DO.
TO BE CONCL

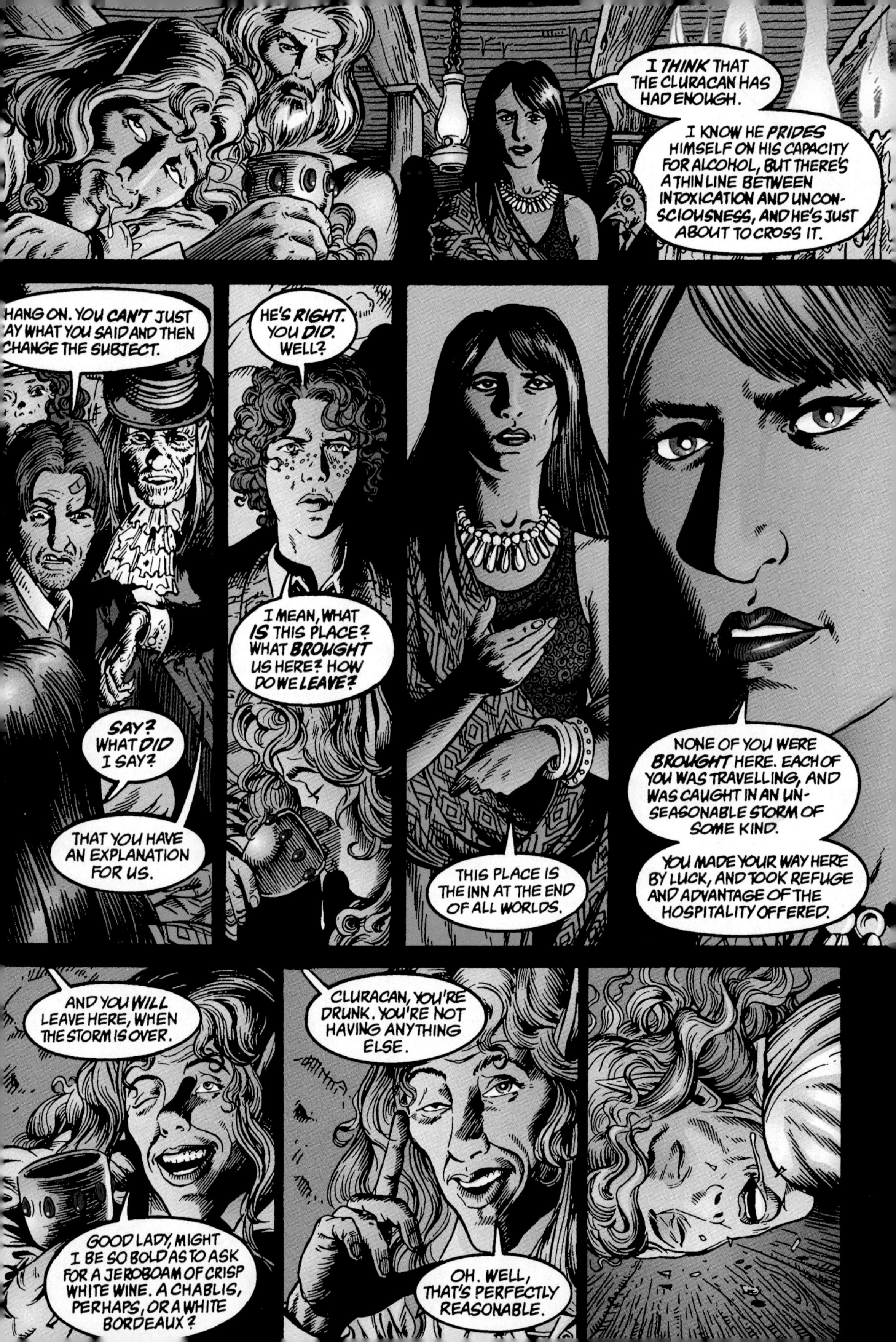
I THINK THAT THE CLURACAN HAS HAD ENOUGH.
I KNOW HE PRIDES HIMSELF ON HIS CAPACITY FOR ALCOHOL, BUT THERE'S A THIN LINE BETWEEN INTOXICATION AND UNCONSCIOUSNESS, AND HE'S JUST ABOUT TO CROSS IT.
HANG ON. YOU CAN'T JUST SAY WHAT YOU SAID AND THEN CHANGE THE SUBJECT.
SAY? WHAT DID I SAY?
THAT YOU HAVE AN EXPLANATION FOR US.
HE'S RIGHT. YOU DID. WELL?
I MEAN, WHAT IS THIS PLACE? WHAT BROUGHT US HERE? HOW DO WE LEAVE?
THIS PLACE IS THE INN AT THE END OF ALL WORLDS.
NONE OF YOU WERE BROUGHT HERE. EACH OF YOU WAS TRAVELLING, AND WAS CAUGHT IN AN UNSEASONABLE STORM OF SOME KIND.
YOU MADE YOUR WAY HERE BY LUCK, AND TOOK REFUGE AND ADVANTAGE OF THE HOSPITALITY OFFERED.
AND YOU WILL LEAVE HERE, WHEN THE STORM IS OVER.
GOOD LADY, MIGHT I BE SO BOLD AS TO ASK FOR A JEROBOAM OF CRISP WHITE WINE. A CHABLIS, PERHAPS, OR A WHITE BORDEAUX?
CLURACAN, YOU'RE DRUNK. YOU'RE NOT HAVING ANYTHING ELSE.
OH. WELL, THAT'S PERFECTLY REASONABLE.

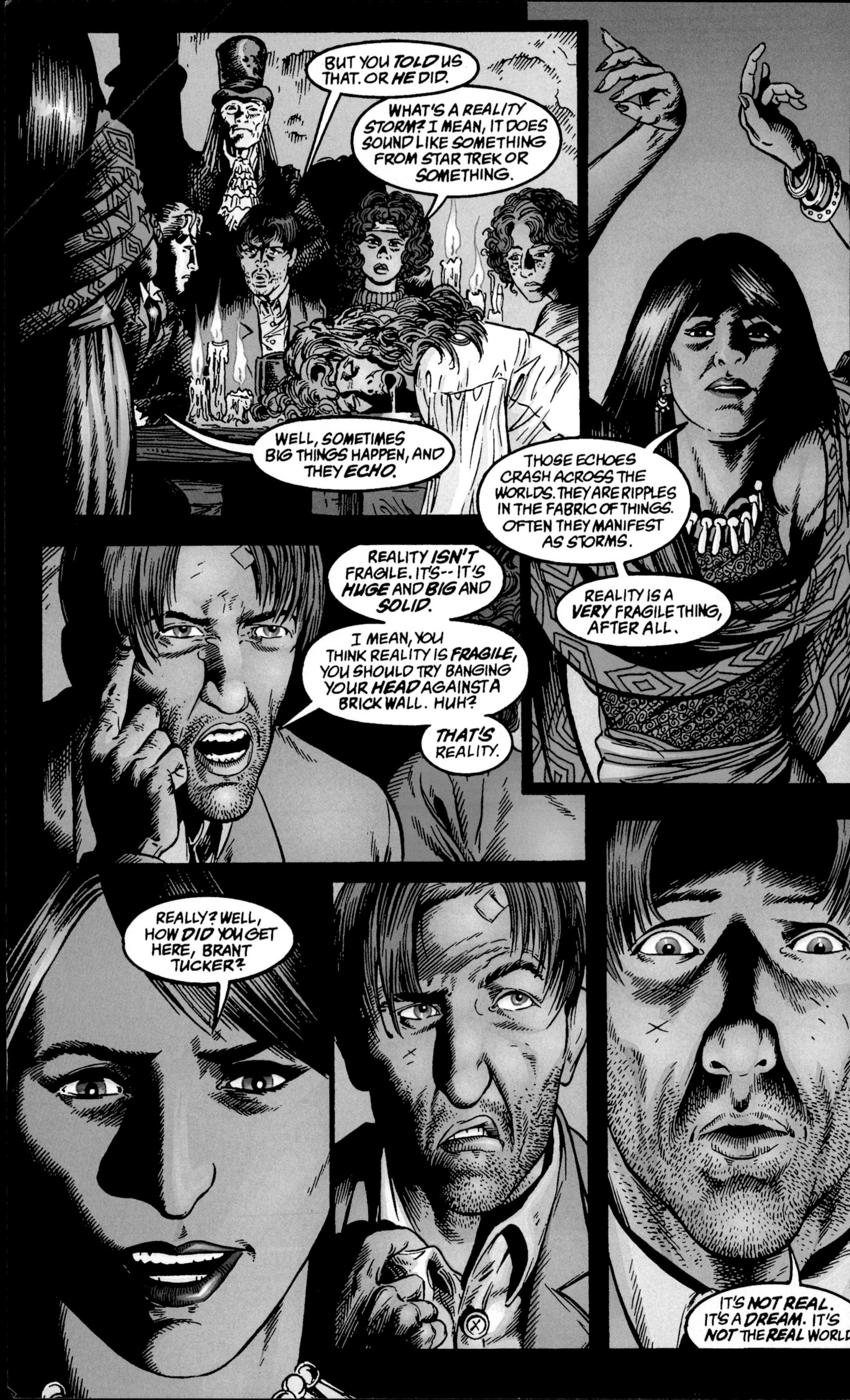
BUT YOU TOLD US THAT. OR HE DID.
WHAT'S A REALITY STORM? I MEAN, IT DOES SOUND LIKE SOMETHING FROM STAR TREK OR SOMETHING.
WELL, SOMETIMES BIG THINGS HAPPEN, AND THEY ECHO.
THOSE ECHOES CRASH ACROSS THE WORLDS. THEY ARE RIPPLES IN THE FABRIC OF THINGS. OFTEN THEY MANIFEST AS STORMS.
REALITY IS A VERY FRAGILE THING, AFTER ALL.
REALITY ISN'T FRAGILE. IT'S--IT'S HUGE AND BIG AND SOLID.
I MEAN, YOU THINK REALITY IS FRAGILE, YOU SHOULD TRY BANGING YOUR HEAD AGAINST A BRICK WALL. HUH?
THAT'S REALITY.
REALLY? WELL, HOW DID YOU GET HERE, BRANT TUCKER?
IT'S NOT REAL. IT'S A DREAM. IT'S NOT THE REAL WORLD

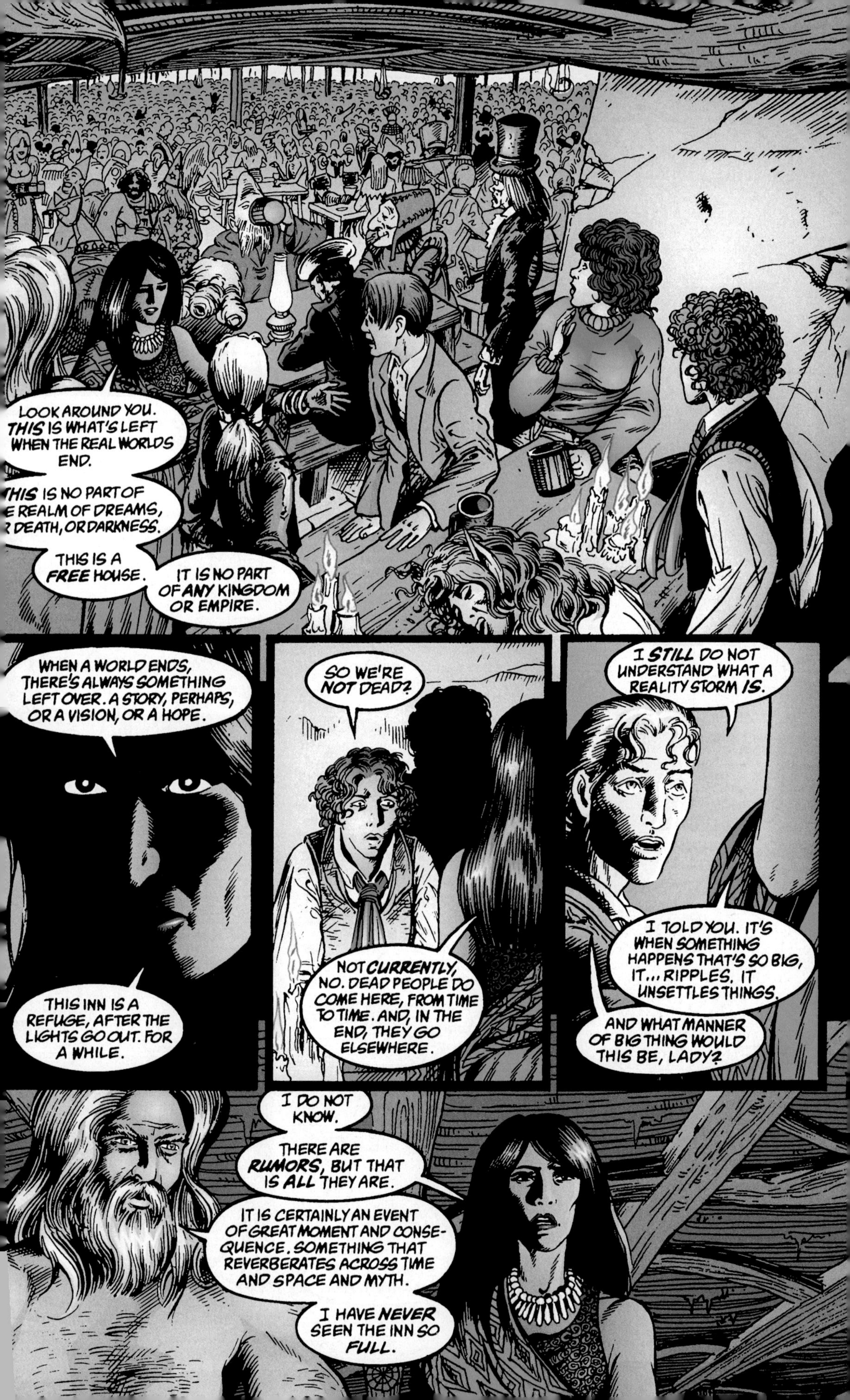
LOOK AROUND YOU. THIS IS WHAT'S LEFT WHEN THE REAL WORLDS END.
THIS IS NO PART OF E REALM OF DREAMS, R DEATH, OR DARKNESS.
THIS IS A FREE HOUSE.
IT IS NO PART OF ANY KINGDOM OR EMPIRE.
WHEN A WORLD ENDS, THERE'S ALWAYS SOMETHING LEFT OVER. A STORY, PERHAPS, OR A VISION, OR A HOPE.
THIS INN IS A REFUGE, AFTER THE LIGHTS GO OUT. FOR A WHILE.
SO WE'RE NOT DEAD?
NOT CURRENTLY, NO. DEAD PEOPLE DO COME HERE, FROM TIME TO TIME. AND, IN THE END, THEY GO ELSEWHERE.
I STILL DO NOT UNDERSTAND WHAT A REALITY STORM IS.
I TOLD YOU. IT'S WHEN SOMETHING HAPPENS THAT'S SO BIG, IT... RIPPLES. IT UNSETTLES THINGS.
AND WHAT MANNER OF BIG THING WOULD THIS BE, LADY?
I DO NOT KNOW.
THERE ARE RUMORS, BUT THAT IS ALL THEY ARE.
IT IS CERTAINLY AN EVENT OF GREAT MOMENT AND CONSE-QUENCE. SOMETHING THAT REVERBERATES ACROSS TIME AND SPACE AND MYTH.
I HAVE NEVER SEEN THE INN SO FULL.

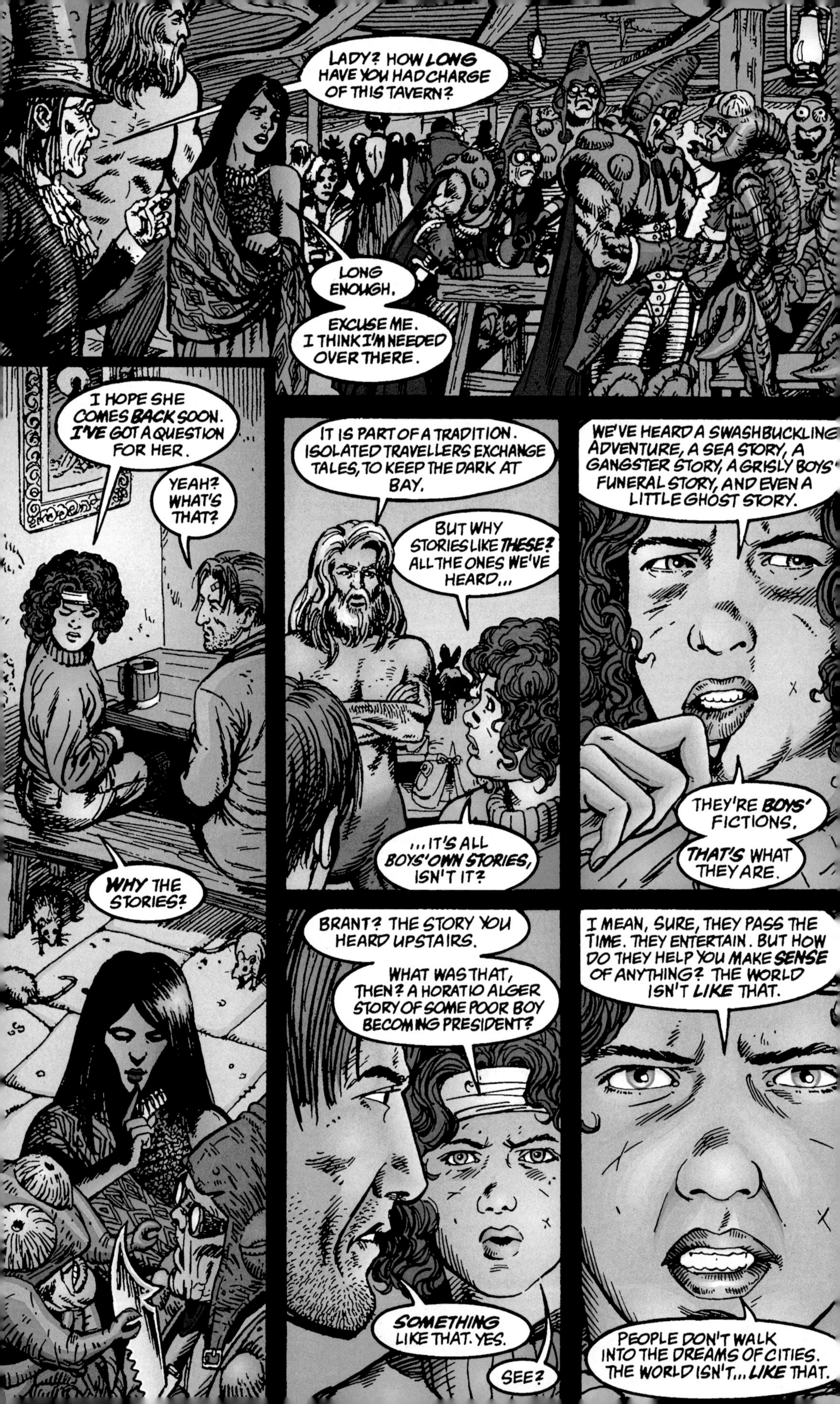
LADY? HOW LONG HAVE YOU HAD CHARGE OF THIS TAVERN?
LONG ENOUGH.
EXCUSE ME. I THINK I'M NEEDED OVER THERE.
I HOPE SHE COMES BACK SOON. I'VE GOT A QUESTION FOR HER.
YEAH? WHAT'S THAT?
WHY THE STORIES?
IT IS PART OF A TRADITION. ISOLATED TRAVELLERS EXCHANGE TALES, TO KEEP THE DARK AT BAY.
BUT WHY STORIES LIKE THESE? ALL THE ONES WE'VE HEARD...
...IT'S ALL BOYS' OWN STORIES, ISN'T IT?
WE'VE HEARD A SWASHBUCKLING ADVENTURE, A SEA STORY, A GANGSTER STORY, A GRISLY BOYS' FUNERAL STORY, AND EVEN A LITTLE GHOST STORY.
THEY'RE BOYS' FICTIONS.
THAT'S WHAT THEY ARE.
BRANT? THE STORY YOU HEARD UPSTAIRS.
WHAT WAS THAT, THEN? A HORATIO ALGER STORY OF SOME POOR BOY BECOMING PRESIDENT?
SOMETHING LIKE THAT. YES.
SEE?
I MEAN, SURE, THEY PASS THE TIME. THEY ENTERTAIN. BUT HOW DO THEY HELP YOU MAKE SENSE OF ANYTHING? THE WORLD ISN'T LIKE THAT.
PEOPLE DON'T WALK INTO THE DREAMS OF CITIES. THE WORLD ISN'T... LIKE THAT.

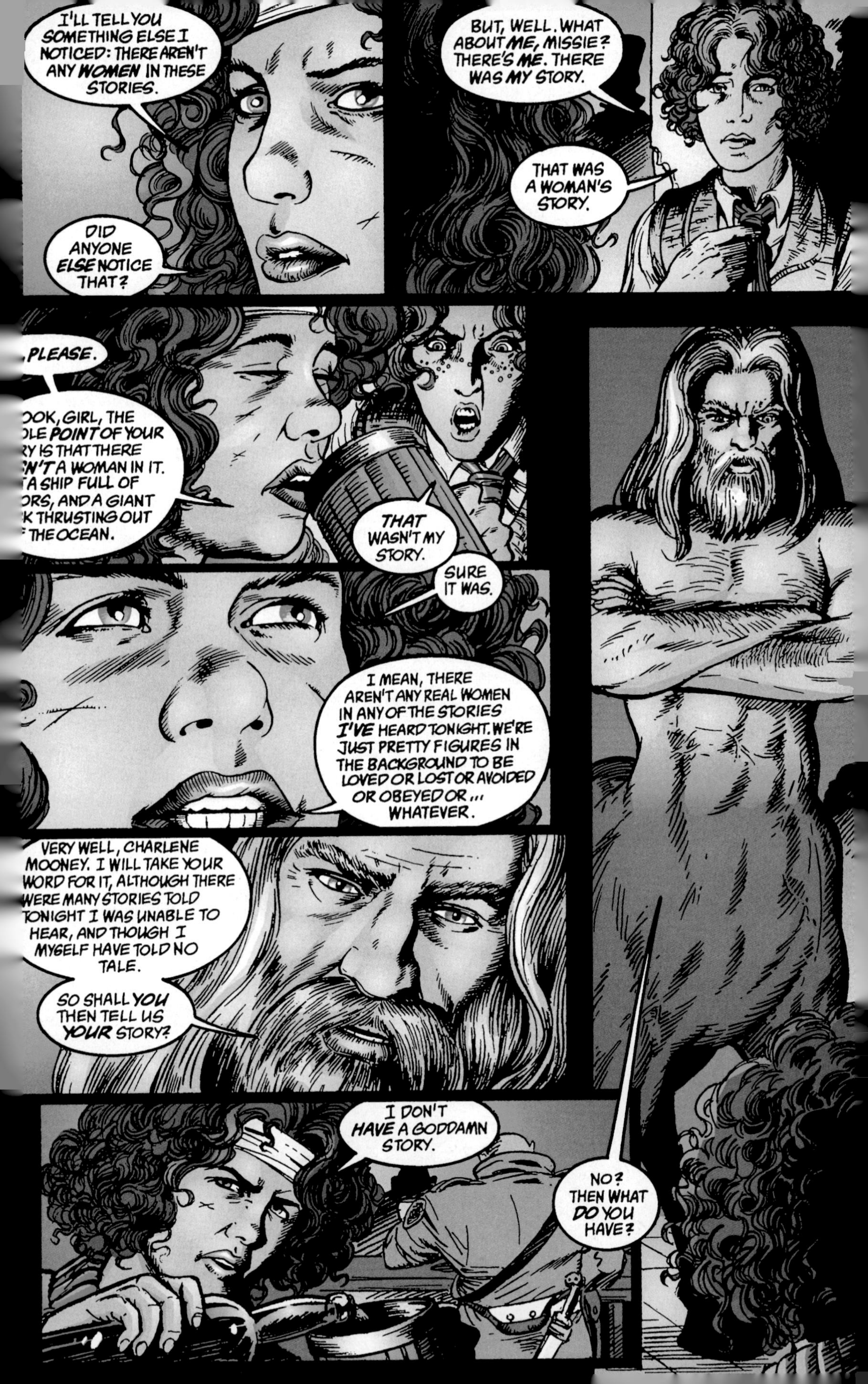

I'LL TELL YOU SOMETHING ELSE I NOTICED: THERE AREN'T ANY WOMEN IN THESE STORIES.
DID ANYONE ELSE NOTICE THAT?
BUT, WELL. WHAT ABOUT ME, MISSIE? THERE'S ME. THERE WAS MY STORY.
THAT WAS A WOMAN'S STORY.
PLEASE.
OOK, GIRL, THE OLE POINT OF YOUR RY IS THAT THERE N'T A WOMAN IN IT. T A SHIP FULL OF ORS, AND A GIANT K THRUSTING OUT F THE OCEAN.
THAT WASN'T MY STORY.
SURE IT WAS.
I MEAN, THERE AREN'T ANY REAL WOMEN IN ANY OF THE STORIES I'VE HEARD TONIGHT. WE'RE JUST PRETTY FIGURES IN THE BACKGROUND TO BE LOVED OR LOST OR AVOIDED OR OBEYED OR ... WHATEVER.
VERY WELL, CHARLENE MOONEY. I WILL TAKE YOUR WORD FOR IT, ALTHOUGH THERE WERE MANY STORIES TOLD TONIGHT I WAS UNABLE TO HEAR, AND THOUGH I MYSELF HAVE TOLD NO TALE.
SO SHALL YOU THEN TELL US YOUR STORY?
I DON'T HAVE A GODDAMN STORY.
NO? THEN WHAT DO YOU HAVE?

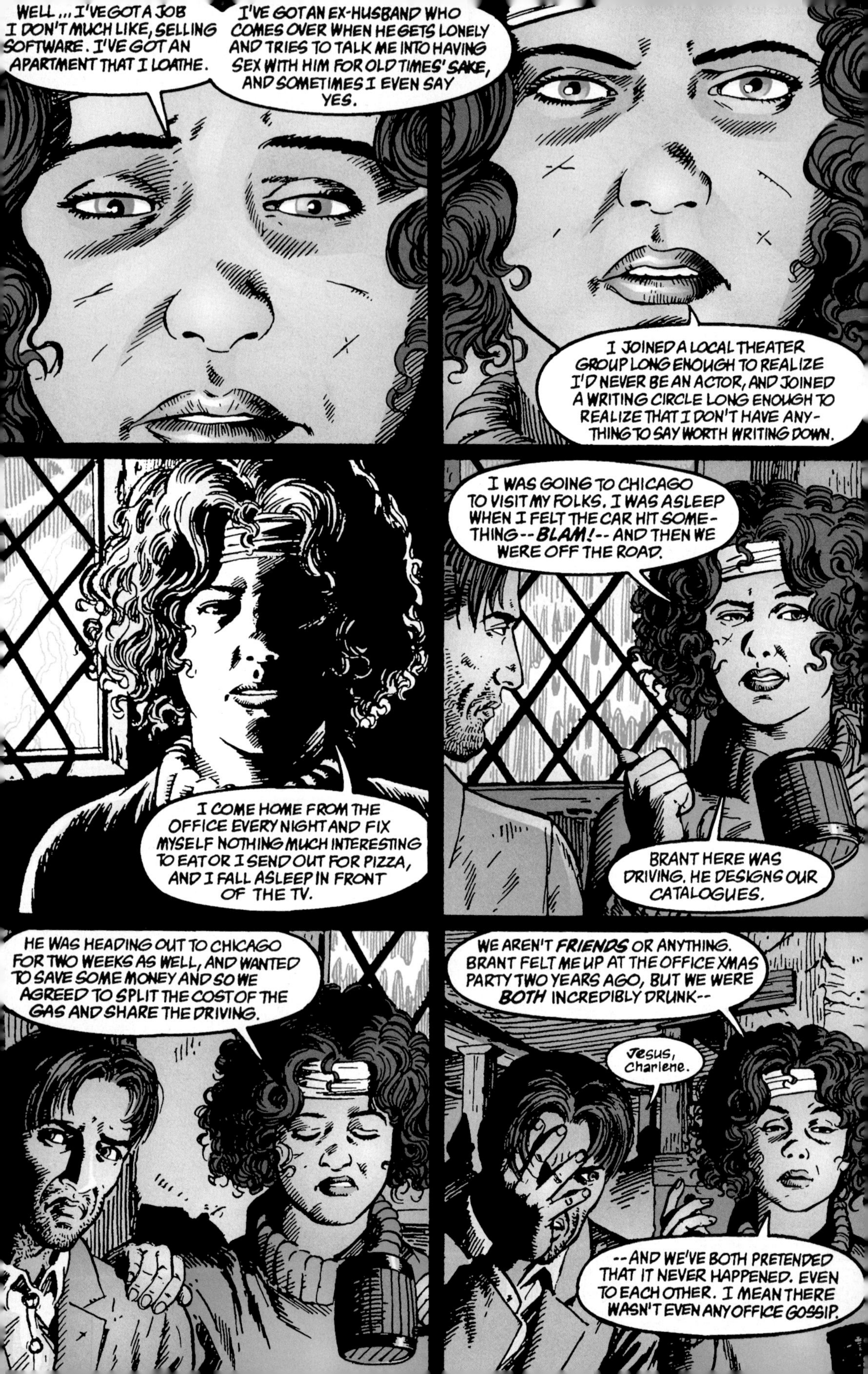
WELL... I'VE GOT A JOB I DON'T MUCH LIKE, SELLING SOFTWARE. I'VE GOT AN APARTMENT THAT I LOATHE.
I'VE GOT AN EX-HUSBAND WHO COMES OVER WHEN HE GETS LONELY AND TRIES TO TALK ME INTO HAVING SEX WITH HIM FOR OLD TIMES' SAKE, AND SOMETIMES I EVEN SAY YES.
I JOINED A LOCAL THEATER GROUP LONG ENOUGH TO REALIZE I'D NEVER BE AN ACTOR, AND JOINED A WRITING CIRCLE LONG ENOUGH TO REALIZE THAT I DON'T HAVE ANYTHING TO SAY WORTH WRITING DOWN.
I COME HOME FROM THE OFFICE EVERY NIGHT AND FIX MYSELF NOTHING MUCH INTERESTING TO EAT OR I SEND OUT FOR PIZZA, AND I FALL ASLEEP IN FRONT OF THE TV.
I WAS GOING TO CHICAGO TO VISIT MY FOLKS. I WAS ASLEEP WHEN I FELT THE CAR HIT SOMETHING--BLAM!--AND THEN WE WERE OFF THE ROAD.
BRANT HERE WAS DRIVING. HE DESIGNS OUR CATALOGUES.
HE WAS HEADING OUT TO CHICAGO FOR TWO WEEKS AS WELL, AND WANTED TO SAVE SOME MONEY AND SO WE AGREED TO SPLIT THE COST OF THE GAS AND SHARE THE DRIVING.
WE AREN'T FRIENDS OR ANYTHING. BRANT FELT ME UP AT THE OFFICE XMAS PARTY TWO YEARS AGO, BUT WE WERE BOTH INCREDIBLY DRUNK--
Jesus, Charlene.
--AND WE'VE BOTH PRETENDED THAT IT NEVER HAPPENED. EVEN TO EACH OTHER. I MEAN THERE WASN'T EVEN ANY OFFICE GOSSIP.

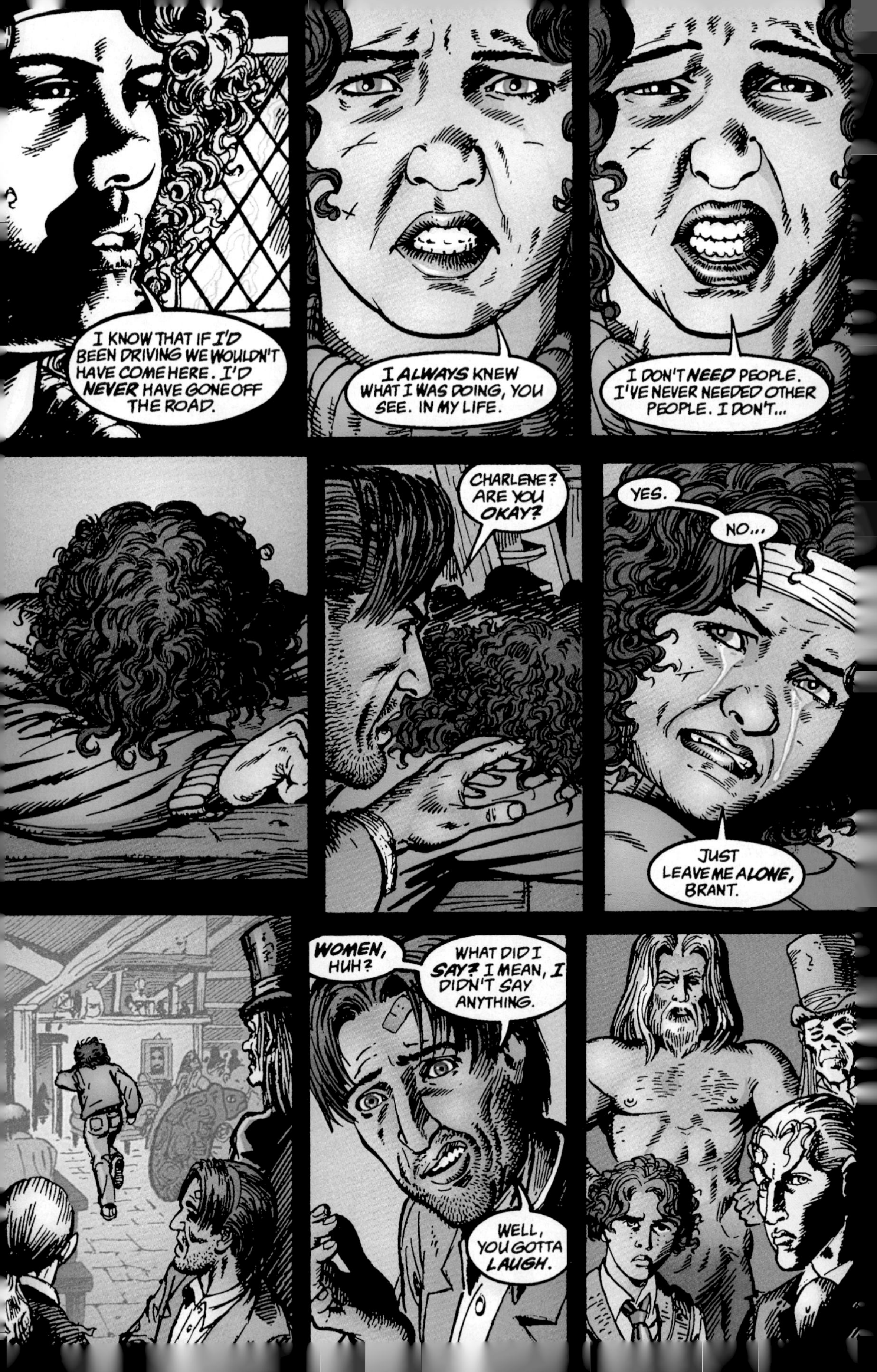
I KNOW THAT IF I'D BEEN DRIVING WE WOULDN'T HAVE COME HERE. I'D NEVER HAVE GONE OFF THE ROAD.
I ALWAYS KNEW WHAT I WAS DOING, YOU SEE. IN MY LIFE.
I DON'T NEED PEOPLE. I'VE NEVER NEEDED OTHER PEOPLE. I DON'T...
CHARLENE? ARE YOU OKAY?
YES.
NO...
JUST LEAVE ME ALONE, BRANT.
WOMEN, HUH?
WHAT DID I SAY? I MEAN, I DIDN'T SAY ANYTHING.
WELL, YOU GOTTA LAUGH.

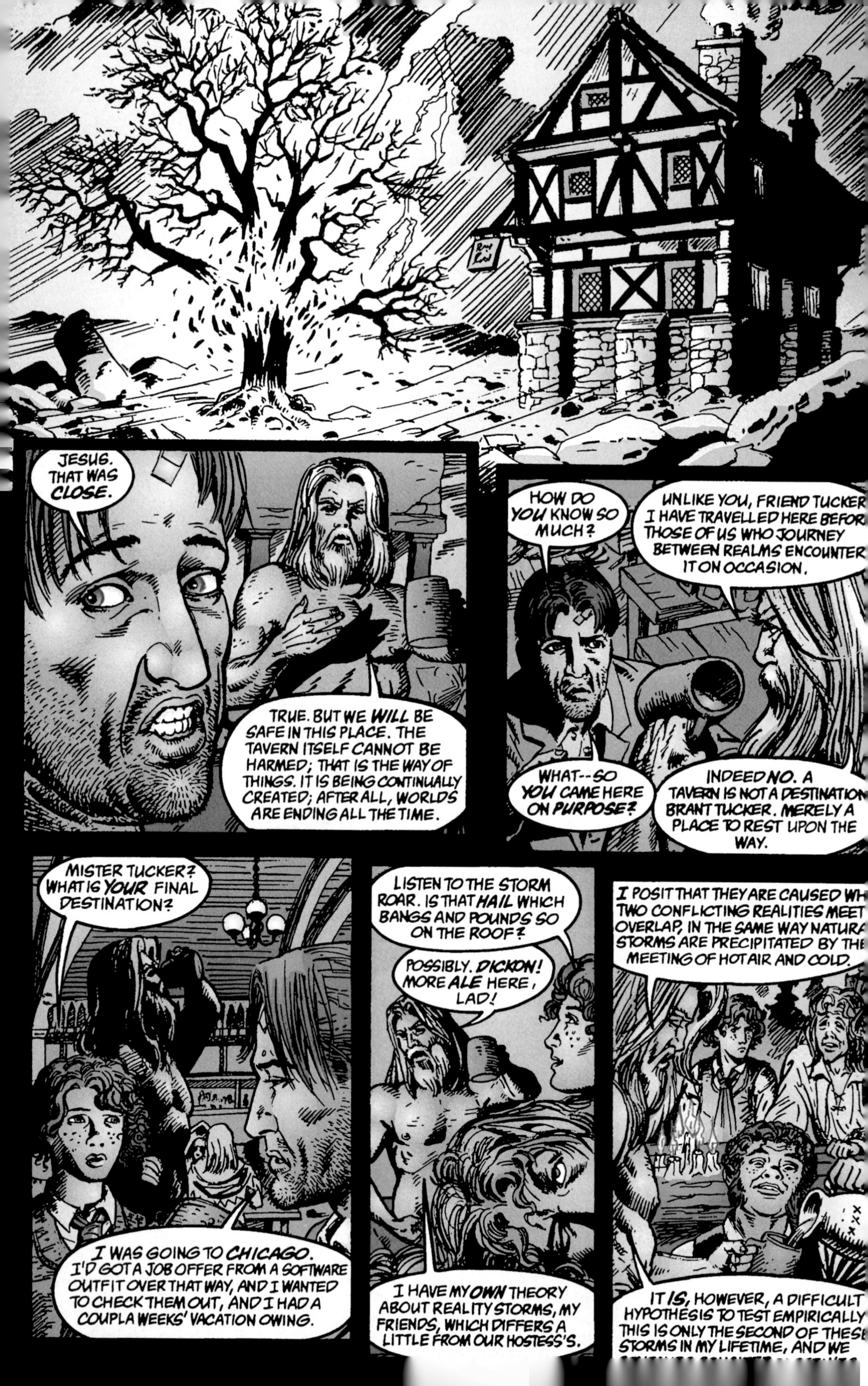

JESUS. THAT WAS CLOSE.
TRUE. BUT WE WILL BE SAFE IN THIS PLACE. THE TAVERN ITSELF CANNOT BE HARMED; THAT IS THE WAY OF THINGS. IT IS BEING CONTINUALLY CREATED; AFTER ALL, WORLDS ARE ENDING ALL THE TIME.
HOW DO YOU KNOW SO MUCH?
UNLIKE YOU, FRIEND TUCKER I HAVE TRAVELLED HERE BEFOR THOSE OF US WHO JOURNEY BETWEEN REALMS ENCOUNTER IT ON OCCASION.
WHAT--SO YOU CAME HERE ON PURPOSE?
INDEED NO. A TAVERN IS NOT A DESTINATION BRANT TUCKER. MERELY A PLACE TO REST UPON THE WAY.
MISTER TUCKER? WHAT IS YOUR FINAL DESTINATION?
I WAS GOING TO CHICAGO. I'D GOT A JOB OFFER FROM A SOFTWARE OUTFIT OVER THAT WAY, AND I WANTED TO CHECK THEM OUT, AND I HAD A COUPLA WEEKS' VACATION OWING.
LISTEN TO THE STORM ROAR. IS THAT HAIL WHICH BANGS AND POUNDS SO ON THE ROOF?
POSSIBLY. DICKON! MORE ALE HERE, LAD!
I HAVE MY OWN THEORY ABOUT REALITY STORMS, MY FRIENDS, WHICH DIFFERS A LITTLE FROM OUR HOSTESS'S.
I POSIT THAT THEY ARE CAUSED WH TWO CONFLICTING REALITIES MEET OVERLAP, IN THE SAME WAY NATUR STORMS ARE PRECIPITATED BY TH MEETING OF HOT AIR AND COLD.
IT IS, HOWEVER, A DIFFICULT HYPOTHESIS TO TEST EMPIRICALLY THIS IS ONLY THE SECOND OF THES STORMS IN MY LIFETIME, AND WE

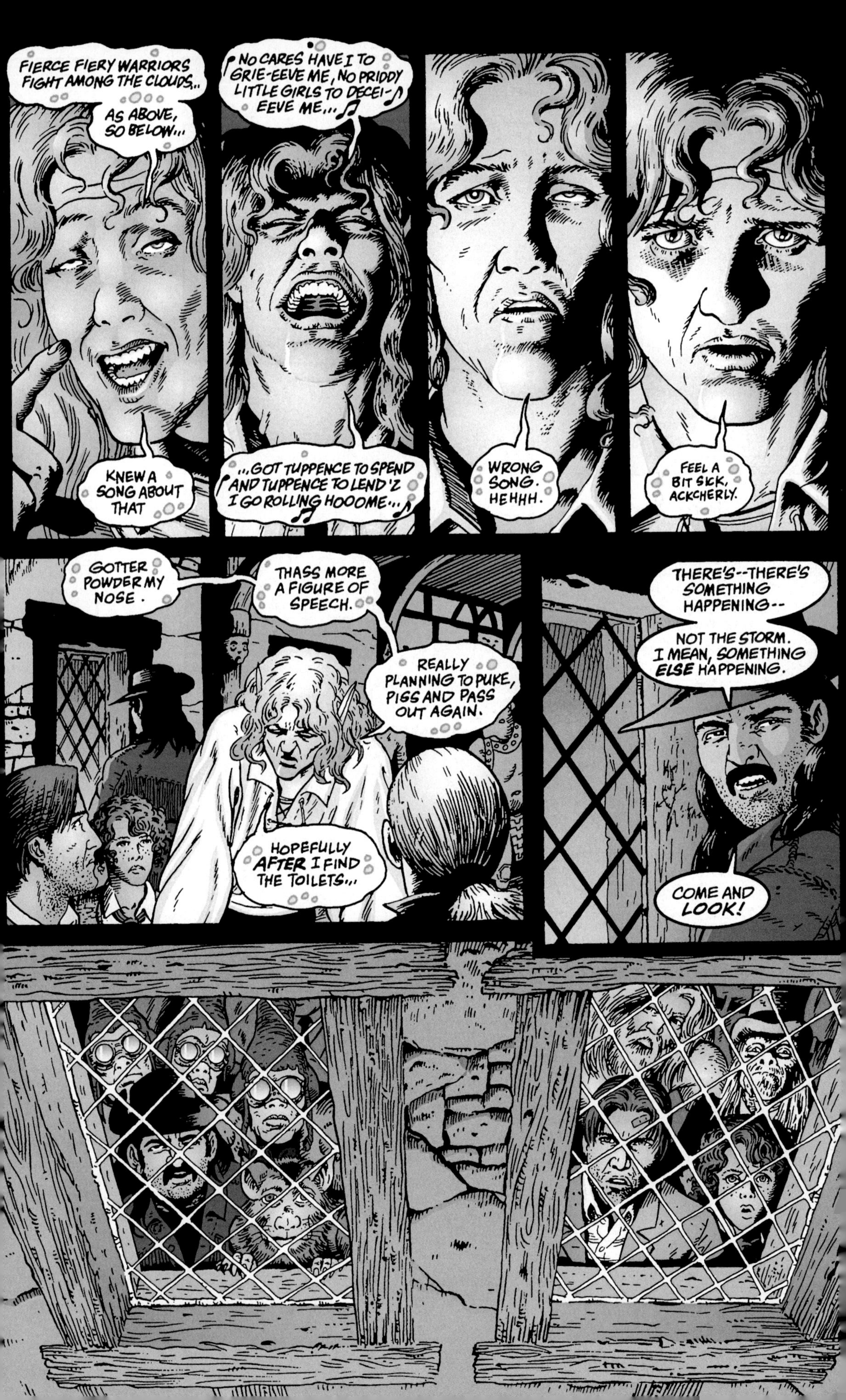
FIERCE FIERY WARRIORS FIGHT AMONG THE CLOUDS...
AS ABOVE, SO BELOW...
KNEW A SONG ABOUT THAT
NO CARES HAVE I TO GRIE-EEVE ME, NO PRIDDY LITTLE GIRLS TO DECEI-EEVE ME...
...GOT TUPPENCE TO SPEND AND TUPPENCE TO LEND 'Z I GO ROLLING HOOOME...
WRONG SONG. HEHHH.
FEEL A BIT SICK, ACKCHERLY.
GOTTER POWDER MY NOSE.
THASS MORE A FIGURE OF SPEECH.
REALLY PLANNING TO PUKE, PISS AND PASS OUT AGAIN.
HOPEFULLY AFTER I FIND THE TOILETS...
THERE'S--THERE'S SOMETHING HAPPENING--
NOT THE STORM. I MEAN, SOMETHING ELSE HAPPENING.
COME AND LOOK!

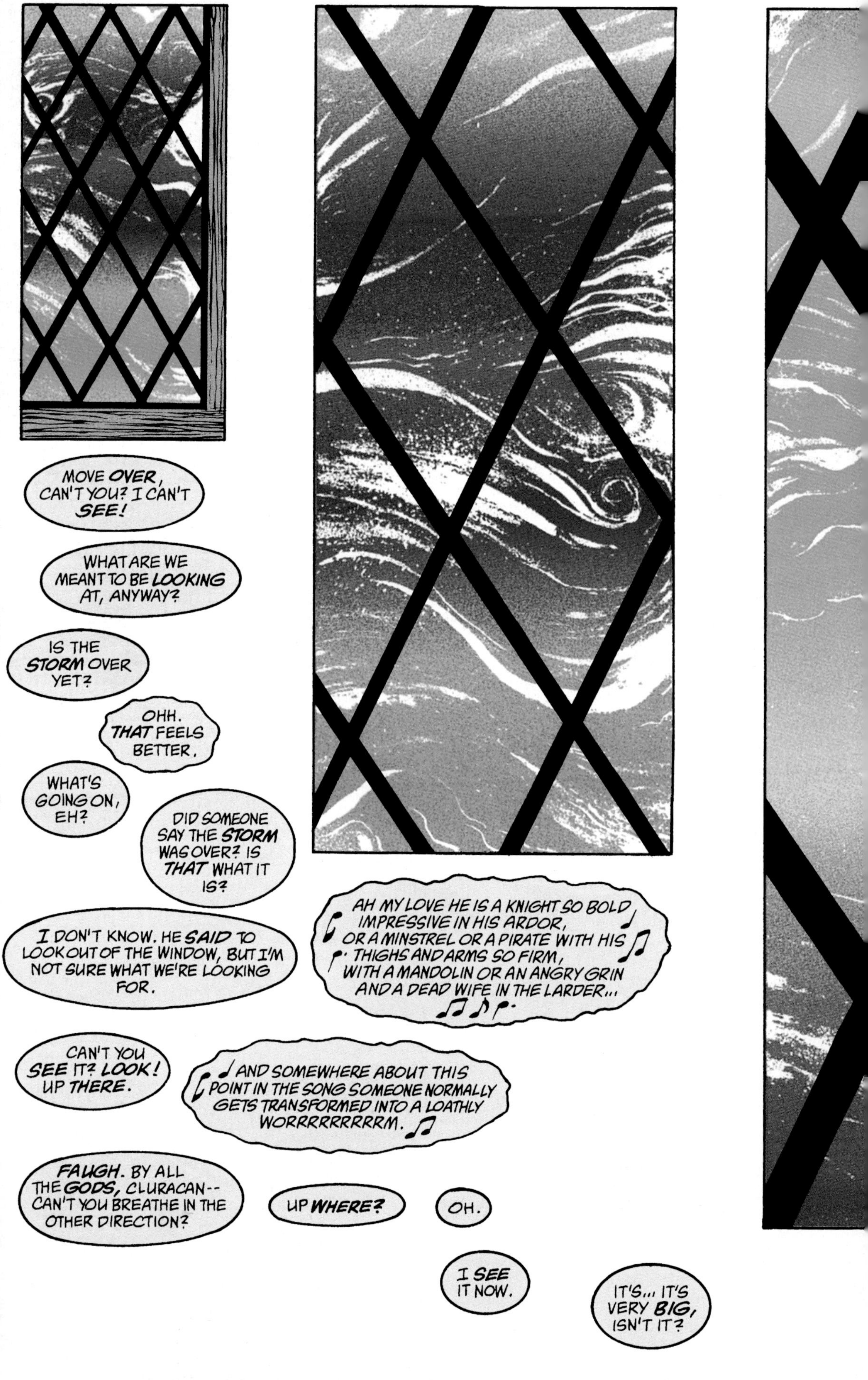
MOVE OVER, CAN'T YOU? I CAN'T SEE!
WHAT ARE WE MEANT TO BE LOOKING AT, ANYWAY?
IS THE STORM OVER YET?
OHH. THAT FEELS BETTER.
WHAT'S GOING ON, EH?
DID SOMEONE SAY THE STORM WAS OVER? IS THAT WHAT IT IS?
I DON'T KNOW. HE SAID TO LOOK OUT OF THE WINDOW, BUT I'M NOT SURE WHAT WE'RE LOOKING FOR.
AH MY LOVE HE IS A KNIGHT SO BOLD IMPRESSIVE IN HIS ARDOR, OR A MINSTREL OR A PIRATE WITH HIS THIGHS AND ARMS SO FIRM, WITH A MANDOLIN OR AN ANGRY GRIN AND A DEAD WIFE IN THE LARDER...
CAN'T YOU SEE IT? LOOK! UP THERE.
AND SOMEWHERE ABOUT THIS POINT IN THE SONG SOMEONE NORMALLY GETS TRANSFORMED INTO A LOATHLY WORRRRRRRRRM.
FAUGH. BY ALL THE GODS, CLURACAN-- CAN'T YOU BREATHE IN THE OTHER DIRECTION?
UP WHERE?
OH.
I SEE IT NOW.
IT'S... IT'S VERY BIG, ISN'T IT?

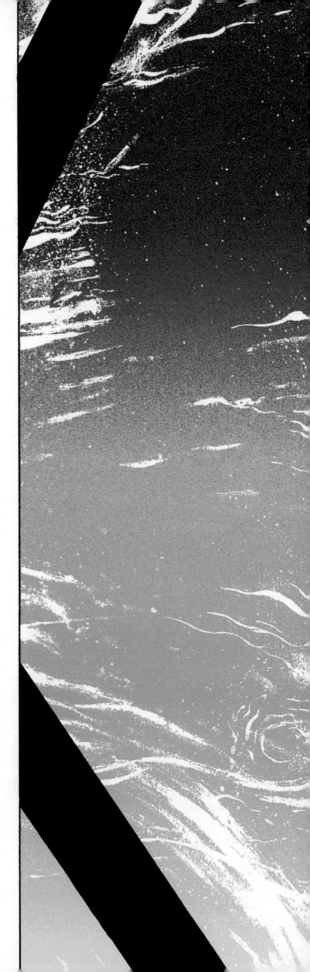

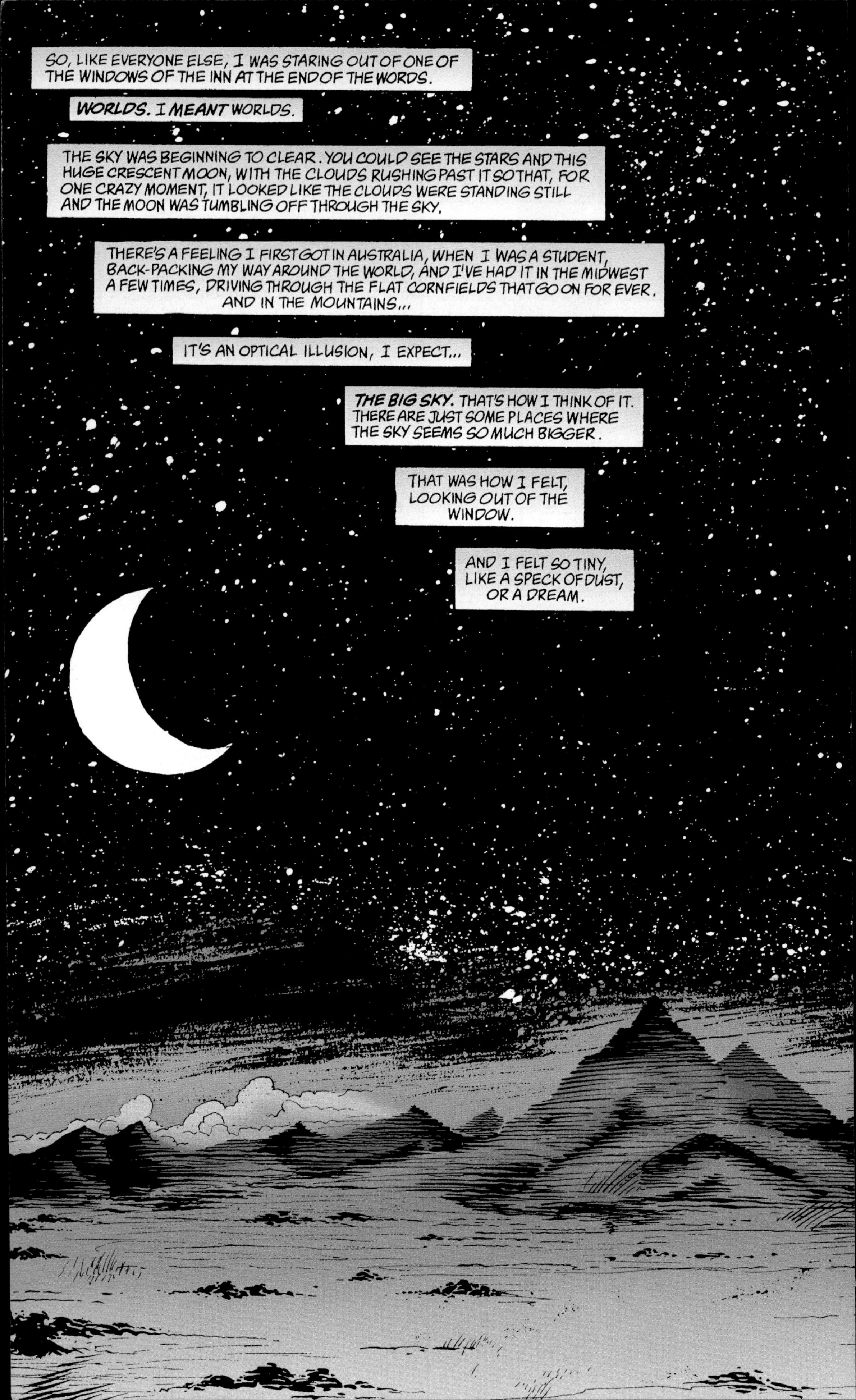
SO, LIKE EVERYONE ELSE, I WAS STARING OUT OF ONE OF THE WINDOWS OF THE INN AT THE END OF THE WORDS.
WORLDS. I MEANT WORLDS.
THE SKY WAS BEGINNING TO CLEAR. YOU COULD SEE THE STARS AND THIS HUGE CRESCENT MOON, WITH THE CLOUDS RUSHING PAST IT SO THAT, FOR ONE CRAZY MOMENT, IT LOOKED LIKE THE CLOUDS WERE STANDING STILL AND THE MOON WAS TUMBLING OFF THROUGH THE SKY.
THERE'S A FEELING I FIRST GOT IN AUSTRALIA, WHEN I WAS A STUDENT, BACK-PACKING MY WAY AROUND THE WORLD, AND I'VE HAD IT IN THE MIDWEST A FEW TIMES, DRIVING THROUGH THE FLAT CORNFIELDS THAT GO ON FOR EVER. AND IN THE MOUNTAINS...
IT'S AN OPTICAL ILLUSION, I EXPECT...
THE BIG SKY. THAT'S HOW I THINK OF IT. THERE ARE JUST SOME PLACES WHERE THE SKY SEEMS SO MUCH BIGGER.
THAT WAS HOW I FELT, LOOKING OUT OF THE WINDOW.
AND I FELT SO TINY, LIKE A SPECK OF DUST, OR A DREAM.

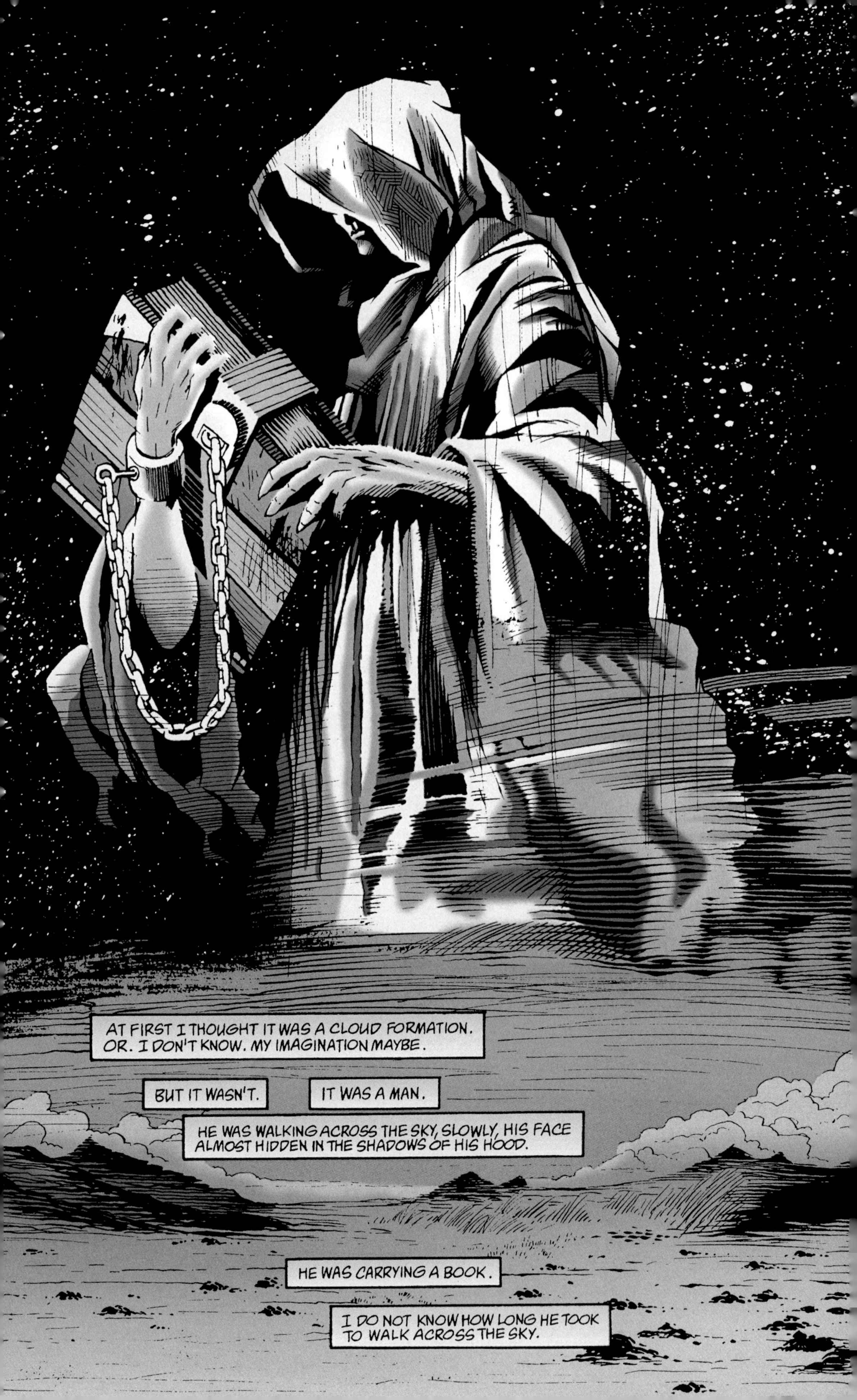
AT FIRST I THOUGHT IT WAS A CLOUD FORMATION. OR. I DON'T KNOW. MY IMAGINATION MAYBE.
BUT IT WASN'T.
IT WAS A MAN.
HE WAS WALKING ACROSS THE SKY, SLOWLY, HIS FACE ALMOST HIDDEN IN THE SHADOWS OF HIS HOOD.
HE WAS CARRYING A BOOK.
I DO NOT KNOW HOW LONG HE TOOK TO WALK ACROSS THE SKY.

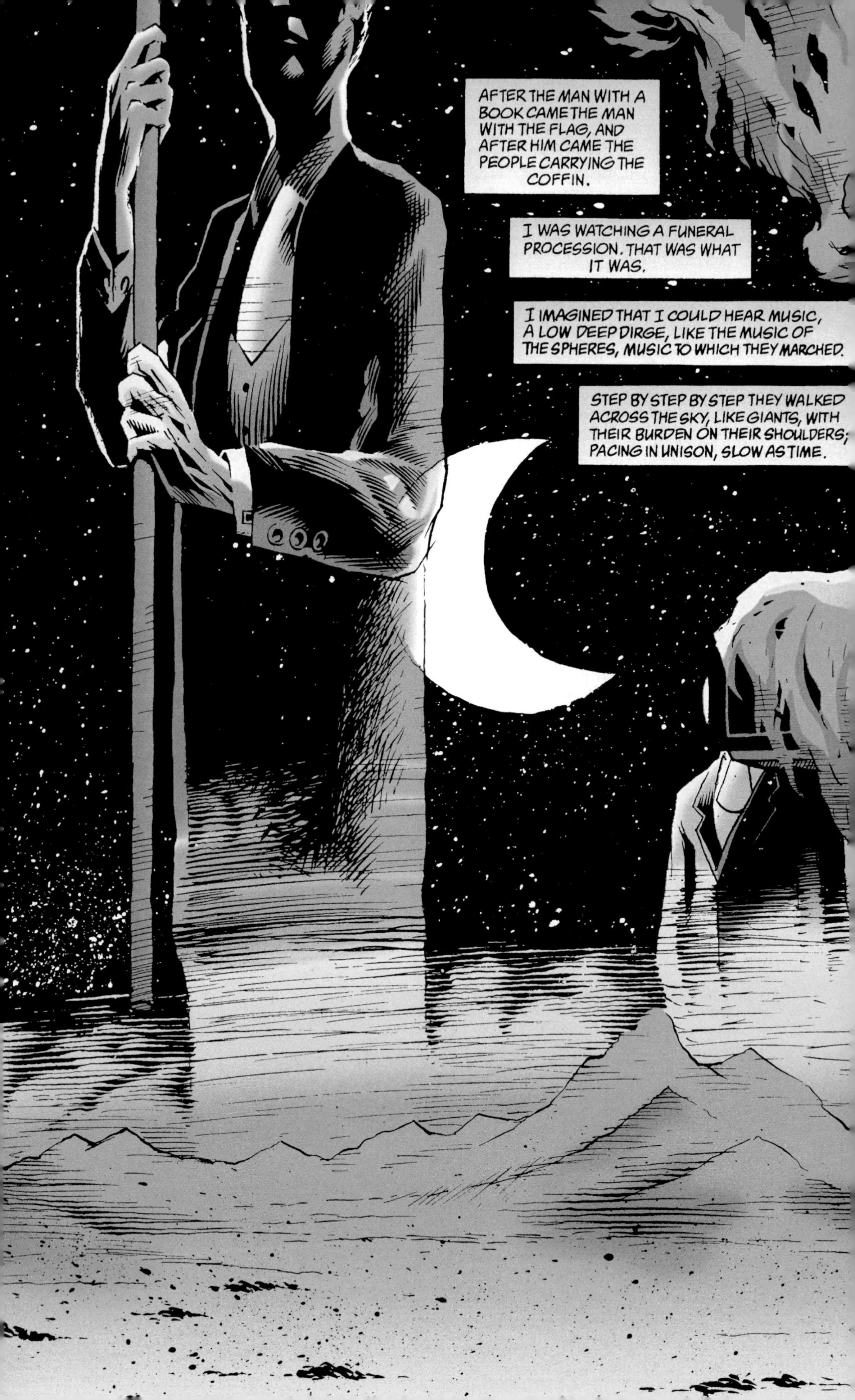
AFTER THE MAN WITH A BOOK CAME THE MAN WITH THE FLAG, AND AFTER HIM CAME THE PEOPLE CARRYING THE COFFIN.
I WAS WATCHING A FUNERAL PROCESSION. THAT WAS WHAT IT WAS.
I IMAGINED THAT I COULD HEAR MUSIC, A LOW DEEP DIRGE, LIKE THE MUSIC OF THE SPHERES, MUSIC TO WHICH THEY MARCHED.
STEP BY STEP BY STEP THEY WALKED ACROSS THE SKY, LIKE GIANTS, WITH THEIR BURDEN ON THEIR SHOULDERS; PACING IN UNISON, SLOW AS TIME.

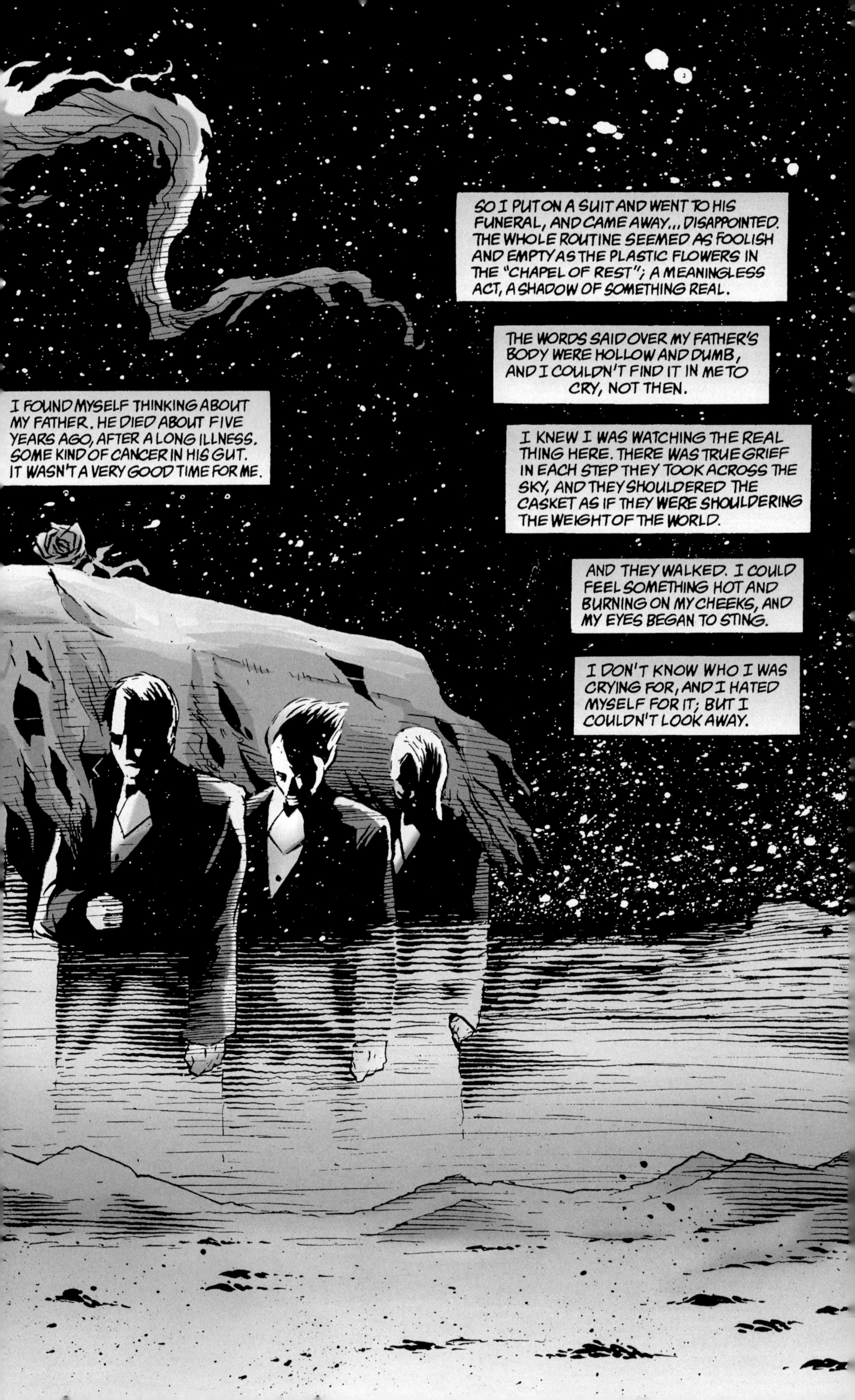
SO I PUT ON A SUIT AND WENT TO HIS FUNERAL, AND CAME AWAY... DISAPPOINTED. THE WHOLE ROUTINE SEEMED AS FOOLISH AND EMPTY AS THE PLASTIC FLOWERS IN THE "CHAPEL OF REST"; A MEANINGLESS ACT, A SHADOW OF SOMETHING REAL.
THE WORDS SAID OVER MY FATHER'S BODY WERE HOLLOW AND DUMB, AND I COULDN'T FIND IT IN ME TO CRY, NOT THEN.
I FOUND MYSELF THINKING ABOUT MY FATHER. HE DIED ABOUT FIVE YEARS AGO, AFTER A LONG ILLNESS. SOME KIND OF CANCER IN HIS GUT. IT WASN'T A VERY GOOD TIME FOR ME.
I KNEW I WAS WATCHING THE REAL THING HERE. THERE WAS TRUE GRIEF IN EACH STEP THEY TOOK ACROSS THE SKY, AND THEY SHOULDERED THE CASKET AS IF THEY WERE SHOULDERING THE WEIGHT OF THE WORLD.
AND THEY WALKED. I COULD FEEL SOMETHING HOT AND BURNING ON MY CHEEKS, AND MY EYES BEGAN TO STING.
I DON'T KNOW WHO I WAS CRYING FOR, AND I HATED MYSELF FOR IT; BUT I COULDN'T LOOK AWAY.

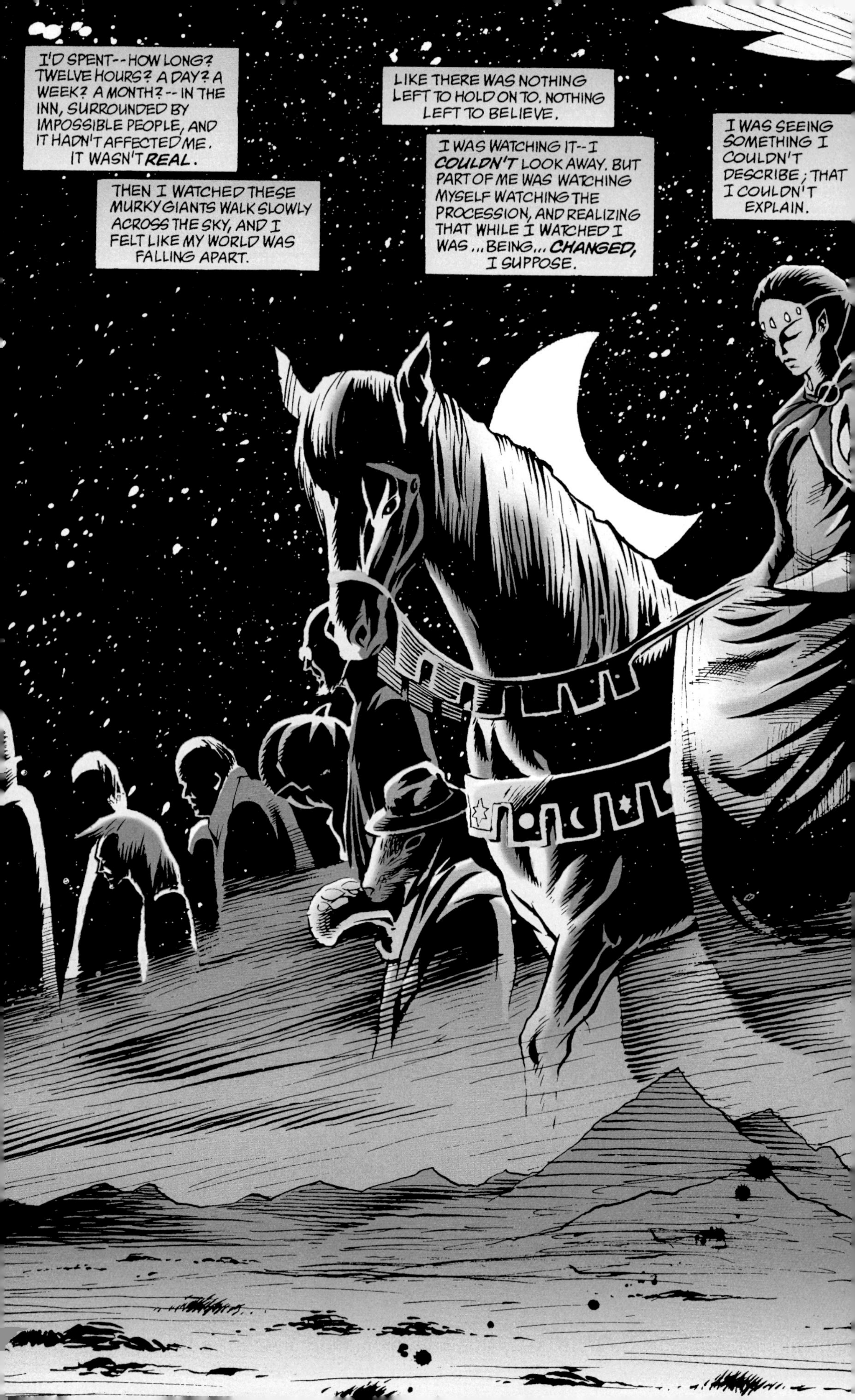
I'D SPENT--HOW LONG? TWELVE HOURS? A DAY? A WEEK? A MONTH? -- IN THE INN, SURROUNDED BY IMPOSSIBLE PEOPLE, AND IT HADN'T AFFECTED ME. IT WASN'T **REAL**.
THEN I WATCHED THESE MURKY GIANTS WALK SLOWLY ACROSS THE SKY, AND I FELT LIKE MY WORLD WAS FALLING APART.
LIKE THERE WAS NOTHING LEFT TO HOLD ON TO. NOTHING LEFT TO BELIEVE.
I WAS WATCHING IT--I **COULDN'T** LOOK AWAY. BUT PART OF ME WAS WATCHING MYSELF WATCHING THE PROCESSION, AND REALIZING THAT WHILE I WATCHED I WAS ...BEING... **CHANGED**, I SUPPOSE.
I WAS SEEING SOMETHING I COULDN'T DESCRIBE; THAT I COULDN'T EXPLAIN.

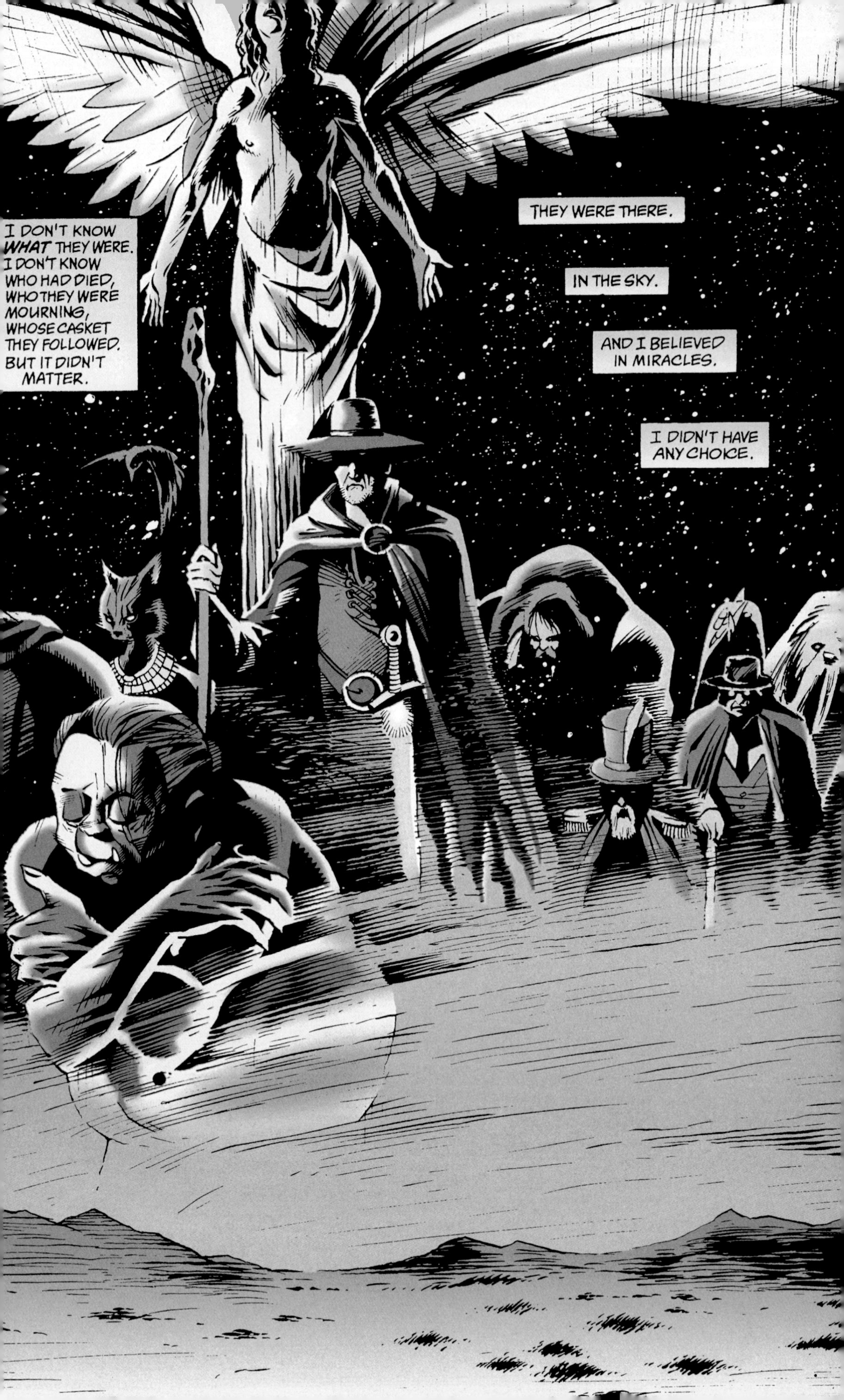
I DON'T KNOW **WHAT** THEY WERE. I DON'T KNOW WHO HAD DIED, WHO THEY WERE MOURNING, WHOSE CASKET THEY FOLLOWED. BUT IT DIDN'T MATTER.
THEY WERE THERE.
IN THE SKY.
AND I BELIEVED IN MIRACLES.
I DIDN'T HAVE ANY CHOICE.

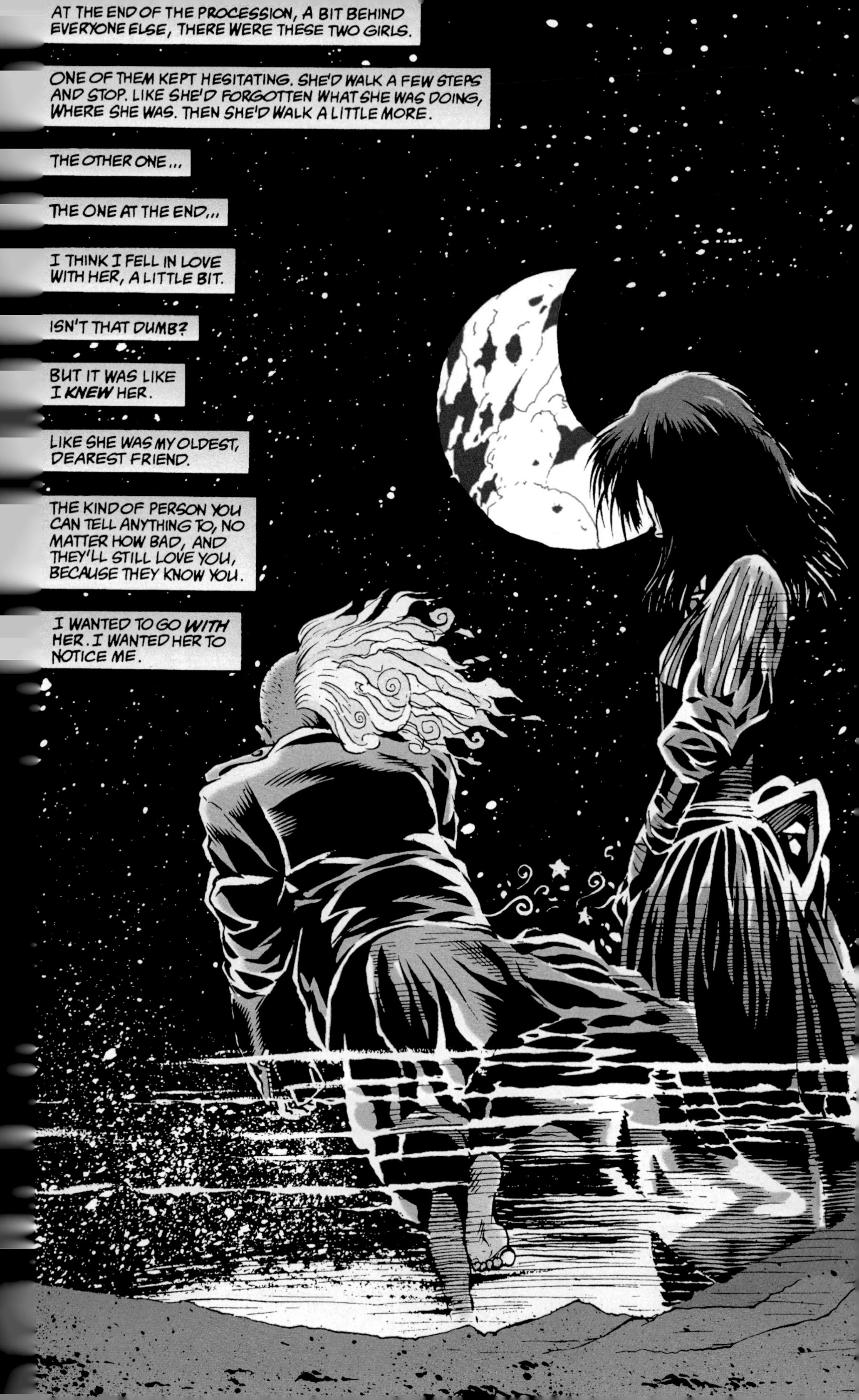
AT THE END OF THE PROCESSION, A BIT BEHIND EVERYONE ELSE, THERE WERE THESE TWO GIRLS.
ONE OF THEM KEPT HESITATING. SHE'D WALK A FEW STEPS AND STOP. LIKE SHE'D FORGOTTEN WHAT SHE WAS DOING, WHERE SHE WAS. THEN SHE'D WALK A LITTLE MORE.
THE OTHER ONE...
THE ONE AT THE END...
I THINK I FELL IN LOVE WITH HER, A LITTLE BIT.
ISN'T THAT DUMB?
BUT IT WAS LIKE I *KNEW* HER.
LIKE SHE WAS MY OLDEST, DEAREST FRIEND.
THE KIND OF PERSON YOU CAN TELL ANYTHING TO, NO MATTER HOW BAD, AND THEY'LL STILL LOVE YOU, BECAUSE THEY KNOW YOU.
I WANTED TO GO *WITH* HER. I WANTED HER TO NOTICE ME.

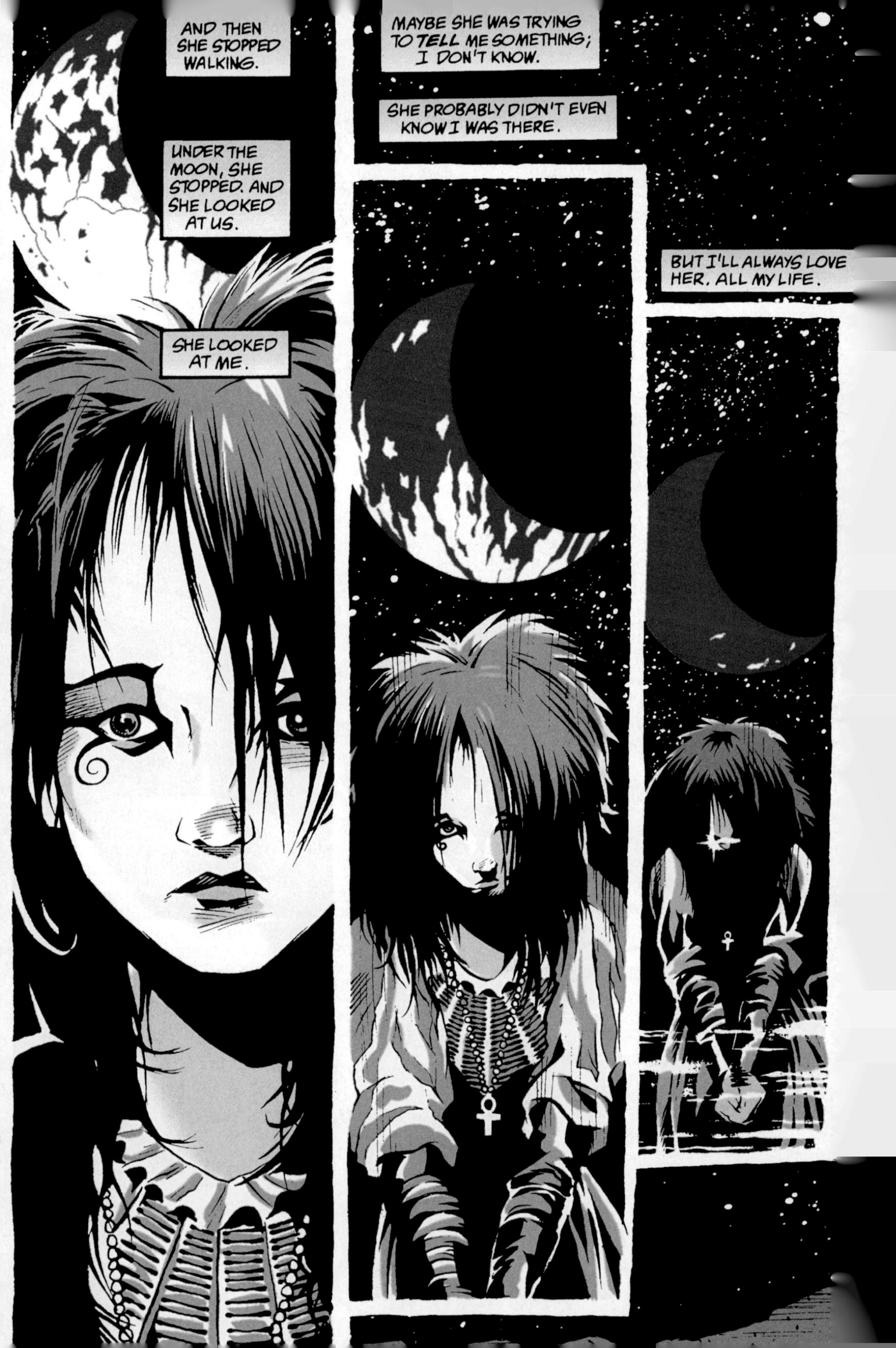
AND THEN SHE STOPPED WALKING.
UNDER THE MOON, SHE STOPPED. AND SHE LOOKED AT US.
SHE LOOKED AT ME.
MAYBE SHE WAS TRYING TO TELL ME SOMETHING; I DON'T KNOW.
SHE PROBABLY DIDN'T EVEN KNOW I WAS THERE.
BUT I'LL ALWAYS LOVE HER. ALL MY LIFE.

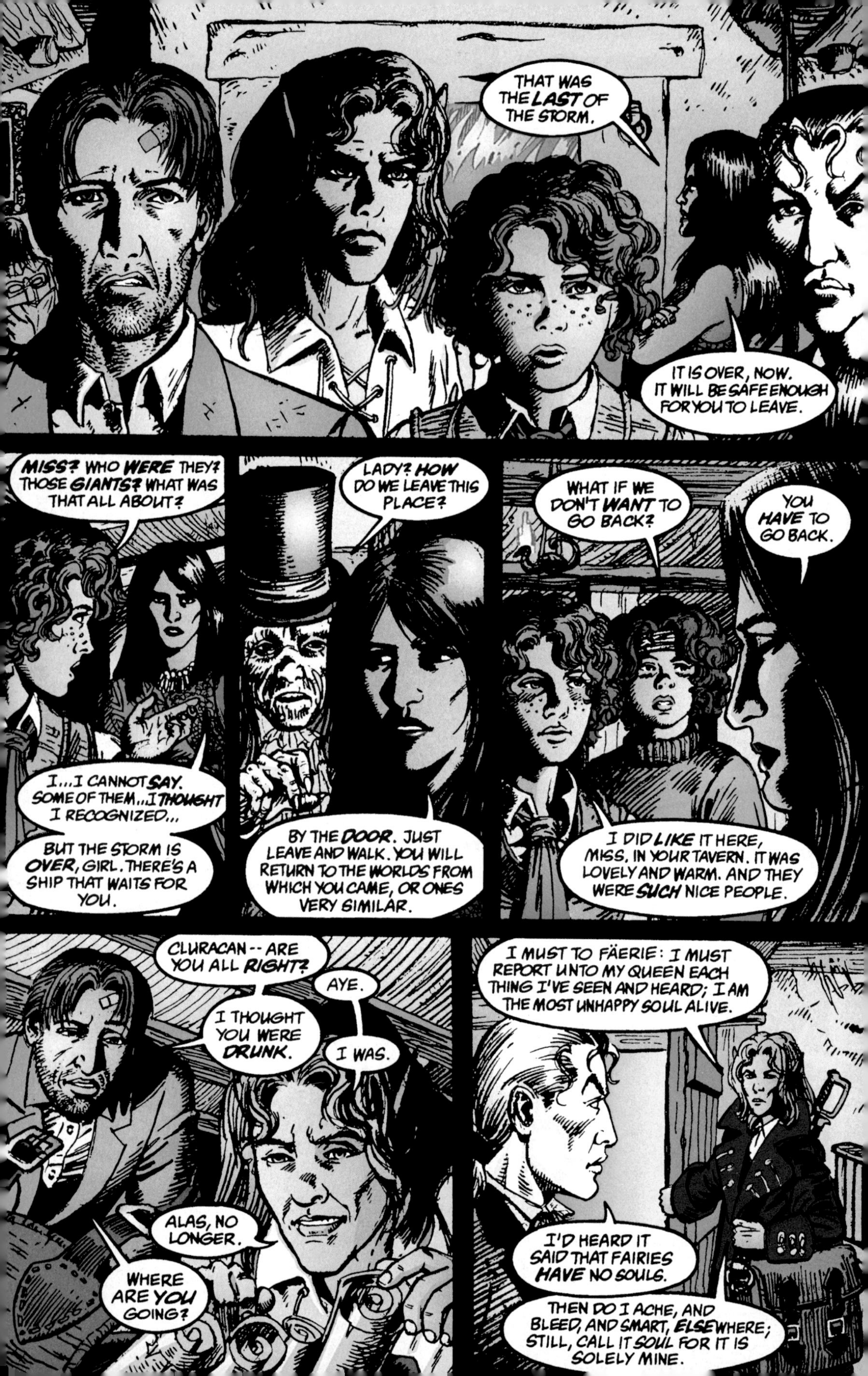
THAT WAS THE LAST OF THE STORM.
IT IS OVER, NOW. IT WILL BE SAFE ENOUGH FOR YOU TO LEAVE.
MISS? WHO WERE THEY? THOSE GIANTS? WHAT WAS THAT ALL ABOUT?
I...I CANNOT SAY. SOME OF THEM...I THOUGHT I RECOGNIZED...
BUT THE STORM IS OVER, GIRL. THERE'S A SHIP THAT WAITS FOR YOU.
LADY? HOW DO WE LEAVE THIS PLACE?
BY THE DOOR. JUST LEAVE AND WALK. YOU WILL RETURN TO THE WORLDS FROM WHICH YOU CAME, OR ONES VERY SIMILAR.
WHAT IF WE DON'T WANT TO GO BACK?
YOU HAVE TO GO BACK.
I DID LIKE IT HERE, MISS, IN YOUR TAVERN. IT WAS LOVELY AND WARM. AND THEY WERE SUCH NICE PEOPLE.
CLURACAN -- ARE YOU ALL RIGHT?
AYE.
I THOUGHT YOU WERE DRUNK.
I WAS.
ALAS, NO LONGER.
WHERE ARE YOU GOING?
I MUST TO FÄERIE: I MUST REPORT UNTO MY QUEEN EACH THING I'VE SEEN AND HEARD; I AM THE MOST UNHAPPY SOUL ALIVE.
I'D HEARD IT SAID THAT FAIRIES HAVE NO SOULS.
THEN DO I ACHE, AND BLEED, AND SMART, ELSEWHERE; STILL, CALL IT SOUL FOR IT IS SOLELY MINE.

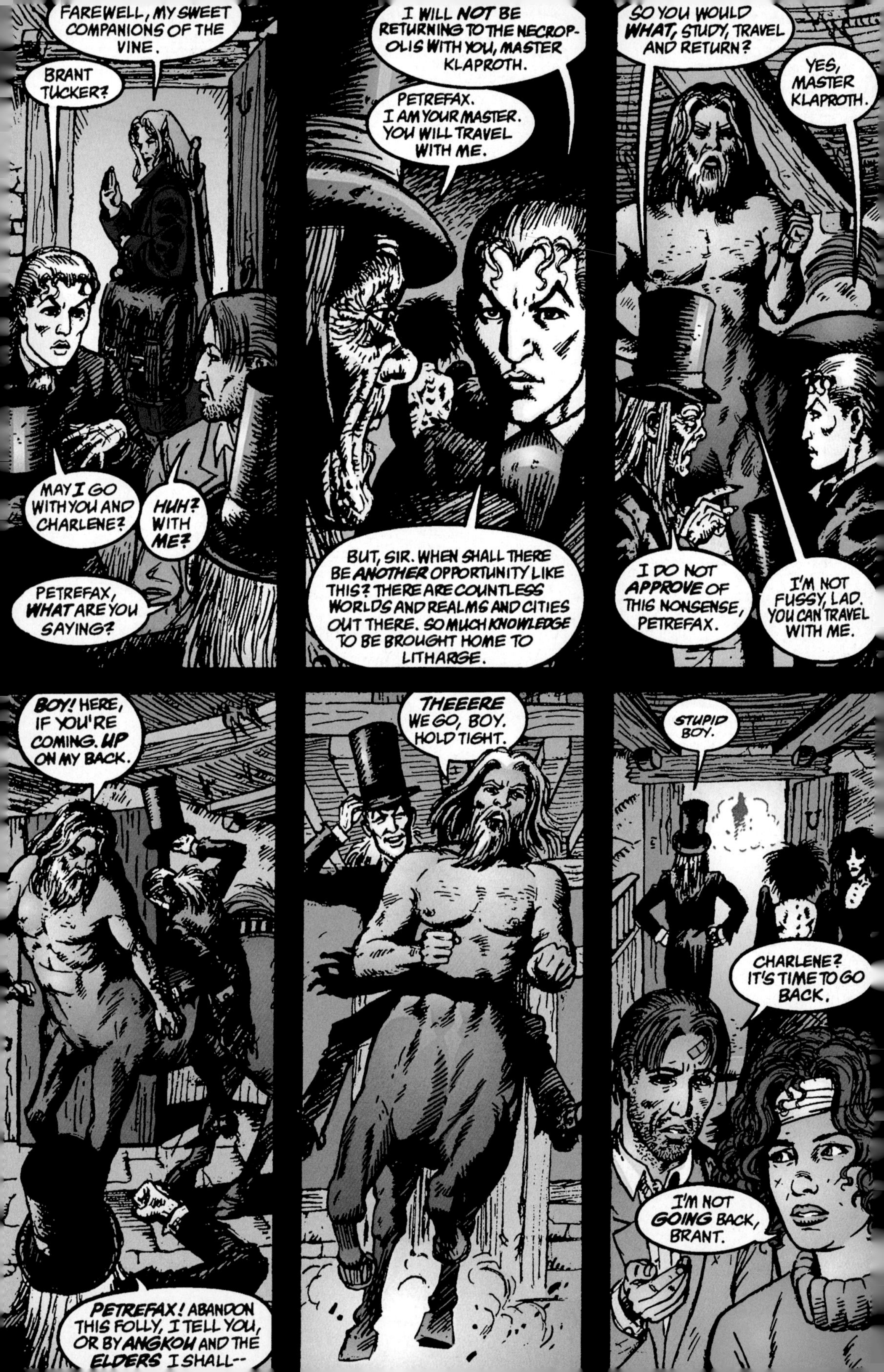
FAREWELL, MY SWEET COMPANIONS OF THE VINE.
BRANT TUCKER?
MAY I GO WITH YOU AND CHARLENE?
HUH? WITH ME?
PETREFAX, WHAT ARE YOU SAYING?
I WILL NOT BE RETURNING TO THE NECROPOLIS WITH YOU, MASTER KLAPROTH.
PETREFAX. I AM YOUR MASTER. YOU WILL TRAVEL WITH ME.
BUT, SIR. WHEN SHALL THERE BE ANOTHER OPPORTUNITY LIKE THIS? THERE ARE COUNTLESS WORLDS AND REALMS AND CITIES OUT THERE. SO MUCH KNOWLEDGE TO BE BROUGHT HOME TO LITHARGE.
SO YOU WOULD WHAT, STUDY, TRAVEL AND RETURN?
YES, MASTER KLAPROTH.
I DO NOT APPROVE OF THIS NONSENSE, PETREFAX.
I'M NOT FUSSY, LAD. YOU CAN TRAVEL WITH ME.
BOY! HERE, IF YOU'RE COMING. UP ON MY BACK.
PETREFAX! ABANDON THIS FOLLY, I TELL YOU, OR BY ANGKOU AND THE ELDERS I SHALL--
THEEERE WE GO, BOY. HOLD TIGHT.
STUPID BOY.
CHARLENE? IT'S TIME TO GO BACK.
I'M NOT GOING BACK, BRANT.

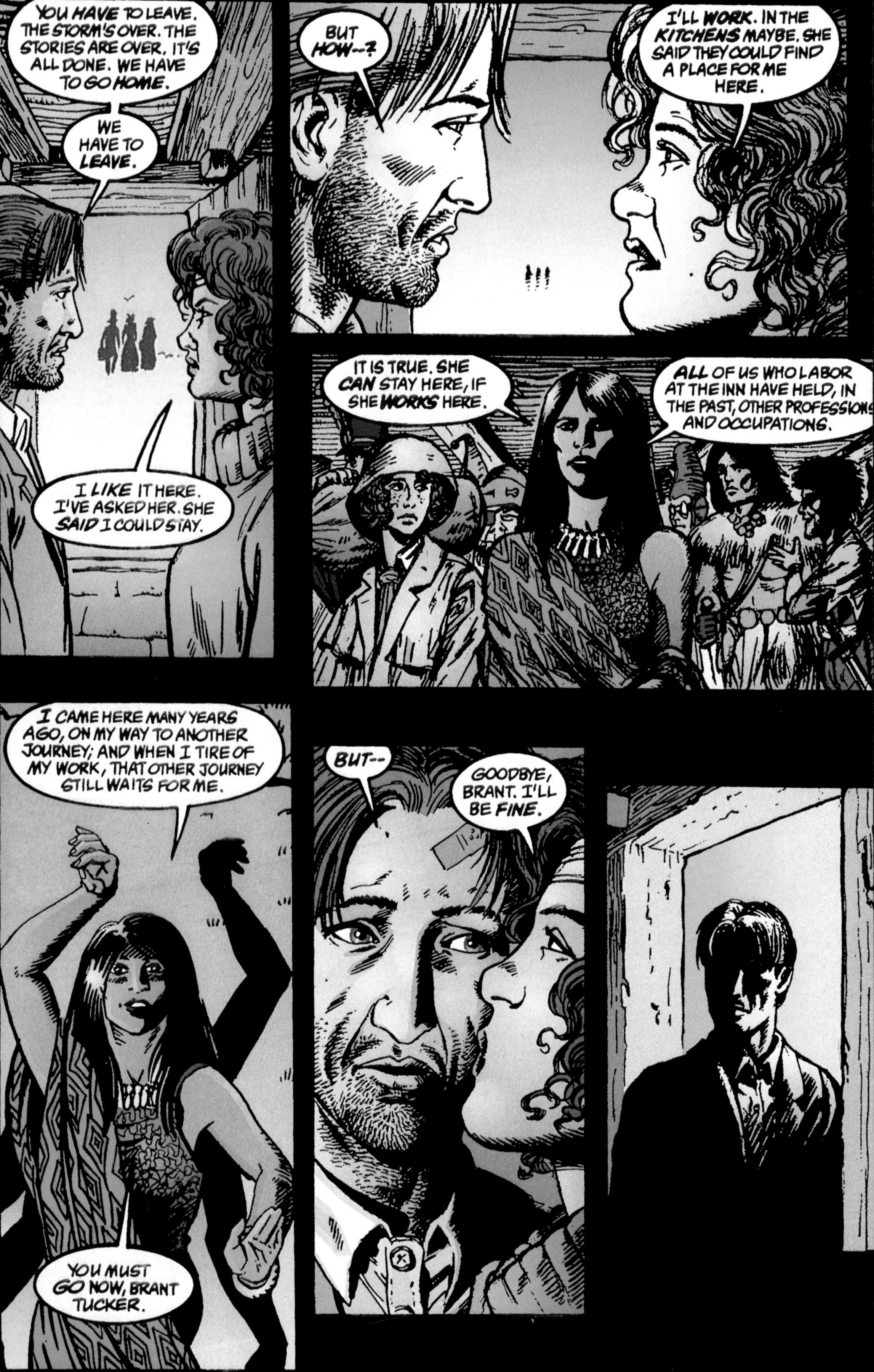
YOU HAVE TO LEAVE. THE STORM'S OVER. THE STORIES ARE OVER. IT'S ALL DONE. WE HAVE TO GO HOME.
WE HAVE TO LEAVE.
I LIKE IT HERE. I'VE ASKED HER. SHE SAID I COULD STAY.
BUT HOW--?
I'LL WORK. IN THE KITCHENS MAYBE. SHE SAID THEY COULD FIND A PLACE FOR ME HERE.
IT IS TRUE. SHE CAN STAY HERE, IF SHE WORKS HERE.
ALL OF US WHO LABOR AT THE INN HAVE HELD, IN THE PAST, OTHER PROFESSIONS AND OCCUPATIONS.
I CAME HERE MANY YEARS AGO, ON MY WAY TO ANOTHER JOURNEY; AND WHEN I TIRE OF MY WORK, THAT OTHER JOURNEY STILL WAITS FOR ME.
YOU MUST GO NOW, BRANT TUCKER.
BUT--
GOODBYE, BRANT. I'LL BE FINE.

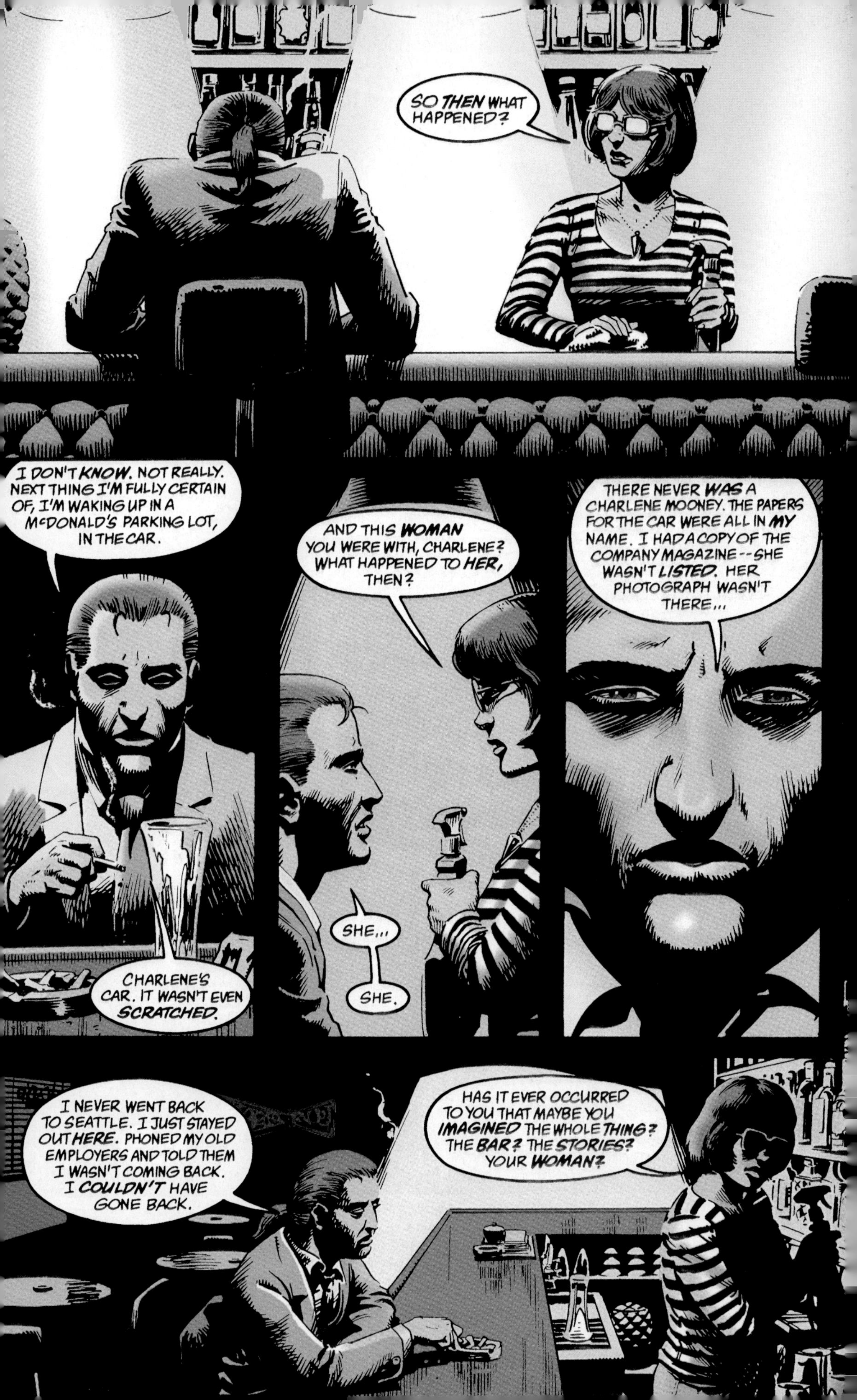
SO THEN WHAT HAPPENED?
I DON'T KNOW. NOT REALLY. NEXT THING I'M FULLY CERTAIN OF, I'M WAKING UP IN A McDONALD'S PARKING LOT, IN THE CAR.
CHARLENE'S CAR. IT WASN'T EVEN SCRATCHED.
AND THIS WOMAN YOU WERE WITH, CHARLENE? WHAT HAPPENED TO HER, THEN?
SHE...
SHE.
THERE NEVER WAS A CHARLENE MOONEY. THE PAPERS FOR THE CAR WERE ALL IN MY NAME. I HAD A COPY OF THE COMPANY MAGAZINE--SHE WASN'T LISTED. HER PHOTOGRAPH WASN'T THERE...
I NEVER WENT BACK TO SEATTLE. I JUST STAYED OUT HERE. PHONED MY OLD EMPLOYERS AND TOLD THEM I WASN'T COMING BACK. I COULDN'T HAVE GONE BACK.
HAS IT EVER OCCURRED TO YOU THAT MAYBE YOU IMAGINED THE WHOLE THING? THE BAR? THE STORIES? YOUR WOMAN?

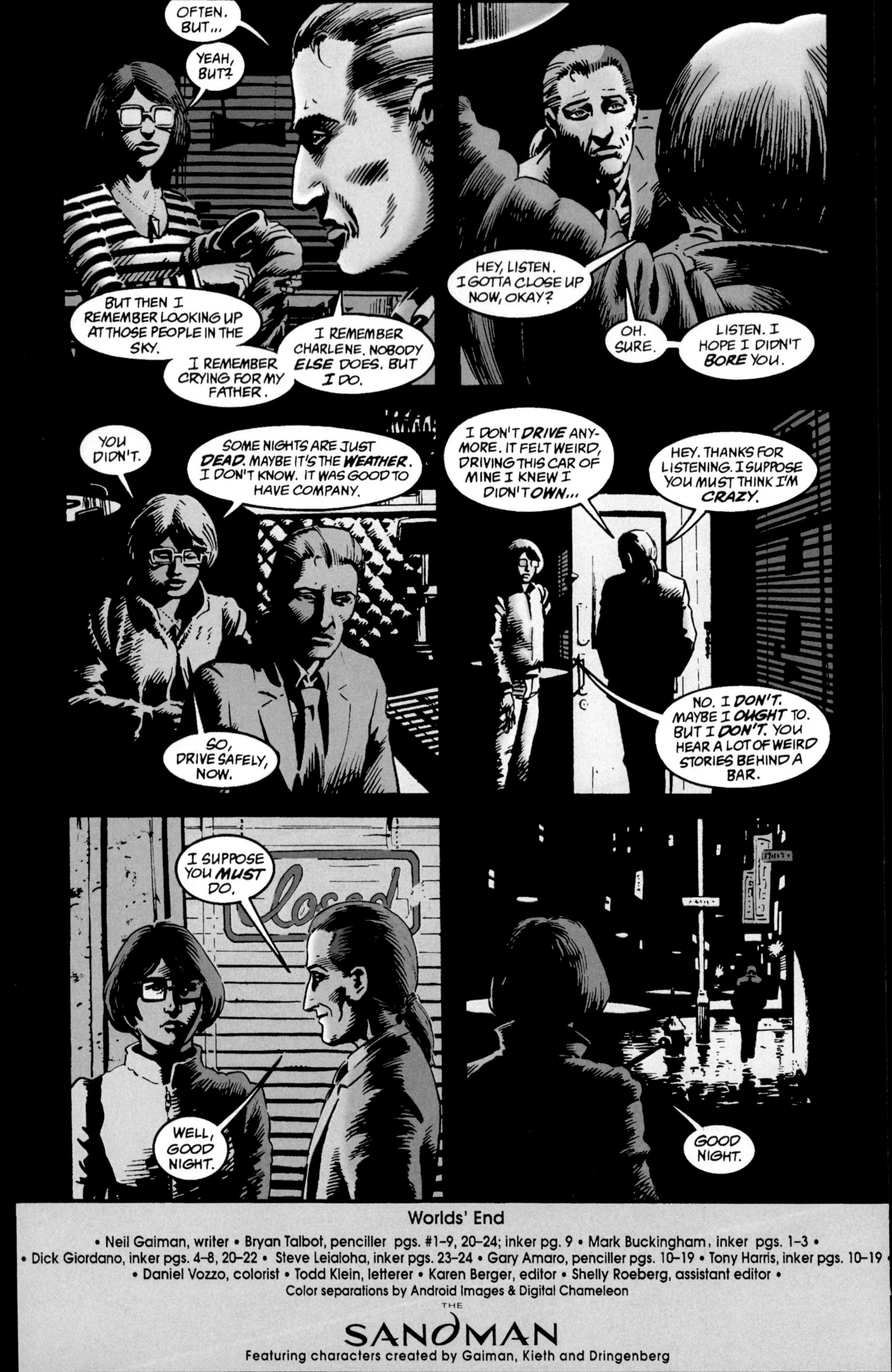
OFTEN. BUT...
YEAH, BUT?
BUT THEN I REMEMBER LOOKING UP AT THOSE PEOPLE IN THE SKY.
I REMEMBER CRYING FOR MY FATHER.
I REMEMBER CHARLENE. NOBODY ELSE DOES. BUT I DO.
HEY, LISTEN. I GOTTA CLOSE UP NOW, OKAY?
OH. SURE.
LISTEN. I HOPE I DIDN'T BORE YOU.
YOU DIDN'T.
SOME NIGHTS ARE JUST DEAD. MAYBE IT'S THE WEATHER. I DON'T KNOW. IT WAS GOOD TO HAVE COMPANY.
SO, DRIVE SAFELY, NOW.
I DON'T DRIVE ANY-MORE. IT FELT WEIRD, DRIVING THIS CAR OF MINE I KNEW I DIDN'T OWN...
HEY. THANKS FOR LISTENING. I SUPPOSE YOU MUST THINK I'M CRAZY.
NO. I DON'T. MAYBE I OUGHT TO. BUT I DON'T. YOU HEAR A LOT OF WEIRD STORIES BEHIND A BAR.
I SUPPOSE YOU MUST DO.
WELL, GOOD NIGHT.
GOOD NIGHT.

Worlds' End

• Neil Gaiman, writer • Bryan Talbot, penciller pgs. #1–9, 20–24; inker pg. 9 • Mark Buckingham, inker pgs. 1–3 •
• Dick Giordano, inker pgs. 4–8, 20–22 • Steve Leialoha, inker pgs. 23–24 • Gary Amaro, penciller pgs. 10–19 • Tony Harris, inker pgs. 10–19 •
• Daniel Vozzo, colorist • Todd Klein, letterer • Karen Berger, editor • Shelly Roeberg, assistant editor •
Color separations by Android Images & Digital Chameleon

THE SANDMAN

Featuring characters created by Gaiman, Kieth and Dringenberg

acknowledgments

The joy of comics, for me at least, is that it is a collaborative medium.

Each of these stories came about because I had a specific artist with whom I wanted to work. 'The Golden Boy,' for example, came partly out of Mike Allred's desire to work with old DC characters and my own fascination with with what people expect from their leaders; but the way the story told itself had much to do with the clean and simple shapes Mike Allred draws, with his people and their movements; 'Hob's Leviathan' came as much from the knowledge that Michael Zulli was about to draw it (and, I suspect, only Michael Zulli could have done) as from my desire to explore an unfamiliar genre and to wave, across the centuries, at Kipling and Burton and Masefield; Alec Stevens' haunting imagery inspired the city story as much as Lovecraft or Dunsany did (but then, the first time I'd noticed Alec's work he was adapting a Lovecraft story); the knowledge that I was writing for John Watkiss helped shape Cluracan's story as much as Shea Anton Pensa's form and line shaped Petrefax's; and through it all Bryan Talbot's ability to ground anything and everything in reality gave me an Inn to return to as each of the tales was told.

I owe them all thanks, as I owe thanks to Todd Klein; to Danny Vozzo - and Android Images, Danny's Partner in crime and colour; to Dick and Mark and Vince and Steve for inks; to Gary and Tony (and digital Lovern) for the rescue; and to the editors, Shelly Roeberg (who does magic) and Karen Berger (who is magic); and to Bob Kahan, who assembled this into a whole.

Dave McKean has, for six years, made the covers to Sandman, and designed these books. He makes me look good, and is my toughest critic. I owe him more than thanks.

There were many things I wanted to do with these stories, and I am uncertain enough that I achieved any of them - my thanks to Stephen King, then, for his kind introduction. He is a master storyteller in his own right, and one for whom I have enormous respect. I have been very lucky in the people who have put pen to paper to introduce these volumes, and I am inordinately grateful.

I'd also like to thank the late Don Thompson, coeditor with his wife Maggie Thompson of the *Comics Buyer's Guide* newspaper. He always supported Sandman, was always kind to my writing. and was, besides, a gentleman. He is much missed.

And lastly my thanks to the staff and patrons of the Worlds' End (A Free House) for allowing me to eavesdrop on their conversations...

NEIL

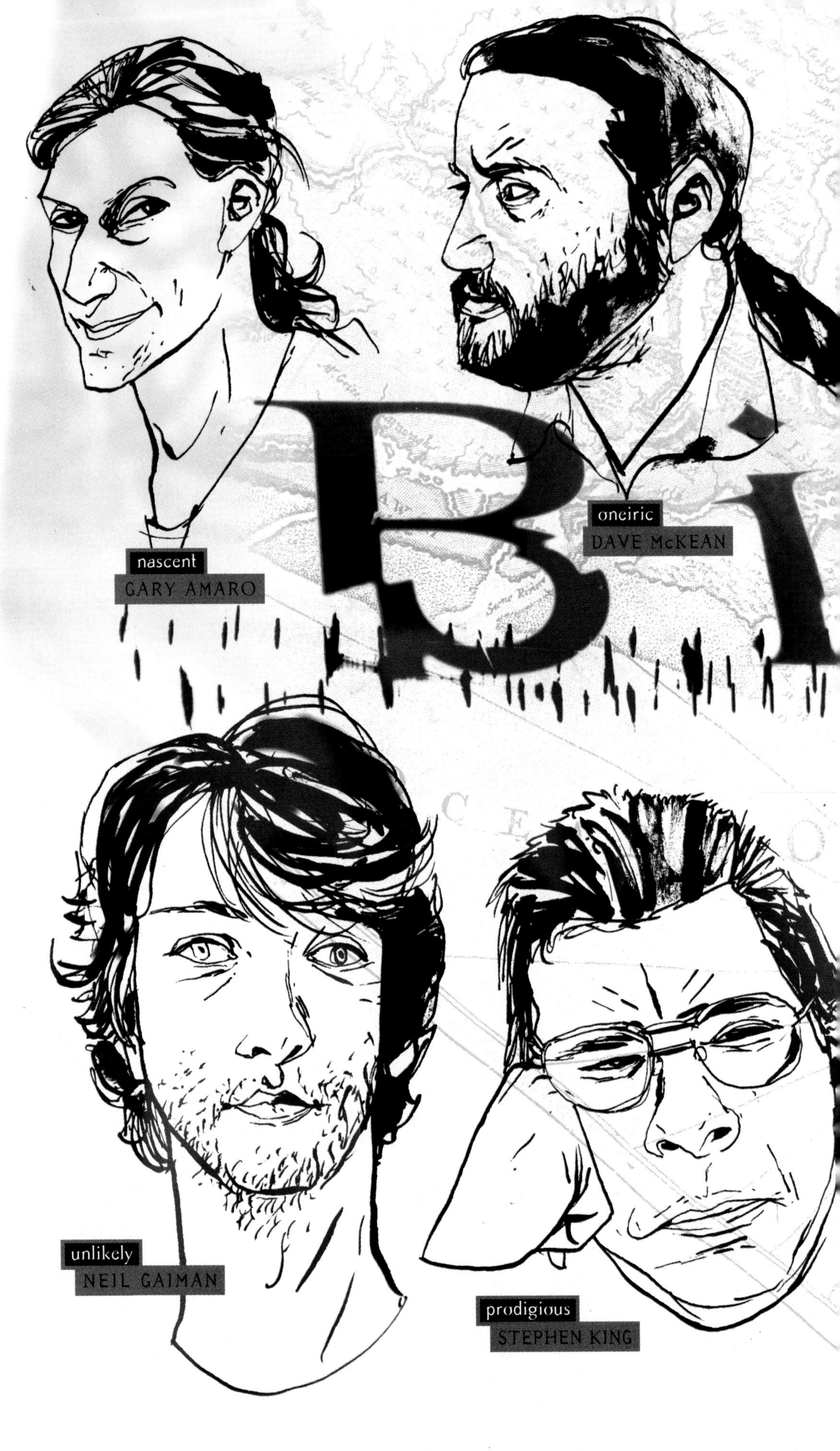
nascent
GARY AMARO
oneiric
DAVE McKEAN
unlikely
NEIL GAIMAN
prodigious
STEPHEN KING

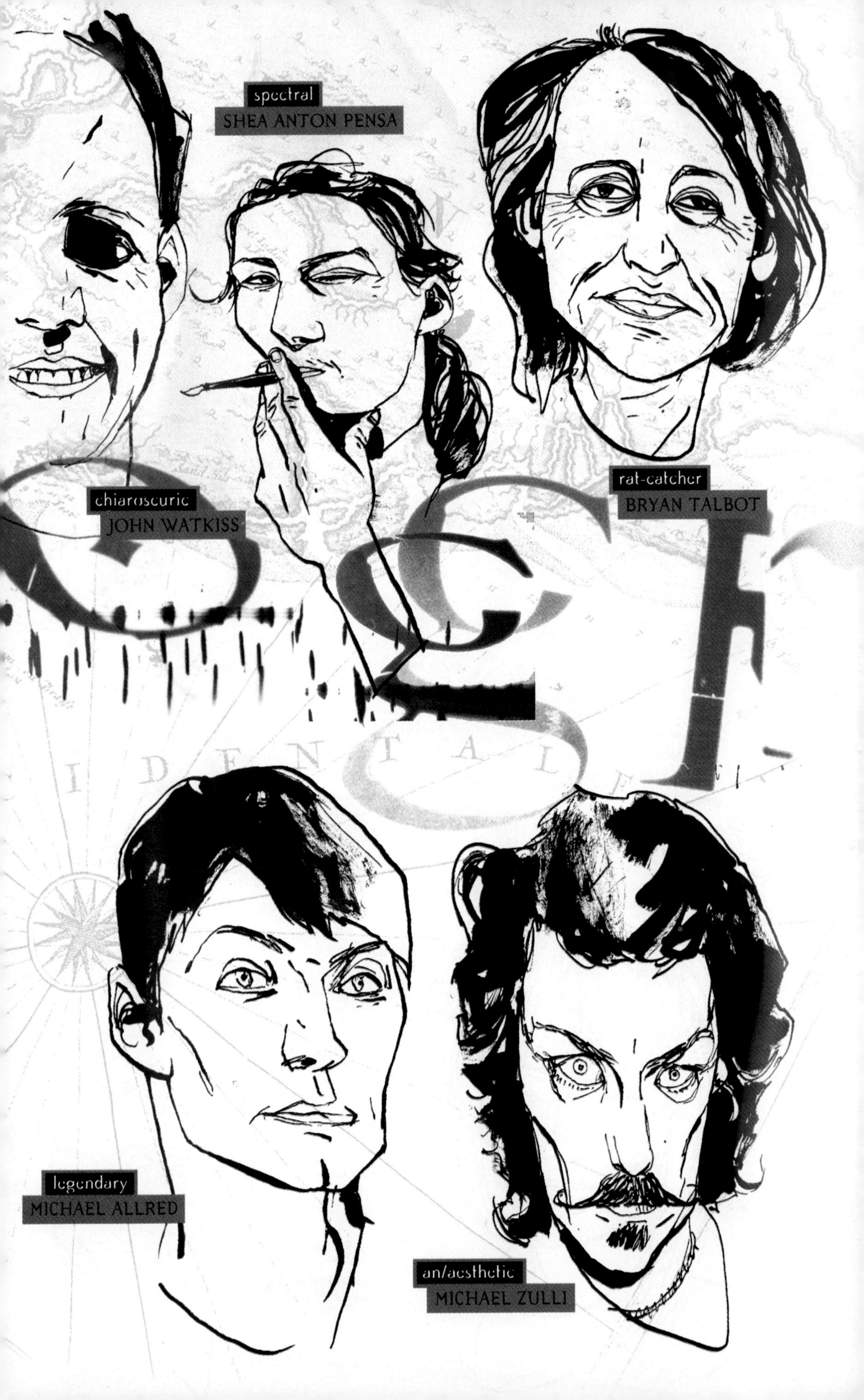

spectral
SHEA ANTON PENSA
rat-catcher
BRYAN TALBOT
chiaroscuric
JOHN WATKISS
legendary
MICHAEL ALLRED
an/aesthetic
MICHAEL ZULLI

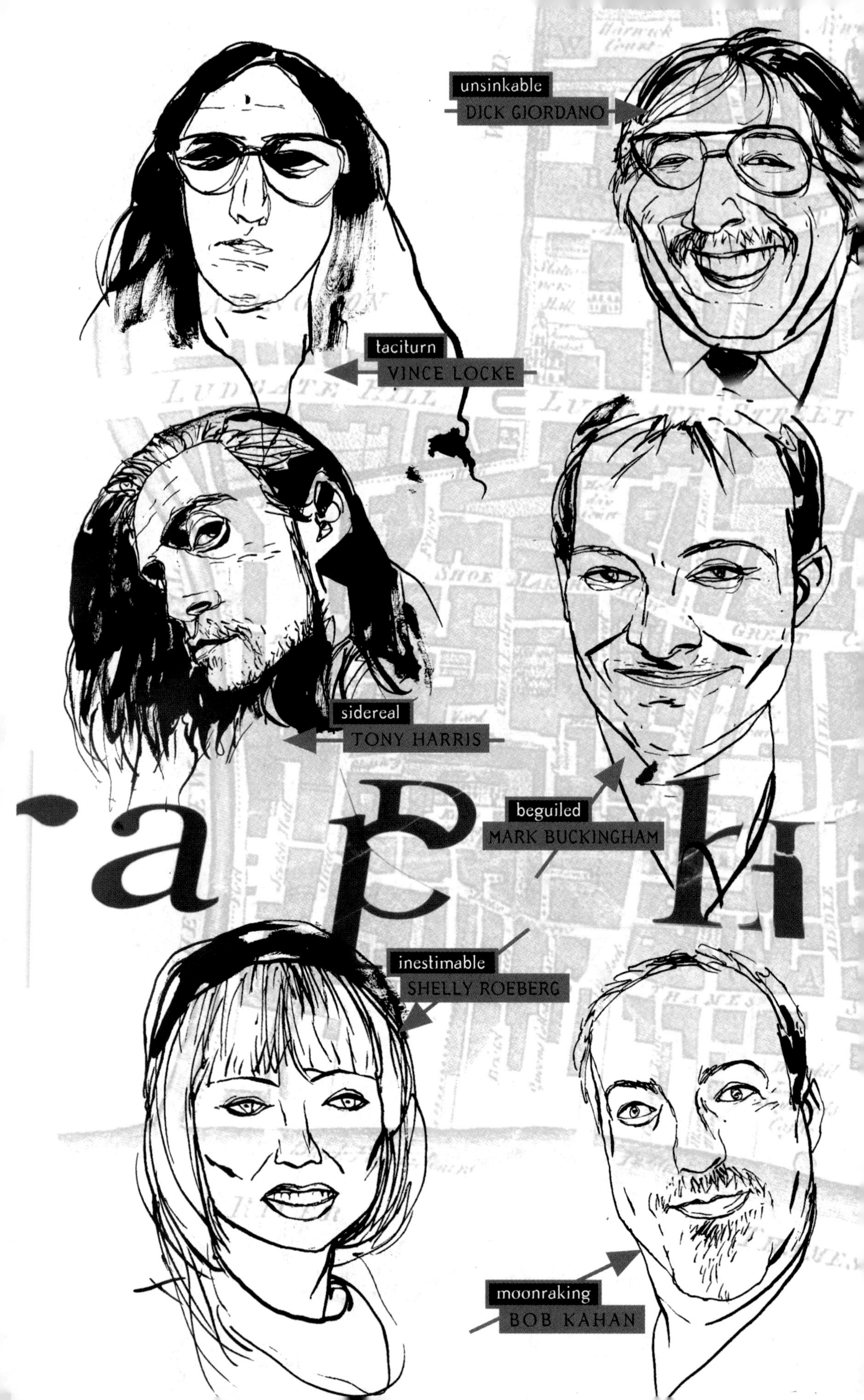
unsinkable
DICK GIORDANO
taciturn
VINCE LOCKE
sidereal
TONY HARRIS
beguiled
MARK BUCKINGHAM
inestimable
SHELLY ROEBERG
moonraking
BOB KAHAN

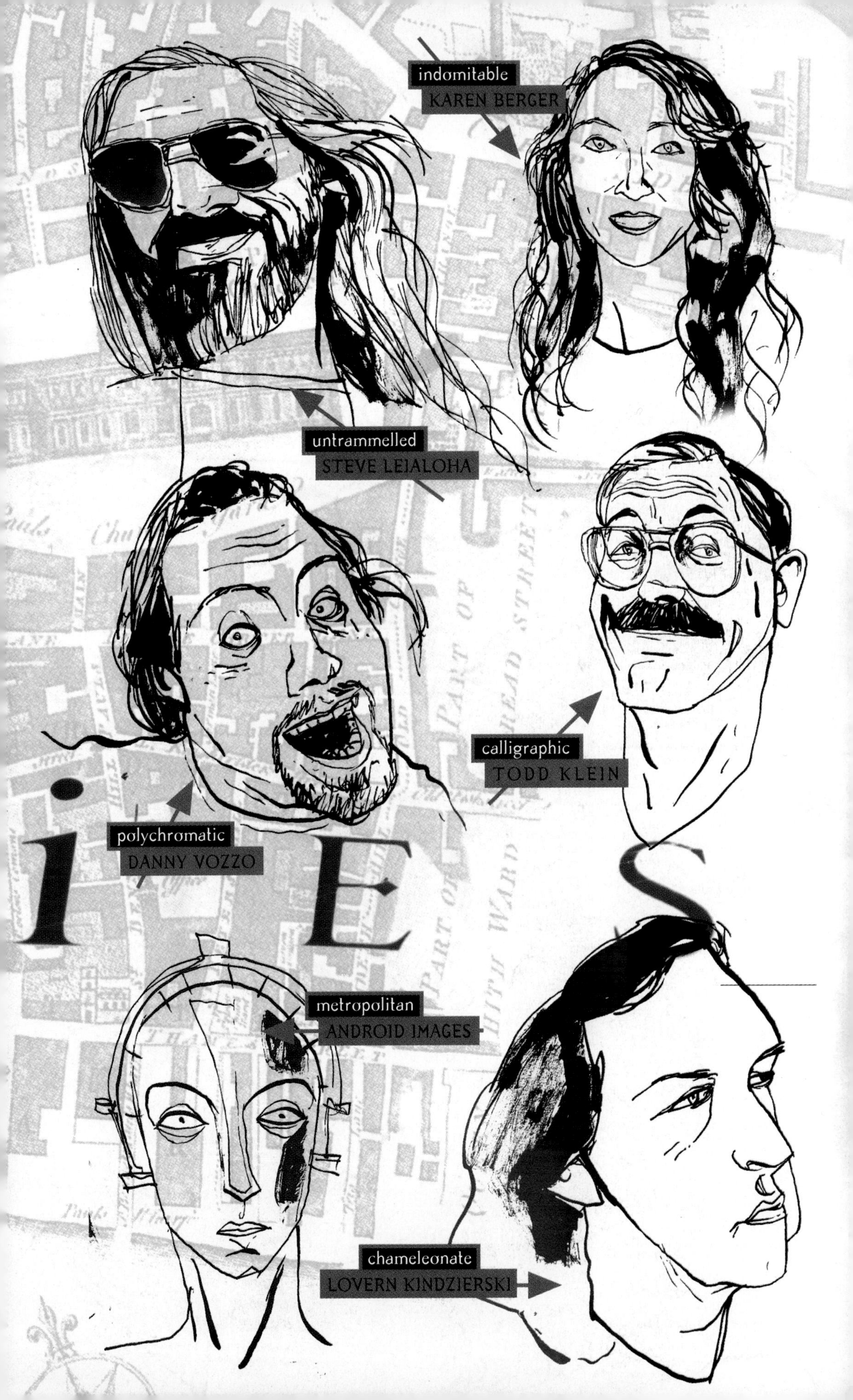
indomitable
KAREN BERGER
untrammelled
STEVE LEJALOHA
calligraphic
TODD KLEIN
polychromatic
DANNY VOZZO
i E S
metropolitan
ANDROID IMAGES
chameleonate
LOVERN KINDZIERSKI

THE SANDMAN VOL. 4:
SEASON OF MISTS

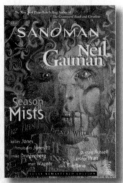

FROM THE NEW YORK TIMES # 1 BEST-SELLING AUTHOR

NEIL GAIMAN

THE SANDMAN

Read the complete series!

THE SANDMAN VOL. 1:
PRELUDES &
NOCTURNES

THE SANDMAN VOL. 2:
THE DOLL'S HOUSE

THE SANDMAN VOL. 3:
DREAM COUNTRY

THE SANDMAN VOL. 4:
SEASON OF MISTS

THE SANDMAN VOL. 5:
A GAME OF YOU

THE SANDMAN VOL. 6:
FABLES &
REFLECTIONS

THE SANDMAN VOL. 7:
BRIEF LIVES

THE SANDMAN VOL. 8:
WORLDS' END

THE SANDMAN VOL. 9:
THE KINDLY ONES

THE SANDMAN VOL. 10:
THE WAKE

THE SANDMAN:
ENDLESS NIGHTS

THE SANDMAN:
THE DREAM HUNTERS

NOW WITH FULLY
REMASTERED
COLORING

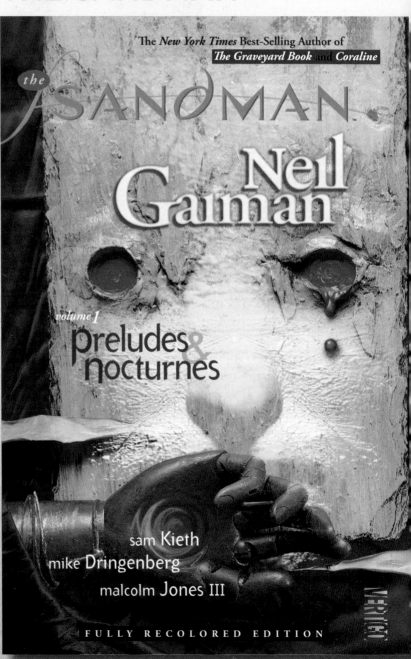